SUBSTANCE ABUSE:

TREATMENT AND REHABILITATION

Edited by

Joseph F. Stano

Springfield College

Aspen Professional Services

2011

PUBLISHED BY
Aspen Professional Services
63 Duffers Drive
Linn Creek, MO 65052

Substance Abuse: Treatment and Rehabilitation
[edited by] Joseph F. Stano

Includes bibliographical references
ISBN 978-0-9721642-5-2

Cover Layout by M. Jean Andrew, Esq.

To Secure Additional Copies, Contact
Aspen Professional Services
63 Duffers Drive
Linn Creek, MO 65052
jandrew@socket.net
573.317.0907
573.286.0418 Cell
573.873.2116 FAX
aspenprofessionalservices.com

ACKNOWLEDGEMENTS

The completion of this text marks the second project that I have completed under Aspen Professional Services and its Publisher, Jason Andrew. Jason's quiet leadership and support is a main reason why this project bore fruit. I also wish to thank Dean David Miller of the School of Health Science and Rehabilitation at Springfield College. I have known David for over twenty years and his friendship and leadership make Springfield College a great place to work.

I would especially like to cite my daughter Kate, Katherine Elizabeth Stano. Kate is currently a doctoral student in Educational Leadership at Argosy University in Seattle. This is the first time that we have been able to work together on a publishing project and we collaborated on four chapters. She is the best daughter any parent could ask for. My wife, Sue, and I consider her the joy of our lives.

This project would not have been possible would it not have been for the fabulous efforts by some of the "usual suspects." Whenever I start a writing project the first person that I e-mail is Dr. Andrea Perkins of Hofstra University. We have known each other for almost twenty years and she, in turn, casts a wide net to bring in other writers. As a result of Andrea's efforts she brought the following folks on to the project: Cindy Robinson, Joshua Carpenter, Katie Sell, Jamie Ghigiarelli, Genevieve Weber Gilmore, Holly Seirup, and Rebecca Rubinstein. Thanks to all for their efforts; I would not have had the pleasure of working with each of you if it were not for Andrea.

I would also like to thank Dr. Arnold Wolf of Hunter College. Arnie is the consummate professional and he has fantastic work habits. He, in turn, brought Joseph Keferl and Jacob Yui Chung Chan on board. Thanks to all. Dr. Sharon Sabik deserves great thanks for completing her chapter while much was happening in her life. Sharon is another person I call early in any writing project. First time collaborators for this project include Dr. Stephanie Lusk of North Carolina A & T and Drs. Debra Homa and David DeLambo of the University of Wisconsin at Stout. Each of these collaborators was thoroughly professional in their approach to this project.

Finally, I would like to thank my Springfield College family for playing very large roles in the completion of this project. Dr. Robert Hewes, friend, and department chair of the Rehabilitation Department is a key contributor. Dr. Michael Accordino is a friend and someone who is like a younger brother. We have several hilarious conversations each day which leave us doubled over in laughter. Mike, in turn, brought Bridget Halpin of the Physical Education department on board. Mike also enlisted our gifted graduate student, Erica Wondolowski, for his chapter. Erica is fabulous and she also collaborated on a chapter with me and my daughter. Melissa Manninen Luse, now a doctoral student at Michigan State University collaborated on this project and she brought Dr. John Kosciulek to the project. Alison Fleming, also at Michigan State collaborated with Robert and Mike on a chapter. Caitlin McInerny Clemons, formally a graduate assistant and now a VRC at the Massachusetts Rehabilitation Commission at Holyoke authored a chapter with me and my daughter.

The work on this project has been long and there were many difficulties but it was all worth it. Thanks again to all.

TABLE OF CONTENTS

THE EDITOR
JOSEPH F. STANO, PH.D., CRC, LRC

Joseph F. Stano is a Professor of Rehabilitation Counseling at Springfield College where he has been a full time professor since 1978. In addition to currently teaching the graduate course Psychosocial Evaluation and Assessment he is coordinator of the undergraduate program in Health Science where he teaches Physiology of Behavior, Human Disease, Genetics, Health and Behavior and Biostatistics.

He is also the editor of the text, Psychology of Disability, which was also published by Aspen Professional Services. Dr Stano is a Member of the American Psychological Association and its divisions, Measurement, Evaluation and Statistics, and Health Psychology.

In addition to working forty years in the field of Substance Abuse, Dr. Stano also has expertise Psychometrics and Psychological Evaluation. He currently assesses consumers in the areas of vocational, cognitive, personal, and neuropsychological functioning for the Massachusetts Rehabilitation Commission.

He and his wife Sue enjoy gardening, travels and movies. Their daughter Kate is a doctoral student is Educational Leadership and she a co-author of three chapter of this text with her dad.

THE CONTRIBUTORS

MICHAEL P. ACCORDINO, Ed.D., CRC, LMHC, is an associate professor and Graduate Coordinator in the Rehabilitation and Disability Studies Department of Springfield College, in Springfield, MA. He has published articles pertaining to vocational rehabilitation of people with disabilities and has conducted communication skills training in community mental health and prison settings.

KACIE M. BLALOCK, Ph.D., CRC, is an Associate Professor of Rehabilitation Counseling in the Department of Human Development and Services at North Carolina A&T State University. She is a certified rehabilitation counselor who earned her Ph.D. in Rehabilitation Counseling Psychology from the University of Wisconsin-Madison, her M.S. in Rehabilitation Counseling from Southern University, and her B.A. in Psychology from Grambling State University. She currently serves as the project director of two long-term training grants from the U.S. Department of Education, Rehabilitation Services Administration. Her research areas include vocational rehabilitation, multicultural counseling, and psychosocial aspects of disability.

QUINTIN BOSTON, Ph.D., CRC, is an Assistant Professor in the Department of Human Development and Services at North Carolina Agricultural and Technical State University. Dr. Boston earned his Ph.D in Rehabilitation from the Rehabilitation Institute at Southern Illinois University-Carbondale. His research interest include multicultural issues in counseling, vocational rehabilitation, and counselor education and supervision.

JOSHUA L. CARPENTER, MS.Ed., CRC, MS.Ed., CRC, received his Bachelor of Science in Psychology from the University of New Orleans and a Master of Science in Education with Distinction in Rehabilitation Counseling in Mental Health from Hofstra University. Mr. Carpenter has been providing intensive psychiatric rehabilitation counseling services for the Clubhouse of Suffolk in Ronkonkoma, NY since 2007. His research interests include human sexuality, social behavior in emergency/crisis situations, recovery from psychosis and thought disorders, and economic self-sufficiency for disadvantaged groups.

JACOB YUI-CHUNG CHAN, Ph.D., is an Assistant Professor of Psychology-Counseling, Ball State University, Muncie, Indiana.

CAITLIN MCINERNY CLEMONS, CRC, is currently employed as a Vocational Rehabilitation Counselor at the Massachusetts Rehabilitation Commission. She has a B.A in psychology from Mount Holyoke College and a M.Ed. in Rehabilitation Counseling and Services with a concentration in pediatric and developmental disabilities from Springfield College.

DAVID DELAMBO, Rh.D., CRC, is an Associate Professor of Rehabilitation at the University of Wisconsin-Stout. He received the Doctor of Rehabilitation degree from Southern Illinois University-Carbondale and has been a rehabilitation educator since 1997. Prior to arriving at UW-Stout, Dave taught for five years in Georgia at Fort Valley State University. Dr. DeLambo's research interests include: psychosocial aspects of disability; substance abuse and disability; privacy issues and social media; work adjustment and behavioral techniques, as well as ethical issues and other counseling related topics in rehabilitation.

ALLISON FLEMING, MS, CRC, is a doctoral student at Michigan State University. Allison is a certified rehabilitation counselor and has experience working in a vocational setting with persons with disabilities, including those with substance abuse histories and co-occurring disorders. She also works as a research assistant for the VR Research and Training Center (VR-RRTC) and the Research and Technical Assistance Center (RTAC) at the Institute for Community Inclusion at U-Mass Boston. At Michigan State, Allison is a research assistant with Project Excellence, a program evaluation partnership between Michigan State University and the Michigan VR agency. Allison teaches a university-level course on substance abuse and has an interest in substance abuse and family issues.

JAMIE GHIGIARELLI, Ph.D., is an assistant professor at Hofstra University in the Department of Health and Human Performance. He received his doctorate in exercise physiology from the University of Pittsburgh. He teaches courses in exercise physiology, kinesiology, and sports nutrition. Dr. Ghigiarelli is a certified strength and conditioning specialist (CSCS), United States level I Olympic club coach (USAW), and sports nutritionist (CISSN). His areas of research are the endocrine responses of salivary testosterone to high intense resistance exercise, the biomechanics of training for explosive power, and sports supplementation.

GENEVIEVE WEBER GILMORE, Ph.D, LMHC, is an assistant professor of counselor education at Hofstra University. She has worked as a substance abuse counselor in community agencies for over ten years. Dr. Weber Gilmore's research focuses on the impact of homophobia on the mental health and substance abuse behaviors of lesbian, gay, bisexual, and transgender individuals.

BRIDGET L. HALPIN, M.S., is an assistant professor in the Physical Education and Health Education Department of Springfield College, in Springfield, Massachusetts. She has worked with individuals with cognitive and physical disabilities in the area physical education. Bridget has also conducted numerous programs for children and adults to attain and maintain lifelong physical fitness. She is a current member of the American Alliance for Health, Physical Education, Recreation, and Dance (AAHPERD) and presented at their national conference. She is also a member of American Association for Physical Activity and Recreation as well as the Research Consortium associated with AAHPERD. Her major research interests are adapted sports, sport participation, motivation, and autism.

ROBERT L. HEWES, RH.D., is a Professor of Rehabilitation and Disabilities Studies and Chair of the Rehabilitation and Disabilities Studies department at Springfield College. Dr. Hewes began at Springfield College in 1997 while completing his dissertation and doctoral degree in rehabilitation counseling at Southern Illinois University (1998). Dr. Hewes has worked as a program evaluator, substance abuse counselor, and substance abuse prevention coordinator. His research interests include substance abuse and family treatment, ethical decision making, and psychology of disability.
Dr. Hewes lives in Three Rivers, MA with his wife and four children and serves as an assistant pastor of a small evangelical Christian church.

DEBRA HOMA, Ph.D., CRC, CVE, is an Associate Professor as well as the online program director for the graduate rehabilitation counseling program at the University of Wisconsin-Stout. Prior to becoming a rehabilitation educator, she worked for over 20 years as a rehabilitation practitioner in a variety of settings, including private rehabilitation agencies, non-profit community-based rehabilitation agencies, and hospital-based programs. Dr. Homa has presented on vocational rehabilitation topics at national conferences and has prior publications regarding disability and substance abuse. Her research interests include: vocational assessment, substance abuse and disability, and outcomes research in vocational rehabilitation.

JOSEPH KEFERL, Ph.D., is an Associate Professor, Rehabilitation Counseling Program for Chemical Dependency, Wright State University, Dayton, Ohio.

JOHN F. KOSCIULEK, PH.D., CRC, is a Professor and Director of the Master of Arts Program in Rehabilitation Counseling at Michigan State University, East Lansing, Michigan.

MELISSA MANNINEN LUSE is a graduate of Michigan Technological University and received her Master's degree in Rehabilitation Counseling from Springfield College. She is currently a doctoral candidate at Michigan State University, East Lansing, Michigan.

STEPHANIE L. LUSK, Ph.D., CRC, is currently an Assistant Professor at the North Carolina Agricultural and Technical State University in Greensboro, North Carolina where she teaches courses in Theories and Foundations of Addictions, Family Counseling and Addictions, Psychopathology, and Psychopharmacology. She earned a doctorate in Rehabilitation and a BA in Psychology from the University of Arkansas and a Master's in Rehabilitation Counseling from Arkansas State University. She has prior work experience in career development and placement, transition planning, and substance abuse treatment. She has also worked with the Substance Abuse and Mental Health Services Administration (SAMHSA) and the Addiction Technology Transfer Center (ATTC) on curriculum development and has pubished work in the *Journal of Vocational Rehabilitation Counseling* and in *Disabilities: Insights From Across the Fields and Around the World*. Her primary areas of research interests includes substance abuse treatment and co-occurring disabilities among African American women, attitudes towards individuals with addictions, and curriculum development for rehabilitation counseling and addictions programs.

MIRIAM REISHUN LYDE is currently a graduate student in the Rehabilitation Counseling program at North Carolina Agricultural and Technical State University. She received a BS degree in Human Development and Family Studies from the University of North Carolina at Greensboro. She is a Rehabilitation Services Administration/Rehabilitation Counseling and Behavioral Addictions scholar, a member of Chi Sigma Iota Counseling, Academic, and Professional Honor Society, and the treasurer of the Rehabilitation Counseling Association. After receiving her Master's of Science degree, she plans to pursue a Doctoral degree in Counseling Psychology.

ANDREA PERKINS, Ph.D., CRC, CVE, is an assistant professor of rehabilitation counseling at Hofstra University. She is also the program director for the CAS for Interdisciplinary Transition Specialists. She completed her doctorate in rehabilitation counselor education from Michigan State University and received a Bachelor and Master's degree in rehabilitation counseling from Springfield College (MA). Dr. Perkins has worked in the private non-profit and for-profit systems as a case manager, program coordinator, and vocational evaluator. She is a nationally certified rehabilitation counselor and certified vocational evaluator. Her research interests include transition services for students with disabilities, interdisciplinary collaboration, and professional development.

CINDY ROBINSON, MS.Ed., CRC, received her Bachelor of Science in Psychology from the University of Connecticut and a Master of Science in Education in Rehabilitation Counseling in Mental Health from Hofstra University. Ms. Robinson is an outpatient counselor at South Oaks Hospital in Amityville, NY and will be entering a doctoral program in counselor education and supervision in the Fall. Her research interests include services for individuals with co-morbid disorders and treatment of eating disorders.

JEREMY ROGERS is a graduate student at North Carolina Agricultural & Technical State University where he is completing coursework to obtain a Master's of Science degree in Rehabilitation Counseling and a certificate in Behavioral Addictions. He was recently inducted into the counseling honor society, Chi Sigma Iota and is a Rehabilitation Services Administration/Rehabilitation Counseling and Behavioral Addictions scholarship recipient. He attended the University of North Carolina, Charlotte where he received a BS degree in Sociology and a minor in Criminal Justice. After completion of his master's program he intends to continue his education in rehabilitation at the doctoral level.

REBECCA RUBINSTEIN, B. A., is a graduate student in the Rehabilitation Counseling in Mental Health program at Hofstra University. She received her B.A. with dual majors in Psychology and Sociology from SUNY Potsdam. She serves as the graduate research assistant to the counseling faculty at Hofstra. Having been a consumer of rehabilitation services, Rebecca found a connection to rehabilitation counseling which lead her to pursue her Master's degree. In the future, she hopes to do research with the adolescents and those with autism and mental illness.

SHARON SABIK, Ph.D., CRC, has been a Certified Rehabilitation Counselor since 1995. She has worked in the field since that time as a caseworker, counselor, researcher, and teacher. Her terminal degree in Rehabilitation Research and Education was obtained from the University of Arkansas at Fayetteville in 2002. Dr. Sabik has a special interest in the impact of chronic illnesses and chronic conditions on individuals; especially in the areas of self-management, quality-of-life, and work accommodations.

HOLLY SEIRUP is currently an Assistant Professor in the Counselor Education program in the School of Education Health and Human Services at Hofstra University. Dr. Seirup is an active member of professional and community organizations serving on the President's Advisory Council for the Nassau County Coalition of Domestic Violence, on the Board of Long Island Lutheran Middle and High School, and on the editorial review board of the Journal of Student Affairs Research and Practice. She has presented at numerous conferences on a variety of topics ranging from the transition from high school to college, professional orientation and ethics, mental health issues on the college campus, and safety issues in schools. Her research interests focus on academic integrity, substance abuse, transition issues, and school engagement.

KATIE SELL, PH.D., is an Assistant Professor in the Department of Health and Human Performance at Hofstra University, where she is the undergraduate Exercise Science Program Director. Dr. Sell currently teaches undergraduate and graduate courses in exercise physiology, physical fitness assessment, and interpretation of research. She is also a certified strength and conditioning specialist (CSCS) through the NSCA, and an ACSM certified health fitness specialist (HFS). Dr. Sell's research interests focus around firefighter health, physical fitness standards, and the impact of NCAA rules and regulations on the professional practice of strength and conditioning coaches and athletic training personnel.

KATHERINE E. STANO is a doctoral student in Educational Leadership at Argosy University at Seattle. Her undergraduate degree is from Smith College and her master's degree is from Springfield College.

ARNOLD WOLF, Ph.D., is a Professor and Coordinator of the Counseling Programs, Educational Foundations and Counseling, Hunter College, City University of New York.

ERICA L. WONDOLOWSKI is a second graduate student in Rehabilitation Counseling at Springfield College. Her undergraduate degree is from Eastern Connecticut State University.

OVERVIEW
OF THE
ADDICTIONS
FIELD

BY **JOSEPH F. STANO**
SPRINGFIELD COLLEGE

Chapter Topics

◊ Introductory Comments
◊ Historical Perspective
◊ Variety of Services
◊ Future Trends

INTRODUCTORY COMMENTS

*T*oday we are bombarded by media. We have 24 hour news channels on television and countless websites. It seems like everyone has a Facebook or other social network account. People "tweet" a running commentary of their lives constantly in bursts of 140 characters or less. We are also obsessed with celebrities. A folksy definition of a celebrity is "someone who is famous for being famous." A person need not accomplish anything – they are just famous. Seemingly, everyone is looking for their 15 minutes of fame as Andy Warhol once stated. As part of this "culture of the personal" we know way too much about way too many people. Forget history or literature when we can live our lives vicariously through others.

Part of the "culture of the personal" is knowledge concerning every aspect of a person's life. So, it is not unusual today to know that _____ (famous person – fill in the blank) has been, or is going to, some type of REHAB program. As rehabilitation counseling practitioners know, REHAB can mean many things. It can include a myriad of treatment protocols. In the vernacular of today's minutiae-obsessed world REHAB has come to mean some type of in-patient treatment for some type of substance abuse. It has not always been this way, either for the concept of in-patient treatment or for treatment at all. To fully understand this, one needs a bit of a recent history lesson.

HISTORICAL PERSPECTIVE

In February of 1974, I accepted a position with the Massachusetts Rehabilitation Commission at Springfield to develop a new caseload in Addictions. This was coincidental with the development of a similar caseload in the Worcester office. At the time, I was completing my master's degree in rehabilitation counseling at Assumption College. It was a time when both the public rehabilitation agency and the field of addictions treatment were expanding rapidly. Alcoholics Anonymous had been started by Bill Wilson and Dr. Bob Smith in 1935 and the American Medical Association (AMA) had recognized Alcoholism as a disease in 1955. In spite of these social trends, the formal treatment of people with alcoholism and other addictions was in its infancy as the 1970s approached.

This was about to change in 1970. Under the sponsorship of Senator Harold Hughes, congress passed, and President Nixon signed, the Comprehensive Alcohol Abuse and Alcohol Prevention, Treatment, and Rehabilitation Act (P.L. 91-616). The passage of this law resulted in the formation of the National Institute of Alcohol Abuse and Alcoholism (NIAAA). It was also the impetus for the funding and development of countless community-based alcoholism treatment agencies across the country. Senator Hughes was himself a person in recovery from Alcoholism, and the strength of his will and commitment was the force that resulted in the passage of this law.

It has to be remembered that when Bill Wilson was attempting to gain sobriety there were no public facilities or programs that could be accessed so that the individual could begin to walk down the path of sobriety. Only through Bill Wilson's wife Lois, and her family's largess, was Bill able to receive treatment in a private facility. These facilities were analogous to a private psychiatric hospital, and entrance to them was based upon the ability to pay. If one did not have the financial resources then one would be denied admission. Health insurance, as we know it today, did not exist, and, even if it did, there were generally no provisions to pay for addiction treatment.

Recognition by the AMA certainly started the movement toward treatment but it was nearly as quick as the yearly movement of a glacier. There existed in the country, and to some degree still exists, a mindset that any form of addiction is a personal failing and essentially a personal morality issue. Within this mindset then, since one was "weak" enough to succumb to the siren call of alcohol and/or other drugs, it was the individual's personal responsibility to stop. Addiction was seen as a personal "choice" and simply as a matter of will. This may well have been one of the last vestiges of the Temperance Movement which resulted in the abolition of alcohol earlier in the Twentieth Century.

So, as I entered the field of Addictions Counseling in the early part of 1974, there was much change happening. By that time, the Commonwealth of Massachusetts had embraced the Hughes Act, and there were public in-patient detoxification centers in several cities, including Springfield. There was an umbrella agency, Alcohol Services of Greater Springfield, which oversaw the operation of the Detoxification Center, an Outpatient Clinic, and a Halfway House for adult males.

I need to digress and discuss the qualifications of persons working in the addictions field at that time. I was then a rehabilitation counselor with a master's degree and trained as a generalist with one course in the area of addictions. I had an intense interest in the field and immediately undertook a personal program of education in addictions. The Director of the Outpatient Clinic in the area had a Master's degree in Psychiatric Nursing. All other individuals working locally in the field had little or no college training or specific addictions training. The major qualification of many individuals working in the field in the local area and I would estimate nationally, was their own personal sobriety. This included persons working as "counselors" in local agencies.

The lack of specially trained individuals was the result of several concurrent factors:

- First, given the newness of the field, many colleges and universities had not yet established curricula focusing on the issues of addiction.
- Second, there was very little health care reimbursement for addiction services.
- Third, the salary ranges for typical professional level positions were inadequate.

- Finally, there was not yet the extensive public awareness that addictions treatment was both a significant medical and public health issue.

Today, there are a variety of mental health professionals who are qualified to provide counseling, therapy, and support to individuals with addiction issues. This is reflective of the growing trend of more and more education required to function in the therapeutic milieu. The addictions professional that the patient sees today generally has a minimum of a master's degree with specific training in addictions. Increasingly, doctoral level psychologists are providing care. A linkage here is that employers of mental health professionals require certain levels of education and licensure in order to seek reimbursement from health insurance providers and government funding sources.

Also available in the 1970s were extensive and long-term, in-patient programs for Veterans of the Armed services. These services were provided by the Veterans Administration. While the primary focus was upon in-patient services, there were the beginnings of outpatient, community-based services.

During the remainder of the 1970s treatment services expanded rapidly. A major factor was the provision in many health insurance policies that up to ninety days in-patient addictions treatment could be provided per calendar year. A major shift occurred, and there was the establishment of hundreds of "Addictions Hospitals" nationwide. I was constantly being called by field representatives of several such programs in the New England area for referrals. As the nature of drug use changed, this was an era when cocaine first became widely available and was widely used, and these facilities established specialty units to deal with other addictive substances. Again, up to ninety days of treatment could be provided under health insurance and, curiously enough, most programs were ninety days in duration.

Over the next 10-15 years, the situation for these facilities changed considerably. Given the cost, such services came under increasing scrutiny. It was eventually determined that ninety days of inpatient treatment was no more effective than thirty days of inpatient treatment. Health insurance carriers adjusted their policies to this new reality. Many programs could not continue to operate in this new environment. Of the four or five such programs that existed in my geographical area at that time only one is still in existence today. This is indicative of a nationwide trend.

For some time now there has been a growing trend to provide as many services on an outpatient basis as is possible. The therapeutic reasons for the trend center around staying in the supportive environment of your life; the financial reasons center upon cost control. Given the high level of deductable expenses in many health insurance policies this trend appears destined to continue. Coupled with this is the fact that millions of individuals lack health insurance. The variety of addiction services is inaccessible to these individuals due to cost alone.

VARIETY OF SERVICES

The variety of services for addiction treatment is extensive. Underlying all else is the presence of the Self-Help Movement, specifically Alcoholics Anonymous (AA). Since its inception in 1935, it has spread around both the country and the world. There are thousands of meetings each week in this country; they literally go on around the clock. The great majority of individuals are just a short drive away from a meeting anywhere that they live. In excess of one million people are sober today in AA in the United States. Before formal treatment existed, a person wishing to attain sobriety would call the AA number in the telephone book asking for assistance. AA members would go to the person's home on what is referred to as a "12 Step Call" in reference to the 12th step of AA's program of recovery. AA members would take turns staying with the person around the clock until they were detoxified. Physicians would assist as possible within the person's means.

Given the relative availability of primary detoxification and other services this routine is rarely practiced today. The foundation of recovery for many individuals is detoxification in an in-patient setting. The public detoxification centers that came into existence as a result of the Hughes Act are still functioning. Admission is available based on space. Typical in-patient stays in detoxification units last from 3-5 days with seven (7) days maximum for persons being detoxified solely from alcohol.

Once the person has successfully completed a detoxification program other treatment options become available. Several options include:

- Return to home with referral to outpatient counseling service; this may be the only option if the individual has no health insurance;
- referral to an in-patient program of up to 28 days in duration;
- if a veteran, referral to an in-patient program at a Veterans Administration Medical Center;
- referral to a halfway house or other similar residential sobriety program where the patient may reside from 3-12 months;
- referral to a psychiatrist, psychologist, or professional counselor for individual therapy;
- a person may be referred to an Employee Assistance Program that is a benefit provided by many employers; and
- a person may refuse any additional services.

There are a myriad of other services; the individual ultimately decides from which to choose, if any.

FUTURE TRENDS

The future of addiction is predicated upon several issues. Certainly, a crucial issue is that of funding. Governmental support, both at the federal and state levels, will continue to drive both the existence of services and the payment of services under both Medicare and Medicaid. This is inextricably coupled with the availability of health insurance. Estimates vary concerning the number of people who have no access to health care in this country at any given time. There may well be 35-50 million Americans who do not have health care and, therefore, lack access to the services needed to help them deal with their addiction. The health insurance reform of 2009 was a good start; more is needed. Mathematical and epidemiological modeling may be indicative of the fact that when money is spent for addiction treatment services, the result is a return to productive living by the individual. The individual returns to work and more than gives back in taxes the money spent on their addiction treatment.

A second issue is the continuing development of medicine and health care as a result of both basic and applied scientific discoveries. Practitioners have long understood the role that genetics plays in addiction and, with the understanding of the human genome, medical advances may be possible over the course of the next generation that were at one time relegated to the realm of science fiction. This includes both a more thorough understanding of brain function and continuing discoveries in the area of neuroplasticity.

Finally, the continued development of psychotherapeutic approaches will result in more efficient use of resources. The growth of Cognitive-Behavioral therapy has led to better treatment outcomes. When the advances in behavioral neuroscience are linked to counseling approaches, more patients will benefit in numerous ways.

The future of addiction treatment is both bright and shrouded in doubt. Yet, in spite of this, one can confidently say that treatment for those individuals with addiction issues in their lives has never been better.

 EPIDEMIOLOGY OF SUBSTANCE ABUSE

BY ERICA L. WONDOLOWSKI

MICHAEL P. ACCORDINO

BRIDGET L. HALPIN

SPRINGFIELD COLLEGE

Chapter Topics

◊ Introduction

◊ Gender

◊ Age

◊ Ethnicity

◊ Genetics

◊ Sexual Orientation

◊ Physical Trauma

◊ Mental Disorders/Co-Morbidity

◊ Conclusion

INTRODUCTION

Epidemiology consists of the study of factors affecting the health and illness of populations; its purpose is to help determine the best interventions that address different populations and to drive public policy. The way that optimal treatments are determined is through evidence-based practice. For the purpose of this chapter, the interaction of substance abuse with different populations is analyzed in order to determine differential patterns of the disease. Throughout the chapter, the substances referred to consist of alcohol, cigarettes, marijuana, cocaine, crack, heroin, and others. Subsequently, subpopulations such as gender, age, race, genetics, sexual orientation, physical trauma, and mental disorder/co-morbidity are all reviewed.

GENDER

Approximately one in 7.5 women are at risk for becoming dependent on an illicit drug after first use. Tobacco, alcohol, and illicit drugs, respectively, are the substances most likely to incite dependence in women. Approximately six percent of women between the ages of 15 and 54 are reported to have met the criteria for a lifetime diagnosis of dependence on an illicit or psychotropic drug.[10] Women are significantly more likely to develop a dependence on psychotropic drugs when used recreationally. Regardless, it has been reported that rates for overall dependence on drugs are significantly higher for men than women. Specifically, alcohol and marijuana dependence are more than twice as high for men as for women, and illicit drug dependence is more than 50 percent higher for men.

It has also been reported that these trends increase with age and that gender differences during adolescence are very small. Individuals within the age range of 15 to 24 reportedly have the highest rate of yearlong dependence on drugs. This rate significantly declines after 24, however. The highest reported drug used during adolescence is tobacco, which, for all ages, is used more by women than men.[10] The use of tobacco is reported to decline after adolescence. Women tend not to progress to illicit drugs unless they have previously used tobacco, whereas men typically progress to illicit drugs after an introduction to alcohol use, regardless of whether or not they have smoked cigarettes.[10] Those adolescents who have experimented with an illicit drug are more likely than their peers to recreationally use prescribed psychotropic drugs. This is especially true for females.

It is reported that when females smoked cigarettes during pregnancy, their children are significantly more likely to adopt the habit of smoking by age thirteen. When mothers experience maternal depression, their adult children are reported to have an increased risk for depression, alcoholism, and cocaine/opioid abuse.[10] This is reported to be more significant in daughters than sons.

AGE

Childhood, Adolescence and Young Adulthood. Age of onset is reported to be one of the most significant factors in the later development of substance use disorders. Particularly, the earlier an individual begins use of a substance, the higher the risk of substance abuse problems later in life. Adolescents who begin to use substances before the age of 15, in conjunction with the emergence of conduct problems, are significantly more likely to develop problems surrounding chronic offending, school failure/unemployment, depression, relational problems, and low self-esteem through adulthood.[16] Physical, emotional, and mental development is at greater risk when substance use behaviors begin in adolescence.

Increased alcohol and drug use in adolescence is strongly associated with various factors such as low socioeconomic status, parental substance abuse, poor family relations, time spent with peers, peer support and risk behavior, lack of interest in school, low self esteem, depressive symptomology, and later development of substance use disorders.[10,16,23,24,27] Genetic factors have been reported to explain a substantial portion of the overlapping risks among alcohol, tobacco, and marijuana use problems in youth.[24] Family situation, peer factors, and school-related factors are also reported to predict problematic substance use.[23] Familial characteristics such as medication within the family for anxiety issues and a father's heavy drinking were strongly associated with problematic alcohol and cannabis use.[27] Individual, family, peer, and school influences all play significant roles in predicting substance abuse issues.

Alcohol was the substance experimented with, repeatedly used, and abused the most by adolescents. Tobacco, however, was reported to elicit the greatest dependency.[24] Adolescent smoking not only increased an individual's odds of developing tobacco/nicotine dependence, but also increased the odds of developing abuse of or dependence on alcohol and marijuana.[24,27] Tobacco smoking, and involvement with police and juvenile authorities during adolescence were associated most strongly with adult alcohol abuse.[27] The likelihood of developing a lifetime diagnosis of an alcohol substance use disorder was at least eight times greater if an individual was dependent on tobacco as opposed to being abstinent. Use or dependence on tobacco during adolescence significantly promotes the likelihood of alcohol and marijuana problems in young adulthood.[24]

Alcohol use, in conjunction with cannabis use during adolescence, is more highly associated with both adult alcohol abuse and adult drug abuse than when used separately during adolescence. Contrary to popular belief, marijuana is not a "gateway drug" and use of this substance does not necessarily indicate the subsequent use of other illicit drugs. However, almost all persistent drug users are reported to have used cannabis, alcohol, and tobacco prior to the use of drugs such as opiates or central stimulants. Use and abuse of these illicit substances have become a widespread issue among adolescents in many industrial countries.[27]

Two out of three adolescents have reported the use of an illicit drug within the past three months.[27] When surveying adolescents currently in treatment, it was reported that a significant number had multiple problems, including concurrent marijuana use and high alcohol consumption. Of these adolescents, those who used multiple drugs rated their addiction as more problematic than did those who used alcohol alone. A broad sampling of substances throughout adolescence generally increases the risk for developing problems of abuse and dependence in young adulthood and into later adulthood.[24]

The combined use of alcohol and cannabis is associated most strongly with adult drug abuse and involvement in other negative behaviors such as criminality, prostitution, and association with drug-using friends.[27] Those who continue using drugs from adolescence through to adulthood are at risk for alcohol and cigarette use, poor mental health, and school problems.

College-aged. In the spring of 1999, O'Malley and Johnston[22] reported that approximately two out of three college students surveyed had reported having at least one alcoholic drink in the thirty days prior to the survey. Furthermore, two out of five students reported having engaged in heavy drinking within the previous two weeks. Concerning gender based use, O'Malley and Johnston[22] reported that alcohol use is generally higher for those male college-aged students who attend school than their female counterparts. It has been posited that two and a half times more male college-aged students than female college-aged students report consuming ten or more drinks per week. Heavy alcohol use has been reported to be more prevalent in the northeast and north central regions of the United States and lowest in the south and western areas. When compared to the west, the southern region has increased alcohol use. Regarding college aged alcohol consumption, O'Malley and Johnson[22] identified that White students, aged 18-22, had the greatest level of alcohol consumption followed by Hispanics and Blacks, respectively.

College aged students currently enrolled in an institution of higher learning are reported to be slightly more likely than their peers who do not attend college to use alcohol, specifically at heavier levels of use. Although alcohol use is higher in matriculated college age students, marijuana, cocaine, and tobacco use are higher in those peers who are not enrolled.[22] High school students who ultimately attend college are lower in frequency and level of drinking than those who do not attend college. Although both groups are at risk of increasing their drinking after graduation, those students who attend college significantly increase their alcohol consumption in comparison to their non-matriculated peers. Whether a student lives on campus also plays a role in alcohol consumption, as those students who live at home and commute to college are reported to drink less than their peers do.

Epler, et al.[8] reported that slightly less than half of college students surveyed reported drinking five or more drinks on at least one occasion within a two week time period. Extensive and frequent drinking is reported to be linked to alcohol related social, legal, and physical problems in college students. These problems include drunk driving, unintended death, injuries, and influences on academic performance. Despite these effects, only 15 percent of students surveyed reported an interest in cutting down on drinking and five percent reported an interest in abstaining from drinking altogether. After alcohol, cigarettes are reported to be the most used substance by college-aged individuals with approximately one third of those surveyed reporting smoking at least one cigarette in the past thirty days. Less than one fifth of those surveyed currently use marijuana and less than one fiftieth currently use cocaine.[22]

The recreational use and abuse of prescription drugs have been a recent development among the collegiate population. More than half of the participants in a 2009 study reported the use of pharmaceutical drugs for non-medical purposes in the past year, and a 342% increase was seen in recreational drug use between the years of 1993 and 2005.[25] Prescription medications are also currently the second most abused drugs by college-aged individuals, second only to marijuana. Reported misused prescription drugs included Demerol, Percocet, OxyContin, and Vicodin, (narcotic analgesics), Adderall, Dexadrine, and Ritalin, (central nervous system stimulants), and Diazepam, Valium, and Xanax (anti-anxiety medications). Quintero[25] reported that 1 in 5 college age students have abused hydrocodone within the last year to achieve a drug induced high.

Participants in the Quintero[25] study reported having a variety of problems related to recreational prescription drug use including nausea, addiction, overdose, effects on relationships, unconsciousness, legal implications, poor academic performance, and death. The ability of users to manage their highs by altering the amount of prescription drug they take and the combination by which they take them, allows the user to produce a specific high and reduce the concern for physical, social and relational consequences.

Middle-Aged and Elderly Adults. Blazer and Wu[3] reported findings that reflected a significant difference in drug use and drug of choice between middle-aged individuals and those who are ages 65 and older. Blazer and Wu[3] also reported that more than half of the adult respondents reported having used alcohol, and a small percentage also admitted using marijuana and/or cocaine in the past year. Those adults classified as middle-aged were reported to be significantly more likely to have used illegal drugs in their lifetime than those aged 65 and older. Active use of illegal drugs was also reported more in middle-aged than elderly adults.

Specifically, marijuana and cocaine use was found to be more prevalent in 50-64 year old men. Alcohol, too, was more prevalent in middle-aged men who were white, had achieved a higher level of education, well employed, married, and lived in large metropolitan areas. Those who used alcohol, marijuana, and cocaine were more likely to be 50-64 years old, male, separated, divorced, or widowed, and to have had major depression in the past year. Trends were identified which showed that those elders who have used illegal drugs for a lengthy period of time in their life tend to move towards excessive use of prescription medications later in life.[3]

ETHNICITY

Caucasian. Whites have higher prevalence rates of substance abuse disorders and drug abuse than other racial and ethnic groups. However, racial and ethnic minorities have been shown to have substance abuse disorders that persist for longer periods of time.[4] Drug abuse rates were found to be lower for Caucasians using crack cocaine and heroin. Higher rates of alcohol consumption are reported in those of Caucasian or Hispanic descent.[3]

African American/Black/Caribbean. African Americans are reportedly more likely to use and abuse alcohol and marijuana than Asians, Pacific Islanders, and Native Hawaiians.[3] Additionally, African Americans are reportedly more likely to use cocaine than Caucasians. Blazer and Wu[3] identify the importance of not grouping persons based on the color of their skin when studying ethnic descent, as it can obscure important distinctions in data collection. The distinction between Caribbean and African descent can produce several important variables in the development and/or cultivation of substance abuse and substance dependence disorders.[4]

American Indian/Alaskan Native. As reported by Young and Joe,[33] American Indians/Alaska Natives have a higher rate of illicit drug use across all age groups when compared to non-Indians. Substance use was reported to be most often initiated before age 18.[26] It has been reported that American Indians/Alaska Natives "have the highest rates of use for marijuana, cocaine, inhalants, hallucinogens, and non-medical use of psychotherapeutics compared to other ethnic groups."[33,p. 223] Despite alcohol consumption being higher in Caucasians, American Indians/Alaska Natives have the highest alcohol-related mortality, substance use, and dependence rates of all ethnic groups.[33] Almost fifty percent of those Native Americans/Alaska Natives who later met the criteria for a substance use disorder had noticeable symptoms prior to 18 years old. Being a male younger than eighteen years of age who has experienced adversity is associated with significantly greater risk of early substance use.[26,33]

Hispanic. Illicit drug abuse or dependence among adult Hispanics is slightly higher than that of Caucasians and lower than rates among African American and American Indian/Alaska Natives.[17] Illicit drug use within the race, however, is highest among those between 18 and 25 years of age, and decreases after this time period. Binge alcohol use is comparable to that of adult Caucasians, whereas lifetime alcohol use was significantly lower in adult Hispanics, when comparing the two groups. Comparison among several Hispanic groups shows significant trends in substance use, abuse, and dependence.

Although the highest prevalence of illicit drug use is among Puerto Rican and Mexican-American men, Cubans between the ages of 18 and 29 have the highest prevalence of alcohol use.[17] Mexican-Americans tend to drink more frequently, in heavier quantities, and have more alcohol-related problems than Cuban-Americans. Cuban-Americans and Central/South -Americans were reported to have the lowest illicit drug use rates among several Hispanic groups. When analyzing for gender, women were consistently more likely to abstain from frequent heavy drinking than men. Puerto Rican women were reported to have the highest heavy drinking rates, whereas Cuban women rate the lowest, although both groups' rates are significantly lower than their male counterparts.[17]

Acculturation plays a large role in Hispanic drug and alcohol use, abuse, and dependence. Hispanics who identified as fully or midway acculturated to America were significantly more likely to develop one or more substance use disorders. Furthermore, Hispanic individuals who were born in the United States, rather than immigrated, were more likely to develop one or more substance use disorders. Hispanic individuals who choose to speak English as their primary language are more likely to engage in illicit drug use.[17] Overall, Hispanic individuals who are first generation immigrants to the United States are less likely to develop one or more substance use disorders than future generations.

GENETICS

Substance use disorders, including abuse and dependence, have been reported to have been exhibited by those individuals who have first-degree relatives and offspring who also have a substance use disorder.[6,11,14] Being a first-degree relative and offspring who has a substance use disorder has also been reported to act as effective pre-morbid predictors of the development of substance abuse.[21,28,31] Specifically, it has been reported that genetic factors appear to be more strongly associated with drug use disorders than drug use,[6,11] and that substance use disorders are now "believed to arise from multiple genes exerting small effects, gene by gene interactions, gene by environment interactions, and/or a host of environmental and risk-conferring behaviors."[6,p.1498]

SEXUAL ORIENTATION

Non-heterosexual persons disclose significantly higher rates of substance use than heterosexuals.[20,18,30] Substance use disorders are more prominent in non-heterosexual females than males,[20] subsequently leading to the report of higher rates of substance use in bisexual and lesbian women than gay or bisexual males.[18,30] One particular study reported a 190% increase in odds of substance use in lesbian, gay, and bisexual persons. The subpopulation of bisexual youth showed a 340% increase and 400% increase for females who classify themselves within lesbian, gay, bisexual, and transgender (LGBT) orientation spectrum.[18]

Bisexual women who reported being a current and solitary substance user, also reported having "stronger pro-drug beliefs and lower resistance self-efficacy, perceived greater parental approval of substance abuse, more exposure to substance using peers, and reported poorer mental health."[30, p. 387] It was also reported that by the age of twenty-three, bisexual women reported higher rates of current substance abuse, including an increase in quantity and frequency, and increased issues revolving around alcohol and drug use.

PHYSICAL TRAUMA

Illicit and licit drug use have been reported in most of those patients presenting with a traumatic physical injury. Drug use, in many cases, was found to precede the trauma and potentially may have contributed to the outcome.[1] In the approximate 2.2 million trauma patients who are hospitalized each year, 19% of them are reportedly due, at least in part, to the use of alcohol and illicit drugs. When admitted for initial medical consultation, more than half of the patients tested positive for alcohol, 1 out of 3 patients tested independently positive for marijuana and cocaine, and 1 out of 10 patients tested positive for opiates. Adults between the ages of 26 and 34 were more likely to be admitted for cocaine and heroin-related traumas, and adolescents for marijuana-related traumas.[15]

For some, substance use is not the basis for their physical trauma, but occurs following initial onset. More than 1 out of 3 respondents with a physical trauma indicated a possible problem with alcohol or drug abuse within the previous month.[2] Substance use was much more prevalent among patients with acute physical trauma than in the general population.[1,15]

A large percentage of individuals with spinal cord injury have reported using both legal and illegal substances within the past 6-12 months–primarily marijuana, cocaine, and opiates.[13] Persons with spinal cord injury are reportedly more likely to drink alcohol daily when compared to persons without. When comparing those individuals with a traumatic brain injury to individuals with a spinal cord injury, those afflicted with a spinal cord injury are more likely to use illicit drugs following the traumatic event.[13]

Post-injury substance use poses significant risks including, but not limited to, "worse rehabilitation outcomes, decreased life satisfaction, increased depression, and increased risk for seizures and re-injury.[13, p.584] This study evaluated the post-injury substance use in individuals with traumatic brain injuries and reported that individuals who continue to use have an inclination towards higher rates of psychiatric disorders, aggressive behavior, arrests, and lower returns to work rates.

MENTAL DISORDERS/CO-MORBIDITY

Mental disorder co-morbidity, or the existence of a mental disorder that is accompanied by a drug use disorder, has been associated with "underachievement, decreased work productivity, poor health, neuropsychological impairment, human immunodeficiency virus infection, hepatitis, social dysfunction, incarceration, poverty, homelessness, a lower probability of recovery, poor treatment outcome, and poor quality of life."[6,p. 566,7] Slightly more than one half of those with a lifetime substance disorder also meet the criteria for at least one lifetime psychiatric disorder, and one in three of those suffering with a psychiatric disorder were reported to have a poly-substance dependence problem.[10,19] Individuals with a poly-substance dependence problem often scored higher for childhood emotional and physical neglect, psychoticism, aggression, and impulsivity.[19]

Research has reported that individuals who abuse only one substance are more likely to be diagnosed with an Axis I psychiatric disorder, and to experience a higher level of depression. Poly-substance users, or those who abuse two or more substances, were significantly more likely to have attempted suicide, self-mutilated, and/or exhibited aggressive behavior.[5,19] Adolescents who identify as former or current daily cigarette smokers, or those who used marijuana often, were more likely to have a history of major depression.[2,6] Individuals with a substance use disorder and physical trauma are reported to have increasingly more depressive symptoms and were additionally more likely to have attempted suicide.[9]

Anxiety and panic disorders are prevalent in individuals with substance use disorders, especially women.[5,7] One in five women has a substance use disorder, one in four has an affective disorder, and one in three women has an anxiety disorder. Individuals with two or more substance use disorders were significantly more likely to have increased occurrence and length of affective episodes, and to be far less compliant with any received treatment.[5] Panic disorders (both with and without agoraphobia) are significantly associated with lifetime drug dependence.[7] Those identifying as current or former daily smokers were more likely to suffer from panic disorders, agoraphobia, and substance use disorders.[6]

Bipolar Disorder I is significantly characterized by drug dependence and/or substance use disorders.[5,7] Overall quality of life is reported to be greatly impaired in those persons with Bipolar Disorder I who additionally have a substance use disorder, which greatly increases the risk for suicide attempts[5,7] Two out of three patients with Bipolar Disorder I have a lifetime history of a drug and/or alcohol use disorder, although alcohol abuse is significantly more prevalent within the population.[5] For patients with Bipolar Disorder II, almost half of the population met the criteria for a lifetime history of a drug and/or alcohol use. Alcohol abuse is significantly more prevalent than drug abuse in those with Bipolar II disorder.

Antisocial personality and conduct disorders are found in slightly more than half of all men suffering with one or more substance use disorders, in comparison to the one in five men who suffer from anxiety or affect disorders[5,7,10] Antisocial personality disorder is also correlated with characteristics such as physical altercations, arguments, telephone harassment, felony convictions, and use of substances on the work site.[32] Subsequently, high levels of attention deficit and hyperactivity disorder and/or conduct disorder are positively correlated with marijuana use between the ages of 13 and 18.[6] Antisocial personality disorder had the highest lifetime prevalence rate among those with a substance use disorder in comparison to those with schizophrenia and major depression.[5] Lifetime drug abuse and dependence were reported to be significantly related to mood, anxiety, and personality disorders.[6,7]

CONCLUSION

Substance abuse is a growing concern for people of all ages and races. Within certain populations, substance abuse is at an alarming rate. Within subpopulations of gender, sexual orientation, age, minority cultures, and mental illnesses, substance abuse has created both personal and social barriers to autonomy and independent living. As the substance abuse problem evolves, so do the interventions that are needed to understand and treat the issue. The epidemiological studies are only an initial step. The more researchers learn about the pattern of behaviors associated with substance use and abuse, the more they can learn about how to help prevent and treat the signs and symptoms associated with substance use and abuse.

There are, however, limitations to epidemiologic research. In order to study large sample sizes over long periods of time, there are significant requirements for time and money in order to obtain intensive and detailed measures. Additionally, the observational nature of most of epidemiologic substance abuse research often prohibits the use of true experimental designs. Improvements in the field of substance abuse epidemiology will require innovations in the areas of research design, statistical analyses, and sociologic and genetic epidemiologic designs to adequately meet the challenges that lie ahead in the constantly evolving substance abuse field. Research is essential to examine contemporary substance abuse trends where varieties of new substances are becoming increasingly available to diverse subpopulations, and in an ever-expanding range of settings. With a social problem as fluid as substance abuse, the challenge to assess the changing availability as well as changing social and cultural trends that influence patterns of use, is enormous.

Lastly, the social and behavioral consequences of substance abuse require additional research to examine the range of behavioral and social consequences that accompany the problem. Such consequences include educational and occupational problems, crime and violence, as well as comorbid medical issues associated with overdose, suicide, and cognitive/neurological impairments. Social consequences such as drug dealing, involvement in gang activities, family dysfunction, and neighborhood disruption all create serious barriers to community cohesion. While there is anecdotal evidence, few studies have assessed how abuse of particular drugs and combinations of drugs affects these consequences. The need to understand retail street drug activity and consumption patterns, as well as to understand drug distribution networks and drug price/purity and availability, are areas for future research. While data exists on the frequency of substance use estimates, data on estimates of drug price/purity, and the quantity of drugs consumed should be mined in future studies.

REFERENCES

[1]Ahmadi, J., Tabatabaee, F., & Gozin, Z. (2006). Physical trauma and substance abuse: a comparative study on substance abuse in patients with physical trauma versus general population. *Journal of Addictive Diseases*, 25(1), 51-63.

[2]Baker, D. G., Heppner, P., Afari, N., Nunnink, S., Kilmer, M., Simmons, A., Harder, L, & Bosse, B (2009). Trauma exposure, branch of service, and physical injury in relation to mental health among u.s. veterans returning from iraq and afghanistan. *Military Medicine*, 174(8), 773-778.

[3]Blazer, D. G., & Wu, L.(2009). The epidemiology of substance use and disorders among middle aged and elderly community adults: national survey on drug use and health. *American Journal of Geriatric Psychiatry*, 17(3), 237-245.

[4]Broman, C. L., Neighbors, H. W., Delva, J., Torres, M., & Jackson, J. S. (2008). Prevalence of substance use disorders among african americans and caribbean blacks in the national survey of american life. *American Journal of Public Health*, 98(6), 1107-1114.

[5]Cerullo, M. A. & Strakowski, S. M. (2007). The prevalence and significance of substance use disorders in bipolar type I and II disorder. *Substance Abuse Treatment, Prevention, and Policy*, 2, 29-37.

[6]Compton, W. M., Thomas, Y. F., Conway, K. P., & Colliver, J. D. (2005). Developments in the epidemiology of drug use and drug use disorders. *American Journal of Psychiatry*, 162, 1494-1502.

[7]Compton, W. M., Thomas, Y. F., Stinson, F. S., & Grant, B. F. (2007). Prevalence, correlates, disability, and comorbidity of DSM-IV drug abuse and dependence in the united states. *Archives of General Psychiatry*, 64, 566-576.

[8]Epler, A. J., Sher, K. J., Loomis, T. B., & O'Malley, S. S. (2009). College student receptiveness to various alcohol treatment options. *Journal of American College Health*, 58(1), 26-32.

[9]Felde, A. B., Westermeyer, J., & Thuras, P. (2006). Co-morbid traumatic brain injury and substance use disorder: childhood predictors and adult correlates. *Brain Injury*, 20(1), 41-49.

[10]Kandel, D. B., Warner, L. A., & Kessler, R. C. (1998). The epidemiology of substance use and dependence among women. In C. L. Wetherington & A. B. Roman (Eds.), *Drug addiction research and the health of women* (pp. 105-130, NIH Publication No. 98-4290). Rockville, MD: National Institute on Drug Abuse.

[11]Kendler, K. S., Jacobson, K. C., Prescott, C. A., & Neale, M. C. (2003). Specificity of genetic and environmental risk factors for use and abuse/dependence of cannabis, cocaine, hallucinogens, sedatives, stimulants, and opiates in male twins. *American Journal of Psychiatry*, 160, 687-695.

[12]Kendler, K. S., Prescott, C. A., Myers, J., & Neale, M. C. (2003). The structure of genetic and environmental risk factors for common psychiatric and substance use disorders in men and women. *Arch Gen Psychiatry*, 60, 929-937.

[13]Kolakowsky-Hayner, S. A., Gourley III, E. V., Kreutzer, J. S., Marwitz, J. H., Meade, M. A., & Cifu, D. X. (2002). Post-injury substance abuse among persons with brain injury and persons with spinal cord injury. *Brain Injury*, 16(7), 583-592.

[14]Langbehn, D. R., Cadoret, R. J., Caspers, K., Troughton, E. P., Yucuis, R. (2003). Genetic and environmental risk factors for the onset of drug use and problems in adoptees. *Drug and Alcohol Dependence*, 69, 151-167.

[15]Li, G. (2000). Epidemiology of substance abuse among trauma patients. *Trauma Quarterly*, 14(4), 353-364.

[16]Liddle, H. A., Rowe, C. L., Dakof, G. A., Henderson, C. E., & Greenbaum, P. E. (2009). Multidimensional family therapy for young adolescent substance abuse: twelve-month outcomes of a randomized controlled trial. *Journal of Consulting and Clinical Psychology*, 77(1), 12-25.

[17]Lipsky, S. & Caetano, R. (2009). Epidemiology of substance abuse among latinos. *Journal of Ethnicity in Substance Abuse*, 8, 242-260.

[18]Marshal, M. P., Friedman, M. S., Stall, R., King, K. M., Miles, J., Gold, M. A., Bukstein, O. G., & Morse, J. Q. (2008). Sexual orientation and adolescent substance use: a meta-analysis and methodological review. *Addiction*, 103, 546-556.

[19]Martinotti, G., Carli, V., Tedeschi, D., Di Giannantonio, Roy, A., Janiri, L., & Sarchiapone, M. (2009). Mono- and polysubstance dependent subjects differ on social factors, childhood trauma, personality, suicidal behaviour, and comorbid axis I diagnoses. *Addictive Behaviors*, 34, 790-793.

[20]McCabe, S. E., Hughes, T. L., Bostwick, W. B., West, B. T., & Boyd, C. J. (2009). Sexual orientation, substance use behaviors, and substance dependence in the united states. *Addiction*, 104, 1333-1345.

[21]Moss, H. B., Lynch, K. G., Hardie, T. L., & Baron, D. A. (2002). Family functioning and peer affiliation in children of fathers with antisocial personality disorder and substance dependence: associations with problem behaviors. *American Journal of Psychiatry*, 159, 607-614.

[22]O'Malley, P. M., & Johnston, L. D. (2002). Epidemiology of alcohol and other drug use among american college students. *Journal of Studies on Alcohol Supplement, 63*(2), 23-39.

[23]Osler, M., Nordentoft, M., & Andersen, A. N.(2006). Childhood social environment and risk of drug and alcohol abuse in a cohort of danish men born in 1953. *American Journal of Epidemiology, 163*, 654-661.

[24]Palmer, R. H. C., Young, S. E., Hopfer, C. J., Corley, R. P., Stallings, M. C., Crowley, T. J., & Hewitt, J. K. (2009). Developmental epidemiology of drug use and abuse in adolescence and young adulthood: evidence of generalized risk. *Drug and Alcohol Dependence, 102*(1-3), 78-87.

[25]Quintero, G. (2009). Rx for a party: a qualitative analysis of recreational pharmaceutical use in a collegiate setting. *Journal of American College Health, 58*(1), 64-70.

[26]Rumbaugh Whitesell, N., Beals, J., Mitchell, C. M., Manson, S. M., Turner, R. J., & The AI-Superpfp Team. (2009). Childhood exposure to adversity and risk of substance-use disorder in two american indian populations: the meditational role of early substance-use initiation. *Journal of Studies on Alcohol and Drugs, 70*, 971-981.

[27]Stenbacka, M. (2003). Problematic alcohol and cannabis use in adolescence – risk of serious adult substance abuse? *Drug and Alcohol Review, 22*, 277-286.

[28]Tarter, R. E., Kirisci, L., Mezzich, A., Cornelius, J. R., Pajer, K., Vanyukov, N., Gardner, W., Blackson, T., & Clark, D. (2003). Neurobehavioral disinhibition in childhood predicts early age at onset of substance use disorder. *American Journal of Psychiatry, 160*, 1078-1085.

[29]Tsuang, M. T. & Tohen, M. (2002). *Textbook in psychiatric epidemiology*, 2nd ed. (Eds.) New York, NY: Wiley-Liss.

[30]Tucker, J. S., Ellickson, P. L., & Klein, D. J. (2008). Understanding differences in substance use among bisexual and heterosexual young women. *Women's Health Issues, 18*, 387-398.

[31]Vanyukov, M. M., Kirisci, L., Moss, L., Tarter, R. E., Reynolds, M. D., Maher, B. S., Kirillova, G. P., Ridenour, T., & Clark, D. B. (2009). Measurement of the risk for substance use disorders: phenotypic and genetic analysis of an index of common liability. *Behavior Genetics, 39*, 233-244.

[32]Westermeyer, J., & Thuras, P. (2005). Association of antisocial personality disorder and substance disorder morbidity in a clinical sample. *The American Journal of Drug and Alcohol Abuse, 1*, 93-110.

[33]Young, R. S., & Joe, J. R. (2009). Some thoughts about the epidemiology of alcohol and drug use among american indian/alaska native populations. *Journal of Ethnicity in Substance Abuse, 8*, 223-241.

MECHANISMS OF

ADDICTION

BY **ARNOLD WOLF**

HUNTER COLLEGE
CITY UNIVERSITY OF NEW YORK

Jacob Yui-Chung Chan

BALL STATE UNIVERSITY

CHAPTER TOPICS

◊ Opening Comments

◊ Medical/ Disease/Genetic Theories

◊ Learning Theory

◊ Relapse Prevention Theory

◊ Personality/Trait Theories

◊ Comorbidity Theory

◊ Biopsychosocial Theory

OPENING COMMENTS

*S*ubstance abuse is a disability and many people believe that there exists an understanding of the causation of the disability. However, there are no clear definitions related to causation to this date. Budziack[4] offers the simplest definition of the disability by implying that a person is either a substance abuser or is not a substance abuser. It is intriguing to note that people who are addicts or alcoholics take drugs and alcohol compulsively in spite of knowing the potential serious consequences of their own behavior that could lead to a loss of life, prison, and destruction of their role within society.

No single theory can fully explain all cases and potential causes of addiction. Each theory appears to contribute to a better understanding of the problems inherent in substance abuse, but each theory lacks a comprehensive overview of the issue.

CASE STUDY

Bill and John grow up in the same neighborhood, attend the same schools, receive the same grades while in school, enjoy the same social activities, and both young men come from home environments where they are loved, supported and no one in their respective families used drugs or alcohol. At 25, Bill is using heroin and has been arrested five times. He is currently awaiting trial for grand theft and will probably go to prison for at least ten years. John, on the other hand, completed his law degree at 24, does not use drugs or alcohol, and he will be defending his friend when Bill's case is presented in court. Given the strong similarities in background and life experiences, what made one person use drugs while the other person never used drugs, or even an occasional alcoholic drink? Could the problem be environmental? Could the problem be genetic since neither family has ever been tested for anything remotely related to drug abuse?

Ralph is another friend of Bill and John. It is well known in the local community that Ralph's grandfather and father were alcoholics. Ralph was abusing alcohol by age 19 and died in a car crash at age 20, where it was determined that his blood sugar was well beyond the limit to drive a car, and he was clearly responsible for the accident. This sounds as if it might be a genetic predisposition toward alcoholic abuse, but it could also be environmental given his familial history of alcohol abuse.

MEDICAL/ DISEASE/GENETIC THEORIES

The "disease" model, sometimes called the "medical" model,[14] proposes that addiction is a medical situation with a strong biological emphasis. Many disease model theorists point to the importance of biological predisposition toward substance abuse and dependence. The model also implies that the disease is progressive. In essence, addiction is regarded as a disease such as diabetes and cancer. This model has social implications. For example, people who are alcoholics are now liberated from the moral blame for their problems since it is a dysfunction of their body or genetic structure. Further, the model strongly implies that such persons are in need of medical treatment and are in fact the victims of a disease. Different biological theories have been established ranging from genetic predisposition to differences in metabolic rates for breaking down the substances in our body.

Indicative of the disease model is research that validates addiction as a chronic progression in which symptoms increase with time. Symptoms include an increased loss of control when using substances over time, physical cravings for the substance that increase with time, increased physical tolerance to the effects of the substance with time, and marked symptoms of withdrawal when the person stops using drugs or alcohol.[24] Medical treatment is considered the appropriate intervention and the person who abuses a chemical does not treat his or her own symptoms or problems without medical help.[5] The treatment goal is total abstinence from using the chemical that caused the abuse.[23] In a similar manner, studies of the human brain indicate that brain functions change with on-going abuse and such changes lead to the compulsion to use drugs.[29]

Recent medical research explores the relationships between abuse of chemicals in relation to genes, proteins, and enzymes with the intent of finding body markers that lead to abuse, and the hope of finding ways to prevent abuse. Many of these studies involve data far beyond the training of persons working in the allied health professions, but a summary of such data leads to an increased awareness that there may well be genetic or other factors that can lead to or cause substance abuse. One study[15] found that certain metabolites significantly contribute to the increased liability of codeine abuse. Nestler[30] reported that diagnosing substance abuse at present is based solely on subjective observations of behavior. This ignores objective methods such as "genomics," or the identification of genes that confer risk for addiction, and simultaneously identify proteins that contribute to the regulation of rewards as in feeling euphoric from use of illicit chemicals. A third study found that a relationship exists between neuropeptides and alcohol dependence.[20] In summation, many of the genetic studies show considerable promise for some future date, but many of the current studies are still exploratory. Some are done with animals versus humans, and others provide research specific to only one chemical in one situation.

CASE STUDY

Imagine yourself in a not too distant future where you are married and have a child. The attending physician requests permission to test your child for various illnesses including substance abuse and alcoholism. The test results indicate a strong potential for alcohol abuse by 20 years of age, but the physician tells you that the hospital can modify a gene to eliminate the risk.

In a more realistic and current setting, a person enters a substance abuse treatment center where urine samples are taken daily and hair samples are taken every week. The tests are done to objectively assess past and current use of an illegal substance. While in treatment, the person is given a regimen of medical and sometimes psychiatric medications to reduce symptoms related to withdrawal from the illegal drug. Upon discharge, the person visits an outpatient clinic weekly where urine and hair tests are done periodically to insure compliance with nonuse of illegal drugs.

LEARNING THEORY

Classical and operant learning theories are applied to the development of substance use and abuse. Bandura[8] reported that maladjustment is an outcome of faulty learning, since a person learns that substance use is rewarding and reinforces behaviors that result in continued substance use or addiction. This is an example of operant conditioning. The classical learning model can be seen when reviewing the social environment of the individual. The person receives cues from drug using friends, family members, and social parties associated with drug use itself that can lead to a conditioned response, such as withdrawal or craving, even without the presence of the drug. Operant learning theory explains addiction by stating that drugs or alcohol can be considered as positive reinforcement that produces euphoria, or as negative reinforcement that produces withdrawal behaviors. Either positive or negative reinforcement triggers the continued use of drugs or alcohol to maintain euphoria, or to avoid the pain of withdrawal.

As an overview of the learning theory approach, a person who is abusing drugs or alcohol will assess the positive and negative value of using drugs as a means of reinforcing mood alterations, lack of punishment or perceived lack of societal punishment for drug or alcohol use, and lack of reinforcement from other sources other than drugs or alcohol to positively alter mood.[9] Treatment that leads to the cessation of drug or alcohol use focuses on learning skills and behaviors that prevent relapse, including learning new and reinforcing behaviors not associated with drug or alcohol use while unlearning old drug or alcohol behaviors

This traditional view of learning, which involves pleasure seeking and withdrawal, has its share of limitations as a comprehensive treatment model. Drug withdrawal may not be as powerful at motivating people to use drugs as people perceive since it was found that the strength of negative reinforcement, such as stress and withdrawal, may not be robust in motivating drug-seeking behavior.[33] Though this might sound contradictory to the common belief of operant learning theory, it fits with the responses from addicts that their sick feelings of withdrawal are not the same as their feelings of craving more drugs or alcohol.

CASE STUDY

Some of the most frightening images that emerged with the advent of crack/cocaine were statements made by drug addicts who reported that no other experiences in the world, including other illegal drugs, came close to the feelings induced by crack/cocaine. Drug addicts reported that it was the most reinforcing feeling that they ever experienced in their lives. Sobriety lacked the reinforcing quality of using crack/cocaine and abusers addicted to this drug are among the most difficult cases, since the abuser refuses to give up the drug.

At age 21, Mary believed that she was not attractive and lacked a personality that would be interesting to men of her age group. Mary decided to have a double martini while attending a party with her friends. Although she had one or two drinks before that time, she never tried a double shot of alcohol before in her life. Within minutes, she felt relief, reduced anxiety, and a new sense of confidence. She found that she could easily talk to men about any topic and when she saw her reflection in a mirror she realized that she was not as unattractive as she thought herself to be at other times. Mary knew that she should not have additional alcohol that evening since it could lead to problems that she did not want to consider. However, she noted that her anxiety returned after an hour or so, and that her confidence was decreasing, especially when talking to men. Mary left the party early, but realized that alcohol was a great way to become social, and to meet eligible men. Mary started having a drink before going to parties and one while at parties and then she realized that three drinks made her feel great and she could stay at the party longer and continue to have fun. To the current day, Mary likes to drink and sometimes even has one with breakfast if she is feeling anxious or upset about something. Mary does not perceive her use of alcohol as an addiction, but as a supportive and reinforcing means of becoming a sociable person.

RELAPSE PREVENTION THEORY

Using the same principles as learning theory, the relapse prevention model perceives drug use as an acquired (bad) habit that can be modified, changed, or eliminated through new learning. It combines classical and operant principles as per learning theory. The one major difference is the addition of two concepts, self-efficacy, and outcome expectancy.[8] These two principles assume that the person has self-control and can be responsible for their own actions, whereas the disease model places responsibility on the illness, and not the person. Relapse prevention uses a three-step model:

◊ The person is expected to be ready to make changes in their life rather than giving in to impulsive decisions.

◊ The person must seek change such as attending treatment or initiating self- change.

◊ The last stage is relapse prevention itself, and it is often considered the most difficult of the stages since people may relapse, may need time to find alternate ways of behaving and/or learn impulse control. Staying sober over the long haul is far more difficult than people realize, and it requires the ability to learn over time with each new constructive learning activity improving the person's ability to cope with substance related stressors while maintaining sobriety.[26]

CASE STUDY

Helen completes a 6-month in-patient treatment program to become drug free. After leaving the program, she selects an out-patient treatment program based on the relapse prevention model. As part of the program, she examines the positive changes she made in treatment coupled with new learning acquired in treatment, and from life in general. She is convinced that she will now remain drug free. She is so convinced that she will remain drug free that she takes a nostalgic trip to visit her old neighborhood where she bought and used drugs. She wakes up the next morning in an alley and realizes that she bought and used drugs! She returns to her out-patient treatment program and learns that she must avoid all previous associations with drug abuse and must develop better coping mechanisms that stop her from doing foolish things such as returning to her old neighborhood. She asks Ralph, a member of her out-patient group, to be her buddy so that she can call him and get his help if she ever feels the urge to return to her old neighborhood. Helen is beginning to realize that recovery and relapse prevention are long roads that may take years to achieve versus days or weeks.

PERSONALITY/TRAIT THEORIES

The study of personality traits was conducted to examine the possibility that some human personality factors or traits can lead to substance abuse. For instance, risk-taking or novelty-seeking traits favor the use of addictive drugs.[12] A somewhat similar study[18] reported a high correlation between novelty, alcohol, and drug dependence. Studies also found that people who seek impulsive acts or exhibit thrill seeking behavior while showing little adherence to traditional moral values are more likely to meet the criteria of substance use disorder.[19] A study of personality traits and substance dependency among college students found that certain core personality traits such as novelty seeking and neuroticism are predictive of multiple types of substance pathology.[10] In addition, the study reported that several personality traits were related to alcohol and drug dependence symptoms. For instance, being an extravert with low openness to experience was found to predict alcohol symptoms, while low conscientiousness was found to predict drug symptoms. These findings provide support to the concept that correlations may exist between different personality traits in relation to distinct forms of substance dependence. Moreover, the study also revealed that high openness to experience uniquely predicts symptoms related to smoking. On the other hand, low openness to experience was found to predict alcohol dependence symptoms by itself.

Whereas such research seems to lend considerable credence to a relationship between personality traits and alcohol/substance abuse disorders, it must be remembered that other variables, such as genetics and environment, may represent key components of personality.

CASE STUDY

Martin and Lee became close friends as teenagers when they realized that they both loved motorcycling. Both of their parents refused to consider buying them motorcycles when they were 18 years old. Instead, the two boys worked part-time after school and saved enough money to buy two used motorcycles. Martin bought an old cruiser and wanted to be just like motorcycle gangsters while Lee bought a small racing bike so that he could practice his skills and perhaps become a grand prix racer one day. Martin joined a motorcycle gang, used drugs and alcohol, and eventually was arrested for driving intoxicated and punching a police officer. Lee never achieved his dream, but he continued to ride motorcycles and sometimes wondered why he and his old friend Martin went different ways when they were such close friends earlier in life. While lighting a cigarette, Lee wondered just how different he and Martin were as teenagers.

COMORBIDITY THEORY

The co-existence of mental disorders and drug addiction is often proposed to be another major contributing factor in drug addiction. According to several epidemiological surveys,[16,17,31] about 22%-23% of the adult population has a psychiatric disorder, while about 15% of those persons are believed to meet the criteria of co-occurring substance abuse disorder. Co-occurring disorder is commonly known as dual diagnosis referring to people who meet the DSM[1] criteria for at least one mental health and one substance use disorder. Psychiatric disorders, particularly schizophrenia, bipolar disorder, depression, and attention-deficit-hyperactivity disorder, are often associated with an increased risk of drug abuse. To explain the etiology of the co-occurring disorders, researchers have proposed different models, such as common factor models, which focus on the common risk factors found in persons with both disorders. The secondary substance abuse disorder model emphasizes the increased risk for substance abuse by a person with mental illness.[28] In essence, the secondary substance abuse disorder model is asserting mental illness as the leading cause of addiction. It is assumed that people with mental health problems often begin using substances as a form of self-medication to deal with negative experiences, to ignore reality, and to feel better or less afraid of the world. In addition to the co-occurring disorders, polydrug use is common among those with drug addiction issues. Many people with addiction issues meet the criteria for dependence on, and abuse of, more than one substance.[21]

Besides mental disorders such as schizophrenia, bipolar disorder, and polysubstance use, some personality disorders have been found to be confounding variables in etiological studies. For instance, in their personality study cited earlier, Grekin and associates (2006)[10] discussed the relationships between personality traits and substance use dependence becoming a less clear relationship when conduct disorder symptoms were added to their proposed structural equation model. They suggested that disinhibited personality traits lead to a conduct disorder while the conduct disorder then leads to substance dependence. As illustrated in this example, the picture of the mechanism of addiction becomes obscure because of the comorbidity, and the confusion it creates. Causal relationships are unclear due to the complexity of the high rate of comorbidity among people with addiction issues. Nevertheless, Grekin and associates (2006)[10] also reported that the predictors of alcohol use remained unchanged after controlling for drug and tobacco symptoms, suggesting that personality traits such as disinhibition and neurotic traits could predict alcohol pathology on top of the effects of comorbid substance use disorder.

Overall, it is safe to conclude that comorbidity issues provide severe challenges for researchers and clinicians to understand the mechanism of addiction. It is projected that large sample longitudinal etiological research will eventually explore and explain the complex layers surrounding these issues.

CASE STUDY

A movement to deinstitutionalize psychiatric hospitals commenced during the latter part of the twentieth century. The movement proceeded despite the lack of consensus that it was appropriate to move people out of psychiatric hospitals into the community, the movement lacked a true philosophical base, the movement failed to provide appropriate and needed community services for persons discharged from hospitals, and there was and remains inadequacies within the mental health system in general.[34] These statements are provided as a backdrop to what happened to persons who were discharged from large psychiatric services to city streets without any clear-cut plan to foster on-going treatment and to provide shelter for such persons. These individuals often wandered city streets without goal or purpose, and their psychiatric symptoms increased since they were not receiving appropriate medications and ancillary services to maintain a functional state of being. Many former psychiatric patients turned to illegal street drugs since the drugs tended to mask their psychiatric symptoms and made them feel less fear. The events surrounding deinstitutionalization led to a tremendous increase in the number of persons diagnosed as comorbid or dually diagnosed with mental illness and substance abuse.

Conversely, many people try illegal drugs as a means of release from their lives, or in the hope of finding a better state of being. Yet, street/illegal drugs are not controlled and tested substances. Many people often take more of an illegal drug than is safe to use, culminating in destruction of brain cells. The person develops psychiatric symptoms due to the use of illegal drugs, and people who were deinstitutionalized became dually diagnosed with mental illness and substance abuse.

BIOPSYCHOSOCIAL THEORY

While some researchers from different disciplines may see the mechanism of addiction from their own knowledge base, most clinicians, as well as family or friends of people with addiction, may possess a more holistic perspective toward the causation. None of the theories presented in this chapter alone can explain all aspects of addiction. Researchers who advocate the biopsychosocial model refer to the multifaceted nature of addiction, and the presence of contextual factors that single theories in medical models or psychological models cannot explain. The biopsychosocial model is a holistic approach to understanding addiction since it encompasses current research and treatment foundations in the fields of psychology, biology, and sociology.

The biopsychosocial model implies that the development and meaning of addiction is unique to each person. A person is exposed to biological, psychological, and social influences that combine differently in each situation, and lead that person toward a belief about addiction and potential drug abuse. A person who is not prepared to cope with multiple variables such as biological, psychological, and social factors may either start using drugs, or the person may relapse if attempting sobriety. To that end, each person who is evaluated for substance abuse should be assessed from a multiple biopsychosocial perspective.[8] Balance of the biological, psychological, and sociological factors determines recovery and relapse prevention while imbalance of these three factors will lead to relapse. As Babor (1993)[2] reported, the adverse risks of substance abuse can be divided into vulnerability to substance abuse along with exposure to substance abuse, and these variables are closely related to biological, psychological, and sociological aspects of life.

Biological and psychological research and theories were presented throughout this chapter, but little direct discussion was provided on the sociological aspects of addiction. The following brief summary of sociological research findings reflects the importance of social factors among the three components of the biopsychosocial theoretical model.

One research team studied deviant peers, and the clear relationship between deviant behavior and substance abuse.[27] A very similar finding appeared in a longitudinal study of young adults.[7] A relationship between early onset of sexual intercourse and relationships with deviant peers was also associated with the early development of substance use disorders. Some of the environmental risks for early substance abuse include poverty and lower socioeconomic status,[32,11,18] the availability of alcohol and drugs within the home, poor parental support, poor parental supervision or neglect,[6] and parental separation or divorce.[22]

The Public health model is an example of the biopsychosocial theory in practice since public health agencies recognize the importance of three broad classes of etiologic factors: agent, host, and environment.[25] Agent would be the substance that one is addicted to, while host would be individual differences, since people are different in their vulnerability to substance abuse. It is safe to say that genetic, physiological, behavioral, and sociocultural factors play a role in influencing an individual's risk to addiction. For instance, factors such as life problems, individual tolerance, neuropsychological impairment, subjective loss of control, or organic damage can all influence the severity of addiction. These factors are not all physiological, nor are they merely psychological and/or social issues. These factors can be regarded as interconnected. Individual differences in the factors presented remain salient, and constitute the host domain of the public health model. Environmental factors, in the context of addiction, would be the environmental interventions and governmental policy aimed at harm reduction, and tackling the supply and demand of illicit chemicals. Miller[25] reported that this model includes all of the various contributing factors to addiction instead of the pointless argument for the supremacy of a single factor or theoretical model.

The value of the biopsychosocial model of addiction includes both clinical practice and research protocols. One clear outcome is the use of the team approach to substance abuse treatment, since no one professional identity can assume the full responsibility of treating drug addiction. Teams that consist of physicians trained in substance use, social workers, psychologists, counselors, and peer counselors can enhance the effectiveness of substance abuse treatment via the use of a holistic and comprehensive approach to identify, treat, and support people with substance abuse problems. Future research must focus on the broader view of addiction that accounts for the influence of biology, genetics, psychology, and sociology.

CASE STUDY

Brad is a 24-year old client with schizoaffective disorder and a history of substance abuse. He is not employed since he has been in and out of the legal system and prison in the past seven years dating back to his adolescence. He is currently working on his substance abuse issue in an assertive community program in the Midwest. He has been "clean" in the past few months, but reluctantly shared in the compulsory group that he is going through a tough time to resist the temptation of using drugs. He mentioned the drug abuse of his elder brother who has been using heroin since his release from prison last month. Brad is happy to see his brother, but does not like his habit of using illegal drugs. Brad told the counseling group about his brother's use of drugs, and then admitted that his mother also uses heroin. He told his case manager last week that he wants to move out of his mother's house since he feels like using drugs with his mother and brother, but he tries to understand the consequences of using, namely, violation of his probation rules and a return to prison. He feels as if he is surrounded by problems that include his living arrangements, family, income status, and community problems that will not give him a chance to succeed in life.

REFERENCES

[1]American Psychiatric Association. (1995). *Diagnostic and statistical manual of mental disorders* (4th ed.), Revised. Washington, DC: Author.

[2]Babor, T. (1993). Substance use and persons with physical disabilities: Nature, diagnosis, and clinical subtypes. In A. W. Heinemann (Ed.), *Substance Abuse and Physical Disability* (pp. 43–56). New York: The Haworth Press.

[3]Bandura, A. (1977). Self-efficacy: Toward a unifying theory of behavior change. *Psychological Review, 84*, 191-215.

[4]Budziack, T. (1993). Evaluating treatment services. In, Heinemann, A. W. (ed.), *Substance abuse and physical disability* (pp.239-255). Binghamton, NY: The Haworth Press.

[5]Chiauzzi, E. J. (1991). *Preventing relapse in the addictions. A biopsychosocial approach.* New York: Pergamon Press.

[6]Clark, D. B., Thatcher, D. L., & Maisto, S. A. (2005). Supervisory neglect and adolescent alcohol use disorders: Effects on AUD onset and treatment outcome. *Addictive Behaviors, 30*(9), 1737-1750.

[7]Cornelius, J. R., Clark, D. B., Reynolds, M., Kirisci, L., & Tarter, R. (2007). Early age of first sexual intercourse and affiliation with deviant peers predict development of SUD: A prospective longitudinal study. *Addictive Behaviors, 32*(4), 850-854.

[8]Donovan, D. M., & Marlatt, G. A. (Eds.). (1988). *Assessment of addictive behaviors.* New York: Guilford.

[9]Fingarette, H. (1991). Alcoholism: The mythical disease. In, Pittman, D. & White, H. (Eds.), Society, culture and Drinking patterns reexamined. Alcohol, culture and social Control monograph series (pp.417- 438). New Brunswick, NJ: Rutgers Center of Alcohol Studies.

[10]Grekin, E. R., Sher, K. J., & Wood, P. K. (2006). Personality and substance dependence symptoms: Modeling substance-specific traits. *Psychology of Addictive Behaviors: Journal of the Society of Psychologists in Addictive Behaviors, 20*(4), 415-424.

[11]Hawkins, J. D., Catalano, R. F., & Miller, J. Y. (1992). Risk and protective factors for alcohol and other drug problems in adolescence and early adulthood: Implications for substance abuse prevention. *Psychological Bulletin, 112*(1), 64-105.

[12]Helmus, T. C., Downey, K. K., Arfken, C. L., Henderson, M. J., & Schuster, C. R. (2001). Novelty seeking as a predictor of treatment retention for heroin dependent cocaine users. *Drug and Alcohol Dependence, 61*(3), 287-295.

[13]Holzer, C. E., Shea, B. M., Swanson, J. W., & Leaf, P. J. (1986). The increased risk for specific psychiatric disorders among persons of low socioeconomic status. *American Journal of Social Psychiatry, 6*(4), 259-271.

[14]Jellinek, E. M. (1945). The problem of alcohol. In, Yale Studies on Alcohol (Ed.), *Alcohol, science, and society* (pp. 13-30). Westport, CT: Greenwood Press.

[15]Kathiramalainathan, K., Kaplan, H., Romach, M., Busto, U., Li, N., Sawe, J., Tyndale, R., & Sellers, E. (2000). Inhibition of cytochrome P450 2D6 modifies codeine abuse liability. *Journal of Clinical Psychopharmacology, 20*(4), 435-444.

[16]Kessler, R. C. (2004). The epidemiology of dual diagnosis. *Biological Psychiatry, 56*(10), 730-737.

[17]Kessler, R. C., McGonagle, K. A., Zhao, S., Nelson, C. B., Hughes, M., Eshleman, S., et al. (1994). Lifetime and 12-month prevalence of DSM-III-R psychiatric disorders in the United States. results from the national comorbidity survey. *Archives of General Psychiatry, 51*(1), 8-19.

[18]Khan, A., Jacobson, K., Gardner, C., Prescott, C., & Kendler, K. (2005). Personality and comorbidity of common psychiatric disorders. *British Journal of Psychiatry, 186*, 190-196.

[19]Krueger, R. F., Hicks, B. M., Patrick, C. J., Carlson, S. R., Iacono, W. G., & McGue, M. (2002). Etiologic connections among substance dependence, antisocial behavior, and personality: Modeling the externalizing spectrum. *Journal of Abnormal Psychology, 111*(3), 411.

[20]Lappalainen, J., Kranzler, H., Malison, R., Price, L., VanDyck, C., Rosenheck, R., Cramer, J., Southwick, S., Charney, D., Krystal, J., & Gelernter, J. (2002). A functional neuropeptide Y Leu 7 Pro polymorphism is associated with alcohol dependence in a large American population sample. *Archives of General Psychiatry, 59*, 825-831.

[21]Leri, F., Bruneau, J., & Stewart, J. (2003). Understanding polydrug use: Review of heroin and cocaine co-use. *Addiction, 98*(1), 7.

[22]Libby, A. M., Orton, H. D., Stover, S. K., & Riggs, P. D. (2005). What came first, major depression or substance use disorder? clinical characteristics and substance use comparing teens in a treatment cohort. *Addictive Behaviors, 30*(9), 1649-1662.

[23]Marlatt, G. A., & Gordon, J. R. (1985). *Relapse Prevention*. New York: Guilford.

[24]Marlatt, G. A. (1992). Substance abuse: Implications of a Biopsychosocial model for prevention, treatment, and relapse prevention. In, Grabowski, J. & Vandenbos, G. (eds.), Psychopharmacology: Basic mechanisms and applied *Interventions (pp. 127-162)*. Washington, D.C.: American Psychological Association.

[25]Miller, W. R. (1993). Alcoholism: Toward a better disease model. *Psychology of Addictive Behaviors, 7*(2), 129-136.

[26]Miller, W. R., & Hester, R. K. (1989). Self-control training. In, Miller, W. R. Miller & Hester, R.K. (Eds.), *Handbook of Alcoholism Treatment Approaches: Effective Alternatives* (pp. 141-149). New York: Pergamon Press.

[27]Moss, H., Lynch, K., & Hardie, T. (2003). Affiliation with deviant peers among children of substance dependent fathers from pre-adolescence into adolescence: Associations with problem behaviors. *Journal of Drug and Alcohol Dependency, 71*(2), 117-125.

[28]Mueser, K. T., Drake, R. E., & Wallach, M. A. (1998). Dual diagnosis: A review of etiological theories. *Addictive Behaviors, 23*(6), 717-734. National Institute on Drug Abuse (1999). *Principles of drug addiction treatment.* NIH Publication No. 99-4180, Washington, DC: Government Printing Office.

[29]National Institute on Drug Abuse (1999). *Principles of drug addiction treatment.* NIH Publication No. 99-4180, Washington, DC: Government Printing Office.

[30]Nestler, Eric. (2001). Psychogenomics: Opportunities for understanding addiction. *Journal of Neuroscience, 21*, 8324-8327.

[31]Regier, D. A., Farmer, M. E., Rae, D. S., Locke, B. Z., Keith, S. J., Judd, L. L., et al. (1990). Comorbidity of mental disorders with alcohol and other drug abuse. *JAMA: Journal of the American Medical Association, 264*(19), 2511.

[32]Reinherz, H. Z., Giaconia, R. M., Lefkowitz, E. S., Pakiz, B., & Frost, A. K. (1993). Prevalence of psychiatric disorders in a community population of older adolescents. *Journal of the American Academy of Child and Adolescent Psychiatry, 32*(2), 369-377.

[33]Stewart, J., & Wise, R. A. (1992). Reinstatement of heroin self-administration habits: Morphine prompts and naltrexone discourages renewed responding after extinction. *Psychopharmacology, 108*(1), 79-84.

[34]Talbott, J. A. (2004). Deinstitutionalization: Avoiding the disasters of the past. *Psychiatric Services, 55*, 1112-1115.

CHAPTER FOUR

ALCOHOL AND ALCOHOLISM: CLINICAL COMPONENTS

BY   STEPHANIE L. LUSK
KACIE M. BLALOCK
QUINTIN BOSTON
MIRIAM LYDE

NORTH CAROLINA AGRICULTURE
AND TECHNICAL STATE UNIVERSITY

Chapter Topics

◊ History of Alcohol and Its Use

◊ Biotransformation and Pharmacology of Alcohol

◊ Consequences of Alcohol Use

◊ Alcohol Use Across the Lifespan

◊ Treatment of Alcohol Dependence

◊ Summary and Implications

◊ Case Study

HISTORY OF ALCOHOL AND ITS USE

$\mathcal{A}$lcohol, second only to caffeine, is one of the most commonly abused substances in the United States. It is produced when sugars or starches from vegetables, fruits, or other substances such as honey are exposed to yeast. When the sugars and yeast are combined, an enzyme is produced that coverts the mixture into ethyl alcohol or ethanol. It is believed that one of the first forms of beer, known as *mead*, was brewed from fermented honey as early as 8000 BC. There is also evidence which purports that another beer-type beverage, *hek,* was prepared by the Egyptians around 3700 BC. Wine is believed to have come from Babylonia around 1700 BC. Wine was deemed as a gift from the gods - the Egyptians called their god of wine Osiris; the Greeks deemed their god Dionysis; and the Romans adopted the name Bacchus.[23] Alcoholic drinks were used for many purposes including rituals, religious ceremonies, and celebrations. Alcohol has been called *aqua vitae*, or the water of life, as well as the fountain of youth, and it quickly became a part of everyday life.

Alcohol was brought over to America by explorers and European colonist. When the Mayflower landed at Plymouth in 1620, alcohol was on board the ship. The colonists constructed distilleries as early as 1640 where whisky, gin and bourbon were made.[23] Left to its own devices, nature can produce a drink that is approximately 15% alcohol. The process of distillation allows for stronger alcoholic beverages, producing solutions with a content of up to 93% alcohol if distilled enough times; however, most alcoholic beverages vary from 40% to 50% alcohol. Rhazes, an Arabian doctor, is credited with having discovered the distillation process when he boiled alcoholic beverages and collected the steam in a cooling tube.

Drinking continued to increase in popularity until the 1830s. Shortly thereafter, the beliefs associated with drinking began to change. Drunkenness was soon to be considered evil and as being the source of crime, broken families, and poverty. As a result of this new perspective, the temperance movement began. In 1917, Congress passed a law which made it illegal to manufacture, sell, and transport liquor; this law became the 18th Amendment in 1920. This amendment was later repealed, as it was quickly noticed that prohibiting the use and distribution of alcohol only led to problems such as organized crime and its illegal production.

ALCOHOLISM AS A DISEASE

E. M. Jellinek began research in the early 1950s which laid the groundwork for designating alcoholism as a disease. A trained biostatistician, his work was mainly based upon surveys he conducted using members of Alcoholics Anonymous (AA). His research resulted in classification systems for the phases of alcoholism as well as the types of alcoholics. Before his classification system individuals who were deemed alcoholics were looked upon negatively and may have been jailed for their behaviors. Because of his research and this new understanding of alcoholism as a disease and that the person had no control over his or her drinking behavior, individuals were to receive medical and nonjudgmental treatment.

Jellinek's research led him to develop four phases of alcoholism:

- prealcoholic;

- prodromal;

- crucial; and

- chronic.

During the prealcoholic phase, individuals usually drink alcohol while engaging in social activities. They quickly notice that drinking relieves stress, and they may eventually begin to seek out occasions in which to drink. Prodromal means warning and individuals within this phase drink much more heavily and can experience blackouts or a loss of memory. The crucial phase is marked by a loss of control over drinking. There is a severe deterioration in everyday functioning, as alcohol becomes the center of their lives. Following this phase is the chronic phase, which is marked by physiological changes and their resulting ailments within the body. Tremors and other withdrawal symptoms are experiences when alcohol is not in the system.

Another result of Jellinek's work included typing alcoholics. He noted that not only were there different phases of alcoholism, but that people themselves were different. As a result of this realization, he developed specific types or categories of alcoholism, which are:

- alpha;

- beta;

- gamma;

- delta; and

- epsilon.

Alpha alcoholism is characterized as a psychological dependence on alcohol. These individuals use alcohol to cope with the stress and discomforts of everyday life. Typical characteristics of *beta* alcoholism include the development of physical problems such as cirrhosis of the liver; however, the person is not psychologically or physically dependent on alcohol. Jellinek noted that individuals in this category may be members of cultures in which heavy drinking is normal. Withdrawal symptoms and a loss of control over drinking is seen in *gamma* alcoholism, as these individuals move from a psychological to a physical dependence on alcohol. This form is considered the most harmful to one's psychological and physiological wellbeing. It is this type that is synonymous with today's definition of alcoholism. *Delta* alcoholism is characterized by psychological and physical dependence, but there is no loss of control over drinking. These individuals can control the amount of alcohol they ingest on any given occasion, but they are compelled to drink everyday in order to avoid withdrawal symptoms. The final type is *epsilon*. Individuals in this category are what would be considered modern day binge drinkers. They are known to drink large amounts of alcohol at any one period of time but are not bothered by withdrawal symptoms or physical and psychological symptoms.

CURRENT USE

Alcohol use disorders are the third leading cause of premature death in the United States.[13] Statistics show that 87.7% of individuals in the United States have used alcohol at least once in their lifetime; 91.1 % of males and 84.4% of females have consumed alcohol.[4] Approximately 17.6 million adults in the United States alone have an alcohol use disorder.[5] Alcohol use plays a large role in the number of injuries seen in emergency rooms each year, domestic violence cases, psychiatric disorders, suicide attempts and completions, and a plethora of other physical, social, and psychological problems. It also is largely associated with the use of other illegal substances as well.

BIOTRANSFORMATION AND PHARMACOLOGY OF ALCOHOL

One standard drink equals one 12-ounce can of beer, four ounces of wine, or 1.5 ounces of liquor. "Whether a person drinks six shots of whisky, six cans of beer, or six glasses of wine, their blood alcohol level will ultimately be the same and the level of intoxication will be similar."[20,p. 37] Substances such as carbonated beverages or seltzer increase the speed in which alcohol's effects are felt, while ingesting food, particularly fatty foods, slows down the rate at which the effects are felt. When alcohol is consumed on an empty stomach, its peak blood level will occur within 30 to 120 minutes after the first drink. When consumed with food, peak effects may not be reached until 1 to 6 hours after the drink is ingested. Even though it takes several minutes to hours for the peak effects to be reached, the first molecules of the alcohol appears in the drinker's blood in as little as one minute after it is ingested.[44] Eventually all of the drink will be absorbed into the person's circulation.

Ethyl alcohol or ethanol, the active ingredient in alcohol, is generally introduced into the body via oral ingestion. Alcohol is considered to be the most popular central nervous system (**CNS**) depressant because of its widespread use, easy access, legal status, and social acceptability.[20] The alcohol molecule is quite small and is both lipid and water soluble. As a result, alcohol is able to quickly penetrate all cells within the body, especially the brain, where its concentration levels can quite rapidly surpass the levels within the blood and the rest of the body.[24] Absorption begins in the stomach, but primarily takes place within the capillary rich walls of the small intestine.

Chemicals that enter the body, such as alcohol and drugs, are biotransformed or metabolized in the liver via zero-order or first-order biotransformation. Biotransformation occurs in order to prepare alcohol for elimination from the body. The liver produces enzymes that are responsible for breaking down the original substance or parent compound into simpler forms known as metabolites. For the most part, metabolites are inactive, but there are exceptions in that some metabolites are more biologically active than the parent compound. This is the case with alcohol. Zero-order biotransformation involves the substance being metabolized at a set rate regardless of its concentration levels in the blood. The antithesis of zero-order biotransformation is first-order biotransformation. When a substance is metabolized based upon its concentration in the blood, this is considered first-order biotransformation. In zero-order biotransformation, the drug concentration levels are irrelevant; however, in first-order biotransformation, elimination is proportional to concentration. Alcohol is biotransformed via the zero-order biotransformation process.

Poisoning can occur when an individual ingests large amounts of alcohol at one time, such as during binge drinking. Binge drinking is defined as consuming five or more drinks (four for women) within a short period of time. Because the alcohol adheres to zero-order biotransformation, the body is not able to metabolize and eliminate enough alcohol to offset what has been ingested. Blood glucose levels can drop so low that seizures result, and it can also interfere with the circulatory and respiratory systems by depressing the heart and breathing rate to the point of death.

When alcohol is ingested, it interacts with enzymes within the liver to begin the process of biotransformation and eventual elimination. In preparation for elimination, two primary enzymes are created - alcohol dehydrogenase (ADH) and aldehyde dehydrogenase (ALDH).[58] First, ADH metabolizes alcohol into acetaldehyde. The second step involves ALDH metabolizing acetaldehyde into acetate. During the final step, acetate is further metabolized into water and carbon dioxide, and from here it is prepared to leave the body through the kidneys, in one's breath, or it can be excreted in sweat.[7] Other enzymes that assist with the breakdown of ethyl alcohol are cytrochrome P450 2E1 (CPY2E1) and catalase. CPY2E1 is active only after a person has ingested large amounts of alcohol (U.S. Department of Health and Human Services et al., 2007). Acetaldehyde, a highly toxic and carcinogenic metabolite of alcohol, is believed to be responsible for the behavioral and physiological effects one experiences as a result of drinking. It is also to blame for the alcohol-flush reaction found most commonly among persons of Asian descent. Because of a genetic mutation, the liver is not able to produce or can produce only small amounts of ALDH. As a result, the acetaldehyde that results during the first stage of metabolism remains in the body and produces unpleasant side-effects such as facial flushing, dizziness, nausea, and heart palpitations as levels in the blood can measure 20 times that of a person whose body can properly metabolize this substance.[7]

PHARMACOLOGY OF ALCOHOL

Alcohol's primary site of action is within the central nervous system (CNS), which includes the brain and spinal cord. It is considered a "dirty" drug in that it affects several neurotransmitters within the brain.[7] Neurotransmitters primarily affected by alcohol use include *gamma amino butyric acid* (GABA), *N-methyl-D-aspartate* (NMDA), dopamine (DA) and serotonin (5-HT).

GABA, the neurotransmitter most affected by alcohol consumption, is considered the main inhibitory neurotransmitter and is primarily responsible for inducing relaxation and sleep. There are two types of GABA receptors, GABA-A and GABA-B; alcohol's primary effect is on GABA-A.[26] GABA receptors are found mainly in the cerebral cortex, cerebellum, hippocampus, amygdala and nucleus accumbens of the brain. Alcohol's interaction with GABA-A changes the functioning within these areas of the brain, and it is assumed that this is what reinforces the effects of ethanol intake.[56] The cerebral cortex is responsible for memory, thought, attention, language, and consciousness. The cerebellum, located near the base of the brain, plays a major role in movement. If injured, a loss of balance and problems with coordination can occur as well as dizziness and nausea. The hippocampus, amygdala, and the nucleus accumbens make up what is known as the limbic system. This system is considered the seat of emotions and the place where memories are created. It is GABA's effect on these areas of the brain that result in the characteristic behaviors noted after alcohol consumption such as relaxation, slurred speech, blackouts, loss of balance, and reduced reaction time.

Other neurotransmitters affected by alcohol are NMDA, dopamine, and serotonin (5-HT). NMDA is an excitatory neurotransmitter. Alcohol is considered an NMDA antagonist in that it slows down the rate at which it is fired throughout the brain and blocks its effects. Dopamine is responsible for producing feelings of pleasure and enjoyment. It is released naturally within the brain as a reward when a person eats, has sex, or engages in other enjoyable activities as a way to entice the person to continue these behaviors in order to survive. It is also released when alcohol is ingested. Serotonin affects feelings of pleasure, perceptions related to pain, memory formation, and sensations related to stimuli within the environment. It also affects sleep and mood. It is alcohol's interaction with these neurotransmitters that cause some of the characteristic behaviors seen when drinking, such as inhibition and an increase in the pain threshold.

CONSEQUENCES OF ALCOHOL USE

PHYSIOLOGICAL EFFECTS

Digestive System. The digestive system is comprised of organs that are involved with food and beverage consumption: the tongue, esophagus, liver, intestine, stomach, pancreas, bladder, and colon are all involved in the process of ingestion and excretion of substances that are consumed by an individual. When alcohol is consumed, the organs in the upper digestive tract are greatly affected by the toxin, as the digestive system immediately begins the process of ridding the body of alcohol when it is swallowed.

There is no nutritional value in alcoholic beverages because the nutrients that the fruits and vegetables contained are lost during the fermentation and distillation process; therefore, instead of gaining nutrients when alcohol is ingested, the digestive organs are poisoned and then have to quickly recover from the mistreatment. When alcohol is consumed, it causes inflammation of the cells in the trachea and causes additional problems such as an increase in cell growth within the digestive tract. Acetaldehyde, the major alcohol metabolite, interferes with the cells of the digestive tract by inhibiting the body's ability to properly replicate new cells, which could lead to complications such as cancer of the mouth and throat as cell growth is interrupted.[49] Alcohol has been associated with 19% of cancer in the mouth, 29% of esophageal cancer, and 25% of cancers in the liver worldwide.[42] Alcohol consumption has also been linked to inflammation of the pancreas, cancers of the rectum,[12,49] gastritis, bleeding of the stomach lining, and ulcers.[7] Once alcohol has passed the organs of the mouth and throat, it travels to the stomach and small intestine where it is absorbed into the blood stream by the body. Damage that ensues can interfere with absorption of nutrients that the body needs from the individual's food and other beverages, which leads to vitamin and nutrient deficiencies.[49]

The liver is the digestive organ that is most affected by the toxicity of alcohol. The liver is responsible for transforming the ethyl alcohol into a substance that can be excreted from the body. Alcohol consumption can cause steatosis, or enlargement of the liver, and once this disease is acquired, the liver can no longer properly function. About 10% to 35% of people who develop steatosis may go on to develop alcoholic hepatitis.[34] The symptoms of alcoholic hepatitis include pain in the abdominal area, fever, dark urine, jaundice, extreme sickness, and even death.[7]

Liver cirrhosis, or scarring of the liver tissue, is the 12th leading cause of death in the United States, and alcohol has been associated with 32% of liver cirrhosis in the world.[55,42] Alcohol causes cirrhosis by damaging the cells of the liver and causing oxidative distress which kills the cells and results in scar tissue.[42] Once the liver is covered in scar tissue, it is no longer able to allow blood to flow through and properly rid the blood of toxins. Also, essential nutrients and vitamins that are normally absorbed through the liver are unable to be taken in. Liver cirrhosis can cause toxins to build up in the blood and nutrient insufficiencies that can cause cancers and disease.

Cardiopulmonary System. The cardiopulmonary system is made up of the heart and the lungs. While moderate drinking has been linked to positive cardiovascular health, excessive alcohol consumption has been linked to increased incidences of coronary heart disease.[42] One to two drinks daily for men has been linked with a reduction of death by 18%, but two drinks or more for women and three drinks or more for men has been associated with premature death.[37] Alcohol increases high blood pressure when drank in excess because of the inflammation of the heart muscle which leads to a decline in the heart's efficiency. The heart begins to struggle to pump blood through the minimized vessels on top of the heart which have been weakened, and then it slows and is inconsistent, which leads to atrial fibrillation.[7]

The heart needs oxygen in order for cells to live and in order to effectively pump blood, and the lungs are greatly affected by the consumption of alcohol. Alcohol is swallowed and the organs of the throat are damaged, which is one of the sites at which oxygen enters the body. If the body is unable to take in air because of the damage that alcohol has done to the cells of the throat, then the cells of the respiratory tract will not be able to absorb oxygen and carry it to the rest of the body.[22] Alcohol abuse decreases the amount of antioxidants available in the lungs, and it also affects the junctions where oxygen and carbon-dioxide are exchanged within the lung cavities.[32]

Another problem that alcohol creates is that it interferes with the production of cells that are responsible for protecting the lungs from infection through the immune response. The toxins that are in alcohol damage cells throughout the lungs and ultimately cause respiratory distress. Acute respiratory distress syndrome has a 40% to 50% mortality rate, and alcohol is a major contributor to this disease because it weakens the defenses of the lungs, which decreases the ability to fight bacterial infections.[22] Pneumonia is another major problem in people who consume alcohol.[22] Following the trauma of lung infection, there is an increase of scar tissue on the lungs, and this scar tissue can lead to the onset of lung disease and cancer.[51] If the body cannot obtain the oxygen that it needs for cells to live, the entire body will suffer and eventually shut down to the point of death.

Central Nervous System. The central nervous system is made up of the brain and the spinal cord. The brain is responsible for controlling the functioning of the entire body including the heart and the lungs. When a person consumes alcohol, the brain's ability to store memory, process incoming information, react to environmental stimuli, and even induce sleep are all effected.[7] The neurotransmitters that signal to the different parts of the brain what it should be doing also are impaired. Damage to the cells of the brain eventually occurs, which stunt the functioning of the brain. Alcohol is toxic and depletes and damages existing cells while causing a decrease in the number of growing cells.[53] Fifteen percent of people who use alcohol heavily have signs of brain damage before they have problems with other organ systems in the body.[7]

It is not uncommon for one to be unable to remember what they did while drinking or be unable to remember information while drinking. The brain is unable to store memories when large amounts of alcohol are in the body. This accounts for the temporary loss of memory.[48] The ability of the body to fall into a deep sleep is also affected. People who use alcohol in excess of the legal dose are likely to experience problems falling asleep and feeling rested after having slept.[21]

Also, the consumption of alcohol depresses the brain's ability to signal to the heart to pump blood and to the lungs to take in oxygen. When the respiratory system is depressed by the brain's inability to control the function of breathing, the body loses oxygen and the heart begins to pump harder to get the oxygen that it needs.[7] The loss of the functioning of the lungs could lead to respiratory distress and heart failure.

Peripheral Nervous System. Alcohol's effects on the nerves outside of the brain and spinal cord usually include loss of sensation and pain or burning in the extremities. Peripheral neuropathy, which is caused by a deficiency of vitamins in the brain and spinal cord, affects the hands and feet; it is found in 10% to 33% of individuals who use alcohol in excess.[48] The brain is connected to the spinal cord and is responsible for the functioning of nerves throughout the body. Therefore, if the functioning of the brain is altered, the entire nervous system is affected.

EMOTIONAL AND PSYCHOLOGICAL EFFECTS

Small amounts of alcohol have been found to alter cognitive functioning. As a result, there is an inability to normally process and evaluate incoming information. When people are unable to understand the information that is being presented to them, there is an increase in overall negative affects because they experience more frustration in trying to control behavior and fulfill tasks.[15] This inability to function normally can lead to irritability, irrational behaviors, and aggressive acts because of the cognitive dysregulation from the effects of alcohol on the brain.

Mental disorders, such as anxiety and depression, are highly correlated with alcohol use.[47] Roughly 20% of individuals diagnosed with a substance use disorder also meet the criteria for major depression.[17] The limbic system of the brain is in charge of regulating the sensory information that is received by the brain. The processing, perception, and evaluation of information is altered because the limbic system of the brain is impaired and judgment is much less clear.[11] Other mental health problems that oftentimes co-occur with alcohol use include personality disorders.[10] Individuals who meet the criteria for alcohol use disorders are also 9 to 17 times more likely to meet the criteria for other substance use disorders.[50] These comorbid conditions lead to increased physical complications, a worse course of the disorders, and a poorer response to treatment.

TOLERANCE AND WITHDRAWAL
As an individual continues to drink, the brain may become insensitive to the effects of alcohol and tolerance develops. When this occurs, the individual may need more in order to become intoxicated or may begin to experience symptoms of withdrawal. Alcohol withdrawal symptoms can be very severe, especially during the 48 hours immediately following the last drink.[57] Withdrawal symptoms may include, but are not limited to, increased heart rate, anxiety, and excessive sweating. There is also the potential for life-threatening complications to occur during the process of withdrawal as well. Because of this, it is important to note that alcohol withdrawal should be treated under the supervision of a physician.[7]

ALCOHOL USE ACROSS THE LIFESPAN

FETUS
Alcohol use among expecting mothers continues to serve as a major concern for the heath community. It is estimated that up to 10% of expecting women utilize alcohol on a regular basis during their pregnancies, placing the fetus in direct danger of birth defects.[6] Prenatal alcohol exposure (PAE) is one of the most preventable causes of birth defects and cognitive impairments.[62] The term Fetal Alcohol Spectrum Disorders (FASD) encompasses a wide variety of issues that can arise due to alcohol use among expecting mothers.[36] The cost of services for individuals with a FASD is more than $1.4 million per individuals across the lifespan.[19] One of the most serious issues within this spectrum is Fetal Alcohol Syndrome (FAS), which was first explained in 1973.[52] FAS is considered the most extreme outcome of alcohol related pregnancy issues. Due to the high prevalence of mothers consuming alcohol, FAS is now the third leading cause of birth defects in the United States.[46]

Not only can physical defects arise because of the use of alcohol among mothers, long term neurological effects can occur as well. Individuals with FASD can demonstrate a wide range of cognitive and behavior impairments that can affect them throughout the lifespan. Impairments such as memory defects, attention function problems, poor visual skills, and reduced IQ are problems associated with FASD.[36] In particular, the most commonly reported neuropsychological deficit is impaired learning.

Unfortunately, studies have shown the even children who have been exposed to special rehabilitation programs designed for children with FASD have had issues achieving normal weight and intelligence.[31] Research has also shown that less than 6% of infants who are enrolled in schools are able to perform in the classroom without some form of special support.[40] Thus, health professionals continue to express to expecting mothers not to place the life of their fetus at risk due to the consumption of alcohol, as the effects and negative impact of alcohol usage among pregnant mothers have lasting effects on children throughout their entire lifespan.

ADOLESCENTS

The rate of substance use among adolescents continues to rise, with alcohol and cannabis being the highest substances of choice.[27] Due to adolescence being a crucial stage of development, heavy usage can alter the body's developmental structure leading to physical and cognitive impairments that persist in adulthood. For instance, the prefrontal cortex and the amygdla of the brain region undergo substantial changes in adolescence. Changes in these two systems have an impact on psychological functioning and behavior. These areas of the brain are not fully developed in adolescence, which leads to poorer decision making and problem solving. Because of this, adolescents may be more prone to engage in risk taking behaviors, such as the usage of alcohol.

A few studies have confirmed that the earlier individuals partake in alcohol use the higher the prevalence of alcohol related problems later in life.[18,1] Socially learned behaviors such as drinking begin very early on, usually with the parents as the first models.[1] In addition to social interactions with parents, peer to peer influences can be a major factor in the prevalence of adolescent drinking. The desire of adolescents to "fit in" among their peers and be socially accepted has help fuel adolescent drinking. As a result of peer pressure and the wanting to be accepted, adolescents tend to engage in heavier episodic drinking such as "binge" drinking.[18]

Another problem associated with adolescent drinking is that young people can be less sensitive to the negative effects of the alcohol, such as lack of coordination and increased sleepiness. Consequently, they are able to consume larger amounts of alcohol in short periods of time. The negative effect of a large consumption of alcohol in adolescents includes problems with complex tasks such as operating a motor vehicle, which makes adolescent alcohol use especially dangerous. Therefore, poor judgment continues to be an issue for adolescents who partake in alcohol use.

Since the body is constantly changing during adolescence, alcohol use among males and females can cause significant physical and psychological changes. For females in particular, depression and body image issues can arise. As a result, levels of stress have been found to be a powerful predictor of use.[59] In addition, heavy alcohol use has been shown to disrupt normal menstrual cycling and the reproduction functions. Puberty has also been shown to be affected by alcohol. Consequently, adolescents who use alcohol are at a greater risk of infertility that can cause prolonged problems in adulthood.

ADULTHOOD

Alcohol related problems among adults are a continuing problem in the 21st century. Young adults, ages 18-24, are at the highest risk of alcohol related problems, as compared to individuals in other age groups. Regardless of sex, individuals belonging to this age group are more likely to engage in risky behaviors such as heavy drinking. One of the many factors associated with the high prevalence of alcohol use by young adults is the transition into college life. Like young adolescents and the issues with peer pressure, young adults tend to face the same pressure from peers as it relates to drinking.

Adults who are not students may continue to engage in heavy drinking and risky activities due to problems related to daily stress. They may utilize alcohol as a coping mechanism. The lack of available treatment programs is another factor in continued use. As a result, the number of deaths linked to risky behaviors, alcohol misuse, and alcohol dependency has reached over 100,000 deaths per year.[60] Continued use of alcohol by adults can have lasting personal, physical, psychological, and social effects. As individuals begin to age, maintaining a healthy lifestyle is paramount. However, some of the negative effects of alcohol can interrupt a person's ability to maintain a healthy lifestyle, as issues of depression, anxiety, and other psychiatric conditions are often associated with dangerous drinking patterns. Adults tend to moderately use or abuse alcohol at an alarming rate, and this can also alter the family structure. Consequently, high usage of alcohol in the family has lead to high divorce rates, violence, and altered family systems.[45]

ELDERLY

The number of elderly individuals engaging in alcohol use has been consistently increasing.[64] One of the common myths associated with the elderly population and alcohol is that individuals with alcohol related problems do not reach old age;[33] however, we know this is not true. A number of elderly individuals actually develop hard drinking patterns during their middle age years, and that pattern continues on into later life.[2] This phenomenon has been termed "*late onset alcoholism* or *reactive alcoholism.*"[33] Research has suggested that over 15% of the elderly who seek medical treatment have alcohol related problems;[9] however, their problems are commonly attributed to complications that may arise due to aging as opposed to alcohol use.

Since elderly individuals are more likely to have additional medical problems than younger individuals, diagnosing alcohol related problems can pose more of a challenge for physicians. This issue is made even more challenging because many elderly individuals with alcohol related issues are less likely to visit the doctor.[8]

Since older individuals metabolize alcohol at a much slower rate than young individuals do, alcohol tends to stay in their system longer. Additionally, elderly individuals are also more likely than other age groups to take prescription medication. When mixed with alcohol, the interactions can be extremely dangerous and even lethal. Alcohol has also been shown to decrease the effectiveness of some medications. Alcohol use can prevent the medication from being metabolized, which can cause toxic levels to build up in the body. It can also cause the drug to be metabolized at a much quicker rate. When this happens, the drug is cleared from the system much too quickly and as a result may not have its desired effect. Continuous education as it related to their health and alcohol use may prove beneficial for individuals who are older.

TREATMENT OF ALCOHOL DEPENDENCE

PHARMACOLOGICAL TREATMENT FOR ALCOHOL DEPENDENCE
Over 700,000 individuals in the United States receive treatment for alcohol dependence each day in either inpatient or outpatient settings.[35] There has recently been a dramatic shift from inpatient to outpatient services for the treatment of alcoholism due to increased costs for services and the emergence of managed health care systems. In all stages of recovery, most services are now provided on an outpatient basis in an effort to reduce costs. Approximately 13.5% of individuals receive treatment for alcoholism in an inpatient (residential or hospital) setting, while 86.5% receive treatment on an outpatient basis.[14] Inpatient and outpatient treatment options may be comprised of medications, psychological approaches, or a combination of both. A number of advancements have been made with medications and psychological approaches that can help individuals achieve and maintain sobriety.

Over the past couple of decades, there have been advancements in the development and clinical testing of medications in the treatment of alcoholism. However, when individuals with alcohol dependence seek help, they may not be prescribed a pharmacological treatment that could be beneficial in preventing relapse. There are a number of treatment programs that do not use pharmacological treatments because providers are often reluctant to substitute one drug for another drug.[14]

Several medications have been proven to reduce alcohol consumption among individuals with alcoholism. Two types of medication primarily used in the treatment of alcohol dependence are aversive medications and anticraving medications. Three medications approved by the Food and Drug Administration (FDA) in the United States, disulfiram, naltrexone, and acamprosate are currently marketed for treating alcohol dependence.

Aversive Medications. The purpose of aversive medication in alcoholism treatment is to deter the individual from drinking. Disulfiram, the most commonly used aversive medication in the treatment of alcohol dependence, has been available since the late 1940s.[14] This was the first FDA approved medication for the treatment of alcoholism in the United States. Disulfiram increases the concentration of acetaldehyde, a toxic byproduct that occurs when alcohol is metabolized in the body. Thus, it alters normal metabolism of ingested alcohol via the liver, which causes acetaldehyde to accumulate in the bloodstream.

Disulfiram causes unpleasant reactions when the individual ingests alcohol, such as nausea, vomiting, flushing, headache, difficulty breathing, and increased blood pressure and heart rate.[14,35,54] Most individuals compliant to the medication completely stop drinking after experiencing aversive reactions. Disulfiram may be beneficial in the abstinence initiation phase because it may eliminate impulsive drinking behavior. This medication has the potential to foster complete abstinence in the treatment of alcoholism. However, individuals must be compliant with adherence to the dosage of the medication.[3]

Anticraving Medications. The use of medication as an adjunct to alcoholism treatment is based on the premise that craving and other manifestations of alcoholism are mediated by neurobiological mechanisms. High levels of craving are associated with increased probability of relapse, particularly during the early stages of the post treatment period. In addition, treatments that reduce craving have been shown to reduce subsequent alcohol use.[54]

Two medications, Naltrexone and Acamprosate, are designed to prevent the pleasant effects and craving of alcohol.[14] These medications are beneficial in suppressing alcohol use by reducing the desire for alcohol, which in turn helps to prevent relapse for those individuals who are in recovery.[16,61] These medications work through different mechanisms in the brain to achieve the same effect. It has been hypothesized that naltrexone may block positive reinforcement and acamprosate may block the effect of negative reinforcement.[16]

Naltrexone. Naltrexone is utilized in alcohol dependence treatment in 19 countries. In 1995, it was approved by the FDA for alcoholism treatment. Naltrexone reduces the urges to drink, which makes any regressions back into drinking less rewarding. When an individual consumes alcohol, endogenous opioids (key brain chemicals) activate certain brain cells and induce some of alcohol's pleasant effects, such as euphoria. Naltrexone interferes with the actions of endogenous opioids by preventing alcohol from releasing its pleasant effects, which in turn reduces the individual's desire for alcohol.[14] Naltrexone may block the reinforcing effect of alcohol by blocking the endogenous opioid activity. Research indicates that individuals who take naltrexone experience less euphoria after consuming alcohol, which helps them to refrain from heavy drinking.[35] Naltrexone does not increase the probability of staying completely abstinent, but rather reduces the intensity or frequency of any drinking that occurs.[41]

Acamprosate. Acamprosate is one of the most promising medications to treat alcoholism. It is approved by the FDA in the United States, and has been used to treat alcohol dependence in more than 30 countries.[3,35] Acamprosate affects two neurotransmitter systems which are involved in maintaining alcohol dependence: the glutamate system and the gamma-aminobutyric acid (GABA) system. Chronic alcohol consumption inhibits both systems, which precipitates changes that may continue for many months following withdrawal. Acamprosate assists with restoring normal activity within these systems.[35] This medication assists individuals with achieving abstinence by reducing alcohol craving and interfering with the processes of reward and conditioning. This helps to improve relapse rates and reduces symptoms of withdrawal.[3]

PSYCHOLOGICAL TREATMENT FOR ALCOHOL DEPENDENCE

There is currently no cure for alcoholism. Although medications are beneficial in the treatment of alcohol dependence; currently, they cannot replace psychological treatments for individuals with alcoholism. These two types of treatment approaches are complementary, and can be used together to improve treatment outcomes.

A broad range of psychological therapies and philosophies are used to treat alcohol dependence. There is not a particular treatment approach which is superior in promoting long-term recovery from alcoholism; rather, a number of different treatment approaches seem to be equally effective.[35] The major behavioral approaches currently used in alcoholism treatment include brief interventions, motivational interviewing, cognitive behavioral therapy, relapse prevention, and Alcoholics Anonymous.

Brief Interventions. Brief, short-term interventions have grown in popularity with alcoholism treatment due to their cost-effectiveness. Some individuals, however, have questioned the feasibility of brief therapy due to the widely held view of the disease concept of alcoholism.[38] These interventions entail time-limited, client centered counseling strategies that focus on behavioral change. Brief intervention sessions can range from 5 to 60 minute sessions. The general steps of brief interventions include: provide assessment and direct feedback; negotiate and set a goal; utilize behavior modification techniques; provide bibliotherapy using informational materials on alcohol use and its consequences; and ensure follow-up and reinforcement to check on progress.[28] Brief interventions are effective in reducing drinking, problems related to alcohol, and reliance on health care services.[14]

Motivational Interviewing. Motivational interviewing is a direct, client centered approach which focuses on helping the client's drinking behavior change via exploration and resolution of ambivalence. An important emphasis in successful treatment of alcoholism is motivation for change. The purpose of motivational interviewing is to increase the probability of treatment continuation and compliance. The five general principles of motivational interviewing that guide the counselor's behavior include:

- expressing empathy through reflective listening;
- developing discrepancy between client's goals and current behavior;
- avoiding argument and direct confrontation;
- adjusting to resistance rather than opposing it directly; and
- supporting self-efficacy and optimism.[30]

Cognitive-Behavioral Therapy. Abstinence is the objective in the treatment of alcoholism from the cognitive-behavioral perspective. Cognitive-behavioral therapists view drinking as a learned behavior which is functionally related to the problems and situations in the individual's life. The goal of therapy is to assist the client with attaining insight into the thoughts and feelings that led to the behavior of alcoholism. The therapist utilizes functional analysis and skills training to help the individual attain new coping skills in regard to reducing relapse risk, maintaining abstinence, and enhancing self-efficacy.[28,39] Clients practice behavioral and cognitive skills to cope with high-risk situations through rehearsal, role playing, and homework. Cognitive-behavioral therapy has proven to be effective in the treatment of alcohol dependence.[25]

Relapse Prevention. Relapse is a common occurrence among individuals addicted to alcohol. The focus of relapse prevention is on reduced drinking behavior. For an individual recovering from alcohol dependence, slip, lapse, and relapse are the terms commonly used to describe a break in abstinence. A slip is a one time occurrence of drinking which may be accidental. A lapse is a brief occurrence of drinking; however, the individual does not return to previous levels of use. Relapse is a return to pretreatment levels of drinking. Slips and lapses are viewed as mistakes from which the person can take the opportunity to correct future behaviors.[29] Relapse prevention is viewed as a harm reduction approach which utilizes interventions to avoid or limit slips or relapses. When planning a relapse prevention program for clients, treatment providers should address the following: identify high-risk situations; develop strategies to cope with high-risk situations; arrange for social support; use a multi-systemic holistic approach; and discuss relapse prevention throughout treatment, beginning with the first session.[20]

Alcoholics Anonymous. Alcoholics anonymous (AA) was founded in 1935 by Bill Wilson and Dr. Bob Smith. The program is based on the premise of one alcoholic helping another, particularly during periods of stress.[29] AA is an organization that promotes fellowship of people whose common goal is recovery from the disease of alcoholism. The philosophy of AA is that individuals who are addicted to alcohol can only be treated by long-term abstinence from drinking.[28] The AA program is based on 12 steps that alcoholics should achieve during the process of recovery. Individuals may participate in AA before engaging in professional treatment, as a part of professional treatment, following professional treatment, or in lieu of professional treatment. Individuals usually have better outcomes when they participate in AA during and following professional treatment.[20,35] AA is the largest and most popular self-help group for individuals with alcohol dependency problems. It has inspired the development of many other self-help groups in the United States.

SUMMARY AND IMPLICATIONS

Alcohol use and its associated disorders are responsible for serious physical, psychological, and social consequences. It is a substance that knows no bounds, as it affects all people regardless of gender, age, or race.

Therapeutic interventions to treat alcoholism have increased in number, including several pharmacological treatments. However, there is still no cure for alcohol dependency disorders. Continued research to refine therapies for alcoholism will have benefits for individuals who are suffering from alcoholism, their families, and society, which incurs the huge economic and social costs of alcohol dependency.[35]

CASE STUDY

Thomas C. is a 69-year-old Hispanic male. He and his wife were married for 40 years; she died approximately a year ago. Thomas had periodically struggled to maintain his mood, as he would sometimes go from feeling depressed to being on top of the world within a matter of days. He always held a job and provided for his family. His wife was a stay-at-home mom. He never really talked to anyone about his mood swings; he just felt they were a normal part of life. There were times, however, that he was physically unable to get up and go to work. He usually attributed it to being tired and needing a day of rest. On the days when his mood was elevated, he would work double shifts making up the time he had missed. During the high periods, Thomas would sometimes drink alcohol in order to bring himself down and get some sleep. If he did not drink, he could stay up for days at a time. Before he retired, he was drinking upwards to 9 or 10 beers a night. Some weekends, he drank even more.

After Thomas' wife passed, he realized that his low periods lasted longer and they seemed to be more severe. After talking to his daughter about this, she suggested that he visit his doctor. She thought that maybe he was just grieving. During Thomas' doctor's visits he talked to his doctor about feeling depressed, but did not mention the manic periods or his drinking. His doctor prescribed an antidepressant as well as another medication, Ambien, to help him sleep.

Shortly after Thomas began taking the antidepressant, he experienced one of his manic states, but it was unlike any he had ever experienced before. He rambled, and his speech was incomprehensible, his thoughts continuously raced, and as he claims, "I had one brilliant idea after another one!" This was the best he had felt since his wife passed; however, after feeling this way for four days, he decided to take the Ambien in order to get some sleep. He washed the pills down with a few cans of beer.

The next thing Thomas knew was that he was waking up in the emergency room. His daughter came over to find him unconscious; she thought he had tried to commit suicide. After answering questions, the doctors realized that his mixing alcohol with the antidepressant and

Ambien has caused a severe depression of his respiratory system. Had his daughter not come to check on him, Thomas may have died. After being released from the hospital, he met with his doctor to discuss his mood swings and his alcohol use. His doctor was able to explain to him the dangers of mixing medications with alcohol. He was diagnosed with Bipolar I disorder and alcohol dependence, and the doctor talked to him about treatment for both problems. Thomas initially resisted because he thought he was fine because he had dealt with this problem all of his life. He also thought that he was too old to be in treatment until his doctor discussed treatment options. After speaking with his daughter, he decided to seek therapy.

REFERENCES

[1]Barnes, G. M., Reifman, A. S., Farrell, M. P., Dintcheff, B. A. (2000). The effects of parenting on the development of adolescent alcohol misuse: A six-wave latent growth model. *Journal of Marriage and the Family, 62*, 175-186.

[2]Brennan, P. L., & Moos, R. H. (1996). Late-life drinking behavior: The influence of personal characteristics, life context, and treatment. *Alcohol Heath & Research World, 20*, 197-204.

[3]Buonopane, A., & Petrakis, I. L. (2005). Pharmacotherapy of alcohol use disorders. *Substance Use & Misuse, 40*, 2001-2020.

[4]Center for Disease Control and Prevention. (2009). *Vital and health statistics: Summary health statistics for US adults: National health interview survey, 2009.* Retrieved from http://www.cdc.gov/nchs/data/series/sr_10/sr10_249.pdf

[5]Center for Disease Control and Prevention. (2003). Alcohol consumption by persons 18 years of age and older according to selected characteristics. *Health United States.* DHHS Publication Number 2004-0152.

[6]Cohen, M. (2000). *Counseling addictive women.* Thousands Oaks, CA: Sage.

[7]Doweiko, H. E. (2009). *Concepts of chemical dependency (7th ed.).* Belmont, CA: Brooks/Cole Cengage.

[8]Doweiko, H. E. (2006). *Concepts of chemical dependency (6th ed.).* Belmont, CA: Brooks/Cole Cengage.

[9]Dunne, F. J. (1994). Misuse of alcohol or drugs by elderly people. *British Medical Journal, 308*, 608-609.

[10]Echeburua, E., de Media, R., & Aizpri, J. (2007). Comorbidity of alcohol dependence and personality disorders: A comparative study. *Alcohol & Alcoholism, 42*, 618-622.

[11]Feldstein Ewing, S. W., Filbey, F. M., Chandler, L. D. & Hutchison, K. E. (2010). Exploring the relationship between depressive and anxiety symptoms and neuronal response alcohol cues. *Alcoholism: Clinical and Experimental Resesearch, 34,* 396-404.

[12]Fleming, M., Mihic, S. J., & Harris, R. A. (2001). *Ethanol. The pharmacological basis of therapeutics (11th ed.).* New York, NY: McGraw-Hill.

[13]Freiberg, M. S., & Samet, J. H. (2005). Alcohol and coronary heart disease: The answer awaits a randomized controlled trial. *Circulation, 112,* 1379-1380.

[14]Fuller, R. K., & Hiller-Sturmhofel, S. (1999). Alcoholism treatment in the United States: An overview. *Alcohol Research & Health, 23,* 69-7.

[15]Godlaski, A. J. & Giancola, P. R. (2009). Executive functioning, irritability and alcohol-related aggression. *Psychology of Addictive Behavior, 23,* 391-403.

[16]Gordis, E. (2009). Contributions of behavioral science to alcohol research: Understanding who is at risk and why. In A. G. Marlatt & K. Witkiewitz (Eds.), *Addictive behaviors: New readings on etiology, prevention, and treatment* (pp. 19-32). Washington, DC: American Psychological Association.

[17]Grant, B., Stinson, F., Dawson, D., Chou, P., Duforu, M., Compton, W., Pickering, R., & Kaplan, K. (2004). Prevalence and co-occurrence of substance use disorders and independent mood and anxiety disorders: Results from the national epidemiologic survey on alcohol and related conditions. *Archives of General Psychiatry, 61,* 807-816.

[18]Grant, B. F., & Dawson, D. A., (1997). Age at onset of alcohol use and its association with DSM-IV alcohol abuse and dependence: Results from the National longitudinal alcohol epidemiological survey. *Journal of Substance Abuse, 9,* 103-110.

[19]Hardwood, H. (2000). Updating estimates of the economic costs of alcohol abuse in the United States: Estimates update methods and data. *Report prepared by The Levin Group for the National Institute on Alcohol Abuse and Alcoholism.*

[20]Johnson, J. L. (2004). *Fundamentals of substance abuse practice.* Belmont, CA: Brooks/Cole Cengage.

[21]Karam-Hage, M. (2004). Treating insomnia in patients with substance use/abuse disorders. *Psychiatric Times 21,* 55-56.

[22]Kershaw C. D. & Guidot, D. M. (2008). Alcoholic lung disease. *Alcohol Research and Health, 31,* 66-75.

[23]Kinney, J. (2004). *Loosening the grip. A handbook of alcohol information.* New York: McGraw Hill.

[24]Kranzler, H. R., & Ciraulo, D. A. (2005). *Clinical manual of addiction pharmacology.* Arlington, VA: American Psychiatric Publishing, Inc.

[25]Litt, M. D., Kadden, R. M., Cooney, N. L., & Kabela, E. (2003). Coping skills and treatment outcomes in cognitive-behavioral and interactional group therapy for alcoholism. *Journal of Consulting and Clinical Psychology, 71,* 118-127.

[26]Lovinger, D. M. (2008). Communication networks in the brain: Neurons, receptors, neurotransmitters, and alcohol. *Alcohol Research & Health, 31(3),* 196-214.

[27]Manhood, O. M., Jocobus, J., Bava, S., Scarlett, A., & Tapert, S. (2010). Learning and memory performances in adolescent users alcohol and marijuana: Interactive effects. *Journal of Studies on Alcohol and Drugs, 71,* 885-894.

[28]McCaul, M. E., & Petry, N. M. (2003). The role of psychosocial treatments in pharmacotherapy for alcoholism. *The American Journal on Addictions, 12,* S41-S52.

[29]Miller, G. (2005). *Learning the language of addiction counseling (2nd ed.).* Hoboken, NJ: John Wiley & Sons.

[30]Miller, W. R. (2008). *Enhancing motivation for change in substance abuse treatment.* Rockville, MD: U.S. Department of Health and Human Services.

[31]Mirin, S. M., Weiss, R. D., & Greenfield, S. F. (1991). Psychoactive substances use disorders. In A. J. Galenberg, E. L. Bassuk, & S. C. Schoonover (Eds.), *The practitioner's guide to psychoactive drugs* (3rd ed). (pp. 291-353). New York: Plenum Medical Book Co.

[32]Molina, P. E., Happel, K. I., Zhang, P., Kols, J. K., Nelson, S. (2010) Focus on: Alcohol and the immune system. *Alcohol Research and Health, 33,* 97-108.

[33]Mundle, G. (2000). Geriatric patients. In G. Zerig, A. Saria, M. Kurz, & S. S. O'Malley (Eds.), *Handbook of Alcoholism* (pp. 137-150). New York: CRC Press.

[34]Nace, E. P. (2005) *Alcohol. Clinical textbook of addictive disorders* (3rd ed.). New York. NY: Guilford.

[35]National Institute on Alcohol Abuse and Alcoholism [NIAAA]. (2000). Research refines alcoholism treatment options. *Alcohol Research & Health, 24,* 53-61.

[36]Niccols, A. (2007). Fetal alcohol syndrome and the developing socio-emotional brain. *Brain and Cognition, 65,* 135-142.

[37]O'Keefe, J. H., Bybee, K. A., & Lavie, C. J. (2010). Alcohol and cardiovascular health: The razor-sharp double-edged sword. *Journal of the American College of Cardiology, 50,* 1009-1014.

[38]Osborn, C. J. (1997). Does disease matter? Incorporating solution-focused brief therapy in alcoholism treatment. *Journal of Alcohol and Drug Education, 43,* 18-30.

[39]Rahill, G. J., Lopez, E. P., Vanderbiest, A., & Rice, C. (2009). What is relapse? A contemporary exploration of treatment of alcoholism. *Journal of Social Work Practice in the Addictions, 9,* 245-262.

[40]Renner, J. A. (2004). Alcoholism and alcohol abuse. In T. A. Stern & J. B. Herman (Eds.), *Massachusetts General Hospital psychiatric update and board preparation* (2nd ed.) (pp. 73-84) . New York: McGraw-Hill.

[41]Rohsenow, D. J. (2004). What place does naltrexone have in the treatment of alcoholism? *CNS Drugs, 18*, 547-560.

[42]Room, R., Babor, T., Rehm, J. (2005). Alcohol and public health. *The Lancet, 365*, 529-530.

[43]Ropper, A. H., & Brown, R. H. (2005). *Adams and victor's principles of neurology (8th ed.).* New York, NY: McGraw-Hill.

[44]Rose, K. J. (1988). *The body in time.* New York: John Wiley.

[45]Rubin, D. H. (2001). *Treating adult children of alcoholics.* New York: Academic Press.

[46]Sadock, B. J., & Sadock, V. A. (2003). *Kaplan and Sadock's synopsis of psychiatry* (9th ed). New York: Lippincott, Williams & Wilkins.

[47]Samokhvolov, A. V., Papova, S., Room, R., Ramonas M., & Rehm, J. (2010). Disability associated with alcohol abuse and dependence. *Alcoholism: Clinical and Experimental Research, 34*, 1871-1878.

[48]Schuckit, M. A. (2005). Alcohol related disorders. In H. I. Kaplan & B. J. Sadock (Eds.), *Comprehensive textbook of psychology* (8th ed.). Baltimore, MD: Williams and Wilkins.

[49]Seitz, H., & Becker, P. (2007). Alcohol metabolism and health risk. *Alcohol Research and Health, 30*, 38-47.

[50]Sintov, N., Kendler, K., Walsh, D., Patterson, D., & Prescott, C. (2009). Predictors of illicit substance dependence among individuals with alcohol dependence. *Journal of Studies on Alcohol and Drugs, 70*, 269-278.

[51]Sisson, J. H. (2007). Alcohol and airways function in health and disease. *Alcohol, 41*, 293-307.

[52]Sokol, R. J., Delaney-Black, V., & Nordstrom, B. (2003). Fetal alcohol spectrum disorder. *Journal of the American Medical Association, 290*, 2996-2999.

[53]Sullivan, E. V., Harris, R. A., Pfefferbaum, A. (2010). Alcohol's effects on brain and behavior. *Alcohol Research and Health, 33*, 127-143.

[54]Swift, R. M. (1999). Medications and alcohol craving. *Alcohol Research & Health, 23*, 207-213.

[55]Szabo G., & Mandrekar, P. (2010). Focus on: Alcohol and the liver. *Alcohol and Health, 33*, 87-96.

[56]Tsurugizawa, T., Uematsu, A., Uneyama, H., & Torii, K. (2010). The role of the GABAergic and dopaminergic systems in the brain response to an intragastric load of alcohol in conscious rats. *Neuroscience, 171*, 451-460.

[57]U.S. Department of Health and Human Services, National Institutes of Health, National Institute on Alcohol Abuse and Alcoholism. (2009). Neuroscience: Pathways to alcohol dependence. *Alcohol Alert, 77*. Retrieved from http:// www.niaaa.nih.gov/Publications/AlcoholAlerts/Documents/AA77.pdf

[58]U.S. Department of Health and Human Services, National Institutes of Health, National Institute on Alcohol Abuse and Alcoholism. (2007). Alcohol metabolism: An update. *Alcohol Alert, 72.* Retrieved from http://pubs.niaaa.nih.gov/publications/aa72/aa72.htm

[59]Wagner, E. F. (1993). Delay of gratification, coping with stress, and substance use in adolescents. *Experiments in Clinical Psychopharmacology, 1,* 27-43.

[60]Whitlock, E. P., Polen, M. R., Green, C. A., Orleans, T., & Klien, J. (2004). Behavioral Counseling interventions in primary care to reduce risky/harmful alcohol use by adults: A summary of the evidence for the U.S. preventive services task force. *Annals of Internal Medicine,* 140(7) 556-580.

[61]Wilbourne, P. L., & Miller, W. R. (2002). Treatment for alcoholism: Older and wiser? *Alcoholism Treatment Quarterly, 20,* 41-59.

[62]Willoughby, K. A., Sheard, E. D., Nash, K., & Rovet, J. (2008). Effects of prenatal alcohol exposure on hippocampal volume, verbal learning, and verbal and spatial recall in late childhood. *Journal of the International Neuropsychological Society, 14,* 1002-1033.

[63]Zoethout, W. E. M., Schoemaker, R. C., Zurrman, L., van Pelt, H., Dahan, A., Cohen, A. F., & van Gerven, J. M. A. (2009). Central nervous system effects of alcohol at a pseudo-steady-state concentration using alcohol clamping in healthy individuals. *British Journal of Clinical Pharmacology, 68,* 524-534.

[64]Zisserson, R. N, & Oslin, D. W. (2004). Alcoholism and at-risk drinking in the older population. *Psychiatric Times, 21(2),* 50-53.

Chapter Five

OPIOID ADDICTION & DEPENDENCE: CLINICAL COMPONENTS

BY   **STEPHANIE L. LUSK**
NORTH CAROLINA AGRICULTURAL
AND TECHNICAL STATE UNIVERSITY

CHAPTER TOPICS

◊   A History of Opiates

◊   Mechanism of Action

◊   Popular Opiates of Abuse

◊   Prevalence of Opiate

◊   Special Considerations

◊   Treatment of Opioid Addiction

◊   Summary and Implications

◊   Case Study

A HISTORY OF OPIATES

*T*he use of opium, once referred to as the "joy plant" by the Sumerians, can be traced back to 4000 BC, but is believed to have been used well before this time, even as early as 10,000 years ago.[33] Opium is from the Greek work *opion* meaning "juice" or "sap."[15] It was originally chewed, eaten, or mixed with different drinks and used to treat a variety of diseases including colic in infants,[6] pain, and diarrhea. In 460 BC, Hippocrates, recognizing the benefits of this drug, prescribed it for sleep and other ills such as melancholy, coughing, asthma, and headaches. Its use quickly spread to Persia, India, and China thereafter. The popularity of opium waned for a period of time during the 1300s due to the Holy Inquisition and its banning by Emperor Cheng of China, however, its resurgence was recognized in the 1500s. The invention of the hypodermic needle in 1853 by Dr. Alexander Wood continued to herald it as a wonder drug as the results of the drug were experienced instantaneously and much more strongly. This allowed for a more effective way to administer the drug. It was noticed that by administering the drug in this manner, a stronger and much more pleasurable effect or high was experienced.

Pain, which involves complex processes and sensations within the body, has always plagued humankind. With the discovery of opium and subsequently its ability to relieve pain, it was considered a gift from the gods.[4] Opiates/opioids are produced from a substance found in the white, milky juice of the opium poppy (*Papaver Somniferun*), which turns brown or black when it is exposed to the air. There are over 20 different alkaloids of opium, but the two most abundant derivatives are morphine and codeine.[4] Morphine, first isolated in 1806 by the German scientist Friedrich Serturner, is named for Morpheus the Greek god of dreams. Morphine is 10 times more powerful than opium and was used early on to treat wounded soldiers. Morphine is the active ingredient of opium. Codeine, which got its name from the Greek word *kodeida,* means "poppyhead" and was isolated in 1832.[15] It is still currently used as a cough suppressant. The isolation of morphine and codeine allowed for the study of their positive properties. This led to the further development of derivatives from opium, one being heroin. Heroin was first isolated in 1874, and in 1898 was marketed as a cough suppressant and treatment for chest pain, tuberculosis, and pneumonia by Bayer and Company.[25] The isolation of these derivatives proved to be beneficial to the medical community. Initially drugs such as morphine were used in many elixirs and individuals who drank these concoctions were not sure of its true composition. The identification of the many derivatives finally allowed for the processing of drugs that were pure and of known potency, which greatly benefited physicians, patients, and society as a whole. This resulted in the ability to prescribe, test, and modify treatment for individuals to whom opiates were prescribed.

Even though there are numerous positive aspects of opium and its derivatives, the associated problems, namely addiction, were quickly becoming noticeable. Opioid addiction was prevalent during the early part of the 19th century. Soldiers who had been injured during the American Civil War were given morphine to treat injuries. Because the drug dosages were not closely regulated, addiction to morphine ran rampant and was eventually referred to as the "soldier's disease[3]". Heroin, because it was considered less harmful than morphine, was then prescribed as a cure for those who were addicted to morphine. Shortly thereafter, addiction to heroin was also ubiquitous and its non-medical use was banned.

Specific laws and closer follow-up by physicians, counselors and other professionals have been put into place to better control problems associated with opiate use, abuse, and addiction. After the realization of the highly addictive properties of heroin, in 1906, the US Congress passed the Pure Food and Drug Act which required makers of elixirs and other medicines to provide a listing of ingredients. In 1914, the government imposed heavy taxes on heroin via the Harrison Act and this act also prevented the use of opiates without a prescription. In 1924, opiates were banned for non- medical use, and in 1970, the Federal Controlled Substance Act classified heroin as a schedule I drug and banned its use completely. Schedule I drugs are those identified as being highly addictive and having no identified medicinal purpose. Opioids, other than heroin, are still used today to help control pain, suppress coughs, and treat diarrhea and in spite of the aforementioned laws and regulations, they remain one of the most used, abused, and addictive substances today.

Table 1

SCHEDULE OF DRUGS

Description	Drugs
Schedule I High potential for abuse; no accepted medical use	Heroin, LSD, peyote, ecstasy
Schedule II High potential for abuse with psychological and/or physical dependence	cocaine, morphine, oxycodone (OxyCotin®, Tylox®), Ritalin ®, hydromorphone, fentanyl, methadone, meperidine (Demarol®)
Schedule III Less substance abuse abuse potential	codeine, Tylenol® with codeine, hydrocodone (Vicodin ®, Lortab ®, Lorcet®)
Schedule IV Even less abuse potential	meprobormate, diazepam (Valium®), pentazocine (Talwin®), propoxyphene (Darvon®)
Schedule V Very low abuse potential; sold over the counter	Robitussin AC ®, buprenorphine, (Buprenex® Subotex®)

Mechanism of Action

Drugs cannot cause the body to communicate, react, or experience feelings and sensations unless they have a specific position or place on which to act. The body produces endogenous pain killers and mood enhancers known as endorphins, enkephalins, and dynorphins for which there are specific positions of action within the brain, spinal cord, and other areas throughout the body. These substances are considered neurotransmitters and are used as communication devices or messengers within the body. These substances are released not only when the body needs to be notified of pain, but also after pleasurable experiences such as exercise and during orgasm. They produce a feeling of overall well being and contentment. Opiates, because of their similar chemical structure, have the ability to infiltrate the specific areas that are normally activated by these naturally occurring substances and cause the body to act. Not only do opiates mimic these naturally occurring substances and "trick" the body into acting and feeling a sense of well being, but they generate an even greater sense of pleasure as they cause the endogenous substances to be produced in amounts.

The body, especially the brain, contains many activation stations or receptor sites that assist with communicating messages such as pain and pleasure. These receptor sites receive the message and are then responsible for sending it forward in the communication process. These receptors can only be unlocked by a specific key or message. Pain and pleasure receptors can act and continue the communication process only when it receives pain and pleasure messages. For opioid receptors, messengers are not only considered the endogenous substances (endorphins, enkephalins, and dynorphins), but opioid derived drugs such as morphine, heroin, and codeine as well.

Pain is a signal that indicates that something within the body has gone awry; therefore, the proper functioning of the communication process is imperative. This allows for immediate attention to the matter so that the feeling of pain is addressed and alleviated as quickly as possible. When endogenous substances are allowed to react to pain messages, a flood of endorphins, enkephalins, and dynorphins within the brain and spinal cord are released. If this does not work to alleviate the pain, opioid derived drugs may be necessary.

The primary receptors within the brain and spinal cord upon which the endogenous substances and opioid drugs act are *mu*1, *mu*2, *kappa*, and *delta*. Opioids, in the form of drugs, are able to fit into these receptor sites and cause a reaction that is more pleasurable than what would be produced by the endogenous opioids. When *mu* receptors are affected, pain is blocked and euphoria is experienced while the autonomic nervous system is depressed and constipation results.[8] These receptors are involved in many of the negative side effects associated with opiates including sweating, nausea, and vomiting. They are also implicated in increased tolerance and dependence. *Kappa* receptors control pain within the spinal cord by causing sedation[9] and activation of these receptors also help to control cough and diarrhea. Doweiko[9] also noted that activation at the *delta* receptors causes feelings of pleasure as well.

Table 2

Type of Opioid	Name
Natural*	Opium
	Morphine
	Codeine
	Thebane
Semi-Synthetic**	Diacetylmorphine (heroin)
	Hydrocodone (Vicodin®, Lortab®, Lorcet®)
	Oxycodone (OxyCotin®, Percodan®)
	Hydromorphone (Dilaudid®)
	Oxymorphone
	Desomorphine
	Micomorphine
	Dipropanoylmorphine
	Benzylmorphine
	Ethylmorphine
Fully Synthetic***	Meperidine (Demerol®)
	Methadone
	Propoxyphene (Darvon®)
	Fentanyl
	Pethidine
	Tramadol
Endogenous****	Endorphins
	Enkephalins
	Dynorphins
	Endormorphins

* Natural opiates are direct products of the opium poppy plant.
** Semi-synthetic opiates are made by modifying the chemicals contained in opium.
***Synthetic opiates are made entirely in laboratories.
****Endogenous opiates are produced in the body by the body.

PHYSICAL EFFECTS OF OPIOID USE

No part of the body is spared from the effects of opiates. As noted earlier, primary side effects involve the digestive system (nausea, vomiting, and constipation), the respiratory system (depressed breathing, lowered blood pressure), and the central nervous system (brain and spinal cord). Doweiko[9] noted that other problems include strokes, pulmonary edema, kidney damage, seizures, and cotton fever which results when cotton is used to filter out impurities from the heroin. Tiny particles of cotton are injected into the body when the drug is taken, which can lead to pulmonary arthritis. Other problems encompass sexual dysfunction, including erectile dysfunction, constriction of the pupils, memory loss, slowing of the heart rate, lowering of body temperature, and pruritus or itchiness, especially with morphine use. Other less serious physical effects include dizziness and loss of balance, but these minor effects can lead to more serious consequences, such as falls. It should also be noted that severe withdrawal symptoms, addiction, and death are also serious side effects of drug use.

PSYCHOLOGICAL EFFECTS OF OPIOID USE

Doweiko[8] noted that there are several factors that may affect the psychological or subjective effects of opiates, including:

◊ Route of administration (whether it was injected, snorted, smoked, etc.);
◊ time between doses;
◊ amount taken;
◊ anxiety level (higher levels of tension and anxiety usually require a larger dosage);
◊ positive or negative expectations of the drug's effect;
◊ amount of time the drug has been used.

Although opiates reduce tension and help to alleviate pain, numerous psychological effects can result. These drugs interfere mental functioning which can lead to delayed thinking and reaction time. Other psychological problems can result as decision making and problem solving abilities are diminished and self-control is lowered.

POPULAR OPIATES OF ABUSE

Doweiko[9] noted that there are several factors that may affect the psychological or subjective effects of opiates, including:

◊ Route of administration (whether it was injected, snorted, smoked, etc.);
◊ time between doses;
◊ amount taken;

◊ anxiety level (higher levels of tension and anxiety usually require a larger dosage);
◊ positive or negative expectations of the drug's effect;
◊ amount of time the drug has been used.

Each of these factors should be considered individually as they will differ for each opiate derivative.

MORPHINE

Morphine, originally isolated by Fredrick Serturner in 1806, is considered the standard by which other pain relievers are measured.[15] Morphine is 10 times as strong as opium and is considered a much better pain reliever. Morphine is generally prescribed to those who have experienced a myocardial infarction (heart attack) and for its cardiovascular effects in the treatment of acute pulmonary edema.[10] Morphine is the active ingredient in opium and is used in the development of other derivatives of the drug.

HEROIN

Heroin, a derivative of morphine, is considered the most addictive and fastest acting of the opiates. Heroin has a schedule I classification and has no recognized medicinal purposes; therefore, its possession and manufacture is illegal. Heroin can be taken by mouth, injected into the muscles or directly into the blood stream, sniffed/snorted, or smoked. When heroin is injected intravenously, it acts almost immediately upon the system, usually within 7 to 8 seconds; when injected into the muscle, its peak effects are experienced within 5 to 8 minutes. If heroin is snorted, it generally takes 10 to 15 minutes to experience its pleasurable effects. Smoking heroin or "chasing the dragon," originated in China and causes effects within 7 to 10 seconds. Approximately 13 to 18 metric tons of heroin are consumed each year,[22] and current estimates suggest that nearly 600,000 people are in need of treatment for heroin addiction.[18] They also note that in the 25 to 49 age group, illicit drug overdose is the fourth leading cause of death. The term "junkie" was created in the 1920s specifically for heroin addicts who searched through junk yards and trash heaps to collect scraps of metal in order to support their drug habit.[24] It is estimated that there are approximately nine million individuals addicted to this substance with one million of those individuals living in the United States.[26] Barnett, et al.[2] also found that the majority of new heroin users were young individuals between the ages of 12 and 25.

CODEINE

Codeine is also a direct derivative of morphine, is about twice as strong, and is the most constipating of all opioids. It accounts for approximately 12% of all drug related deaths[17] Doweiko[8] states that these deaths may be the result of heroin addicts overestimating the amount of this drug they will need in order to alleviate their negative withdrawal symptoms, so deaths by overdosing are more likely.

Codeine is most commonly used to control coughs. Its abuse potential is lower, it is sometimes used to help alleviate withdrawal symptoms from morphine or heroin when they cannot be obtained. Codeine containing medicines are easier to obtain, some may be purchased over-the-counter.

METHADONE

Methadone was originally developed over 30 years ago to replace morphine use. It is currently utilized to treat heroin addiction. It works by reducing an individual's cravings for the drug. Individuals who utilize methadone in this way must still be cautioned about it addictive properties. Because it is useful in helping to alleviate withdrawal symptoms, it is used for detoxification as well.

FENTANYL

Fentanyl was first isolated in 1968 and is considered the most powerful of the opioids. Because it is a shorter acting opiate, it is generally used during and immediately following surgery to provide quick pain relief which is experienced only minutes after injection. There is some disagreement in relation to the strength of this drug. Some argue that it is 50 to 100 times more potent than morphine,[11] while Kirsch[18] states that it is 1000 to 3000 times more potent. Side effects of fentanyl include those common to all opioids as well as dizziness, hallucinations, anxiety, and depression. Lollipops for children and oral-transmucosal versions provide additional options for administration.

PRESCRIPTION DRUGS OF ABUSE

Hydrocodone (Vicodin®). Hydrocodone is currently considered the most widely abused prescription opioid in the United States[15] and has posed many serious problems. Vicodin® is produced by Abbott Laboratories and was approved in 1984 by the Federal Drug Administration (FDA) for pain relief. Considered a schedule II drug, it is commonly prescribed as a pain reliever.

Oxycodone (OxyCotin®, Percocet®). Oxycodone is a synthesized form of the opium derivative thebaine and is produced by Purdue Pharma. OxyContin was first produced in 1995 and is classified as a schedule II drug. Percocet is a combination of oxycodone and Acetaminophen (or Tylenol). Using the combination of these two drugs increases its pain relieving abilities. It is also considered a schedule II drug.

PREVALENCE OF OPIATE

DIAGNOSING OPIATE USE AND ITS RELATED DISORDERS

According to the Diagnostic and Statistical Manual (DSM) opioid-related disorders can fall into two categories, opioid use disorders and opioid-induced disorders. Opioid use disorders include dependence and abuse. Opioid-induced disorders include intoxication with and without delirium, withdrawal, intoxication delirium, psychotic disorders with delusions and/or hallucinations, mood disorders, sexual dysfunction, sleep disorders, and those not otherwise specified.[1] When using the DSM as a guide for diagnosing an individual with an opioid use disorder, it is important to rule out any other possible substance use disorder, mental disorder, or medical condition that could mimic symptoms similar to those listed below.

Criteria for opioid abuse and dependence are outlined by the American Psychiatric Association.[1] Abuse is characterized by maladaptive patterns of opiate use that leads to significant problems in one or more of the following areas within a 12-month timeframe:

◊ Major role obligations at home, work, or school;
◊ use in physically hazardous situations;
◊ legal problems related to the substance use; and/or
◊ exacerbation of social and interpersonal problems.

Opioid dependence (addiction) is differentiated from abuse in two primary ways:

◊ tolerance (the need for increased amounts of the opiate in order to experience the same effects);
◊ withdrawal (unpleasant side effects experienced as a result of discontinuing the drug or needing to ingest the drug in order to alleviate and/or avoid the negative effects) are prevalent.

With dependence, the individual may also experience:

◊ a desire to cut down or discontinue the drug;
◊ huge amounts of time, effort and energy are spend on obtaining, preparing, ingesting, and recovering from drug use;
◊ important activities are discontinued;
◊ use is continued even after the realization of the negative consequences associated with the drug's use.

Behaviors associated with opioid intoxication include:

◊ euphoria;
◊ slowing down of thought and physical functioning;
◊ drowsiness or coma;
◊ incoherent speech;
◊ impaired memory.

Opioid withdrawal results when the drug is discontinued and the individual experiences three or more of the following:

◊ dysphoric mood;
◊ nausea or vomiting;
◊ muscle aches;
◊ lacrimation or rhinorrhea;
◊ pupillatory dilation and sweating;
◊ diarrhea;
◊ yawning;
◊ fever;
◊ insomnia.[1]

These symptoms are severe enough that they cause distress and impairment in the individual's life.

USE, ABUSE, AND ADDICTION

Simply put, people use opiates because they make them feel good, especially if the individual is in pain. According to the United Nations, there has been a steady increase in heroin use worldwide totaling upwards to 15 million users of which half live in Asia, 25% are in Europe, and only 16.7% are in the United States.[26] Inaba and Cohen[14] noted that even though the use of heroin is illegal, the production of the opium plant has more than doubled with major production in Afghanistan (produces more than 70% of the world's supply), Pakistan, Myanmar, Thailand, and Laos. The United States receives the majority of this drug from Mexico and Columbia, and it is estimated that between 13 and 18 metric tons of heroin are consumed each year.[22] In 2001, opioid dependence accounted for approximately 18% of substance abuse treatment admissions.[23]

Heroin abuse and addiction. Heroin, processed from morphine is considered the most commonly abused and rapidly acting opiate. As stated in the Research Report Series on Heroin Abuse and Addiction published by the National Institute on Drug Abuse, the National Survey on Drug Use and Health estimated that 3.7 million people had use heroin at some time in their lives.[21] The United Nations estimates that there are approximately 1.4 million Americans addicted to heroin.[26] Addiction to this substance leads to a plethora of associated physical, psychological, social, and legal problems. Withdrawal from narcotics is not fatal, but is extremely uncomfortable.

SPECIAL CONSIDERATIONS

WOMEN

Women who abuse substances encounter numerous problems that are unique to them. As noted by the US Department of Health and Human Services[32] one-forth to one-half of men who engage in domestic violence have substance abuse problems themselves and those women who abuse substances are more likely to be victims of domestic violence. A study of California prisons conducted by Bloom[28] found that 29% of women reported being physically abused as children and 60% as adults; 31% reported being sexually abused as a child and 23% as adults; and 40% of women reported some form of emotional abuse as a child and 48% as an adult. Domestic abuse not only includes violence between partners, but expands to include children and the elderly as well. The abuse is not limited to physical force such as battering, but encompasses sexual, verbal, and psychological components as well. When these women enter treatment, their safety needs to be ensured and a treatment plan needs to be developed that not only addresses the addiction and any underlying psychological issues, but domestic violence as well. These women also face problems of Post Traumatic

Stress Disorder (PTSD), low self-esteem, shame, and guilt.

Another problem unique to women is the birth of infants who are premature, have low birth weight, or are addicted to substances. These infants are dealing with withdrawal symptoms immediately after birth and are more likely to die from Sudden Death Syndrome (SIDS).[19] Also noted in older children who were exposed to drugs in vitro were problems associated with poor eye sight, delayed language development, lower intelligence, and hyperactivity. These problems can lead to additional stress for the mother which in turn could perpetuate the continued abuse of substances. Mothers of these children require additional supports to help them address their needs as well as the special needs of their children.

Also noted as an issue that is not necessarily unique to women are legal problems, and how women are impacted by this problem produces unique circumstances. The US Department of Health and Human Services[28] noted that most of the women entering the criminal justice system are under the age of 40 and 8 out of every 10 are parents. The majority of these women enter prison for drug related offenses such as possession or for activities employed to support their drug habit such as theft and prostitution. These women enter the prison system with major substance abuse problems that are generally more advanced and at a more severe stage than men do. Oftentimes this is their first opportunity for treatment; therefore, treatment that is comprehensive and addresses their unique needs is necessary while follow-up care is paramount for the maintenance of abstinence.

ADOLESCENTS

According to Hopfer, er al.[14] the age of first time users of heroin has dropped from 27 in 1988 to 19 by the mid-1990s. Even though there has been a decrease in the use of heroin by adolescents, other opioids, including hydrocodone, oxycodone, and codeine, has stepped up to take its place. These drugs may be attractive for use because they may be easy to obtain and are considered less harmful than heroin because they are prescribed by physicians and originate from pharmaceutical companies. Even though created in pill form and designed to be administered orally, these pills are usually crushed and snorted or mixed to be injected intravenously. These methods result in a quicker, more intense high.

Approximately 13% of the 2003 graduating senior class reported having abused an opiate other than heroin at least once and 1.5% reportedly used heroin at least once.[15] According to the Monitoring the Future survey conducted by the National Institute on Drug Abuse, between 2003 and 2004, heroin use among 8th graders measured 1.6% and 1.5% among 10th and 12th graders. Adolescents with severe behavioral and emotional problems may have higher rates of use and abuse.

In order to decrease substance use and subsequent dependence, protective factors such as school involvement, stable family settings, community and church activities, etc., can be employed. Another option includes creating partnerships with social services, mental health practitioners, and even the juvenile justice system in an effort to help thwart problems related to addiction.[30,31]

ELDERLY

Barriers associated with diagnosing and treating the elderly with substance use disorders includes ageism, lack of awareness, the behavior of physicians and mental health professionals, and co-morbidity. According to the US Department of Health and Human Services,[28] adults over the age of 65 consume more prescribed and over-the-counter medications than any age group. Noted factors that contribute to the misuse and abuse of these drugs include old age, poor physical health, and being female. They may misunderstand the directions, negative drug interactions may occur which can lead to unpleasant side effects, overdose, and even death. Life changes may also serve as a catalyst that leads to substance abuse. Some of the life changes include emotional and social problems such as death and loneliness, medical problems such as chronic pain and sensory reduction (loss of sight, hearing, etc.), and practical problems such as loss of income, homelessness, and the inability to care for oneself.

It is important for professionals to properly screen patients in order to identify symptoms of abuse and dependence. A physical as well as a psychological exam are oftentimes necessary to tease out problems that may otherwise be missed or masked as another problem. Appropriate referrals to treatment are necessary. Treatment should not only address the addiction, but should address problems related to underlying psychological problems and life changes as well. These individuals should also have treatment that is age appropriate, focus on rebuilding social networks and support, and provides linkages to services necessary for maintaining sobriety.[28]

INDIVIDUALS WITH DISABILITIES

According to the Rehabilitation Research and Training Center on Drugs and Disability approximately 49 million Americans have some form of disability. Research conducted by the US Department of Health and Human Services[29] found that approximately 20% of individuals who qualify for state vocational rehabilitation services have a diagnosis of substance abuse or dependence. Research has indicated that substance abuse may be higher among this group because of unemployment, lack or recreational opportunities, isolation, homelessness, and abuse. These individuals may be more likely to also experience mental health problems as well which serves to create a "triple whammy" for them. These individuals may be less likely to access appropriate treatment and for those who do, they may still be underserved as indicated in a lack of referrals to abuse treatment. Each of these problem increase the likelihood of substance use disorders to occur, and because of the numerous diagnoses, treatment is oftentimes more complex requiring more services, resources, and time.

Individuals with disabilities face barriers related to treatment that include negative attitudes, discrimination and stereotypes, communication, and architectural; therefore, treatment and service professionals will need to be diligent in addressing these additional needs. Because modifications to treatment programs may be necessary, accommodations will need to be considered as well as the cognitive and emotional functioning of each individual.

CO-OCCURRING MENTAL DISORDERS

The US Department of Health and Human Services[30,31] noted that serious mental illness (SMI) is highly correlated with substance abuse, finding that among adults with SMI 23.2 % were dependent on alcohol or some other illicit drug while only 8.2% of individuals who did not have SMI had problems with drug abuse. They also found that these individuals were more likely to be hospitalized. Those with opioids dependence and a co-occurring diagnosis of schizophrenia were more likely to experience premature death. Other studies have identified higher rates of mental illness including personality disorders with narcissistic-antisocial disorders representing the highest percentage from their sample followed by dependent.[6] Additional problems that would require additional attention within this population include homelessness, legal issues, infectious diseases, and trauma.

INFECTIOUS DISEASES

Because Opioids are oftentimes administered via hypodermic needles and little thought is given to the cleanliness of said needle, the transmission of diseases is a problem. Higher incidences of blood borne pathogens such as HIV/AIDS and Hepatitis B and C have been found within this population. Other diseases such as sexually transmitted infections are likely to be passed along as well.

TREATMENT OF OPIOID ADDICTION

PATIENT SCREENING AND ASSESSMENT

In order to appropriately plan and address the numerous needs of individuals with opioid addictions, it is important to screen and utilize assessments that will allow for better treatment planning. The screening process involves making an initial diagnosis of opioid abuse and/or addiction as well as looking for other problems, including other addictions, mental health problems other than addictions, and physical maladies. This process ends with initial recommendations for testing, treatment, and biopsychosocial needs.

The next part of the process includes assessing patients in order to establish what was determined during the initial screening process. During this time, an appropriate diagnosis is provided and determinations for treatment are made. Instruments that can be used to determine opioid addictions include the Clinical Opiate Withdrawal Scale (COWS) and the Subjective Opiate Withdrawal Scale

(SOWS). Other instruments can be used to determine or rule out additional disorders and mental illnesses such as depression, bipolar I or II, anxiety disorders. This process should include a physical examination as well in order to diagnose and treat problems that could hinder the addiction treatment process, such as HIV/AIDS, Hepatitis B and C. These diseases frequently co-occur among intravenous opiate drug users.

TREATING OPIOID ADDICTION WITH DRUGS

Several prescription medications have been developed in order to assist individuals addicted to opiates. These drugs block the pleasurable effects the individual once felt. They allow for a greater probability of return to life prior to the addiction or at least permit the individual to gain some control over his or her life. Several medications have been developed including methadone, LAAM®, and Subutex®.

Methadone. Methadone maintenance therapy has been in place for over 30 years. It works by suppressing withdrawal effects from opiates. About 20% of the estimated 810,000 heroin addicts in the United States receive MMT. It is considered safer because it can be administered in controlled doses under the supervision of trained personnel and individuals can continue this treatment continuously for 10 or more years. Another benefit of methadone is that individuals are able to experience pain and emotions, something they were not able to do when addicted to heroin. This is a benefit particularly for those who are also undergoing psychotherapy and/or have co-occurring conditions that result in pain. A dose of methadone lasts approximately 1 to 2 days, much longer than the effects of heroin; therefore, individuals being treated with this drug are able to function. Other benefits include its lower cost and the role it plays in helping to reduce the spread of infectious diseases such as HIV and AIDS. Individuals receiving methadone maintenance therapy should be warned of the perils of addiction as this substance is highly addictive itself.

Levomethadyl acetate (LAAM®). Methadone is generally considered the first choice for treating individuals addicted to opiates; however LAAM has proven to been a good alternative for individuals who do not respond positively to methadone.[4] Levomethadyl acetate is considered a better replacement therapy in that it prevents withdrawal symptoms for 2 to 3 days as opposed to methadone, which only prevents the symptoms from returning for 1 to 2 days.

Naltrexone/Buprenorphine (Subutex®). Buprenorphine was originally introduced in the 1960s and is 25 to 50 times more potent than morphine,[17] and it was originally used to treat cancer pain. It was approved in Australia in 2001 to treat opioid addiction and approved in the US in 2002 for general use, and approved in 2003 for opioid dependence.[23] This drug works in the same way as the aforementioned drug by blocking the pleasurable effects of opiates. Some of its major benefits include:

◊ A lesser likelihood for dependence to develop;
◊ detoxification, which allows for the reduction of severe withdrawal symptoms;
◊ stabilization and maintenance, which allows the individual to quickly return to normal daily activities.[5]

PSYCHOTHERAPY

There are other reasons individuals may be attracted to opiates besides their ability to alleviate physical pain. One of those reasons could very well be to alleviate psychological pain. According to the self-medication theory of addiction, individuals who are experiencing severe mood states related to depression, mania, anxiety, personality disorders, or psychotic disorders such as schizophrenia, may be inclined to utilize illicit drugs as a way to assuage the negative feelings. These individuals choose a drug that will cause feelings and mood states that are the exact opposite of what they currently experience. Because the underlying psychological issue is not correctly addressed and treated, they may continue to indulge in the use of these drugs to rid themselves of the pain. This cycle can only lead to more severe problems; eventually not only will they experience the negative mood states associated with the underlying psychological problem, but abuse and eventually dependence to this substance could occur. When dependence is added to the mix, numerous other problems are the result.

Individuals who are considered to have a dual diagnosis or co-occurring disorders (addiction plus psychological diagnosis) require treatment that is integrated and addresses all problems at one time as opposed to addressing each individually. Along with psychopharmacology, psychotherapy is considered to be an important part of the recovery process for individuals addicted to opiates. The psychopharmacological part of treatment helps to address withdrawal symptoms and allows the individual to clear their systems and their minds from the drug. Once the body and mind are detoxified, psychotherapy then assists in allowing the individual to effectively address the underlying problems that may have lead to their use and subsequent addiction to the opiate.

Behavior therapy has proven to be useful in helping individuals to achieve abstinence, with cognitive-behavior therapy (CBT) being most commonly employed[12] CBT provides opportunities for cognitive restructuring whereby the individual changes his or her way of thinking which in turn affects their behavior. If a person thinks differently about their problems, an automatic change in their response or behavior to their problems results. Also incorporated in psychotherapy is the identification of triggers. Trigger can be people, places, or things that may lead a person back to drug use. When the individual has identified their triggers, an appropriate plan can be developed to help them avoid these things. This decreases the likelihood of them returning to the use of drugs.

Other recommendations or outcomes from psychotherapy may include participation in group therapy and in support groups such as 12-step programs.

According to Dziegielewski and Suris[12] support groups provide a sense of community and belonging. Not only are individuals able to share their stories and not feel judged, but they can also learn from others. Groups also provide an opportunity for the practicing of social skills that may have been lost or neglected during addiction and for giving and receiving appropriate support and encouragement.

SUMMARY AND IMPLICATIONS

The discovery of Opioids and its derivatives have proven to be a blessing and a curse. There are obvious benefits to the drugs when they are prescribed and utilized with care; however, when one steps outside of the intended uses of the drug, disaster can be the result. It is obvious that the misuse of these drugs can be related back to numerous problems such as physical/sexual abuse, mental illness, severe pain, and sheer boredom just to name a few, but it is imperative to understand the many negative consequence that may result. The American Pain Society (APS) and the America Academy of Pain Medicine (AAMP) created new guidelines that serve to address concerns physicians may have when it comes to prescribing these drugs. These guidelines provide a balanced approach to screening, diagnosing, and treating chronic pain conditions while taking abuse and addiction into consideration. These guidelines are only the beginning in the process of prevention, intervention, and treatment for opioid addiction.

Addiction affects us all in one way or another and as a society, we cannot afford to ignore the plight of those suffering from this disease. The responsible use of opiates is imperative if we are to help curtail its associated problems. However, when addiction results, intervention and treatment programs that address all of the unique issues and needs of these individuals is paramount.

CASE STUDY

Tamara E. is a 30-year-old African American female who has just been admitted for Opioids dependence. During her intake interview, this is the story she relays:

I grew up in a family that was loving and caring. I had two older sisters and one younger brother. My father worked in construction and provided a good life for us, while my mother stayed at home. The day my father was killed at work was the day my entire life changed. I was only 12 at the time, but I remember it like it was yesterday. There were flowers and people everywhere. I remember my mother crying and my grandmother comforting her. A few weeks later, I overhead my mother saying that she would need to find a job in order to keep the apartment and pay the bills. She went out a few days later and found a night job as a cashier and stocker. She would leave for work before we got home from school and return in the morning before we left for school.

While she worked at night, our neighbor, Fred, came over to check on us. My mother trusted him because he had been really good friends with my father. He was okay, but he made me feel creepy when he looked at me. A couple of years later, my mother hurt her back at work and was prescribed some medicine for pain, but it did not seem to work. She went back to the doctor several times, but complained because of the cost. Frank told my mom that he knew someone who could get the medicine she needed for a better price. My mom agreed.

Eventually she was not able to get up and go to work because she said the medicine made her really sleepy. She lost her job because she missed so many days at work. Frank offered to marry my mom and help take care of her, and she agreed. When Frank moved in, that's when the real problems began. Frank would come into our room each night and touch my sisters and me. He even began to have sex with my older sisters. Later we found out that he had been molesting my brother, too. During this time my mom was usually out of it. We tried to talk to her, but she fussed and said no one would take care of us if Frank left. After this I realized that I had to do something. I began taking my mother's medicine and found that it didn't bother me too much when Frank came into my room at night. It was not long before I was taking the pills everyday and then several times a day. I finally got the courage to talk to my school counselor. We were immediately removed from my mother's care.

After being placed in foster care, I suffered from more sexual abuse as well as physical and emotional abuse. Some of the children were able to get different drugs and I would take whatever they had. I was so strung out that I often passed out for days at a time. I ran away constantly and ended up working as a prostitute to support my drug habit. I ended up in jail a few times and after my third strike, I was sent to prison. This was the best thing that could have happened to me. I was able to get into treatment and begin turning my life around. It's been hard, but in here you don't have too much choice about what you do. I have been clean and sober for a few years now, and I feel better than ever.

REFERENCES

[1]American Psychiatric Association. (2000). *Diagnostic and Statistical manual* (4th ed., text revision). Washington, DC: Author.

[2]Barnett, P. G., Rodgers, J. H., & Bloch, D. A. (2001). A meta-analysis comparing buprenorphine to methadone for treatment of opiate dependence. *Addiction, 96,* 683-690.

[3]Booth, M. (1996). *Opium: A history.* New York: St. Martin's Griffin.

[4]Brink, W., & Haasen, C. (2006). Evidence-based treatment of opioid-dependent patients. *Canadian Journal of Psychiatry, 51,* 635-646.

[5]Byrne, M. H., Lander, L., & Ferris, M. (2009). The changing face of opioid addiction: Prescription pain pill dependence and treatment. *Health & Social Work, 34,* 53-56.

[6]Calsyn, D. A., Fleming, C., Wells, E. A., & Saxon, A. J. (1996). Personality disorder subtypes among opiate addicts in methadone maintenance. *Psychology of Addictive Behaviors, 10,* 3-8.

[7]Darton, L. A., & Dilts, S. L. (1998). Opioids. In J. R. Frances & S. I. Miller (Eds.), *Clinical textbook of addictive behaviors (2^{d} ed.).* New York: Guilford.

[8]Doweiko, H. E. (2006). *Concepts of chemical dependency,* (6th ed.). Belmont, CA: Thompson Brooks/Cole.

[9]Doweiko, H. E. (2009). *Concepts of chemical dependency,* (7th ed.). Belmont, CA: Brooks/Cole Cengage Learning.

[10]Drug Enforcement Administration (DEA). (2008). *Morphine.* Retrieved June 15, 2009 from, http://www.streetdrugs.org/morphine.htm

[11]Drummer, O. H., & Odell, M. (2001). *The forensic pharmacology of drug abuse.* New York: Oxford University Press, Inc.

[12]Dziegielewski, S. F., & Suris, N. (2005). Heroin and other opiates. In S. F. Dziegielewski (Ed.), *Understanding substance addictions: Assessment and intervention,* (pp. 150-173). Chicago, IL: Lyceum Books, Inc.

[13]Heroin Addiction Drug Rehab. (2008). *Heroin statistics.* Retrieved June 15, 2009 from, http://www.heroinaddictiondrugrehab.com/h-statistics.htm

[14]Hopfer, C. J., Mikulich, S. K., & Crowley, T. J. (2000). Heroin use Among adolescents in treatment for substance use disorders. *Journal of the American Academy of Child and Adolescent Psychiatry, 39,* 1316-1323.

[15]Inaba, D. S., & Cohen, W. E. (2000). *Uppers, downers, and all arounders: Physical and mental effects of psychoactive drugs,* (5th ed.). Ashland, OR: CNS Publications, Inc.

[16]Johnson, L. D., O'Malley, P. M., & Bachman, J. G. (2003). *National survey results on drug use from the monitoring the future study, 1975-2003 (Vol. I).* Rockville, MD: US Department of Health and Human Services.

[17]Karch, S. B. (2002). *The pathology of drug abuse*, (3rd ed.). New York: CRC Press.

[18]Kirsch, M. M. (1996). *Designer drugs*. Minneapolis: Comp-Care Publications.

[19]Lall, Abhimanu. (2008). Neonatal abstinence syndrome. *British Journal of Midwifery, 16,* 220-223.

[20]Marlow-Ferguson, R. (2009). *Encyclopedia of drugs, alcohol, and addictive behavior: Opiates/opioids*. Retrieved June 10, 2009, from http://www.enotes.com/drugs-alcohol- encyclopedia/opiates-opioids.

[21]National Institute on Drug Abuse (2005). *Research report series: Heroin abuse and addiction*. NIH Publication Number 05-4165.

[22]Office of National Drug Control Policy. (2004). *National drug control strategy*. Washington, DC: US Government Printing Office.

[23]Reckitt Benckiser Pharmaceuticals, Inc. (2007). *History of opioids*. Retrieved June 10, 2009, from http://suboxone.com/patients/opioiddependence/history.aspx.

[24]Scott, I. (1998) A hundred-year habit. *History Today, 48,* 6-8.

[25]Trebach, A. (1981). *The heroin solution*. New Haven, CT: Yale University Press.

[26]United Nations. (2004). *World drug report. Volume I: Analysis*. Retrieved June 10, 2004, from http://www.unodoc.org/unodc/en/world_drug_report.html.

[27]US Department of Health and Human Services/National Institute of Health. (2005). *Research report series: Heroin abuse and addiction*. NIH Publication Number 05-4165.

[28]US Department of Health and Human Services/Substance Abuse and Mental Health Services Administration/Center for Substance Abuse Treatment. (2004). *Substance abuse treatment for women offenders: Guide to promising practices. Technical Assistance Publication (TAP) Series, 23.*

[29]US Department of Health and Human Services/Substance Abuse and Mental Health Services Administration/Center for Substance Abuse Treatment. (2005). *Substance use disorder treatment for people with physical and cognitive disabilities. Treatment Improvement Protocol (TIP) Series, 29.*

[30]US Department of Health and Human Services/Substance Abuse and Mental Health Services Administration/Center for Substance Abuse Treatment. (2007). *Combining alcohol and other drug abuse treatment with diversion for juveniles in the justice system.* Treatment Improvement Protocol (TIP) Series, 21.

[31]US Department of Health and Human Services/Substance Abuse and Mental Health Services Administration/Center for Substance Abuse Treatment. (2007). *Substance abuse treatment for persons with co-occurring disorders.* Treatment Improvement Protocol (TIP), 42.

[32]US Department of Health and Human Services/Substance Abuse and Mental Health Services Administration/Center for Substance Abuse Treatment. (2008). *Substance abuse treatment and domestic violence.* Treatment Improvement Protocol (TIP) series, 25.

[33]Walton, S. (2002). *Out of it: A cultural history of intoxication.* New York: Harmony Books.

Chapter Six

COCAINE & CRACK ADDICTION: CLINICAL COMPONENTS

BY **STEPHANIE L. LUSK**

NORTH CAROLINA AGRICULTURAL
AND TECHNICAL STATE UNIVERSITY

CHAPTER TOPICS

◊   A Brief Overview of Cocaine

◊   Routes of Administration

◊   Mechanism of Action

◊   Prevalence of Cocaine: Use, Abuse, and Dependence

◊   Crack Cocaine

◊   Treatment of Cocaine Dependence

◊   Summary and Implications

◊   Case Study

A BRIEF OVERVIEW OF COCAINE

Cocaine is produced from a member of the plant species *Erythroxylon coca.* The plant grows as green and yellow shrubs and gets as tall as six to eight feet. The use of cocaine can be traced back at least 5,000 years where it was noted that Incan workers chewed on its leaves and noticed that they were able to work for longer periods of time.[13] Other early forms of ingesting cocaine include chopping it and placing it on the gums under the tongue and mixing it with drinks. The coca plant was used extensively by the Incans and was initially reserved for the upper classes of society where it was used in social and religious ceremonies. When the Conquistadors conquered the Inca Empire in the 16th century, the use of cocaine spread and was then used by all individuals. Spanish explores took the plant back to their homeland, and the drug was eventually banned and regarded as an "evil agent of the devil" and was found to "destroy the natives."[7] After being banned for a while, it was quickly noticed that workers could not produce as much or work as long without ingesting the coca plant, so its cultivation and use picked up once again and from there it spread all across Europe.

The medicinal properties of cocaine were identified as early as the 1400s; however, it was not isolated until much later. The active ingredient was first isolated by Friedrich Gaedcke in 1855, and he named the product erythroxyline. Albert Nieman, a German graduate student, improved upon the purification process as part of his dissertation studies and called the product cocaine. At this time, the drug was used as an anesthetic during surgeries. As others became aware of cocaine's properties, its use was extended and encouraged. Sigmund Freud experimented with this product and even prescribed it for ailments such as depression, gastric disorders, asthma, and morphine and alcohol addiction. He discussed its therapeutic properties at length in his book *Uber Coca.* Other individuals who were noted to have used cocaine include Sherlock Holmes and Robert Louis Stephenson who reportedly wrote *The Strange Case of Dr. Jekyll and Mr. Hyde* during a six-day cocaine binge.[7]

Cocaine's popularity waxed and waned for years and during each decade of the 1990s a cocaine epidemic seemed to emerge. In the 1970s and 1980s a new form of cocaine, freebase and crack, appeared and its popularity increased yet again.[9] Cocaine was a drug that was generally associated with a more affluent group of individuals, but with the advent cheaper forms of cocaine, namely freebase and crack, its use and abuse spread even more so. As a result of its widespread use and associated problems, its addictive properties and negative side effects could no longer be ignored. The Food and Drug Act of 1906 as well as the Harrison Narcotic Act of 1914 helped somewhat to regulate its use. The Food and Drug Act required a listing of all ingredients used to make medicinal concoctions and, as a result, cocaine was removed as a product The Harrison

Narcotic Act banned all non-medical uses of cocaine and severely restricted its legal uses.

Cocaine is classified as a stimulant and works by increasing the activity of the central nervous system. It also works as a local anesthetic and is used during surgeries. It is the only known drug that possesses both of these properties. When individuals ingest cocaine a surge of energy as well as increased heart rate, blood pressure, alertness, confidence, and restlessness results. Cocaine is classified as a schedule II substance which means it has a high potential for abuse and some approved medical uses (See Table 1, Chapter 6). Other side effects of cocaine use include decreased appetite and weight loss.

How Cocaine is Produced

The production of cocaine has remained relatively unchanged. It is generally produced in five to six steps:

◊   Cocaine leaves are harvested, soaked in lime, and watered for three to four days, then dried;

◊   The dried leaves are placed in a pit and mixed with water, sulfuric acid, gasoline, kerosene, or acetone to remove alkaloids;

◊   The mixture is crushed by individuals who wade in the pits with their bare feet. The liquid is drained and lime is added to the residue forming a paste known as the cocaine base (it takes 500 kg of leaves to produce one kg of cocaine);[4]

◊   Water, gas, ammonia, potassium permanganate and acids are added, which results in a reddish brown paste that is dried;

◊   Hydrochloric acid and acetone are added to the paste. A white solid, cocaine hydrochloride, forms and settles to the bottom of the container;

◊   This substance is dried under heating lamps which causes a crystalline powder to result; this is the cocaine that will be distributed for use.

ROUTES OF ADMINISTRATION

Drinking

After the active ingredient from the *Erythroxylon coca* plant was identified and refined, cocaine could be absorbed in water and other liquids and drank. In the 1960s cocaine wine was extremely popular. When alcohol and cocaine are ingested together, the body produces a metabolite or by-product, cocaethylene. This metabolite produces an effect that lasts longer and is more intense than either one of the drugs produced on its own. Besides alcoholic drinks, cocaine can be mixed with other liquids in order to produce prescriptions medicines to control pain. Another drink that was popular during the 1880s which contained cocaine was Coca-Cola®. Invented in 1886 by John Pemberton, a Georgia pharmacist, Coca-Cola® was sold as a cure for headaches and as a stimulant. Cocaine was a major ingredient in this soda until 1903.

SNORTING

Snorting cocaine, also known as tooting, blowing, or horning, was first used as a method of ingestion in the early 1900s. Karch[11] stated that smoking or insufflating cocaine can be traced back to 1903 when reports of septal perforation were noted in doctor's offices and medical journals. Cocaine is snorted into the nasal passages by using tubes or tightly rolled dollar bills. Its effects are experienced within 3-5 minutes and the high lasts for 10-20 minutes. Snorting cocaine leads to problems such as the swelling of nasal tissue and its subsequent dying, perforation of the nasal septum that divides the nostrils, and a runny nose.

SMOKING

During the 1890s cocaine plants were burned, and the smoke was used to treat whooping cough, bronchitis, and asthma.[17] Cocaine was introduced in cigarettes in 1914 by Parke-Davis Pharmaceuticals. Because a high temperature was needed in order to convert the cocaine into smoke, less than desirable outcomes were produced. This resulted in a quick discontinuation of using cocaine in this manner. However, in the mid 1970s smoking cocaine was tried again. Cocaine was converted to freebase cocaine so that it could be smoked. Freebase cocaine is created by combining cocaine hydrochloride with ammonia and ether so that it can be smoked while still maintaining its psychoactive properties. Freebase cocaine led to the development of crack cocaine. This form of cocaine took off in the 1980s and was referred to as crack because of the crackling sound it makes while it is being smoked. Crack is a rock form of cocaine that uses cocaine hydrochloride with baking soda and water. Crack is less pure cocaine and is cheaper and easier to obtain. This form of administration allows the effects of cocaine to be felt within 5-8 seconds; however, the high lasts for only 5 to 20 minutes. As quickly as its effects are experienced, it is metabolized or broken down and excreted from the body. This rapid high and subsequent low is why crack is considered the most addictive forms of cocaine.

INJECTION

Just as with opioid administration, the invention of the hypodermic needle in 1857 helped to increase the use and abuse of cocaine. When injected, cocaine reaches the brain within 15 to 30 seconds. This method allows for the majority of the cocaine to be absorbed by the body. Its effects last for only 10 to 20 minutes. Doweiko[4] noted that this is the least common form of administration.

MUCOSAL AND SUBLINGUAL

Mucosal ingestion use involves cocaine being absorbed in the nose, gums, cheeks, rectum, or vagina. In this way cocaine can be used as a topical anesthetic. Karch[11] noted an increasing trend in male homosexuals who use cocaine in this manner. Cocaine can also be absorbed by the outer skin, but not as quickly and the effects are not as intense. Sublingual administration involves the drug being absorbed under the tongue.

MECHANISM OF ACTION

Cocaine works by mainly affecting the neurotransmitter dopamine as well as serotonin and norepinephrine. All three of these neurotransmitters serve to regulate mood. Dopamine receptors are found mainly in the limbic system within the brain. The limbic system is considered the reward center and is also responsible for movement, cognition, the formation of memories, and motivation. The limbic system is comprised primarily of the hypothalamus, hippocampus, and amygdala. The primary function of the hypothalamus is to maintain homeostasis or balance within the body. It regulates balance, pain, pleasure, and aggressive behaviors as well as blood pressure and breathing. The hippocampus is responsible for converting short-term memory into long-term memory. Damage to the hippocampus results in a person being unable to form or build new memories. Finally, the amygdala helps to control anger and stress responses.

When one is excited or engaged in pleasurable experiences, dopamine being released within the limbic system is responsible for these feelings. Cocaine causes a release of dopamine and then prevents it from being reabsorbed by its receptors. This results in feelings of pleasure for a longer period of time. The individual may also experience increased movement and racing thoughts. There are negative side effects associated with the dysregulation of dopamine including irritability and paranoia with associated hallucinations; this is generally how an individual may feel when coming down from a cocaine high. Too little dopamine can result in tremors and paralysis as seen in Parkinson's disease. Individual who severely abuse cocaine, can begin to exhibit these symptoms. There are five types of dopamine receptors within the brain D1, D2, D3, D4, and D5. D1 seems to be the dopamine receptor most affected by cocaine. The D1 receptors are more plentiful in the limbic system which is why the pleasurable feelings are experienced. Cocaine also affects the *mu* and *kappa* opioid receptors which may contribute to its craving and addictive properties.[4]

THE OPPONENT PROCESS THEORY
The Opponent Process Theory can be used to explain how cocaine use can eventually lead to dependence with continued use. This theory asserts that before an individual begins to use cocaine or any drug, their mood state remains somewhere around "normal." When individuals ingest a drug such as cocaine for

the first time, they experience a feeling that will more than likely never be re-experienced. Individuals continue taking the drug, or chasing the high only to realize they cannot get back to the initial feeling. At this point they may begin to take larger amounts of the drug or switch to a different drug altogether. This pleasurable, positive state is known as Process A. Process B, or the negative state, results when the individual comes down from the drug and is experiencing withdrawal symptoms such as agitation and irritability. These feeling are generally below normal, and the longer an individual uses the drug, the lower he or she will "sink" into Process B. After repeated use, usually when dependence occurs, Process A does not get much higher and will eventually not go past what was considered their normal mood. The individual at this point no longer experiences a high, but requires the drug now just to function and feel somewhat normal. At the same time as individuals continue to take the drug, they continue to descend further into the negative mood state of Process B. Depression usually has settled in at this point. This process works as the dopamine receptors are continuously stimulated (Process A) and huge surges of dopamine are left to float around in the synapses or spaces within the brain between receptors. Eventually the dopamine receptors become depleted and no more or very little is being produced. As a result the individual no longer experiences the pleasure they once felt. The low levels of dopamine lead to depression and other negative mood states (Process B).

PREVALENCE OF COCAINE: USE, ABUSE, AND DEPENDENCE

The coca plant is mainly grown in South America which produces approximately 97% of the world's crop.[9] The remaining percentage is grown in the Amazon Jungle and in Indonesia. The Drug Enforcement Agency noted that the United States consumes 70% of the cocaine that is produced and that $36.1 billion is spend on this drug. In 2004 the United Nations estimated that approximately 687 metric tons of cocaine were produced and used around the world and noted high rates of cocaine abuse to go along with the amount produced. It noted that there were 13.4 million abusers worldwide with 6.5 million in the United States, 3.5 million in Europe, and 2.3 million in South America, while the remaining 1.8 million lived in other areas around the world.[9] Interestingly, even as late as the 1980s, cocaine was considered incapable of causing addiction because of its differences in abuse and withdrawal patterns when compared to other drugs.[5] However with further research and a better understanding of the problems associated with cocaine ingestion, its addictive properties have now been recognized and respected.

DIAGNOSING COCAINE USE AND ITS RELATED DISORDERS

According to the Diagnostic and Statistical Manual (DSM) cocaine disorders can fall into two categories: cocaine use disorders and cocaine-induced disorders. Cocaine use disorders include abuse and dependence. Cocaine-induced disorders include intoxication, withdrawal, intoxication with delirium, psychotic disorder with delusions and/or hallucinations, mood disorders, anxiety disorders, sexual dysfunction, sleep disorder, and those not otherwise specified.[2] When using the DSM as a guide for diagnosing an individual with a cocaine use disorder, it is important to rule out any other possible substance use disorder, mental disorder, or medical condition that could mimic symptoms similar to those listed below.

Criteria for cocaine abuse and dependence are outlined by the American Psychiatric Association.[2] Abuse is characterized by maladaptive patterns of opiate use that leads to significant problems in one or more of the following areas within a 12-month timeframe:

◊ Major role obligations at home, work, or school;
◊ use in physically hazardous situations;
◊ legal problems related to the substance use; and/or
◊ exacerbation of social and interpersonal problems.

Cocaine dependence (addiction) is differentiated from abuse in two primary ways: 1) tolerance (the need for increased amounts of the opiate in order to experience the same effects); and 2) withdrawal (unpleasant side effects experienced as a result of discontinuing the drug or needing to ingest the drug in order to alleviate and/or avoid the negative effects).

With dependence, the individual may also experience:

◊ A desire to cut down or discontinue the drug;
◊ huge amounts of time, effort and energy are spend on obtaining, preparing, ingesting, and recovering from drug use;
◊ important activities are discontinued; and
◊ use is continued even after the realization of the negative consequences associated with the drug's use.

Behaviors associated with cocaine intoxication include:

◊ tachycardia or bradycardia
◊ papillary dilation
◊ elevated or lowered blood pressure
◊ perspiration or chills
◊ nausea or vomiting
◊ evidence of weight loss
◊ psychomotor agitation or retardation

◊   muscular weakness, respiratory depression, chest pain, or cardiac arrhythmias
◊   confusion, seizures, dyskinesias, dystonias, or coma.

Cocaine withdrawal results when the drug is discontinued and the individual experiences two or more of the following:
◊   Fatigue
◊   vivid, unpleasant dreams
◊   insomnia or hypersomnia
◊   increased appetite
◊   psychomotor retardation or agitation.[2]

These symptoms are severe enough that they cause distress and impairment in the individual's life.

CROSS ADDICTIONS AND DRUG INTERACTIONS

Alcohol. Cross addiction is quite common among individuals who abuse cocaine which serves to produce interactions and side effects that can be quite dangerous. Gold and Jacobs[6] noted that 62-90% of individuals who abuse cocaine also abuse alcohol. When cocaine is combined with alcohol the liver has to work harder in order to rid the body of these substances. The production of *cocaethylene* is another problem that results from combining these two drugs. This by-product is toxic and functions as a calcium channel blocker in the heart which could lead to death. Alcohol use has been associated with poorer treatment outcomes and more severe cocaine dependence. When treating these individuals, it is important to ensure that the alcohol abuse or dependence is considered as well.

Opiates. Speedballing, which is the process of combining cocaine with a depressant, usually an opiate, is yet another problem. According to speedballers, combining cocaine with an opiate helps to balance out the negative effects of each drug.

Smoking. Poling, et al.[16] noted that upwards to 80% of individuals who use cocaine also smoke cigarettes. It was found that these individuals exhibit heavier cocaine use and are more likely to ingest cocaine via injection or smoking which puts them at greater risk for other complications.

PHYSICAL AND PSYCHOLOGICAL EFFECTS OF COCAINE

Individuals who abuse cocaine generally suffer from ailments such as complications to the respiratory and cardiovascular systems. Respiratory problems include chest pain, damage to the lungs, wheezing, pneumonia, and chronic bronchiolitis. However, it is believed that the cardiovascular system is most affected by cocaine use. Common problems include coronary artery disease, hypertension, increased heart rate, cardiac arrhythmias, and heart attack, damage to the heart muscles and blood vessels, and stroke. Other physical problems include sexual dysfunction (including problems associated with high-risk sexual behaviors), liver damage, and hyperthermia (restriction of blood flow to the extremities).

After the pleasurable feelings of well-being and euphoria wear off, the individual experiences the opposite of these feelings. Depression, decreased activity, slowed thoughts, and an increased need for food and sleep are experienced. Severe psychological effects may include psychosis, paranoia, and suicidal ideation.[20]

Because cocaine is a stimulant, its effects are exhibited as euphoria and an increase in activity, thinking, and talking. Once the drug effects wear off, individuals experience the opposite of these feelings. As individuals continue to use cocaine, and in accordance to the Opponent Process Theory as described above, they eventually reach a point where they are completely consumed by the more negative effects of the drug. According to the US Department of Health and Human Services,[20] the following are a list of physical and psychological side effects of chronic drug abuse:

◊   Extreme fatigue
◊   nutritional disorders (extreme weight loss, anemia, anorexia, body wasting)
◊   poor hygiene
◊   skin disorders (itching, hives)
◊   hair loss
◊   muscle pain
◊   cardiovascular damage
◊   hypertension or renal failure
◊   difficulty breathing
◊   heart attack
◊   headaches, strokes, seizures, vision loss
◊   choreoathetoid disorders (involuntary movement disorders)
◊   impaired sexual performance
◊   gastrointestinal problems
◊   paranoia (hallucinations and delusions)
◊   apprehension
◊   depression
◊   acute anxiety
◊   eating disorders.[Pg. 95]

CRACK COCAINE

The emergence of crack was seen during the 1980s and its popularity soared because of its easy access and cheaper price. Crack seemed to be initially concentrated in larger cities with large Black populations and has since spread to all areas. Crack cocaine is made by mixing cocaine hydrochloride with baking soda and water. When this substance dries, hard smokable "rocks" are formed. This substance contains much less pure cocaine, but still produces a quick, intense high that last for only about 15 minutes. Because this high lasts for only a few minutes, the smoker almost immediately desires more of the drug. This fleeting feeling lends itself to the high tendency to binge and eventually become addicted to crack. Another problem associated with the usage of crack cocaine includes diminished personal care which leads to a plethora of social, physical, and psychological problems, such as HIV/AIDS from unprotected sex and prostitution in order to obtain the drug, co-occurring mental illnesses, violence, crime, and legal problems.

SPECIAL POPULATIONS AND ISSUES RELATED TO CRACK COCAINE

Women and Babies. Women face unique problems when it comes to cocaine abuse and dependence. Oftentimes, desire for the drugs causes women to neglect personal care and engage in activities that will allow them access to the drug including high risk sexual behaviors. This can lead to the spread of blood borne diseases such as hepatitis and HIV/AIDS. Other problems include domestic violence, child neglect and abuse, and the birth of babies who are addicted to crack cocaine and suffer physical and cognitive disabilities as a result. These babies experience lower birth weight and a smaller head circumference. Higher rates of mental retardation, developmental and cognitive delays, and learning problems have also been noted.[18] Other studies have noted that children born after being exposed to crack cocaine in vitro have fewer stress-reducing coping strategies, and as a result are less able to regulate their emotional reactions or comfort themselves.[15]

Legal Disparities. The Anti-Drug Abuse Act, signed into law on October 27, 1986, by President Ronald Regan, established a first time mandatory minimum sentence for individuals charged with cocaine related offenses. This act established consequences that were much tougher for crack cocaine than for powder cocaine. Distribution of just 5 grams of crack cocaine carries a 5-year minimum sentence while distribution of 500 grams of powder cocaine carries the same sentence. In 1988 the Omnibus Anti-Drug Abuse Act allowed for a 5-year mandatory and 20-year maximum sentence for the possession of 5 grams or more of crack cocaine. The American Civil Liberties Union (ACLU) reported that in 2003 whites made up 7.8% and blacks composed 80% of the defendants sentenced for crack related offenses even though statistics show that more than 66% of crack cocaine users in the United States are white or Hispanic. Legal problems for black women soared as a result of this law as well. The ACLU reported that women's incarceration, generally related to drug related offences, increased by 800% since the Act was passed compared to only 400% for all other races. There have been increasing concerns with the extensive disparities among sentencing for drug related offenses among black and white offenders. Because of these concerns, the Sentencing Reform Act of 1984 was enacted in order to address the associated problems.

TREATMENT OF COCAINE DEPENDENCE

According to Gawin,[5] there are three phases to cocaine abstinence: crash; withdrawal; and extension. The crash phase generally begins within nine hours to four days after the last ingestion of cocaine. The individual may experience agitation, depression, and a need to sleep and eat.

The withdrawal phase includes low anxiety, high cocaine cravings as the individual remembers the euphoric high from the cocaine rush, and anhedonia.

The extension phase is characterized by normal pleasure responses, good mood, and low cravings. These three phases can lead to abstinence if relapse is prevented. Relapse is more likely to occur during the second phase. Other important parts of treatment include family and group counseling, frequent drug testing to ensure abstinence, and a 12-step program participation as well as the following pharmacological and psychological treatment options. Worley, et al.[21] found that patients who received a combination of treatment services such as therapy for co-occurring mental disorders or physical disabilities, pharmacotherapy, and medical and legal services along with treatment for cocaine dependence were more likely to have positive outcomes as compared to those who did not receive additional services.

PHARMACOLOGICAL TREATMENT FOR COCAINE DEPENDENCE

Disulfiram. Initially approved to treat alcohol dependence, Disulfiram has been found to work effectively for individuals with cocaine dependence. Common side effects include headaches, anxiety, and fatigue.

Baclofen (Lioresal®). Baclofen, a muscle relaxant and antispastic agent, has been approved and prescribed for years to treat patients with muscle symptoms caused by muscular sclerosis, tardive dyskinesia, and intractable hiccups. Major side effects include fatigue and headache. Baclofen may help cocaine addicts by causing the release of the neurotransmitter gamma aminobutryic acid (GABA) which then inhibits the release of dopamine in the brain. GABA is the most abundant inhibitory neurotransmitter in the brain. It works by helping to balance the brain and prevent overexcitement; it also helps to regulate anxiety and controls vision and motor activity. This drug works by preventing the high caused by cocaine.

Topiramate. Currently used to treat seizures, Topiramate has shown promise in treating individuals who are dependent on cocaine. This drug seems to work similarly to Baclofen in that it affects the production of GABA and glutamate. Because these are both inhibitory neurotransmitters, dopamine is prevented from being released when cocaine is ingested. Research using this drug to treat cocaine dependence is in its early stages, but looks promising. Results have shown that individuals taking this drug versus a placebo have been able to remain abstinent three or more continuous weeks.[12]

Modafinil. Modafinil, a medication currently used to treat narcolepsy, seems to enhance levels of glutamate produced in the brain. Studies conducted by Dackis et al.[3] found that individuals who received Modafinil as behavioral therapy during an eight week trial were more likely to remain abstinent that those who received a placebo along with behavior therapy.

Cocaine Vaccines. According to the Harvard Mental Health Letter,[8] vaccines for cocaine dependence have been in the works since 1974. The cocaine vaccine, also known as TA-CD combines "inactivated cholera toxin B protein with inactivated cocaine molecules."pg. 6 Antibodies to cholera as well as to cocaine are expected to form which will serve to prevent the individual from contracting either disease. This vaccine is currently in phase II of clinical trials.

PSYCHOLOGICAL TREATMENT FOR COCAINE DEPENDENCE *Behavioral therapy.* Behavioral therapy or cognitive behavior therapy changes thoughts and their following behaviors related to cocaine dependence. Those with cocaine dependence generally have co-occurring disorders that either led to their use and consequent dependence or develop these disorders as a result of long term use. Depression and personality disorders, particularly Antisocial Personality Disorder (ASPD), are common occurrences.[16]Among those seeking treatment, upwards to 32% have a diagnosis of depression compared to 7% of the general population. The same study also found that between 45 to 55% of cocaine users also have a diagnosis of ASPD. This disorder is associated with more severe cocaine use and poorer treatment outcomes. Other disorders that have been associated with cocaine dependence include dysthymia, bipolar disorder, post-traumatic stress disorder (PTSD), attention deficit hyperactivity disorder (ADHD), and schizophrenia. These disorders need to be treated concurrently with cocaine dependence in order to prevent sabotaging treatment efforts. Behavior therapi0000es include teaching individuals to recognize triggers and learning new ways of coping during recovery and after abstinence is achieved.[10]

Contingency management. This process involves utilizing rewards and incentives, usually in the form of vouchers, to encourage abstinence. This form of treatment seems to work really well as it sets concrete short and long-term goals and provides immediate gratification for meeting these goals. Other rewards may include monetary awards, gift certificates, and even issuing gold stars. This process also involves counseling, training in social skills, and vocational training.

Relapse prevention. Relapse prevention should be part of any treatment program. Lapse and relapse are generally considered part of the recovery process

as large numbers of individuals return to drug use. According to the US
Department of Health and Human Services,[20] these programs should focus on
five areas:

◊   Coping with cravings;
◊   learning refusal and assertiveness skills;
◊   strengthening decision making skills;
◊   coping and problem solving skills;
◊   applying strategies that will help to prevent lapse and relapse.

Matrix model. This model was originally referred to as the neurobehavioral
model, and was developed during the 1980s. This program combines relapse
prevention, motivational interviewing, psychoeducation, family therapy, and
participation in 12-step programs. Outpatient programs are generally based on
this model and include a network of agencies and other resources to meet the
treatment needs of its clients.

SUMMARY AND IMPLICATIONS

Over the years, the use and abuse of cocaine has waxed and waned. Initially used
to provide strength and energy to the Incas working long hours its use quickly
turned to medicinal and curative purposes to pleasurable pursuits. Having both
anesthetic and stimulant properties, it is the only known drug that possesses both.
There are different forms of cocaine that can be ingested via snorting, ingestion,
and smoking, but all are dangerously addictive and damaging to an individual's
mental, physical, social, occupational, and emotional well-being. Even though this
drug is considered illegal, problems with its use and abuse still continue today. In
order for treatment to be effective, attention must not only focus on the abuse or
addiction issue, but any co-occurring disorder should be addressed as well.

CASE STUDY

*Jenna T. is a married 37-year-old White female with two children. She
and her husband Tim have been married for 10 years. Jenna met Tim
20 years ago when she was a senior in high school He is 15 years older
and he was immediately attracted to her. He agreed to pay for her to go
to college if she agreed to marry him. Seeing this as her only way to
pursue her dream of becoming a high school teacher, she took him up
on his offer.*

*The first few months of their marriage were good for the most part,
but she did note that Tim would get jealous sometimes when she stayed
late on campus studying. Their first child was born during the spring
semester of her first year of college, and she stated that, "Tim gets really*

upset a lot now. He says I have no time for him now that I am studying and taking care of the baby. I am usually so tired when I come home that all I want to do is sleep." A few months later she was pregnant with their second child. She relayed that the marriage got even worse.

Because of the demands of school and taking care of two toddlers, Jenna stated that she barely had enough energy to do anything anymore. She relayed that she and Tim fight even more now and he's started staying out late, not even coming home some nights.

She said, "With all of this going on, I needed something to help me concentrate. My mind was scattered all over the place and I needed to get through finals. I could not afford to fail. I needed to care for my children and deal with the problems with Tim, so I asked a few students about ways to cope with all of this.

I never thought in my wildest dreams that I would eventually be addicted to crack cocaine. It started with just a little cocaine; a guy in my class, Thomas, got it for me, and I thought I'd just use it to get me through finals. I was able to stay up for long periods of time, and I did well on my exams. I realized that I had more energy and was not as aggravated about having to care for the kids. I was happy again, not worried about my problems, and playing with the kids, so I kept using it thinking that I would take the summer off and regroup. When I wasn't using it, I missed the way I felt and would soon call my classmate the get more for me. Tim became suspicious because I was asking for more money for groceries and was stopping by the ATM more often. He started questioning me and making comments about money being withdrawn. I could not afford to continue buying cocaine much longer, so I asked Thomas about something else I could use that was as effective, but cheaper. He suggested crack, and this is where my nightmare begins!

Thomas came over with the drugs one day while Tim was at work. I wanted him to show me how to use the drug. I was anxious and excited at the same time. I remember how I felt the first time I smoked the crack; it's like all of my cares went away. I was floating, I felt so good. I continued to use crack throughout the summer and into the beginning of the fall semester. I got to the point of caring more about smoking crack than studying, doing homework, or caring for my home. I did not do too well that semester. Because of that, Tim and I fought even more because he thought I was wasting his money. He said I wasn't keeping the house clean, taking care of the kids, or acting like a wife towards him. The more we argued, the more I smoked and the more he stayed out drinking. He even began drinking in the mornings before he left for work.

One morning during the holiday break, I thought Tim had left for work, and I went out to the garage to smoke before the kids woke up. Tim had forgotten his wallet and walked into the garage to find me lighting up. He was furious. That was the first time he ever hit me. He called me all sorts of names and told me he wanted me out of the house before he returned from work. I didn't know what to do. I told him that I needed help, that we both needed help. He just looked at me like he was disgusted with me. All I could do was cry."

References

[1]American Civil Liberties Union. (2006). *Crack in the system: Twenty years of the unjust federal crack cocaine law.* Author.

[2]American Psychiatric Association. (2000). *Diagnostic and Statistical manual* (4th ed., text revision). Washington, DC: Author.

[3]Dackis, C. A., Kampman, K. M., Lynch, K. G., Pettinaiti, H. M., O'Brien, C. P. (2005). A double-blind, placebo-controlled trial of modafinil for cocaine dependence. *Neuropsychopharmacology, 30,* 205-211.

[4]Doweiko, H. E. (2009). *Concepts of chemical dependence (7th ed.).* Belmont, CA: Brooks/Cole Cengage.

[5]Drug Enforcement Agency (DEA). (2001). www.usdoj.gov/dea/pubs/cn-grtest/ct041301.html.

[5]Gawin, F. H. (1991). Cocaine addiction: Psychology and neurophysiology. *Science, 251,* 1580-1586.

[6]Gold, M. S, & Jacobs, W. S. (2005). Cocaine and crack: Clinical aspects. In J. H. Lowinson, P. Ruiz, R. B. Millman, & J. G. Langrod (Eds.). *Substance abuse: A comprehensive textbook (4th ed.).* New York: Lipponcott, Williams & Wilkins.

[7]The Good Drug Guide. (n.d.). *In search of the big bang.* Retrieved June 10, 2009, from http://www.cocaine.org/.

[8]Harvard Mental Health Letter. (2009). *Overcoming cocaine or stimulant addiction: Medications offer modest help; vaccines are in development.* Retrieved June 9, 2009, from http://www.health.harvard.edu.

[9]Inaba, D. C., & Cohen, W. E. (2000). *Uppers, downers, all arounders: Physical and mental effects of psychoactive drugs (4th ed.).* Ashland, OR: CNS Publications, Inc.

[10]Kalivas, P. W. (2007). Neurobiology of cocaine addiction: Implications for new pharmacotherapy. *The American Journal on Addictions, 16,* 71-78.

[11]Karch, S. B. (2002). *The pathology of drug abuse (3ᵈ ed.)*. New York: CRC Press.

[12]Kampman, K. M., Pettinait, H., Lynck, K. G., Dackis, C., Sparkman, T., Weigley, C., & O'Brien, C. P. (2004). A pilot trial of topiramate for the treatment of cocaine dependence. *Drug and Alcohol Dependence, 75*, 233-240.

[13]Levis, J. T., & Garmel, G. M. (2005). Cocaine-related chest pain. *Emergency Medical Clinics of North America, 23*, 1083-1103.

[14]Mann, J. (1994). *Murder, magic, and medicine*. New York: Oxford.

[15]Medical News Today. (2009). *Prenatal cocaine exposure impairs infant's response to stress*. Retrieved June 6, 2009, from http://www.medicalnewstoday.com/articles/136089.hph.

[16]Poling, J., Kosten, T. R., Sofuoglu, M. (2007). Treatment outcomes for cocaine dependence. *The Journal of Drug and Alcohol Abuse, 33*, 191-206.

[17]Siegel, R. K. (1982). Cocaine smoking disorders: Diagnosis and treatment. *Psychiatric Annals, 14*, 728-732.

[18]Stamatis, G. (2002). *At 2 years, cocaine babies suffer cognitive developmental effects*. Retrieved June 6, 2009, from http://www.cocaine.org/crackbaby/cocaine-babies.html.

[19]United Nations. (2004). *World drug report. Volume I: Analysis*. Retrieved June 9, 2009, from, http://www.unodc.org/unodoc/en/world_drug_report.html.

[20]US Department of Health and Human Services/Substance Abuse and Mental Health Services Administration/Center for Substance Abuse Treatment. *Treatment for stimulant use disorders: Treatment improvement protocol (TIP) series, 33*.

[21]Worley, M., Gallop, R., Gibbons, M. B., Ring-Kurtz, S., Present, J., Weiss, R. D., & Crits-Christoph, P. (2008). Additional treatment services in cocaine treatment study: Level of services obtained and impact on outcome. *The American Journal on Addictions, 17*, 209-217.

Chapter Seven

MARIJUANA

ABUSE

BY   **JOSEPH F. STANO**
SPRINGFIELD COLLEGE

KATHERINE E. STANO
ARGOSY UNIVERSITY

Chapter Topics

◊ Marijuana
◊ Future Issues
◊ Case Study #1
◊ Case Study #2

PREFATORY NOTE

The majority of the material for this chapter is taken directly from the National Institute on Drug Abuse (NIDA) Research Report Series on Marijuana Abuse and the NIDA InfoFacts: Marijuana sheet.

MARIJUANA

Marijuana goes by many names in the vernacular. These include: *pot, grass, reefer, weed, herb, maryjane, or MJ.* It is a greenish-gray mixture of the dried, shredded leaves, stems, seeds, and flowers of *Cannabis sativa*, the hemp plant. Most users smoke marijuana in hand-rolled cigarettes called *joints*, among other names; some use piper or water pipes called *bongs.* Marijuana cigars called *blunts* have also become popular. To make blunts, users slice open cigars and replace the tobacco with marijuana, often combined with another drug, such as crack cocaine. Marijuana also is used to brew tea and is sometimes mixed into foods.

The major active chemical is marijuana is delta-9-tetrahydrocannabinol (THC), which is the cause of the mind-altering effects of marijuana intoxication. The amount of THC, which is the active ingredient in hashish, determines the potency and, therefore, the effects of marijuana. Between 1980 and 1997, the amount of THC in marijuana available in the United States rose dramatically.[9]

SCOPE OF UNITED STATES MARIJUANA USE

Marijuana is the nation's most commonly used illicit drug. More than 94 million Americans, 40 percent of the population, age 12 and older have tried marijuana at least once, according to the 2003 National Survey of Drug Use and Health (NSDUH).[28]

Marijuana use is widespread among adolescents and young adults. The percentage of middle school students who reported using marijuana increased throughout the early 1990s. In the past few years, according to the 2004 Monitoring the Future Survey, an annual survey of drug use among the nation's middle and high school students, illicit drug use by 8th, 10th, and 12th-graders has leveled off. Still, in 2004, 16 percent of 8th-graders reported that they had tried marijuana, and six percent were current users. This was defined as having used the drug in the 30 days preceding the survey. Among 10th-graders, 35 percent had tried marijuana sometime in their lives, and 16 percent were current users. As would be expected, rates of use among 12th-graders were higher still. Forty-six percent had tried marijuana at some time, and 20 percent were current users.

The Drug Abuse Warning Network (DAWN),[29] a system for monitoring the health impact of drugs, estimated that, in 2002, marijuana was a contributing factor in over 119,000 emergency department (ED) visits in the United States, with about 15 percent of the patients between the ages of 12 and 17, and almost two-thirds male.[29]

In 2002, the National Institute of Justice's Arrestee Drug Abuse Monitoring (ADAM) Program,[21] which collects data on the number of adult arrestees testing positive for various drugs, found that, on average, 41 percent of adult male arrestees and 27 percent of adult female arrestees tested positive for marijuana. On average, 57 percent of juvenile male and 32 percent of juvenile female arrestees tested positive for marijuana.

NIDA's Community Epidemiology Work Group (CEWG), a network of investigators that track trends in the nature and patterns of drug use in major U.S. cities, consistently report that marijuana frequently is combined with other drugs, such as crack cocaine, phencyclidine (PCP), formaldehyde, and codeine cough syrup, sometimes without the user being aware of it. Thus, the risks associated with marijuana use may be compounded by the risks of added drugs.

MARIJUANA AND THE BRAIN

Scientists have learned a great deal about how THC acts in the brain to produce its many effects. When someone smokes marijuana, THC rapidly passes from the lungs into the bloodstream, which carries the chemical to the brain and other organs throughout the body.

THC acts upon specific sites in the brain, called cannabinoid receptors, kicking off a series of cellular reactions that ultimately lead to the "high" that users experience when they smoke marijuana. Areas having many cannabinoid receptors are found in parts of the brain that influence pleasure, memory, thoughts, concentration, sensory and time perception, and coordinated movement.

Not surprisingly, marijuana intoxication can cause distorted perceptions, impaired coordination, difficulty in thinking and problem solving, and problems with learning and memory. Investigators have shown that marijuana's adverse impact on learning and memory can last for days or weeks after the acute effects of the drug wear off.[25] As a result, someone who smokes marijuana every day may be functioning at a suboptimal intellectual level all of the time.

Investigation of the long-term effects of marijuana abuse indicates some changes in the brain similar to those seen after long-term abuse of other major drugs. For example, cannabinoid withdrawal in chronically exposed animals leads to an increase in the activation of the stress-response system[27] and changes in the activity of nerve cells containing dopamine.[8] Dopamine neurons are involved in the regulation of motivation and reward, and are directly or indirectly affected by all drugs of abuse.

ACUTE EFFECTS OF MARIJUANA USE

When marijuana is smoked, its effects begin immediately after the drug enters the brain and last from one to three hours. If marijuana is consumed in food or drink, the short-term effects begin more slowly, usually in one-half to one hour, and last longer, for as long as four hours. Smoking marijuana deposits several times more THC into the blood than does eating or drinking the drug.

Within a few minutes after inhaling marijuana smoke, an individual's heart begins beating more rapidly, the bronchial passages relax and become enlarged, and blood vessels in the eyes expand, making the eyes look red. The heart rate, normally 70 to 80 beats per minute, may increase by 2 to 50 beats per minute or, in some cases, even double. This effect can be greater if other drugs are taken with marijuana.

As THC enters the brain, it results in a user feeling euphoric, or "high," by acting in the brain's reward system, areas of the brain that respond to stimuli such as food and drink, as well as most drugs of abuse. THC activates the reward system in the same way that nearly all drugs of abuse do, by stimulating brain cells to release the chemical dopamine.

A marijuana user may experience pleasant sensations, colors and sounds may seem more intense, and time appears to pass very slowly. Users' mouths feel dry, and they may suddenly become very hungry and thirsty. Their hands may tremble and grow cold. The euphoria passes after awhile, and then a user may feel sleepy or depressed. Occasionally, marijuana use produces anxiety, fear, distrust, or panic.

Heavy marijuana use impairs a person's ability to form memories, recall events, and shift attention from one thing to another.[26] THC also has a disruptive effect upon coordination and balance by binding to receptors in the cerebellum and basal ganglia, parts of the brain that regulate balance, posture, coordination of movement, and reaction time. Through its effects on the brain and body, marijuana intoxication can result in accidents. Investigators show that approximately 6 to 11 percent of fatal accident victims test positive for THC. In many cases, alcohol is detected as well.[7]

In an investigation conducted by the National Highway Traffic Safety administration, a moderate dose of marijuana alone was shown to impair driving performance; however, the effects of even a low dose of marijuana combined with alcohol were markedly greater than for either drug alone.[22] Driving indices measured included reaction time, visual search frequency, that is, the driver checking side streets, and the ability to perceive and/or respond to changes in the relative velocity of other vehicles.

Marijuana users who have taken high doses of the drug may experience acute toxic psychosis, which includes hallucinations, delusions, and depersonalization – a loss of the sense of personal identity, or self-recognition. Although the specific etiologies of these symptoms remain unknown, they appear to occur more frequently when a high dose of cannabis is consumed in food or drink rather than smoked.

MARIJUANA, MEMORY, AND THE HIPPOCAMPUS

96

Marijuana's damage to short-tem memory seems to occur because THC alters the way in which information is processed by the hippocampus, a brain area responsible for memory formation. Laboratory rats treated with THC displayed the same reduced ability to perform tasks requiring short-term memory as other rats showed after nerve cells in their hippocampus were destroyed. In addition, the THC-treated rats had the greatest difficulty with the tasks precisely during the time when the drug was interfering most with the normal functioning of cells in the hippocampus.

As people age, they normally lose neurons in the hippocampus, which decreases their ability to remember events. Chronic THC exposure may hasten the age-related loss of hippocampus neurons. In one series of studies, rats exposed to THC every day for eight months – this is approximately 30 percent of their lifespan – when examined at 11 to 12 months of age, showed nerve cell loss equivalent to that of unexposed animals twice their age.

MARIJUANA'S EFFECTS ON PHYSICAL HEALTH

Marijuana use has been shown to increase users' difficulty in trying to quit smoking tobacco.[10] This was reported in an investigation comparing smoking cessation in adults who smoked both marijuana and tobacco with those who smoked only tobacco. The relationship between marijuana use and continued smoking was particularly strong in those who smoked marijuana daily at the time of the initial interview, thirteen years prior to the follow-up interview.

An investigation of 450 individuals found that people who smoke marijuana frequently but do not smoke tobacco have more health problems and miss more days of work than nonsmokers do. Many of the extra sick days used by the marijuana smokers in the investigation were for respiratory illnesses.

Even infrequent marijuana use can result in burning and stinging of the mouth and throat, often accompanied by a heavy cough. Someone who smokes marijuana regularly may have many of the same respiratory problems that tobacco smokers do, such as daily cough and phlegm production, more frequent acute chest illnesses, a heightened risk of lung infection, and a greater tendency toward obstructed airways.

Cancer of the respiratory tract and lungs may also be promoted by marijuana smoke.[30] Investigators compared 173 cancer patients and 176 healthy individuals; they produced strong evidence that smoking marijuana increases the likelihood of developing cancer of the head and neck, and that the more marijuana smoked, the greater the increase. A statistical analysis of the data led to the suggestion that marijuana smoking doubled or tripled the risk of these cancers.

Marijuana has the potential to promote cancer of the lungs and other parts of the respiratory tract because it contains irritants and carcinogens. In fact, marijuana smoke contains 50 percent to 70 percent more carcinogenic hydrocarbons than does tobacco smoke. It also produces high levels of an enzyme that converts certain hydrocarbons into their carcinogenic form; levels that may accelerate the changes that ultimately produce malignant cells. Marijuana users usually inhale more deeply and hold their breath longer than tobacco smokers do, which increases the lungs' exposure to carcinogenic smoke. These facts suggest that, puff for puff, smoking marijuana may increase the risk of cancer more than smoking tobacco does.

Some adverse health effects caused by marijuana may occur because THC impairs the immune system's ability to fight off infectious diseases and cancer. In laboratory experiments that exposed animal and human cells to THC or other marijuana ingredients, the normal disease-preventing reactions of many of the key types of immune cells were inhibited.[1] In other investigations, mice exposed to THS or related substances were more likely than unexposed mice to develop bacterial infections and tumors.

One investigation has led to the indication that a person's risk of heart attack during the first hour after smoking marijuana is four times his or her usual risk. The investigators suggest that a heart attack might occur, in part, because marijuana raises blood pressure and heart rate and reduces the oxygen-carrying capacity of blood.

HEALTH CONSEQUENCES OF MARIJUANA ABUSE

Acute [present during intoxication]
- Impairs short-term memory.
- Impairs attention, judgment, and other cognitive functions.
- Impairs coordination and balance.
- Increases heart rate.

Persistent [lasting longer than intoxication, but may not be permanent]
- Impairs memory and learning skills.

Long-Term [cumulative, potentially permanent effects of chronic abuse]
- Can lead to addiction.
- Increases risk of chronic cough, bronchitis, and emphysema.
- Increases risk of cancer of the head, neck, and lungs.

MARIJUANA'S EFFECTS ON SCHOOL, WORK, AND SOCIAL LIFE

Students who smoke marijuana get lower grades and are less likely to graduate from high school compared with their non-smoking peers.[3,17] Workers who smoke marijuana are more likely than their co-workers to have problems on the job. Several investigators have associated workers' marijuana smoking with increased absences, tardiness, accidents, Workers' Compensation claims, and job turnover. An investigator examining postal workers found that employees who tested positive for marijuana on a pre-employment urine drug test had 55 percent more industrial accidents, 85 percent more injuries, and a 75 percent increase in absenteeism compared with those who tested negative for marijuana use.

Depression, anxiety, and personality disturbances are all associated with marijuana use. Investigators indicate that marijuana use has the potential to cause problems in daily life or make a person's existing problems worse. Because marijuana compromises the ability to learn and remember information, the more people use marijuana the more they are likely to fall behind in accumulating intellectual, job, or social skills. In one investigation of cognition, adults were matched on the basis of their performance in the 4th grade on Iowa Test of Basic Skills. They were evaluated on a number of cognitive measures including the 12th grade version of the Iowa Test. Those who were heavy marijuana smokers scored significantly lower on mathematical skills and verbal expression than nonsmokers.

Moreover, investigators have shown that marijuana's adverse impact on memory and learning can last for days or weeks after the acute effects of the drug wear off.[25] For example, an investigation of 129 college students found that among heavy users of marijuana – those who smoked the drug at least 27 of the preceding 30 days – critical skills related to attention, memory, and learning were significantly impaired, even after they had not used the drug for at least 24 hours.[26] The heavy marijuana users in the investigation had more trouble sustaining and shifting their attention and in registering, organizing, and using information than did the participants who had used marijuana no more than three of the previous thirty days. As a result, someone who smokes marijuana once daily may be functioning at a reduced intellectual level all of the time. More recently, the same investigators demonstrated that a group of long-term heavy marijuana users' ability to recall words from a list was impaired one week following cessation of marijuana use, but returned to normal by four weeks.[25] An implication of this finding is that even after long-term heavy marijuana use, if an individual quits marijuana use, some cognitive abilities may be recovered.

Another investigation produced additional evidence that marijuana's affects on the brain can result in cumulative deterioration of critical life skills, in the long run. Investigators gave students a battery of tests measuring problem-solving and emotional skills in 8th grade and again in 12th grade. The results were indicative of the fact that the students who were already drinking alcohol plus smoking marijuana in the 8th grade started off slightly behind their peers, but that the distance separating these two groups grew significantly by their senior year in high school. The analysis was used to link marijuana use, independent of alcohol use, to reduced capacity for self-reinforcement, a group of psychological skills that enable individuals to maintain confidence and persevere in the pursuit of goals.

Marijuana users themselves report poor outcomes on a variety of measures of life satisfaction and achievement. A recent investigation was used to compare current and former long-term heavy users of marijuana with a control group who reported smoking cannabis at least once in their lives, but not more than 50 times. Despite similar education and incomes in their families of origin, significant differences were found in educational attainment and income between heavy users and the control group: fewer of the cannabis users completed college and more had household incomes of less than $30,000. When asked how marijuana affected their cognitive abilities, career achievements, social lives, and physical and mental health, the overwhelming majority of heavy cannabis users reported the drug's deleterious effect on all of these measures.

MARIJUANA AND PREGNANCY

Investigators have shown that some babies born to women who used marijuana during their pregnancies display altered responses to visual stimuli, increased tremulousness, and a high-pitched cry, which may be indicative of problems with neurological development. During the preschool years, marijuana-exposed children have been observed to perform tasks involving sustained attention and memory more poorly than non-exposed children do. In the school years, these children are more likely to exhibit deficits in problem-solving skills, memory, and the ability to remain attentive.[11]

MARIJUANA AND ADDICTION

Long-term marijuana use can lead to addiction for some people; that is, they use the drug compulsively even though it often interferes with family, school, work, and recreational activities. According to the 2003 National Survey on Drug Use and Health (NSDUH),[28] an estimated 21.6 million Americans aged 12 or older were classified with substance dependence or abuse; this is 9.1 percent of the total population. Of the estimated 6.9 million Americans classified with dependence on or abuse of illicit drugs, 4.2 million were dependent on or abused marijuana. In 2002, 15 percent of people entering drug abuse treatment programs reported that marijuana was their primary drug of abuse. Along with craving, withdrawal symptoms can make it hard for long-term marijuana smokers to stop using the drug. People trying to quit report irritability, difficulty sleeping, and anxiety. They also displayed increased aggression on psychological tests, peaking approximately one week after they last used the drug.

In addition to its addictive liability, investigation is indicative of the fact that early exposure to marijuana can increase the likelihood of a lifetime of subsequent drug problems. A recent examination of over 300 fraternal and identical twin pairs, who differed on whether or not they used marijuana before the age of 17, found that those who had used marijuana early had elevated rates of other drug use and drug problems later on, compared with their twins who did not use marijuana before age 17. These investigators re-emphasize the importance of primary prevention by showing that early drug initiation is associated with increased risk of later drug problems and they provide more evidence for why preventing marijuana experimentation during adolescence could have an impact on preventing addiction.[16]

THE BODY'S NATURAL THC-LIKE CHEMICALS

THC owes many of its effects to its similarity to a family of chemical called *endogenous cannabinoids,* which are natural Cannabis-like chemicals.

Because a THC molecule is shaped like these endogenous cannabinoids, it interacts with the same receptors on nerve cells, the cannabinoid receptors, that endogenous cannabinoids do, and it influences many of the same processes. Research has shown that the endogenous cannabinoids help control a wide array of mental and physical processes in the brain and throughout the body, including memory and perception, fine motor coordination, pain sensations, and immunity to disease, and reproduction.

When someone smokes marijuana, THC over-stimulates the cannabinoid receptors, leading to a disruption of the endogenous cannabinoids' normal function. This overstimulation produces the intoxication experienced by marijuana smokers. Over time, it may alter the function of cannabinoid receptors, which along with other changes in the brain, can lead to withdrawal symptoms and addiction.

MARIJUANA TREATMENT

Treatment programs directed solely at marijuana abuse are rare, partly because many who use marijuana do so in combination with other drugs such as cocaine and alcohol. With more people seeking help to control marijuana abuse, investigative work has focused on ways to overcome problems with abuse of this drug.

One investigation of adult marijuana users found comparable benefits from a 14 session cognitive-behavioral group treatment and a two session individual treatment that included motivational interviewing and advice on ways to reduce marijuana use. Participants were mostly men in their early thirties who had smoked marijuana daily over ten years. By increasing patients' awareness of what triggers their marijuana use, both treatments were used to help them devise avoidance strategies. Use, dependence symptoms, and psychosocial problems decreased for at least one year after both treatments. About 30 percent of users were abstinent during the last three month follow-up period. Other investigators suggest that giving patients vouchers for abstaining from marijuana can improve outcomes.[4] Vouchers can be redeemed for rewards such as movie passes, sports equipment, or vocational training.

No medications are now available to treat marijuana abuse. However, recent discoveries about the workings of THC receptors have raised the possibility that scientists may eventually develop a medication that will block THC's intoxicating effects. Such a medication might be used to prevent relapse to marijuana abuse by reducing or elimination its appeal.

FUTURE ISSUES

Perhaps the largest issues facing drug abuse, in general, and marijuana abuse, in particular, are the dual growing trends of decriminalization and legalization with respect to marijuana. One can certainly understand the trend toward decriminalization. Personal use, or abuse, of marijuana should not be seen primarily as a criminal justice issue. When personal use results in habitual and addictive behavior with the consequent effects upon performance in many areas of life, this becomes both a health care and public health issue. The line that exists between use of a mind-altering substance and abuse of said substance is certainly not clear in all cases. Given that marijuana continues to be an illicit substance, one can certainly understand how an individual determined by law enforcement authorities to be in possession of small quantities of marijuana, even for personal use, will be held responsible. In many states, the resultant "ticket" is analogous to a large traffic fine.

Many states have essentially decriminalized the personal possession of marijuana. As judged solely by anecdotal evidence, the use of marijuana appears to be both wide-ranging across the population, and it involves a considerable proportion of the population. The current generation of high school aged individuals is essentially the third American generation in which marijuana use has become a "fact" of life for a sizable proportion of the cohort. Their elders, who came of age during the 1960s, were the first generation to widely use marijuana; a sizable proportion continues regular or occasional use today. Judging simply by the sale of inexpensive cigars and cigar wrappers at convenience stores, the use of marijuana is widespread.

The legalization of the marijuana movement has been steadily gaining momentum since the drug came into widespread use. In November 2010, there was a ballot question for the State of California. The intent of the ballot initiative, if passed, was to legalize marijuana in the state. The question failed by a small margin. It appears to be inevitable that first one state then another will pass ballot initiatives to fully legalize marijuana. It could be argued that this will result in a cascade of other states eventually following suit. This possibility may result in a new paradigm in society. If marijuana becomes legal in a state, issues revolving around sales, purity, distribution, accessibility, and many others will need to be confronted.

Also complicating matters is the fact that if even one state legalizes marijuana, there will be ramifications if the federal government continuing to classifying it as an illicit substance. It would appear that prolonged legal battles will be in the offing. These may well be concerned with states' rights issues rather than the medical or health care issues. Regardless, a long and protracted series of events appear to be on the horizon.

CASE STUDY

Basil Smetna is a 21 year old college student at Ye Olde State University in a Midwestern state. Basil is majoring in biology with the hope of gaining acceptance to medical school. Mr. Smetna was first introduced to marijuana use by his older brother Bogdan. Basil was 12 years old at the time. At first, he was an occasional opportunistic user; when he was offered marijuana, he used it. Throughout the final three years of high school, he was a regular user on both Friday and Saturday nights. He occasionally sold small quantities to friends to help with his personal purchase costs. By this time, Bogdan was selling widely to an increasing circle of friends and acquaintances.

Throughout high school, Basil remained a strong student, especially in mathematics and the sciences. The state university was his first choice of schools for a variety of reasons; first, it was affordable for him and his family, second, the biology program had a very good track record of placing strong students in both graduate and professional programs, and third, the university was also known for the wide spread use of marijuana among its students.

Initially, in college, Basil's marijuana use continued much as it did while in high school. His personal and academic adjustment to college was relatively uneventful. During the first two years of college, both his overall grade point average and his grades in his major and allied courses were well above average. Marijuana usage in the residence hall was forbidden, and this rule was rigorously enforced. This essentially limited his marijuana use to off campus parties, of which there were many, and other opportunistic occasions.

Basil decided to move off campus with three of his male friends for his junior year. The ostensible reason was financial; it would be less expensive than university housing. Realistically, all four of the roommates were regular marijuana users, and the move gave them more latitude for regular use. Basil's use became daily, and there has been a resultant plunge in his grade point average. His academic advisor has had several conversations with him regarding his deteriorating academic performance. While he is not yet in jeopardy of either being dismissed from the major or the university, Basil's chances of obtaining a medical education are sinking quickly. Basil states that the courses have become markedly more difficult this year. He sees no relationship between his marijuana use and his grade point average. He says that he only smokes after he finishes studying each night.

CASE STUDY

Florence Denholm is a 54 year dental hygienist who was diagnosed with fibromyalgia approximately four years ago. The resultant chronic and severe pain has had a devastating effect upon her life. It has affected her ability to work as many hours as she wishes, and it has affected the 20 year cohabitation relationship she has had with her transsexual partner "Syd." Over the course of the four years since her diagnosis, Florence has had consultations with a variety of physicians representing several medical specialties. She has repeatedly gone through regimens of care with little or no improvement. Of course, as is often the case with fibromyalgia, there was a protracted period of time before the diagnosis could definitely be established. The pain has increased in intensity over that time.

In addition to traditional scientific medicine, Florence has also used a variety of complementary medical modalities in a search for resolution of her difficulties. These included various bodywork techniques, meditative strategies, and herbal solutions. None were effective in her case. As time has progressed, a variety of friends in Syd's and her social circle, suggested the use of medical marijuana. Florence was initially condemning of this possibility; she was raised in a home where one of the consistent messages was that "all drugs were bad and that they would destroy your life." Eventually, out of a growing sense of desperation, Florence did begin to contemplate the use of medical marijuana. Given her background, it was important to her that she interface with the health care community regarding this decision. Her primary care physician, Dr. Sharon Baselow, recommended that she see Dr. Floyd Hammersmill, a psychologist, regarding the possibility of a prescription for medical marijuana. In her state, Dr. Hammersmill is classified as a health care provider and, therefore, capable of writing this type of prescription.

As the result of this consultation, Florence did receive a prescription. She also agreed to continue to see Dr. Hammersmill on a quarterly basis and maintain her continuing relationship with Dr. Baselow. The next day Florence and Syd went to a recommended marijuana dispensary to purchase her supply. It was suggested that she use a water pipe as the delivery system. Using the behavioral regimen suggested by Dr. Hammersmill, Florence found significant relief on almost an immediate basis. Eight months post the start of this regimen Florence reports that she continues to experience significant relief; she has returned to full time work, and her relationship with Syd has returned to its prior healthy state.

The only cause for concern on Florence's part is the conflicted state that she experiences about her regular marijuana use. This stems from the lessons learned during her childhood yet, on the other hand, she believes that she could not function and perform her expected responsibilities without the drug.

REFERENCES

[1]Adams, I. B. and Marin, B. R. (1996). Cannabis: Pharmacology and toxicology in animals and humans. Addiction *91*, 1585-1614.

[2]Breivogel, C. S., Scates, S. M., Beletskaya, I. O., Lowery, O. B., Aceta, M. D., and Marin, B. R. (2003). The effects of delta-9 tetrahydrocannabinol physical dependence on brain cannabinoid receptors. Euro J Pharmacology *459*, 139-150.

[3]Brook, J. S., Balka, E. B. and Whiteman, M. (1999). The risks for late adolescence of early adolescent marijuana use. Am J Public Health *89*(10), 1549-1554.

[4]Budney, A. J., Higgins, S. T., Radonovich, K. I. and Novy, P. L. (2000). Adding voucher-based incentives to coping skills and motivational enhancement improves outcomes during treatment for marijuana dependence. J Consult Clin Psychol *68*(6), 1051-1061.

[5]Budney, A. J., Moore, B. A., Vandrey, R. G. and Hughes, J. R. (2003). The time course and significance of cannabis withdrawal. J Abnorm Psychol *112*(3), 393-402.

[6]Budney, A. J., Vandrey, R. G., Hughes, J. R., Thostenson, J. D. and Bursac, Z. (2008). Comparison of cannabis and tobacco withdrawal: Severity and contribution to relapse. J Subst Abuse Treat, e-publication ahead of print, March 12.

[7]Cimbura, G., Lucas, D. M., Bennett, R. C. and Donelson, A. C. (1990). Incidence and toxicological aspects of cannabis and ethanol detected in 1,394 fatally injured drivers and pedestrians in Ontario (1982-1984). J Forensic Sci *35*, 1035-1041.

[8]Diana, M., Melis, M., Muntoni, A. L. and Gessa, G. L. (1998). Mesolimbic dopaminergic decline after cannabinoid withdrawal. Proc Natl Acad Sci, USA, *95*(17), 10269-10273.

[9]ElSohly, M. A., Ross, S. A., Mehmedic, Z., Arafat, R., Yi, B. and Banahan, B. (2000). Potency trends of delta-9-THC and other cannabinoids in confiscated marijuana from 1980-1997. J Forensic Sci, *45*(1), 24-30.

[10]Ford, D. E., Vu, H. T. and Anthony, J. C. (2002). Marijuana use and cessation of tobacco smoking in adults from a community sample. Drug Alc Depend *67*, 243-248.

[11]Fried, P. A. and Smith, A. M. (2001). A literature review of the consequences of prenatal marijuana exposure: An emerging theme of a deficiency in aspects of executive function. Neurotoxicology and Teratology *23*(1), 1-11.

[12]Gruber, A. J., Pope, H. G., Hudson, J. I. and Yurgelun-Todd, D. (2003). Attributes of long-term heavy cannabis users: A case control study. Psychological Med *33*(8), 1415-1422.

[13]Hashibe, M., Morgenstern, H., Cui, Y., et al. (2006). Marijuana use and the risk of lung and upper aerodigestive tract cancers: Results of a population-based case-control study. Cancer Epidemiol Biomarkers Prev 15(10), 1829-1834.

[14]Herkenham, M., Lynn, A., Little, M.D., et al. (1990). Cannabinoid receptor localization in the brain. Proc Natl Acad Sci, USA 87(5), 1932-1936.

[15]Johnston, L. D., O'Malley, P. M., and Bachman, J. G. (2005). Monitoring the future: National results on adolescent drug use, overview and key findings, 2004. NIH Pub. No. 05-5506. Bethesda, MD: NIDA, NIH, DHHS.

[16]Lynskey, M. T., Heath, A. C., Bucholz, K. K., Slutske, W. S., Madden, P. A. F., Nelson, E. C., Statham, D. J., and Martin, N. G. (2003). Escalation of drug use in early-onset cannabis users vs. co-twin controls. JAMA 289, 427-433.

[17]Lynskey, M. and Hall, W. (2000). The effects of adolescent cannabis use on educational attainment: A review. Addiction 95(11), 1621-1630.

[18]Maldonado, R., and de Fonseca, F. R. (2002). Cannabinoid addiction: Behavioral models and neural correlates. J Neuroscience 22(9), 3326-3331.

[19]Mittleman, M. A., Lewis, R. A., Maclure, M., Sherwood, J. B., and Muller, J. E. (2001). Triggering myocardial infarction by marijuana. Circulation 103(23), 2805-2809.

[20]Moore, T. H., Zammit, S., Lingford-Hughes, et al. (2007). Cannabis use and risk of psychotic or affective mental health outcomes: A systematic review. Lancet 370(9584), 319-328.

[21]National Institute of Justice, Arrestee Drug Abuse Monitoring Program. (2002). Preliminary Data on Drug Use & Related Matters Among Adult Arrestees & Juvenile Detainees, 2002. Washington, DC: U.S. Department of Justice.

[22]National Highway traffic Safety Administration (NHTSA) Notes. (2000). Marijuana and alcohol combined severely impede driving performance. Annals Emer Med 35(4), 398-399.

[23]Piomelli, D., Giuffrida, A. Calignano, A. and Rodriquez de Fonseca, F. (2000). The endocannabinoid system as a target for therapeutic drugs. TIPS 21, 218-224.

[24]Polen, M. R., Sidney, S., Tekawa, I. S., Sadler, M., Friedman, G.D. (1993). Health care use by frequent marijuana smokers who do not smoke tobacco. West J Med 158(6), 596-601.

[25]Pope, H. G., Gruber, A. J., Hudson, J. I., Huestis, M. A. and Yurgelun-Todd, D. (2001). Neuropsychological performance in long-term cannabis users. Arch Gen Psychiatry 58(10), 909-915.

[26]Pope, H. G. and Yurgelun-Todd, D. (1996). The residual cognitive effects of heavy marijuana use in college students. JAMA 275(7), 521-527.

[27]Rodrigues de Fonseca, F., Carrera, M. R. A., Navarro, M, Koob, G. F. and Weiss, F. (1997). Activation of corticotrophin-releasing factor in the limbic system during cannabinoid withdrawal. Science 276(5321), 2050-2054.

[28]Substance Abuse and Mental Health Services Administration. (2004). Results from the 2003 National Survey on Drug Use and Health: National Findings. NHSDA Series H-25.DHHS Pub. No. (SMA) 04-3964. Rockville, MD: DHHS.

[29]Substance Abuse and Mental Health Services Administration. (2003). Office of Applies Studies. Emergency Department Trends from DAWN: Final Estimates 1995-2002. DAWN Series D-24; DHHS Pub No. (SMA) 03-3780. Rockville, MD: SAMHSA.

[30]Tashkin, D. P. (2005). Smoked marijuana as a cause of lung injury. Monaldi Arch Chest Dis *63*(2), 92-100.

[31]Tashkin, D. (1990). Pulmonary complications of smoked substance abuse. West J Med *152*, 525-530.

Chapter Eight

STIMULANTS:
AMPHETAMINE
&
METHAMPHETAMINE

By **MELISSA MANNINEN LUSE**

JOHN F. KOSCIULEK
MICHIGAN STATE UNIVERSITY

Chapter Topics

◊ Introduction
◊ The Amphetamines
◊ Methamphetamine
◊ MDMA Ecstasy: A Club Drug

INTRODUCTION

*T*his chapter's focus is on stimulants, specifically on amphetamines and methamphetamines. Stimulant is an umbrella term for cocaine and amphetamines, chemicals that are able to stimulate the central nervous system (CNS) in a host of ways: increasing alertness, energy, creating euphoria and increased perception of power, and decreasing fatigue and appetite. Stimulants are used legally for certain medical conditions such as narcolepsy and hyperactivity, and illegally for a variety of reasons: by athletes to keep weight down and increase energy, by people with depression as a way to self-medicate, by students to help increase focus, memory, and maintain concentration, and in combination with other drugs to enhance or elevate certain effects.

RELEVANT DRUGS COVERED

Amphetamine was the first member of a group of chemical compounds collectively called *amphetamines.* Amphetamines also include *methamphetamine,* synthesized in 1893, and *3-4 methylenedioxy-methamphetamine (MDMA* or *ecstasy),* developed in the early 1900s and patented in 1914. *Methcathinone* (cat) is another amphetamine. It is derived from cathinone, a stimulating ingredient in Catha Edulis, a plant grown in East Africa and the Saudi Arabia Peninsula. Catha Edulis is better known for the derived stimulant *khat* (pronounced *cot).* While often known for its hallucinogenic effects, the designer drug, MDMA, is also a stimulant.

Today, some of the most abused amphetamines are prescription stimulants, such as Ritalin and Adderall, prescribed for attention deficit-hyperactivity disorder, with teenagers and young adults the largest population abusing these drugs. The rapidly increasing use of Ritalin and Adderall in teens and college students must be discussed as these drugs are capable of causing effects similar to illegal amphetamine and cocaine, and have the potential to cause the same types of physical and psychological effects.

HISTORY OF AMPHETAMINES

The first recorded use of stimulants dates back to over 5000 years ago, Chinese physicians produced Ma Huang from the ephedra plant, its active ingredient ephedrine. Ephedrine was first isolated and used in the late 1800s to treat asthma, and was available without prescription. In a desire to create a synthetic version, amphetamine was first synthesized in 1887, and was first used as a hay fever medication in the United States in the early 1930s as the Benzedrine Inhaler. Amphetamine later became a cure-all for a plethora of conditions, and were used extensively during World War II; administered to soldiers to increase alertness and decrease fatigue. After WWII, amphetamines became popular with long-haul truckers, allowing drivers to go farther without stopping to rest. As an appetite suppressant, amphetamines also became very popular, and were highly effective as a quick way to lose weight. With their energizing effects, amphetamines were also prescribed as "pep" pills by doctors to millions of people to elevate mood, and as a remedy for psychosomatic conditions; the majority of people being "unhappy housewives" looking for relief from boredom. In the 1960s, amphetamine exploded onto the American youth scene along with methamphetamine, and other drugs such as marijuana and LSD.

THE PHARMACEUTICAL INDUSTRY AND AMPHETAMINE SALES
As a result of intense competition between pharmaceutical companies and ignorance of the dependence potential of the drug, the US experienced an amphetamine epidemic lasting from the early 1940s until the 1970s.

Since its development, amphetamine was marketed as a remedy for all ailments. As a decongestant and bronchodilator, then later in its base form as the Benzedrine Inhaler, the patient was to inhale the amphetamine vapor every hour as needed. Benzedrine was available over-the-counter until 1971. In 1937, Benzedrine sulfate was approved for sale as a remedy for narcolepsy, postencephalitic Parkinsonism, and minor depression. *Dextroamphetamine* later became the main treatment option for narcolepsy, and it is still widely used today. During the 1940s, amphetamines became the first anti-depressant, a popular diet pill, prescribed for relief of menopausal symptoms, and used in WWII by millions of US, British, German, and Japanese soldiers. During Vietnam, the total number of US troops taking speed was more than all WWII troops combined.

Through intense industry competition in the 1950s, consumption sky-rocketed. One amphetamine, Dexamyl, a blend of dextroamphetamine and amobarbital, was successfully marketed for everyday "mental and emotional distress" and also as a weight loss remedy "striking at the emotional causes of overeating.[30] By 1941, annual sales of Benzedrine tablets reached $500,000. In 1945, over 30 million amphetamine tablets were produced monthly in the US alone. By 1947, amphetamine sales reached over $5.5 million, just one decade after the drug was introduced to medicine. By the early 1960s, amphetamine production reached a staggering 8–10 billion 10-mg doses.[30]

WOMEN AND AMPHETAMINES
Since the introduction of amphetamines in the 1930s, women have been the largest population of consumers. In 1960, in the UK alone, 85% of all amphetamine users were women. The drug was prescribed for "mental adjustment" and to relieve boredom, and by 1967, over 30 million prescriptions for amphetamine diet pills were written, again the majority of users being women. Today, women still are more likely than men to use prescription amphetamines illicitly because of their ability to suppress the appetite.[30,36]

Amphetamine is highly addictive, with serious health conditions. As a result, its use has been severely reduced since 1965, with newer and more effective derivatives taking its place. However, amphetamine is now a popular black market drug, its chemicals cheap and easy to purchase, and production so simple that many communities across the US have seen an epidemic of laboratories springing up. Such kitchen laboratories have created their own health hazards separate from the actual use and dependence of the drug.

HOW AMPHETAMINES WORK AND THERE EFFECTS

Amphetamine can be taken orally in pill form, smoked, or injected. Taken orally, effects occur within 30-60 minutes, and last about 30 to 45 minutes, much slower than if smoked or injected. In oral form, at least half of the substance is destroyed by the liver. Effects from smoking amphetamine occur within five minutes, peaking at about 10 minutes and wearing off after almost an hour. Injecting the substance directly into the blood stream results in almost immediate effects that are very intense, but last only 10 to 20 minutes.

Amphetamines produce their focus and energizing effects primarily by increasing synaptic levels of dopamine within the brain, but also by increasing biogenic amines, norepinephrine, and serotonin levels. Dopamine, an *excitatory* neurotransmitter, increases focus, memory, motivation, alertness, mood, pleasure, excitement, and decreases depression. Amphetamines are *agonist* drugs, enhancing dopamine's effects. Dopamine is affected through various mechanisms. Similar in structure to the neurotransmitter, ampheta-mines are able to enter the terminal button of the presynaptic neuron via its dopamine transporters. Amphetamines then force dopamine out of its storage vesicles and into the synaptic gap, the brain receiving more dopamine than needed, resulting in a stimulating and euphoric effect. Amphetamines also affect dopamine by hindering it from reuptake back into the presynaptic neuron, and keeping the neurotransmitter in the synapse longer than needed. Norepinephrine is another primary neurotransmitter affected by amphetamines by competing with each other for post-synaptic receptors.

With increases in excitatory neurotransmitters, the CNS becomes stimulated. Brain activity, such as in the Reward or Pleasure Center, is amplified. Packed with dopamine and norepinephrine, feelings of euphoria and desire for drugs is enhanced; adrenalin is released; the nervous system speeds up; as do heart, respiratory rates, and blood pressure; appetite decreases; and the "fight or flight" response is jump started, which can be very dangerous.

Side effects of amphetamine include: restlessness, insomnia, agitation, anxiety, bruxism (teeth grinding), tremor, stereotyped behavior, increased blood pressure and heart rate, dry mouth, sweating, headaches, muscle rigidity, intense emotional lability, paranoia, and violent outbursts.[35] Serious adverse effects include dangerously high heart rate and blood pressure; and increased body temperature, resulting in cardiovascular shock, fatal arrhythmia, heart attack, or stroke.

THE AMPHETAMINES

Today, the US is experiencing an epidemic in amphetamine abuse, the most commonly abused drug after marijuana,[15] affecting between 1 to 3% of the nation.[35] This comes out to be about 3 million Americans who have used amphetamines just within 2007, or 600,000 in one week, and approximately 300,000 people are addicted, with the number of heavy users with addiction problems doubling between 2002-04. While at first it may seem obvious to point fingers at the illegal amphetamine drug market, this is not where amphetamine addiction is stemming from. According to 2006 survey data, the illicit use of prescription amphetamines has peaked and reached a plateau.[30]

However, amphetamine abuse may be increasing at a decreasing rate. According to 2007 data from the National Institute on Drug Abuse (NIDA), amphetamine use has dropped among middle and high school students: by more than half among 8th graders; by a third among 10th graders; and by a third among 12th graders. Prescription amphetamines are most commonly abuse by teens and young adults in college; however, according to a recent study, emergency rooms are seeing an increase of 700% from 1995-2002 in patients 55 and older with amphetamine induced health problems.[5,3]

AMPHETAMINES IN THE MAJOR LEAGUE BASEBALL

According to an MLB team doctor, amphetamines should be more of a concern than steroids. In 2006, there were only 28 players who were granted therapeutic use exemptions, increasing to 103 just by 2007! This means that almost 8% of major league baseball players have ADD/ADHD when only 1-3% of the general population is diagnosed with these disorders.

Dr. Gary Wadler, chairman of the committee that determines the banned-substances list for the World Anti-Doping Agency further stated: "This is incredible. . .There seems to be an epidemic of ADD in major league baseball. . .I've been in private practice for a lot of years. I can count on one hand the number of individuals that have ADD."[26]

In its pure form, illicit amphetamine, also known as *uppers* or *speed,* is a white, odorless, bitter-tasting crystalline powder. Illicit amphetamines vary in purity, which is noticeable by sight, texture, and smell: from whitish with traces of gray, to pink color in a coarse powder, crystals or chunks, and may smell "fishy" or like ammonia. Methamphetamine resembles shaved glass slivers or clear rock salt. Amphetamines are injected, smoked, sniffed, or taken as pills. Amphetamines have many slang names such as "beanies," "black beauties," "crank," and "lid poppers." Poly-drug use, stimulants commonly used with other drugs such as heroin, alcohol, or depressants to enhance or elevate effects of these drugs or the amphetamine, is significant in amphetamine abuse.

PRESCRIPTION AMPHETAMINES: RITALIN AND ADDERALL

Attention deficit/hyperactivity disorder (ADHD) is a common mental health condition that affects approximately 8 to 9 percent of children ages 4-17 and 3 to 4 percent of adults. Diagnosis for ADHD includes "...persistent pattern of inattention and/or hyperactivity-impulsivity that is more frequently displayed and more severe than is typically observed in individuals at a comparable level of development."[22] Such behavior is normally evident during preschool/early elementary years, with age seven the average time of diagnosis, and 75% of children diagnosed are male.[37] Most individuals experience improvement in symptoms by adulthood.

Since the 1930's, the stimulants *methylphenidate* (e.g., Ritalin and Concerta) and amphetamine (e.g., Adderall, a mix of amphetamine salts) have been the primary treatment option in ADHD symptom management. Investigators have found stimulant treatment to be more effective than behavioral therapy alone, or even when combined with medication. In the 1970's, investigators found children without ADHD also show improvements in attention and focus when taking amphetamines. Just how amphetamines improve focus and impulsive behavior is still not well understood, however. In small amounts, amphetamines can produce a paradoxical calming and "focusing" effect. It is hypothesized that because methylphenidate and amphetamine intensifies the release of dopamine, these substances can improve attention and focus, especially in individuals who have dopamine signals that are weak.[37]

There has been much concern about serious side effects of stimulant treatment for ADHD, especially since most drug testing has been performed on adults, not children, and there are few long-term investigations of stimulant use for ADHD. Common side effects include delayed sleep onset, reduced appetite, abdominal pain, weight loss, tics, jitteriness, and headache. Other adverse effects include induced psychological changes, such as anxiety, irritability, sadness, over focusing. Such side effects are commonly reported with the initiation of stimulant treatment, and decrease within a few months. In a five year study of the effects of stimulant medication for ADHD, the most common sustained side effect reported was appetite loss, with the majority of children reporting that side effects were mild.[18] Other side effects include nervousness, nausea, vomiting, skin rashes, itching, digestive problems, dizziness, headaches, blood clots, toxic psychosis, psychotic episodes, drug dependence, severe depression upon withdrawal, tremors, muscle twitching, fevers, convulsions, irregular respirations, stereotyped behavior, and skin and circulatory problems. In addition, snorting Ritalin causes the membrane separating the nasal passage and the brain to deteriorate, resulting in nosebleeds and damage to nasal cartilage.

Stimulant medication has been in the news lately concerning potential cardiovascular effects on children, with 12 cases of sudden death within five years reportedly due to stimulant medication. Health Canada was so concerned about such a potentially significant effect, that in 2005, it discontinued the marketing of Adderall. Later, this was reversed after it was determined that the rate of cardiac events was actually lower for those taking stimulants than the base rate for the general population. Investigators continue to find mixed results regarding cardiovascular effects of stimulant use in the treatment of ADHD.[18] Until the late 1990's, many medications prescribed for children have been studied on adults and animals rather than children. Just within the last 10 years, pharmaceutical companies have begun testing medications such as Ritalin and Adderall on children. Slowly, long-term studies are beginning to be published. For many years, stimulant medication has been associated with slowed growth and weight in children. After years of mixed results, and newly conducted long-term investigations, it appears that such effects are now being discounted. A recent study failed to find evidence for reduced long-term height and weight in children treated during the 80's, and then followed to their ultimate adult height. This study, and other long-term investigations, report slowed weight and height are limited to the first few months to one year of treatment, in most cases.[18]

COLLEGE USE OF PRESCRIPTION AMPHETAMINES

The United States Drug Enforcement Agency (DEA) classifies Ritalin as a schedule II drug, a substance with a large potential for misuse. In recent years, this drug has become one of the substances and medications most abused by college students who use it as an aid in retaining information and cramming for exams. Amphetamines have replaced minor stimulants such as caffeine as the number one study aid of college students. Ritalin allows students to stay awake for hours, increase focus, and maintain high levels of concentration. A survey of 2087 college students revealed that over five percent admitted non-medical use of amphetamines. Young adults are not beginning the use of Ritalin when they reach college, but are coming to college campuses already using it. In 2006, almost four and-a-half percent of 12th graders admitted annual use of amphetamines, as did over 3.5% of 10th graders. A study of 6000 high school students in Massachusetts revealed that 13% abused Ritalin, and 4% of middle school children had also abused Ritalin.[36]

Amphetamines are easily accessible across US college campuses through online pharmacies, where the majority offer prescription drugs without a doctor's prescription, and from students who have a prescription. Students may sell the medication, each tablet costing about $2, or may provide them for free to a select few. One college senior at a Midwestern university takes Adderall for ADD (attention deficit disorder), and gives her pills to a few close friends to help study for exams, but says she does not sell them or give them to just anyone. "I give it to my very close friends who need it in tough situations, as in finals week, midterms–the big stuff." However, she also expressed how she does not like doing it. "I hate doing it," she said, and also conveyed a common misperception about prescribed amphetamines: "but, I mean, it's not going to kill you. It's just going to help you get your work done."[36] Using a prescription drug non-medically can be dangerous. Everyone is different, body weight, chemistry, drug interactions, medical history, and health. All of this is important in determining how much of a drug an individual can safely take. Taking a drug, and at a dose meant for someone else, poses potentially serious affects.

METHAMPHETAMINE

Societies around the world experience cycles of stimulant epidemics. Currently in the US, methamphetamine (*meth* or *crystal meth*) use has increased significantly, and is now the most abused amphetamine. According to Haney,[14] the number of admissions for methamphetamine treatment increased more than four times from 1994 to 2004, and in many areas of the US, the number of people enrolled for meth treatment surpasses the number of people in treatment for cocaine or heroin. Until the 1980's, most meth production and abuse occurred in California. Today, production and use has heavily affected the rest of the West coast. While only .6% of individuals nationwide age 12 and over used meth in 2005, over 2% of individuals on the West coast used meth in the same year.[22]

Originally, suppliers were motorcycle gangs and independent trafficking groups from Mexico. Although California produces 85 percent of the Nation's methamphetamine, the expansion of Mexico-based meth traffickers and independent U.S.-based laboratories has increased meth availability and abuse, specifically in the Pacific Northwest. To help counter use, Multnomah County Sheriff's Office in Oregon began to keep booking pictures of meth users, and now displays on the Internet the progressive changes people incur. Meth use has rapidly spread throughout the Mid West and portions of the Southeast. Georgia, Tennessee, and Alabama have experienced high rates of meth abuse, with the infamous Meth Mountain being located in Alabama. The Mid-Atlantic States and New England have not yet experienced a meth epidemic, with less than .4% of the population in these areas using meth in 2005.[22]

PRODUCTION OF METHAMPHETAMINE
First produced in Japan in 1919, meth is a synthetic stimulant. Smoking is the most common route of administration, but it can be injected, snorted, and taken orally. Along with amphetamine, meth was prescribed for depression and obesity for many years. During the 60s, meth was used by some doctors to treat heroin addiction. The federal government began regulating the drug in 1970. Today, meth is still prescribed for some medical conditions. It is a Schedule II stimulant, which means it has a high potential for abuse, and is available only through a prescription. Medical uses are limited, with very low doses prescribed.

States are increasingly experiencing more local meth producers who make smaller amounts of the drug in less complex laboratories using homemade or

Internet recipes of uncertain origin. Meth is easy, cheap, and quick to make; its ingredients easily available in pharmacies and hardware stores. This has resulted in significant FDA changes for procuring over-the-counter medications, as well as regulations for obtaining hardware store products. The simplicity of meth making has now resulted in mobile labs, people making the drug out of the trunk of a car, or in an RV. Meth is important to discuss as it is a relatively new drug and the depth of this epidemic is unknown by most people. Investigators have traditionally paid little attention to this drug, focusing on other stimulants such as cocaine and Ritalin.

While Meth production is simple, quick, and ingredients are cheap with relative easy access, most ingredients used are highly toxic, as is the actual cooking of meth. Meth is manufactured using the ephedrine, or pseudoephedrine reduction method. Cold and allergy tablets containing ephedrine, or pseudoephedrine, are cooked until the ephedrine or pseudoephedrine is separated. Other ingredients include red phosphorous, acetone, iodine, ammonia, paint thinner, toluene, ether, lye, camping fuel, drain cleaner, anhydrous ammonia or farm fertilizer, and lithium from batteries. These products can be purchased at any pharmacy or hardware store and recipes can be found on the Internet. As the government continues to crack down on the products to produce meth, meth makers continue to find substitutes. For example, meth makers are now turning to products such as shower gel, extracting certain chemicals by cooking the soap.

The actual cooking of meth is dangerous because many of these products are highly explosive, and generate gallons of toxic waste. The waste is usually dumped onto the ground, or into sewage systems or rivers. The vapors from meth production are toxic, soaking into walls and carpeting, making the site of the meth lab uninhabitable. Cleaning up just one meth lab costs between $2000 and $4000, and requires specialized cleaning crews.

HOW METHAMPHETAMINE WORKS AND ITS EFFECTS

Meth stimulates the neurons to release high amounts of dopamine, serotonin, and norepinephrine into the synaptic gap, and decrease reuptake ability. Meth results in sensations of euphoria and a "rush" feeling, lowered inhibitions, feelings of invincibility, increased wakefulness, heightened sexual experiences, increased energy, and hyperactivity. Metabolism of meth is very slow–the drug staying in the body for a long period of time, its effects lasting much longer than other stimulants, upwards to 24 to 36 hours. When other stimulants, such as cocaine, have very short periods of effect, meth's long lasting effects are a significant factor for its use. Combine this with its low cost–about $20 for a hit, ease, and low expense to make, and high accessibility, makes meth a highly dangerous adversary for society to deal with, and stop the growing epidemic.

Other short-term effects of meth include increased attention, decreased fatigue, decreased appetite, increased respiratory rate, chest pains, dangerously high body temperature, and convulsions. The meth abuser can remain awake for days, and as the high wears off, or as the individual begins to crash, the individual enters the *tweaking* stage. During the tweaking stage, the individual becomes irritable, and is prone to violence, delusions, and paranoia. While individuals are in this stage, they often are unpredictable, and can become physically violent over seemingly minor events. Meth abusers often try to counter the effects of the crash with other drugs, such as cocaine or heroin.

Long-term effects include:

◊   Anxiety and anxiousness,
◊   changes to the brain and central nervous system,
◊   damage to the heart or other major organs,
◊   tremors or uncontrolled motor activities,
◊   physical deterioration of the body,
◊   severe weight loss,
◊   sores and rashes known as *meth mites,*
◊   deterioration of the teeth and gums.

Cognitive impairments and changes in the brain also occur, which result in symptoms similar to those of Parkinson's disease, and neurotoxicity and neurodegeneration.

People also experience psychological problems:

◊   Hallucinations,
◊   mood disturbances,
◊   homicidal or suicidal thinking,
◊   violent and/or paranoid behavior, and
◊   amphetamine psychosis.

Psychological effects will be discussed later in this chapter.

Meth, as well as other stimulants, also changes the body's core temperature. Individuals experiencing hypothermia at higher than normal body temperatures and hyperthermia at lower than normal temperatures. Both conditions can result in their own serious conditions. Hyperthermia can further exacerbate neurophysiologic deficits that individuals already experience due to methamphetamine. Children born of meth-addicted women can have developmental conditions such as mental retardation, hyperactivity, premature birth, learning disorders, and aggression.

RISK FACTORS FOR USE

Investigators report many risk factors for meth addiction. Haney[14] reported that impulse control is a significant precursor, and is intensified with meth use. The prefrontal cortex, which is involved in judgment and decision-making, may be already inhibited prior to drug use, and further inhibited with addiction. Furthermore, the amygdala (critical component in emotional regulation and addiction), and the ventral tegmental area (the VTA, which is part of the Reward Center of the brain) may not function appropriately prior to meth use, and are significantly more affected by chronic use. Chronic meth use results in long-lasting affects in dopamine levels and metabolic activity in the frontal cortex that persist for months after use. Such alterations affect decision-making and judgment for months, but do improve the longer an individual remains sober.

Other risk factors for meth use include negative association with education; ethnic background (Caucasian and Hispanic youth are more likely to use meth), positive association with opiate use and family use of meth, and a history of violence.[33]

EFFECTS OF METHAMPHETAMINE

Methamphetamine is not a victimless crime, it affecting many innocent people. The effects can be seen throughout Cumberland County, TN. The local jail is overcrowded, and the jail gymnasium and library are used for sleeping quarters for inmates, most held on charges related to methamphetamine. The county spends $300,000 a year on medical costs at the jail, largely because of meth abuse. Area hospitals have seen a rise in ER admissions, and doctors and staff are trained on how to handle meth abusers. Ambulance drivers and firefighters responding to scenes where methamphetamine is produced now face the dangers of toxic and volatile chemicals.

Children are significantly affected. Known as "meth orphans," hundreds of children have been found neglected and living in squalor — parents too consumed by addiction to care for their children. Taken from their parents and placed in foster care, many of these children face physical, developmental, and emotional problems. County schools are bracing for a wave of meth-affected children soon to enter kindergarten. "The symptoms that we've been told about so far are hyperactivity, and impulsivity and possible learning problems," said Dr. Pattie Ragsdale, director of schools. Despite knowing how methamphetamine affects individuals and families, the cycle of addiction is continuing with the children, with reports that junior and high school students are already using the substance.[29]

MDMA/ECSTASY: A CLUB DRUG

The term *club drug* refers to a variety of synthetic substances that have stimulant and/or hallucinogenic effects. Drugs that have both such effects include *MDMA/Ecstasy* (methylenedioxymethamphetamine). While these drugs have existed for almost 100 years, it was not until recently that teens and young adults began using them in clubs or at raves.

MDMA or ecstasy is chemically similar to methamphetamine and mescaline (a hallucinogen). Since the 1980s it has been used recreationally, most often used in the club and rave scenes where people often party for days at a time without sleep. Ecstasy produces a stimulating effect, allowing people to dance for long periods of time, and have intense tactile sensations. One ecstasy user explains "It was as though my whole life I had been wearing gloves and for the first time was free to feel the infinite variety of the touch of things. . ."[34]

MDMA was first developed in the early 1900s in Germany, used as the main compound to develop other drugs. Even though the drug never went through formal clinical trials, and did not have FDA approval, US psychiatrists began using MDMA as a psychotherapeutic medication in the 1970s. It was believed that MDMA enhanced communication between client and therapist, and client and spouse, and allowed the client to have more insight into his or her problems. In the early 80s, MDMA found its way to the streets, and began to be abused. In 1985, the US Drug Enforcement Administration (DEA) banned the drug, listing it as Schedule I drugs, a substance with no proven therapeutic value. In 2000, the FDA approved the first clinical trials for MDMA to determine if the drug can be used safely in conjunction with two sessions of ongoing psychotherapy under carefully monitored conditions, to treat post-traumatic stress disorder.

HOW MDMA WORKS AND ITS EFFECTS

MDMA is usually taken orally, by tablet or capsule, and its effects last 3 to 6 hours. Users report intense feelings of pleasure, empathy, happiness, increased sensitivity to music, and emotional openness, along with the stimulating effect. Effects are usually felt within one hour of administration, beginning with tingling and rushes of exhilaration, and building to physical pleasure, euphoria, empathy, and muscle relaxation. Effects come on in waves, building each time, although depression, sleep problems, and anxiety have been reported for days to weeks afterwards.[8]

MDMA has a two-phase effect on the CNS, and wreaks havoc on the neurotransmitter serotonin. Shortly after administration, there is an increase of serotonin, dopamine, and norepinephrine. After use, MDMA does not allow for the reuptake of serotonin in the synaptic gap, and causes a long-term reduction in serotonin. MDMA also does not allow for the release of GABA (the chief inhibitory neurotransmitter) to help regulate the other neurotransmitters.[13]

This disruption of neurotransmitters can result in aggression, anxiety, impulsivity, memory problems, insomnia, and other harmful effects when taken in high doses.[8,13] MDMA can interfere with the body's ability to regulate temperature, sometimes leading to a sharp increase in body temperature (hyperthermia), resulting in liver, kidney, and cardiovascular system failure, and death. MDMA users also risk increases in heart rate and blood pressure, and symptoms such as muscle tension, involuntary teeth clenching, nausea, blurred vision, faintness, and chills or sweating. Psychological effects of MDMA use can include confusion, delusions, hallucinations, depression, sleep disturbances, and drug craving. Additionally, these problems can occur during, as well as days or weeks after, using the drug. Animal studies link MDMA use to long-term damage to serotonin neurons. Primates who were administered MDMA for four days experienced damage to serotonin nerve terminals that was still evident over six years later.

It is difficult to determine the exact effects MDMA has on the body, as it is often taken with other substances such as ketamine, cocaine, metham-phetamine, and dextromethorphan (DXM, a cough suppressant that has PCP-like effects at high doses). Complications or deaths associated with MDMA are often confounded due to other such substances, heat exhaustion, severe dehydration, and hyperthermia. The combination of MDMA with other drugs is highly dangerous, significantly enhancing what are already harmful effects. Furthermore, individuals ingesting MDMA do not know what drugs and chemicals are used in its production. Underground chemists often use cheap and toxic substitutes in production, and even sell other drugs as MDMA.

EXTENT OF USE

An estimated 12.4 million Americans aged 12 or older tried ecstasy at least once in their lifetimes, representing 5% of the U.S. population in that age group.[22] Ecstasy use in 2007 was approximately 2.1 million (0.9% of the population aged 12 or older), and the number of past month ecstasy users was 503,000 (0.2%). Ecstasy use is most popular among young adults. Approximately .3% reported past month ecstasy use among 12–17 year olds; .7% of 18–25 year olds, and 0.1% of those aged 26 or older reported past month use of ecstasy. Survey results from Monitoring the Future[23] indicate that 2.4% of eighth graders, 4.3% of tenth graders, and 6.2% of twelfth graders reported lifetime use of MDMA.

WITHDRAWAL AND AMPHETAMINE PSYCHOSIS

It was not until the 1980s that a plethora of research indicated that heavy use of amphetamines produces dependence. About 90% of users report a significant and highly uncomfortable physiological withdrawal syndrome involving depression, somnolence, and intense hunger.[35]

Withdrawal syndrome can be divided into two main phases. The first nine hours to several days is the "crash" phase. Individuals experience craving, drug seeking behavior, agitation, depression, decreased appetite, concentration problems, and fatigue associated with insomnia.[14,35] During the second stage, there is a normalization of sleep, lower levels of craving, and normalization of mood. Withdrawal is extreme during the first 3-5 days following abstinence, though individuals report symptoms for months afterward.

Amphetamine psychosis is difficult to distinguish from organic psychosis. Symptoms include deep depression, hallucinations, delusions of grandeur or persecution, antisocial behavior, violence, paranoia, hypochondria, hyperactivity, and panic. For years, debates raged whether or not amphetamines caused psychosis, or whether amphetamines triggered psychosis in individuals prone to mental illness. Investigations from the 1970s indicate that amphetamines can cause psychosis in individuals with no family history of mental illness.[31] Clinicians must conduct a thorough assessment of client drug use history, and family history of mental illness before making a diagnosis.

Unfortunately, because there is usually a very gradual development of psychotic symptoms, loved ones associate these symptoms with effects of the substance used, so professionals often do not see clients until they are in advanced psychotic stages. Amphetamine psychosis is not permanent, but can last for months, and even at least one year after abstinence.[35] Chronic users with a history of at least one major episode of amphetamine psychosis have reported repeated reoccurrence of psychosis promptly after relapse, even with administration of only a small dose of the substance.[14]

ONCE IN ADVANCED STAGES OF AMPHETAMINE PSYCHOSIS, CLIENTS CAN BE VERY DIFFICULT TO TREAT DUE TO SYMPTOMS THAT ENHANCE THE RISK OF RELAPSE.[31]

Symptoms	Clinical Challenges
Paranoia	Increased treatment dropout rate
Fatigue	Paranoia
Cognitive Impairment	Increased relapse rate
Anxiety	Reoccurring or ongoing psychosis
Agitation	Craving

There are signs to be watched for that distinguishes amphetamine psychosis from the drug's normal effects. A hallmark characteristic of the beginning stages of amphetamine psychosis is intense curiosity for objects, words, and trying to find meaning in thoughts, or spoken and written words. This leads to a repetitious or stereotyped behavior in which individuals perform repeated movements, become intensely curious about how objects, such as a radio, clock or television work, and take things apart. This is also called "punding" or "hung-up" behavior. Often people perform odd "grooming behavior," compulsive examining of one's self, spending hours in front of a mirror. They may perform repeated compulsive actions. They may develop tactile hallucinations of bugs crawling underneath the skin (*meth mites*), and pick at one's self, often resulting in blemishes and scars. Individuals may repeatedly rub their fingers together, or rub their hand across a leg or arm, or another surface.

People may also become involved in "speed art," where they may simply string beads together for hours, or perform more complicated actions such as taking apart objects; sorting, analyzing, and arranging the pieces in specific patterns. People may also become intensely curious about the actions of others, and how society and the world work. Individuals may become obsessed with finding meaning in the actions of others, search for patterns and hidden messages in written material, and develop highly complicated synopses of patterns they find. There is suspiciousness of one's surroundings that people enjoy during the early stages of psychosis. They take pleasure in this feeling, and in the actual dismantling of things, and the looking for and explaining of hidden meanings. As the disorder progresses, people often develop insight or "eureka experiences." Delusions of grandeur develop. Individuals believe they are able to understand the inner workings of the world, and predict the future.

Feelings of joy do not last forever. As the disorder progresses, an individual moves into the next stage where suspiciousness turns to paranoia, and delusions of persecution develop. Individuals begin to think others are watching and analyzing them. The once pleasurable feelings of suspiciousness turn to agitation, fear, hyperactivity, panic, isolation, and even violence. It is often during this stage when treatment is sought.

TREATMENT

Despite the current epidemic in meth abuse and treatment, approaches to treatment are limited. Therapies such as cognitive behavioral and rational emotive behavior therapy are standard, as are 12-step, self-help groups such as Narcotics or Cocaine Anonymous. These therapies and programs will continue to be the standard for many years to come.

Individuals experiencing serious health conditions or psychosis must be hospitalized. Detoxification in an inpatient facility, or treatment through an out-patient facility is preferred where an individual can be closely monitored for physical health effects, withdrawal symptoms, craving, drug seeking behavior (associating with drug using friends and places), and suicide ideation. Users receive much needed support to stay clean, and begin to receive therapy. There is an ongoing debate whether in-patient or outpatient treatment is better.

In-patient treatment is highly beneficial because of the constant monitoring individuals receive, and the level of support. On the other hand, they are in a well-controlled environment that is much different from the outside world. They are kept active, are away from the stresses of life, and they are separated from drugs and triggers to use drugs.

Outpatient treatment is beneficial for the amount of family support one can receive, and earlier learning of how to deal with reality, stress, and triggers. Yet clinicians are limited in the amount of monitoring they can do, and the level of support they can provide. Individuals may have to rely much more heavily on themselves for relapse prevention.

Pharmacological treatment in the management of cravings and withdrawal is in its infancy. Benzodiazepines, antipsychotics, and antidepressants are currently used with limited effectiveness. A newer antidepressant, Mirtzpine, appears to be more effective than other medications, is safer to take, is well tolerated with limited side effects, decreases withdrawal symptoms, and helps in the establishment of normal sleep patterns[20] Other research indicates that the use of non-addictive stimulants may be beneficial.[24] This replacement approach is similar to narcotic treatment, where methadone, a non-addictive narcotic, is used to treat heroin addiction.

Substance abuse and dependence have followed human evolution for thousands of years, and is not going away anytime soon. There is no magic pill to take to cure addiction. Addiction is highly complex, involving the natural workings of the brain for pleasure and reward, genetic makeup, attitude/beliefs towards drugs and life, the environment, and how one was raised. All of this must be taken into consideration when treating drug addiction. What success with addiction treatment comes down to is hope for the future, and being convinced that one has something to stay clean and live for. Individuals who believe they have too much to lose–spouse, children, their profession–are more likely to seek treatment and stay clean than individuals who are homeless, jobless, have no family, and no hope for the future.[13]

REFERENCES

[1]A brief history of methamphetamine. (2008). Retrieved March 20th, 2009 from the Vermont Department of Health web site: http://healthvermont.gov/adap/meth/brief_history.aspx

[2]Anglin, M., Burke, C., Perrochet, B., Stamper, E., & Dawud-Noursi, S. (2000). History of the methamphetamine problem. *Journal of Psychoactive Drugs, 32*(2), 137-41.

[3]Berman, S., O'Neill, J., Fears, S., Bartzokis, G., & London, E. (2008). Abuse of amphetamines and structural abnormalities in the brain. Annals of the New York Academy of Sciences, *1141*(31), 195-208.

[4]Billing, L, Eriksson, M., Jonsson, B., Steneroth, G., & Zetterstrom, R. (1994). The influence of environmental factors on behavioral problems in 8 year old children exposed to amphetamine during fetal life. *Child & Neglect, 18*, 3-9.

[5]Charach, A., & Gajaria, A. (2008). Improving psychostimulant adherence in children with ADHD. *Expert Review of Neurotherapeutics, 8*(10), 1563-71.

[6]Club drugs. (2008). Retrieved May 5th, 2009 from the National Institute on Drug Abuse (NIDA) web site: http://www.nida.nih.gov/pdf/infofacts/ClubDrugs07.pdf

[7]Club drugs facts & figures. (2008). Retrieved May 5th, 2009 from the Office of National Drug Control Policy web site: http://www.whitehousedrugpolicy.gov/drugfact/club/club_drug_ff.html

[8]Ecstasy (MDMA). (2008). Retrieved May 5th, 2009 from the Focus Adolescent Services web site: http://www.focusas.com/Ecstasy.html

[9]Ellinwood, E., Sudilovsky, A., & Nelson, L. (1973). Evolving behavior in the clinical and experimental amphetamine (model) psychosis. *American Journal of Psychiatry, 130*(10), 1088-1094.

[10]Faraone, S., Biederman, J., Morley, C., & Spencer, T. (2008). Effects of stimulants on height and weight: A review of the literature. *Journal of American Academy of Child & Adolescent Psychiatry, 47*(9), 994-1009.

[11]Field, M., & Cox, W. (2008). Attentional bias in addictive behaviors: A review of its development, causes, and consequences. *Drug and Alcohol Dependence, 97*, 1-20.

[12]Grinspoon, L. (1993). Update on cocaine: Parts 1 and 2. *Harvard Mental Health Letter 10, August-September,* 1-4.

[13]Gyongyosi, N., Balogh, B., Kirilly, E., Kitka, T., Kantor, S., & Bagdy, G. (2008). MDMA treatment 6 months earlier attenuates the effects of CP-94,253, a 5-HT1B receptor agonist, on motor control but not sleep inhibition. *Brain Research, 1231*, 34-46.

[14]Haney, M. (2008). Neurobiology of Stimulants. In M. Galanter & H. Kleber (Ed.s), *The American Psychiatric Publishing Textbook of Substance Abuse Treatment* (pp. 143-155). Arlington, VA: American Psychiatric Publishing.

[15]Hall, W., Doran, C., Degenhardt, L., & Shapard, D. (2006). Illicit opiate abuse. In Disease Control Priorities Related to Mental, Neurological, Developmental and Substance Abuse Disorders (pp. 77-100). Geneva: World Health Organization.

[16] Hepis, T., & Krischnan-Sarin, S. (2008). Characterizing adolescent prescription misusers: A population-based study. *Journal of American Academy of Child & Adolescent Psychiatry, 47*(7), 745-754.

[17]Kalechstein, A., Jentsch, J., & Kantak, K. (2008). Stimulant-associated cognitive abnormalities: Mechanisms and impact on reward-related behavior and addiction. *Drug and Alcohol Dependence, 97*, 276-280.

[18]Lerner, M., & Wigal, T. (2008). Long-term safety of stimulant medications used to treat children with ADHD. *Journal of Psychosocial Nursing, 46*(8), 39-48.

[19]McCabe, S., Cranford, J., & West, B. (2008). Trends in prescription drug abuse and dependence, co-occurrence with other substance use disorders and treatment utilization: Results from two national surveys. *Addictive Behaviors, 33*, 1297-1305.

[20]McGregor, C., Srisurapanont, M., Mitchell, A., Wickes, W., & White, J. (2008). Symptoms and sleep patterns during inpatient treatment of methamphetamine withdrawal: A comparison of mirtazapine and modafinil with treatment as usual. *Journal of Substance Abuse Treatment, 35*, 334-342.

[21]Merkin, S. (2009). Selig defends role in dealing with PEDS. Retrieved March 7th, 2009 from: MLB.com

[22]Methamphetamine. (2008). Retrieved March 11th, 2009 from the National Institute on Drug Abuse (NIDA) web site: http://www.nida.nih.gov/InfoFacts/methamphetamine.html

[23]Methamphetamine trends in the United States. (2007). Retrieved March11th, 2009, from the US Department of Justice web site: http://www.ojp.usdoj.gov/ovc/publications/bulletins/children/pg4.html

[24]Moeller, F., Schmitz, J., Herin, D., & Kjome, K. (n.d.). Use of stimulants to treat cocaine and methamphetamine abuse. *Substance Abuse Disorders*, 386-391.

[25]Myles, B., Jarrett, L., Broom, S., Speaker, H., & Sabol, K. (2008). The effects of methamphetamine on core body temperature in the rat - Part 1: Chronic treatment and ambient temperature. *Psychopharmacology, 198*, 301-311.

[26]Nightengale, B. (2009). MLB discloses drug-testing info on stimulants, ADD drugs. Retrieved March 7th, 2009 from the *USA Today* web site: http://www.usatoday.com

[27]Paulus, M., Lovero, K., Wittmann, M., & Leland, D. (2008). Reduced behavioral and neural activation in stimulant users to different error rates during decision making. *Biological Psychiatry, 63*, 1054-1060.

[28]Piran, N., & Robinson, S.R. (2007). The association between disordered eating and substance use and abuse in women: a community based investigation. *Women & Health, 44*, 1-20.

[29]Potter, M. (2004). Meth labs, a toxic threat to rural America. Retrieved on April 21st, from MSNBC web site: http://www.msnbc.msn.com/id/4489307/

[30]Rasmusson, N. (2008). *On Speed: The Many Lives of Amphetamine.* New York, NY: New York University Press.

[31]Rawson, R., & Ling, W. (2008). Clinical management: Methamphetamine. In M. Galanter & H. Kleber (Ed.s), *The American Psychiatric Publishing Textbook of Substance Abuse Treatment* (pp. 169-179). Arlington, VA: American Psychiatric Publishing.

[32]Rodvelt, K., Kracke, G., Schachtman, T., & Miller, D. (2008). Ketamine induces hyperactivity in rats and hypersensitivity to nicotine in rat striatal slices. *Pharmacology, Biochemistry, and Behavior, 91*, 71-76.

[33]Russell, K., Dryden, D., Liang, Y., Friesen, C., O'Gorman, K., Durec, T., et al. (2008). Risk factors for methamphetamine use in youth: A systematic review. *BMC Pediatrics, 8*(48), 1-10.

[34]Saunders, N., & Doblin, R. (1996). Ecstasy: Dance, Trance, and Transformation. Quick American Archives: San Francisco, CA.

[35]Schuckit, M. (2006). Stimulants: Amphetamines and Cocaine. In *Drug and Alcohol Abuse* (6th ed., pp. 137-163). New York, NY: Springer Science + Business Media.

[36]Singer, D. (2009). Students use prescriptions to survive finals. Retrieved from: http://www.duclarion.com

[37]Singh, I. (2008). Beyond polemics: Science and ethics of ADHD. *Neuroscience, 9*, 957-964.

[38]Starr, M.A., Page, E., & Waterhouse, B.D. (2008). MDMA(3,4-Methylenedioxymethamphetamine)-Mediated distortion of somatosensory signal transmission and neurotransmitter efflux in the ventral posterior medial thalamus. *The Journal of Pharmacology and Experimental Therapeutics, 327*, 20-31.

[39]Stein, M. (2008). Treating adult ADHD with stimulants. *CNS Spectrums, 13*(9), 8-11.

[40]Towbin, K. (2008). Paying attention to stimulants: Height, weight, and cardiovascular monitoring in clinical practice. *Journal of American Academy of Child & Adolescent Psychiatry, 47*(7), 977-980.

Chapter Nine

HALLUCINOGENS AND DISSOCIATIVE DRUGS

BY **JOSEPH F. STANO**
SPRINGFIELD COLLEGE

KATHERINE E. STANO
ARGOSY UNIVERSITY

CAITLIN MCINERY CLEMONS
MASSACHUSETTS REHABILITATION COMMISSION

Chapter Topics

◊ The Nature of Hallucinogens

◊ The Nature of Dissociative Drugs

◊ General Overview of Substances

◊ Dissociative Drugs

◊ Case Studies

PREFATORY NOTE

The majority of the material for this chapter is taken directly from the National Institute on Drug Abuse (NIDA) Research Report Series on Hallucinogens and Dissociative Drugs and the NIDA InfoFacts: Hallucinogens - LSD, Peyote, Psilocybin, and PCP sheet.

THE NATURE OF HALLUCINOGENS

*H*allucinogens are drugs that cause hallucinations - profound disturbances in a person's perceptions of reality. Under the influence of hallucinogens, people see images, hear sounds, and feel sensations that seem real but do not exist. Some hallucinogens also produce rapid, intense emotional swings.

Hallucinogens cause their effects by disrupting the interaction of nerve cells and the neurotransmitter serotonin. Distributed throughout the brain and spinal cord, the serotonin system is involved in the control of behavioral, perceptual, and regulatory systems, including mood, hunger, body temperature, sexual behavior, muscle control, and sensory perception.

Lysergic acid diethylamide (LSD) is the drug most commonly identified with the term "hallucinogen" and the most widely used in this class of drugs. It is considered the typical hallucinogen, and the characteristics of its action and effects apply to other hallucinogens including mescaline, psilocybin, and ibogaine.

THE NATURE OF DISSOCIATIVE DRUGS

Drugs such as phencyclidine (PCP) and ketamine, which were initially developed as general anesthetics for surgery, distort perceptions of sight and sound and produce feelings of detachment - dissociation - from the environment and self. But these mind-altering effects are not hallucinations. PCP and ketamine are therefore more properly known as "dissociative anesthetics." Dextromethorphan, a widely available cough suppressant, when taken in high doses can produce effects similar to those of PCP and ketamine.

The dissociative drugs act by altering distribution of the neurotransmitter glutamate throughout the brain. Glutamate is involved in perception of pain, responses to the environment, and memory. PCP is considered the typical

dissociative drug, and the description of PCP's actions and effects largely applies
to ketamine and dextromethorphan as well.

GENERAL OVERVIEW
OF SUBSTANCES

Hallucinogenic compounds are found in some plants and mushrooms (or their
extracts) have been used – mostly during religious rituals – for centuries. Almost
all hallucinogens contain nitrogen and are classified as alkaloids. Many
hallucinogens have chemical structures similar to those of natural
neurotransmitters, for example, acetylcholine-like, serotonin-like, or
catecholamine-like. While the exact mechanisms by which hallucinogens exert
their effects remain unclear, investigators suggest that these drugs work, at least
partially, by temporarily interfering with neurotransmitter action or by binding to
their receptor sites. Four common types of hallucinogens are described below:

- *LSD* (d-lysergic acid diethylamide) is one of the most potent mood-
  changing chemicals. It was discovered in 1938 and is manufactured
  from lysergic acid, which is found in ergot, a fungus that grows on
  rye and other grains.

- *Peyote* is a small, spineless cactus in which the principal active
  ingredient is mescaline. The plant has been used by natives in
  northern Mexico and the southwestern United States as a part of
  religious ceremonies. Mescaline can also be produced through
  chemical synthesis.

- *Psilocybin* (4-phosphoryloxy-N,N-dimethyltryptamine) is obtained
  from certain types of mushrooms that are indigenous to tropical and
  subtropical regions of South America, Mexico, and the United
  States. These mushrooms typically contain less than 0.5 percent
  psilocybin plus trace amounts of psilocin, another hallucinogenic
  substance.

- *PCP* (phencyclidine) was developed in the 1950s as an intravenous
  anesthetic. Its use has since been discontinued due to adverse
  effects.

REASONS FOR TAKING HALLUCINOGENS
Hallucinogenic drugs have played a role in human life for thousands of years.
Cultures from the tropics to the arctic have used plants to induce states of
detachment from reality and to precipitate "visions" thought to provide mystical
insight. These plants contain chemical compounds, such as mescaline,
psilocybin, and ibogaine, that are structurally similar to serotonin, and they
produce their effects by disrupting normal functioning of the serotonin system.

Historically, hallucinogenic plants were used largely for social and religious ritual, and their availability was limited by the climate and soil conditions they require. After the development of LSD, a synthetic compound that can be manufactured anywhere, abuse of hallucinogens became more widespread, and from the 1960s it increased dramatically. All LSD manufactured in this country is intended for illegal use, since LSD had no accepted medical use in the United States.

A BRIEF HISTORY OF LSD

Chemist Albert Hofmann, working at the Sandoz Corporation pharmaceutical laboratory in Switzerland, first synthesized LSD in 1938. He was conducting research on possible medical applications of various lysergic acid compounds derived from ergot, a fungus that develops on rye grass. Searching for compounds with therapeutic value, Hofmann created more than two dozen ergot-derived synthetic molecules. The 25th was called, in German, Lyserg-Säure-Diäthylamid 25, or LSD-25. Five years after he first created the drug, Hofmann accidentally ingested a small amount and experienced a series of frightening sensory effects:

> *"My surroundings...transformed themselves in more terrifying ways. Everything in the room spun around, and the familiar objects and pieces of furniture assumed grotesque, threatening forms. They were in continuous motion, animated, as if driven by an inner restlessness.*
>
> *...Even worse were the alterations that I perceived in myself, in my inner being. Every exertion of my will, every attempt to put an end to the disintegration of the outer world and the dissolution of my ego, seemed to be wasted effort. A demon had invaded me, had taken possession of my body, mind, and soul."*

PHYSICAL CHARACTERISTICS OF HALLUCINOGENS

LSD is sold in tablets, capsules, and occasionally, liquid form; thus, it is usually taken orally. LSD is often added to absorbent paper, which is then divided into decorated pieces, each equivalent to one dose. The experiences, often referred to as "trips," are long; typically, they end after about 12 hours.

Peyote. The top of the peyote cactus, also referred to as the crown, consists of disc-shaped buttons that are cut from the roots and dried. These buttons are generally chewed or soaked in water to produce an intoxicating liquid. The hallucinogenic dose of mescaline is about 0.3 to 0.5 grams, and its effects last about 12 hours. Because the extract is so bitter, some individuals prefer to prepare a tea by boiling the cacti for several hours.

Psilocybin. Mushrooms containing psilocybin are available fresh or dried and are typically taken orally. Psilocybin and its biologically active form, psilocin, cannot be inactivated by cooking of freezing preparations. Thus, they may also be brewed as a tea or added to other foods to mask their bitter flavor. The effects of psilocybin, which appear within 20 minutes of ingestion, last approximately six hours.

PCP is a white crystalline powder that is readily soluble in water or alcohol. It has a distinctive bitter chemical taste. PCP can be mixed easily with dyes and is often sold on the illicit drug market in a variety of tablet, capsule, and colored powder forms that that normally snorted, smoked, or orally ingested. For smoking, PCP is often applies to a leafy material such as mint, parsley, oregano, or marijuana. Depending upon how much and by what route PCP is taken, its effects can last approximately 4-6 hours.

LSD's Effects as an Example of an Hallucinogen

The precise mechanism by which LSD alters perceptions is still unclear. Evidence from laboratory investigations is suggestive of the fact that LSD, like hallucinogenic plants, acts on certain groups of serotonin receptors designated the 5-HT_2 receptors, and that its effects are most prominent in two brain region. The first is the cerebral cortex, an area involved in mood, cognition, and perception; the other is the locus ceruleus, this area receives sensory signals from all areas of the body and it has been described as the brain's "novelty detector" for important external stimuli.

LSD's effects typically begin within 30 to 90 minutes of ingestion and may last as long as 12 hours. Users refer to LSD and other hallucinogenic experiences as "trips" and to the acute adverse experiences as "bad trips." Although most LSD trips include both pleasant and unpleasant aspects, the drug's effects are unpredictable and may vary with the amount ingested and the user's personality, mood, expectations, and surroundings.

Users of LSD may experience some physiological effects, such as increased blood pressure and heart rate, dizziness, loss of appetite, dry mouth, sweating, nausea, numbness, and tremors; but the drug's major effects are emotional and sensory. The user's emotions may shift rapidly through a range from fear to euphoria, with transitions do rapid that the user may seem to experience several emotions simultaneously.

LSD also has dramatic effects on the senses. Colors, smells, sounds, and other sensations, seem highly intensified. In some cases, sensory perceptions may blend in a phenomenon known as synesthesia, in which a person seems to hear or feel colors and see sounds.

Hallucinations distort or transform shapes and movements, and they may give rise to a perception that time is moving very slowly or that the user's body is changing shape. On some trips, users experience sensations that are enjoyable and mentally stimulating and that produce a sense of heightened understanding. Bad trips, however, include terrifying thoughts and nightmarish feelings of anxiety and despair that include fears of insanity, death, or losing control.

LSD users quickly develop a high degree of tolerance for the drug's effects. After repeated use, they need increasingly larger doses to produce similar effects. LSD use also produces tolerance for other hallucinogenic drugs such as psilocybin and mescaline, but not drugs such as marijuana and amphetamines, and PCP, which do not act directly on the serotonin receptors affected by LSD. Tolerance for LSD is short-lived – it is lost if the user stops taking the drug for several days. There is no evidence that LSD produces physical withdrawal symptoms when chronic use is stopped.

Two long-term effects – persistent psychosis and hallucinogen persisting perception disorder (HPPD), more commonly referred to as "flashbacks" – have been associated with use of LSD. The causes of these effects, which in some users occur after a single experience with the drug, are not known.

Psychosis. The effects of LSD can be described as drug-induced psychosis – distortion or disorganization of a person's capacity to recognize reality, think rationally, or communicate with others. Some LSD users experience devastating psychological effects that persist after the trip has ended, producing a long-lasting psychotic-like state. LSD-induced persistent psychosis may include dramatic mood swings from mania to profound depression, vivid visual disturbances, and hallucinations. These effects may last for years and can affect people who have no history or other symptoms of psychological disorder.

Hallucinogen Persisting Perception Disorder. Some former LSD users report experiences known colloquially as "flashbacks" and called "HPPD" by physicians. These episodes are spontaneous, repeated, sometimes continuous recurrences of some of the sensory distortions originally produced by LSD. The experience may include hallucinations, but it most commonly consists of visual disturbances such as seeing false motion on the edges of the field of vision, bright or colored flashes, and halos or trails attached to moving objects. This condition is typically persistent and in some cases remains unchanged for years after individuals have stopped using the drug.

Because HPPD symptoms may be mistaken for those of other neurological disorders such as stroke or brain tumors, these individuals may consult a variety of clinicians before the disorder is accurately diagnosed. There is no established treatment for HPPD, although some antidepressant drugs may reduce the symptoms. Psychotherapy may help patients adjust to the confusion associated with visual distraction and to minimize the fear, expressed by some, that they are experiencing brain damage or psychiatric disorder.

DISSOCIATIVE DRUGS

PCP's FORM AND EFFECTS

PCP, developed in the 1950s as an intravenous surgical anesthetic, is classified as a dissociative anesthetic. It has sedative and anesthetic effects; they are trance-like, and patients experience a feeling of being "out of body" and detached from their environment. PCP was used in veterinary medicine but was never approved for human use because of problems that arose during clinical studies, including delirium and extreme agitation experienced by patients emerging from anesthesia.

During the 1960s, PCP in pill form became widely abused, but the surge in illicit use receded rapidly as users became dissatisfied with the long delay between taking the drug and feeling its effects, and with the unpredictable and often violent behavior associated with its use. Powdered PCP – known as "ozone," "rocket fuel," "love boat," "hog," "embalming fluid," or "superweed" – appeared in the 1970s. in powdered form, the drug is sprinkled on marijuana, tobacco, or parsley then smoked, and the onset of effects is rapid. Users sometimes ingest PCP by snorting the powder or by swallowing it in tablet form. Normally a white crystalline form, PCP is sometimes colored with water-soluble or alcohol-soluble dyes.

When snorted or smoked, PCP rapidly passes to the brain to disrupt the functioning of sites known as NMDA (N-methyl-D-aspartate) receptor complexes, which are receptors for the neurotransmitter glutamate. Glutamate receptors play a major role in the perception of pain, in cognition – including learning and memory – and in emotion. In the brain, PCP also alters the actions of dopamine, a neurotransmitter responsible for the euphoria and "rush" associated with many abused drugs.

At low PCP doses (5 mg or less), physical effects include shallow, rapid breathing, increased blood pressure and heart rate, and elevated temperature. Doses of 10 mg or more cause dangerous changes in blood pressure, heart rate, and respiration, often accompanied by nausea, blurred vision, dizziness, and decreased awareness of pain. Muscle contractions may cause uncoordinated movements and bizarre postures. When severe, the muscle contractions can result in bone fracture or in kidney damage or failure as a consequence of muscle cells breaking down. Very high doses of PCP can cause convulsions, coma, hyperthermia, and death.

PCP's effects are unpredictable. Typically, they are felt within minutes of ingestion and last for several hours. Some users report feeling the drug's effects for days. One drug-taking episode may produce feelings of detachment from reality, including distortions of space, time, and body image; another may produce hallucinations, panic, and fear. Some users report feelings of invulnerability and exaggerated strength. PCP user may become severely disoriented, violent, or suicidal.

Repeated use of **PCP** can result in addiction, and recent research suggests that repeated or prolonged use of **PCP** can cause withdrawal syndrome when drug use is stopped. Symptoms such as memory loss and depression may persist for as long as a year after a chronic user stops taking **PCP**.

STREET NAMES FOR HALLUCINOGENS
AND DISSOCIATIVE DRUGS

LSD
- ◊ Acid
- ◊ Blotter
- ◊ Blotter acid
- ◊ Dots
- ◊ Microdot
- ◊ Pane
- ◊ Paper acid
- ◊ Sugar
- ◊ Sugar cubes
- ◊ Trip
- ◊ Window glass
- ◊ Window pane
- ◊ Zen

Ketamine
- ◊ Bump
- ◊ Cat Valium
- ◊ Green
- ◊ Honey oil
- ◊ Jet
- ◊ K
- ◊ Purple
- ◊ Special k
- ◊ Specialla coke
- ◊ Super acid
- ◊ Super C
- ◊ Vitamin K

PCP
- ◊ Angel
- ◊ Angel dust
- ◊ Boat
- ◊ Dummy dust
- ◊ Love boat
- ◊ Peace
- ◊ Supergrass
- ◊ Zombie

NATURE AND EFFECTS OF KETAMINE

Ketamine is a dissociative anesthetic developed in 1963 to replace PCP and currently used in human anesthesia and veterinary medicine. Much of the ketamine sold on the street has been diverted from veterinarians' offices. Although it is manufactured as an injectable liquid, in illicit use ketamine is generally evaporated to form a powder that is snorted or compressed into pills.

Ketamine's chemical structure and mechanism of action are similar to those of PCP, and its effects are similar, but ketamine is much less potent than PCP with effects of much shorter duration. Users report sensations ranging from a pleasant feeling of floating to being separated from their bodies. Some ketamine experiences involve a terrifying feeling of almost complete sensory detachment that is likened to a near-death experience. These experiences, similar to a "bad trip" on LSD, are called the "K-hole."

Ketamine is odorless and tasteless, so it can be added to beverages without being detected, and it induces amnesia. Because of these properties, the drug is sometimes given to unsuspecting victims and used in the commission of sexual assaults referred to a "date rape."

NATURE AND EFFECTS OF DEXTROMETHORPHAN

Dextromethorphan (sometimes called "DXM" or "robo") is a cough-suppressing ingredient in a variety of over-the-counter cold and cough medications. Like PCP and ketamine, dextromethorphan is "extra-strength" cough syrup, which typically contains three milligrams of the drug per milliliter of syrup. At the doses recommended for treating coughs (1/6 to 1/3 ounce of medication, containing 15 mg to 30 mg dextromethorphan), the drug is safe and effective. At much higher doses (four or more ounces), dextromethorphan produces dissociative effects similar to those of PCP and ketamine.

The effects vary with dose, and dextromethorphan users describe a set of distinct dose-dependent "plateaus" ranging from a mild stimulant effect with distorted visual perceptions at low (approximately 2-ounce) doses to a sense of complete dissociation from one's body at doses of 10 ounces or more. The effects typically last for six hours. Over-the-counter medications that contain dextromethorphan often contain antihistamine and decongestant ingredients as well, and high doses of these mixtures can seriously increase risks of dextromethorphan abuse.

ABUSE OF HALLUCINOGENS

According to the National Survey on Drug Use and Health (NSDUH), there were approximately 1.1 million persons aged and 12 or older in 2007 who reported using hallucinogens for the first time within the past 12 months.

CASE STUDY

Lola Danek is a 61 year old electrical engineer who has been using a variety of Hallucinogenic drugs since she was an undergraduate college student. She has worked for over 30 years for a major utility and she plans to retire in the next year or two. She is quite financially secure. Her drug of choice continues to be LSD but she also uses Peyote, Psilocybin and mescaline as the opportunity presents itself. Lola has always considered herself to be a "counterculture" type of individual; she was, and continues to be, heavily influenced by the search for "self." She has been twice divorced; both of her former husband's eventually found fault with her drug use. Lola has two grown daughters; Twinkle and Melody. They do not agree with their mother's lifestyle but feel powerless to change her or to even debate her on the subject. She is currently sharing her home with her friend Lois. Lois is of a similar mind with regard to hallucinogen use. Lola considers herself a social drinker and an occasional user of marijuana.

Lola believes that use of hallucinogens leads to much greater insight and that they contribute to a deep degree of spirituality. She had read widely on the subject. She states that human beings have always searched for mystical experiences and many peoples, across time and culture, have used hallucinogens to enhance their mysticism. Lola, and like-minded friends, have travelled extensively across the globe to areas where hallucinogens are still used. From the age of eighteen to the present, Lola states that she has used hallucinogens 1-2 per week. At brief times in her life she reports using every day for 1-2 weeks.

She often feels misunderstood by her family. Her health history is unremarkable but she has been experiencing "flashbacks" on a regular basis. She continues to believe that personal nirvana is within reach. She feels that her journey has been worth all of the travails.

CASE STUDY

Fred Burns is a 20 year old male who is currently living with his parents. He is also currently on $50,000 bail while awaiting trial for rape and associated charges. There are several conditions attached to his bail, including the wearing of an electronic monitoring device. Until the middle of last semester Mr. Burns was a college sophomore at East Southwest State University majoring in Physics. When the charges were brought against him, Mr. Burns was suspended by the University until the case is adjudicated. Upon the resolution of the case, his final status at the university will be determined.

The charges were brought against Mr. Burns by Miss Lucille Marmesan. Miss Marmesan and friends were at an off-campus party at the apartment of Mr. Burns and his roommates. Alcohol was plentiful and marijuana was openly being used. Persons at the party were "hooking up" over the course of the evening. The next day Mr. Burns was arrested by the town of Ashfield detectives; he spent the night in jail and he was arraigned the next day. His parents posted bail and he went to his parents' home. His roommates packed his possessions and subsequently brought them to the house of his parents.

In the early hours of the next morning, after the "party" ended Miss Marmesan was transported back to her dormitory by her friends. She awoke several hours later in pain and with the feeling of being "drugged." Her Residence Director heard the details of her situation and called the campus police. The officers transported Miss Marmesan to the Emergency Room where a physical examination and laboratory testing was performed. The physical examination was indicative of the fact of extensive vaginal bruising and bites marks in various places on her body. The vaginal smear indicated the presence of semen.

Based upon the preliminary physical evidence and the interviewing of Miss Marmesan's friends and the roommates, including Mr. Burns, the city detectives arrested Mr. Burns. Eventual toxicology results were indicative of the fact that alcohol, THC, and Ketamine were present in Miss Marmesan's system. Mr. Burns agreed to DNA testing and the eventual result was a match between the DNA sample and the semen extracted from Miss Marmesan.

Various drugs were found in the apartment, as the result of a search warrant, including Ketamine, a dissociative drug. Mr. Burns' trial is scheduled to begin in approximately eight months. If convicted on all charges he faces 8-15 years in prison.

BIBLIOGRAPHY

Abraham, H. D., Aldridge, A. M., and Gogia, P. The psychopharmacology of hallucinogens. *Neuropsychopharmacology* 14: 285-398, 1996.

Aghajanian, G. K., and Marek, G. J. Serotonin and hallucinogens. *Neuropsychopharmacology* 21: 16S-23S, 1999.

Attema-de Jonge, M. E., Portier, C. B., and Franssen, E. J. Automutilation after consumption of hallucinogenic mushrooms. *Ned. Tijdschr. Geneeskd.* 151(52): 2869-2872, 2007.

Backstrom, J. R., Chang, M. S., Chu, H. Niswender, C. M., and Sanders-Bush, E. Agonist-directed signaling of serotonin 5-HT$_{2c}$ receptors: Differences between serotonin and lysergic acid diethylamide (LSD). *Neuropsychopharmacology* 21: 77S-81S, 1999.

Carroll, M. E. PCP and hallucinogens. *Advances in Alcohol and Substance Abuse* 9(1-2): 167-190, 1990.

Christopherson, A. S. Amphetamine designer drugs: An overview and epidemiology. *Toxicology Letters* 112-113: 127-131, 2000.

Cunningham, N. Hallucinogenic plants of abuse. *Emerg. Med. Australas* 20(2): 167-174, 2008.

Fantegrossi, W. E., Murnane, K. S., and Reissig, C. J. The behavioral pharmacology of hallucinogens. *Biochem Pharmacol* 75(1): 17-33, 2008.

Frankenheim, J., and Lin, G. C. Hallucinogenic Drugs. In: Craighead, W. E., and Nemeroff, C. eds. *Encyclopedia of Psychology and Neuroscience.* New York: John Wiley & Sons, 2002.

Gilmore, H. T. Peyote use during pregnancy. *S D J Med* 54(1): 27-29, 2001.

Halpern, J. H., Sherwood, A. R., Hudson, J. I., Yurgelun-Todd, D., and Pope, H. G., Jr. Psychological and cognitive effects of long-term peyote use among Native Americans. *Biol Psychiatry* 58(8): 624-631, 2005.

Hofmann, A. *LSD: My problem child.* New York: McGraw-Hill, 1980.

Javitt, D. C., and Zukin, S. R. Recent advances in the phencyclidine model of schizophrenia. *American Journal of Psychiatry* 148: 1301-1308, 1991.

Kosten, T, and Owens, S. M. Immunotherapy for the treatment of drug abuse. *Pharmacol Ther* 108(1): 76-85, 2005.

National Institute on Drug Abuse. *NIDS infofacts: Hallucinogens – LSD, peyote, psilocybin, and PCP. http://drugabuse.gov/*infofacts*/hallucinogens.html, Revised 06/09.*

National Institute on Drug Abuse. Research Report Series – *Hallucinogens and Dissociative Drugs.* NIH Publication Number 01-4209, Printed March 2001.

Sanders-Bush, E. Neurochemical Evidence That Hallucinogenic Drugs are 5-HT$_{2c}$ Receptor Agonists: What Next? In: Lin, G.C., and Glennon, R.A., eds. *Hallucinogens: An update. National Institute on Drug Abuse Research Monograph* No. 146. NIH Pub. No. 94-3872. Washington, D.C.: U.S. Government Printing Office, 1994.

Schwartz, R. H., and Smith, D. E. *Clin Pediatr (Phila)* 27(2): 70-73, 1988.

Ungerleider, J.T., and Pechnick, R.N. Hallucinogens. In: Lowenstein, J.H., Ruiz, P., and Millman, R.B. eds. *Substance abuse: A comprehensive textbook,* second edition, Baltimore: Williams & Wilkins, 1992.

Yago, K. B., Pitts, F. N., Burgoyne, R. W., Aniline, O., Yago, L. S., and Pitts, A. F. The urban epidemic of phencyclidine (PCP) use: Clinical and Laboratory evidence from a public psychiatric hospital emergency service. *J Clin Psychiatry* 42: 193-196, 1981.

Chapter Ten

NICOTINE DEPENDENCE:
CLINICAL COMPONENTS

BY **DEBRA HOMA**

DAVID DELAMBO
UNIVERSITY OF WISCONSIN-STOUT

Chapter Topics

CASE STUDY

*A*lan, *a young child from the Midwest, grew up in the 1950s and 1960s, watching all the popular television shows and listening to rock and roll music. Cigarette smoking appeared so appealing in the movies. His favorite movie actors like William Holden, John Wayne, and Lee Marvin smoked constantly on screen. Each portrayed successful characters in the film, with lavish jobs, money, and women. Smoking was associated with all the positive things that life had to offer. Alan's favorite musician, Keith Richards of the Rolling Stones, was not to be seen without his legendary Marlboro cigarette hanging between his lips. Alan also noticed that the older neighborhood adolescents, as well as their family members, smoked. He watched as someone lit the cigarette. It looked so appealing as they inhaled the cigarette and exhaled the smoke through the mouth and nostrils. The smell was so pleasant, and people looked so natural and mature. Alan could not understand why smoking was supposed to be bad. His parents were non-smokers and told him not to smoke, but he could not believe there was anything wrong with it–so many people smoked and enjoyed it. Alan kept seeing a neighbor driving down the road and throwing out the cigarette butt from the window. One day, as the car sped by, he picked up a cigarette butt from the road. He rushed to nearby woods and finished smoking the half-used cigarette. That was his first cigarette puff. Alan and his friends began purchasing cigarettes from the Supervalu grocery store vending machine. His friends would take cigarettes from their parents and share these with Alan. At 10 years old, he began inhaling the cigarettes. He had a "head" rush. At first, it was nauseating but it still felt good. The taste and the head rush were so stimulating. Plus, it was cool.*

For the first time, Alan felt both mature and cool. He finally found something that made him very similar to the grownups and stars he admired. Smoking soon became a social activity. Alan and his friends would get together and smoke. They would smoke in the school bathrooms, next to the school, and in the woods after school. As Alan grew older, he smoked more. After a while, he was smoking three packs of cigarettes a day. As he moved through his 20's and then 30's he noticed his health was deteriorating. His complexion became very pale; he began getting very noticeable wrinkles, losing his teeth from periodontal disease, and breathing became difficult. He lost weight and looked too skinny, weighing only 140 pounds on a 6'1" frame. He felt bad, looked bad, and had a pessimistic outlook. Alan often said to himself, "Today is the last day of smoking." Unfortunately, in the morning, after coughing profusely, the first thing he would do was light a cigarette. Alan noticed that he would cough to the point of not being able to breathe. As he approached his early 50's Alan was diagnosed with Chronic Obstructive Pulmonary Disease (COPD). He had difficulty catching his breath. It seemed that as he breathed in, he could not get enough air, and he had to use an oxygen tank to breathe. He felt hopeless. Still, the thought of quitting the following day gave him some hope that he could change his situation. However, as soon as Alan woke up the next day, he reached for a cigarette. Once that happened, he knew what the remainder of the day would consist of—cigarette after cigarette with many negative thoughts about this unbearable addiction that showed no sign of defeat. One day in late October, he went for his regular doctor visit. This time, the doctor told him that if he kept smoking, he would be dead by spring. Alan continued the ritualistic behavior that controlled every aspect of his life. The following spring, at age 58, Alan died from complications related to cigarette smoking. The glorifying Marlboro Man commercial was not there to save him. He was yet another death statistic related to smoking.

NICOTINE DEPENDENCE

As the above scenario shows, nicotine can be powerfully addictive, compelling people to continue using it despite its many adverse consequences. Nicotine is a psychoactive substance that stimulates the central nervous system and has a direct impact on the brain, creating physiological dependence. Nicotine dependence typically develops as a consequence of using tobacco products, which are derived from the Nicotiana tabacum plant. In the United States, 90% of tobacco use is from cigarettes.[16] Because nicotine is toxic, it can cause death if consumed in excessive amounts.[35]

Symptoms of nicotine dependence are similar to those of other abused drugs, though some research has suggested that withdrawal symptoms may be a more reliable indicator of dependence than tolerance, as non-dependent smokers show signs of pharmacological tolerance.[41] The *Diagnostic and Statistical Manual of Mental Disorders, Text Revision*[1] is one of the most widely used approaches to diagnosing nicotine dependence in clinical settings.[44] The DSM uses the same criteria for all substance dependence, which recognize a combination of symptoms, including those of a physical as well as behavioral/cognitive nature. According to the DSM, individuals can be diagnosed with nicotine dependence if they meet the criteria for at least three of the following within a 12-month period:

- Tolerance;
- withdrawal;

- using the substance more than intended;
- difficulty cutting down or controlling;
- spends considerable time obtaining, using, or recovering from the substance;
- gives up or reduces important activities;
- continues to use substance despite its harmful effects.[1]

An important criticism of the DSM criteria is that recent research suggests that nicotine dependence can occur in less than one year.[8]

Other widely used assessment measures include the Fagerström Test for Nicotine Dependence (FTND), a six- item test that assesses physical dependence,[13] and the Nicotine Dependence Syndrome Scale (NDSS), a 19-item test designed to provide a multidimensional assessment of dependence.[42] DiFranza[8] maintains that only one symptom is needed to diagnose nicotine dependence," the recurrent and periodic compulsion to use tobacco."[p. 381]

NICOTINE DELIVERY MECHANISMS

The two main forms of nicotine ingestion are through burning (i.e., smoked in cigarettes, cigars, or pipes) and by chewing or snorting (smokeless tobacco). Nicotine products include cigarettes, cigars, pipe tobacco, and smokeless tobacco (i.e., moist snuff, powder snuff, and loose-leaf chewing tobacco). The majority of U.S. tobacco users smoke cigarettes, which are highly efficient mechanisms for delivering nicotine to the central nervous system.[16,35] Although cigarettes are associated with the greatest health risks, all tobacco products are likely to cause serious harm to the user.[24] Cigarettes are uniform in diameter and vary in length (e.g., king size and 100s). Popular cigarette brands in the U.S. include Marlboro, Winston, Camel, Lucky Strike, and New Port.[47] Inhalation of each cigarette introduces 1-2 milligrams of nicotine into the smoker's bloodstream, rapidly crossing the blood-brain barrier to stimulate the central nervous system within five to eight seconds.[16,35] In fact, the speed with which nicotine reaches the brain may contribute to the additive properties of cigarette smoking.[40] In general, the smoker will inhale 10 puffs per cigarette within a 5 minute period. Thus, a two-pack a day smoker takes approximately 400 puffs, ingesting as much as 100-200 milligrams of nicotine per day.[35]

Though advertised by cigarette companies as being less harmful, light cigarettes are as dangerous as full flavor cigarettes, and there is no truth to "less" danger with these cigarettes. Light cigarettes have small pinholes on the end of the cigarette butt. These holes act as air vents to dilute the smoke when tested in a laboratory via a smoking machine and provide misleading data about the levels of tar smokers would actually inhale. Because the holes are millimeters next to where smokers hold the cigarette, their fingers cover these pin holes, causing them to inhale more smoke. When considering whether to smoke light and low tar cigarettes, smokers should also be aware of the titration process. That is, smokers will adjust their smoking behavior to obtain the same stable dose of nicotine; long deep inhales with an increase in puffs occur until the desired nicotine dose is present in the system. Thus, light cigarettes with low tar content actually cause the user to smoke more cigarettes and to cover the pinhole air vents on the cigarette butt to increase the dose of nicotine.[30] Some smokers will even cut the filter in half to increase the dosage.[28]

Cigars contain more nicotine than cigarettes, potentially delivering as much nicotine in a single cigar than in a pack of cigarettes. With cigars, nicotine enters the body through absorption in the lining of the mouth or via the lungs if inhaled.[25,29] Most cigars contain a fermented and air-cured tobacco and are wrapped in a tobacco paper. Three sizes of cigars are available in the United States: little cigars (most have a filter and contain about three grams of tobacco), cigarillos (bigger than little cigars, also with approximately three grams of tobacco), and large cigars (typically seven inches long with between five to 20 grams of tobacco).[29]

Smokeless tobacco is inserted between the cheek and gum, chewed, or snorted via the nasal cavity.[55] The main types of smokeless tobacco products in the US include: plug (chewing tobacco compressed into a brick shape), twist (tobacco is braided in strands, which the user places between the cheek and gums), snuff (finely ground tobacco in a dry or moist format; dry snuff is typically snorted via the nose, and moist snuff is placed between the gums and cheek), snus ("spitless" tobacco placed between the cheek and gum), and dissolvable tobacco products (compressed powered tobacco similar to small hard candies that dissolve in the mouth).[27] Users of smokeless tobacco ingest three to four times more nicotine than from a cigarette. Although the nicotine is absorbed more slowly (three to five minutes, compared to less than ten seconds for cigarettes), the nicotine from smokeless tobacco stays in the bloodstream longer, making it as addictive as smoking tobacco.[16,29]

PREVALENCE OF NICOTINE DEPENDENCE

According to the World Health Organization,[63] tobacco was responsible for the deaths of 100 million people in the world in the 20th century and it is predicted that up to one billion people may be killed by tobacco in the 21st century. Although the rate of smoking in the United States has decreased by about half since 1965, it continues to be a significant health issue.[33] According to the National Survey on Drug Use and Health, (NSDUH), almost 71 million Americans ages 12 and older used tobacco in 2008.[54] Of those, almost 60 million persons reported currently smoking cigarettes, representing approximately 24%

of the population; 13.1 million reported smoking cigars, 8.7 million were current users of smokeless tobacco, and 1.9 million smoked pipes. Results of the survey found that the highest rate of tobacco use was among young adults ages 18 to 25 (41% for all tobacco products and 35.7% for cigarettes). Men were more likely than women to be current users of tobacco products (34.5% versus 22.5% for women). They were closer in their reported use of cigarettes, however, with 26% of men and almost 22% of women being current smokers. A national study conducted in 2006 found that almost 58% of surveyed smokers met the diagnostic criteria for nicotine dependence, with an almost equal proportion of males and females.[53]

People with mental illness are more likely to smoke; approximately 90% of individuals with schizophrenia smoke, and the rates of smoking are two to four times higher for individuals with post-traumatic stress disorder (PTSD), bipolar disorder, and major depressive disorder, than the general population.[35] People are more likely to take up smoking during their teenage years, leading to addiction. About 90% of adult smokers report that they began smoking under the age of 18, and research suggests that individuals who begin smoking during adolescence are more likely to become nicotine dependent and find it more difficult to quit.[35,51] Adolescence appears to be a particularly vulnerable time for the initiation of smoking, possibly due to a combination of biological susceptibility,[7] as well as the powerful influence of smoking peers. Research tracking the smoking behavior of teenagers over time indicates that teenagers with networks of smoking friends were more likely to smoke, when followed up six years later.[43] Comparisons of tobacco use among racial/ethnic groups indicate that use is higher among whites and blacks (30.4% and 28.6%, respectively) and lower for Asians and Hispanics.[54] Cigarette use is also associated with education, with lowest rates reported by college graduates and highest by adults without a high school diploma.[54,51] There is also an association between nicotine dependence and socioeconomic status; rates of dependence are higher for people with annual family incomes less than $25,000 and lowest for those with incomes exceeding $75,000.[53]

PHYSIOLOGICAL IMPACT OF NICOTINE

Nicotine stimulates the central nervous system. When nicotine first takes effect, users may experience a "kick" due to stimulation of the adrenal gland, which causes release of epinephrine (adrenaline), resulting in increased blood pressure, respiration, and heart rate.[35] In addition, nicotine curbs the release of insulin from the pancreas, causing smokers to have elevated blood sugar levels (i.e., hyperglycemia).[32] Nicotine also increases metabolism and suppresses appetite. For this reason, when individuals quit smoking, they tend to gain weight; in fact, women usually gain at least 15 pounds after quitting.[15] Physiologically, nicotine results in very rapid adaptation. Even within only a few hours of smoking, the body begins to adjust, probably via the nervous system. Novice smokers will often initially feel dizzy and even nauseated. After the physiological adaptation occurs, however, smokers tend to build up to a more or less stable level of nicotine intake. In contrast to other addictive substances, the level of tolerance does not continue to increase.[16] Nicotine appears to improve mood, but the extent to which it actually does so is likely influenced by the interaction of personality characteristics and situational factors.[20] Smokers indicate that smoking helps them relax and deal with stress.[64] This perception may be more a matter of dampening the withdrawal symptoms, rather than due to having a true calming effect, especially for smokers who are nicotine-dependent.[17,20]

NICOTINE IN THE BRAIN

Nicotine is highly addictive. Compared to other drugs, nicotine seems to have greater likelihood of dependence, as epidemiological studies indicate that up to 32% of people who have ever used tobacco products become nicotine dependent, versus 15% for alcohol and 23% for heroin.[40] Physiological dependence on nicotine is associated with changes in brain tissue and chemistry that appear to be long-standing.[16] Nicotine stimulates release of neurotransmitters in the brain, especially dopamine, that affect mood, arousal, and pleasure.[3] In fact, much of the addictive properties of nicotine occur because nicotine increases the levels of dopamine, activating the reward circuits in the mid-brain areas, and nicotine causes both direct and indirect stimulation of this reward system.[64] Most important is the action of dopamine in the nucleus accumbens, which is the reward pathway involved in other drugs of abuse.[35,64] Nicotine binds to receptors for the neurotransmitter acetylcholine known as nicotinic acetylcholine receptors. Acetylcholine is involved with a variety of functions, including movement, memory, learning, and mental acuity.[16,23] Cigarette smoking has additional reinforcing effects, as it lowers the activity of monoamine oxidase, an enzyme involved in breaking down dopamine, thus increasing the availability of dopamine.[3] Another substance in tobacco, acetylaldehyde, seems to work synergistically with nicotine to enhance its reinforcing impact.[14]

Compared to acetylcholine, nicotine initially tends to lengthen the activation period of the nicotinic acetylcholine receptors. Afterwards, there is a period of desensitization, causing the receptors to become temporarily inactive. Over time, the desensitization of these receptors continues with chronic use of nicotine, setting off a self-perpetuating cycle. As more receptors are desensitized, smokers experience less pleasure, which means that they need to increase their nicotine intake to experience any positive effect. Repeated exposure to nicotine causes an increase in the number of nicotinic acetylcholine receptors, probably due to the brain's attempt to compensate for the receptors that have been desensitized by nicotine. This process of desensitization of receptors and a corresponding increase in the number of nicotinic receptors appears to occur as users develop tolerance to nicotine and also appears to play a key role in withdrawal symptoms. As nicotine wears off, the inactive receptors return to normal, which means more receptors are available, creating a state of heightened excitability that may be associated with craving (e.g., feelings of irritability and jitteriness).[6,19,64] Recent research using brain imaging technology to examine the impact of nicotine on the nicotinic acetylcholine receptors has highlighted their role in smokers' sensations of craving. For example, one study found that when nicotine took up less than 95% of the nicotinic receptor subsets called α4β2, heavy smokers experienced craving. The feelings of craving decreased as more receptors were saturated with nicotine (after smoking two-and-a-half to three cigarettes), and smokers obtained relief from craving when saturation reached 95%.[33] Significantly, the time lag between the last cigarette and withdrawal symptoms diminishes as the smoker develops increased tolerance for nicotine, and this shorter time period is seen even in relapsed smokers who have not smoked in years, suggesting that the process of developing tolerance to nicotine causes permanent changes in the brain.[11]

IMPACT ON HEALTH

Cigarette use is the leading preventable cause of death and disease in the U.S. Smoking cigarettes causes 400,000 deaths per year, one in five deaths in the U.S.[34] Health-related economic costs to the U.S. caused by smoking are staggering and estimated to be almost $158 billion per year.[61] Smoking reduces the lifespan about 13 years for men and 14 and a half years for women. In addition to its long-term impact on health, smoking also lowers quality of life, particularly due to its effect on the respiratory and cardiovascular systems, which causes breathing and circulation difficulties. A majority of smoking-related diseases are caused by substances in tobacco other than nicotine. In fact, tobacco contains over 4000 chemicals, of which 400 are toxins and 69 are known carcinogens, such as cadmium, cyanide, and arsenic.[16] Smoke also contains tar and carbon monoxide, which are harmful to the body. Tar increases the risk of lung cancer, emphysema, and bronchial diseases. Carbon monoxide lowers the blood's ability to transport oxygen and increases risk for cardiovascular disease.[23,34]

Smoking has been demonstrated to harm almost every of organ in the body.[60] In reviewing the accumulating evidence for the connection between smoking and disease, the 2004 Surgeon General's Report[61] identified links to many forms of cancer, including lung, laryngeal, and oral cancer, esophageal cancer, pancreatic cancer, and acute leukemia. Cancer deaths are two times higher in smokers compared to non-smokers, and cigarette smoking is associated with 90% of lung cancer cases. Smoking causes cardiovascular diseases, including atherosclerosis, coronary heart disease, cerebrovascular disease, and aortic aneurysm. Coronary heart disease is two to four times more likely in smokers.[35]

Smoking has been linked to chronic respiratory diseases, such as chronic obstructive pulmonary disease (COPD), as well as acute respiratory diseases such as pneumonia, and 90% of deaths from COPD are caused by smoking cigarettes. It is also implicated in a variety of other conditions, such as dental disease, low bone density, and cataracts. Smoking creates significant risks during pregnancy; nicotine crosses the placenta and causes higher concentrations of nicotine in the fetus than in the mother. Smoking during pregnancy has been linked to decreases in the growth of the fetus and may be associated with learning and behavioral problems.[35]

The most harmful effects of smoking generally take 20 or more years to develop, and smoking lacks the usual warning signs of other drugs, other than coughing or a decrease in lung capacity with exertion. For smokers to be willing to make the effort needed to quit, they must fully appreciate and recognize the long-term harmful consequences of smoking.[16] Optimistic bias may be a significant reason why individuals continue to smoke even when presented with information pertaining to the grave health consequences of cigarette smoking. Current smokers tend to see themselves personally as being at less risk of health complications (e.g., lung cancer) compared to other smokers in general. In addition, they undervalue the personal benefits of quitting smoking.[62] Such beliefs can be addressed through cognitive behavioral approaches in smoking cessation programs.

Premature skin aging is one effect of smoking that can become apparent some years before the serious health problems previously described. Although skin wrinkling is related to aging and sun exposure, current smokers have significantly more facial wrinkles than non-smokers do. This especially holds true for chronic heavy smokers who have been smoking for many years. Skin changes from smoking may become apparent even at young ages. On the surface, adolescent smokers may not notice a difference in skin aging. Instruments such as Daniell's Skin wrinkle grading method[22] can identify microscopic signs of premature facial wrinkling in young current smokers. The impact on their appearance could provide extra incentive to young people to quit smoking by showing them that such damage is already occurring.

PSYCHOSOCIAL IMPLICATIONS OF SMOKING

Due to advancements in identifying the many health risks associated with smoking, individuals who smoke are often stigmatized in society. Stigma is a social construct in which a person is devalued by others based on particular characteristics that mark them as socially deviant.[20] Social norms in relation to friends and family and their disapproval of smoking also have an impact on smoker stigma. In a survey of current and ex-smokers, NIDA[32] identified stigma-related themes toward smokers. For example, they found that a majority of non-smokers would be disinclined to have a relationship with a current smoker, and non-smokers would not hire a smoker to take care of their children. Van Volkom[62] found that non-smokers were less likely to date, marry, cohabitate or have sexual relations with a smoker. In fact, the majority of non-smoking college students did not smoke because of health concerns and viewed cigarette smoking as a disgusting habit. Moreover, cigarette smoking has been related to divorce rates, with smokers being over 50% more likely to divorce than non-smokers.[9] Other studies have found that, following exposure to antismoking ads, non-smokers viewed cigarette smokers as unglamorous and with faulty common sense because of intentionally harming their health by cigarette smoking.[39] Cigarette smoking is viewed as a "choice" by non-smoking coworkers. A negative bias occurs when smokers congregate and smoke away from their workstation. Smoking has been linked to lower performance appraisals by supervisors,[12] as well as to employee absenteeism and increased occupational and industrial accidents.[46]

Falvo[10] reported that respiratory ailments from smoking (e.g., COPD, asthma) could produce very negative reactions from the public. Excessive coughing with production of sputum can be very displeasing in a social situation. The smoker may also experience depression, guilt, and loneliness as a consequence of social exclusion. Symptoms of COPD (e.g., significant weight loss, barrel chest, breathing struggles, coughing, sputum production, wheezing, fatigue, and oxygen tank use) are stigmatizing and create barriers to social acceptance.[18] For the person experiencing stigma, the consequences can be emotionally painful and include loneliness, lower self-esteem, diminished community or social involvement, and isolation.

Negative attitudes toward smoking may be linked to attributions of personal responsibility.[45] A condition (e.g., lung cancer) that is viewed as caused by the individual's behavior (in this case, cigarette smoking) may decrease society's compassion because the individual is deemed responsible for the condition. Others may increase social distance from cigarette smokers because of aesthetic anxiety and existential anxiety. A heavy smoker with COPD may be viewed as aesthetically unappealing with a barrel chest, wheezing breath, and underweight frame attached to an oxygen tank. Existential anxiety may also occur when nonsmokers are reminded of the fragility of their own human condition, and stay away from the impaired individual.

Research suggests that smokers often experience negative feelings about smoking. A study using an electronic diary to gather "real-time" data of smokers' thoughts and feelings throughout the day found that cigarette smokers, on average, tended to have over four negative thoughts per day about their smoking, typically after smoking a cigarette.[21] The prevailing focus of these thoughts was on the immediate consequences of smoking (e.g., shortness of breath, wheezing), rather than on their possible distant consequences, such as lung cancer or dying. Smokers' negative thoughts increased while smoking at work or in another's vehicle, when in the company of family and friends, and when looking for a smoking-designated area. Feelings that provoked the most worry among smokers were related to self-control (i.e., dislike of being a smoker and wondering if they were addicted) as well as health (e.g., smoking symptoms such as wheezing and shortness of breath). These findings suggest that smoking cessation programs that increase smokers' feelings of worry about smoking and its detrimental consequences may be more effective.

NICOTINE ADDICTION
TREATMENT

Nicotine, a central nervous stimulant, is the primary reason individuals use tobacco. Even though many years of research have demonstrated the harmful impact of tobacco, individuals will continue to smoke. Estimates are that 80% of those who smoke would like to quit, and an additional 10% would like to cut down.[16] In addition to the powerful addictive properties of nicotine, other factors that contribute to continued cigarette use include: concerns about gaining weight, rebellion, acting as an adult, perception that smoking is sexual, and rituals associated with smoking, like lighting the cigarette.[17] One of the most important reasons for continued cigarette use, despite the many grave consequences, is avoidance of withdrawal symptoms (i.e., craving).[16,15] Avoidance of cigarette withdrawal symptoms is the motivating drive behind continued use. Withdrawal symptoms include fatigue, sleep disturbances, extensive irritability, nervousness, and severe craving. In order to feel "normal," the smoker will continue using the drug. Although nicotine is a stimulant, some individuals feel that smoking is very relaxing for them. The relaxing feeling, however, is only the withdrawal symptoms being removed.

According to the Surgeon General, tobacco addiction is a chronic disease with the characteristics of relapse and remission.[60] The majority of individuals who try to quit smoking will likely relapse and require subsequent smoking cessation procedures. Most smoking cessation programs last from one to three months.[32] Unfortunately, within 6 months, approximately 75-80% of smokers relapse, and smokers need four or more attempts to quit before they are successful.[3] Research has demonstrated that by lengthening cessation programs beyond the traditional format, 50 percent of smokers may remain in remission one year after quitting.[35]

Quitting smoking reaps immediate health benefits. Within 24 hours of smoking cessation, chances of heart attack decrease. Immediate benefits also include improvements in blood pressure and circulation, lowered carbon monoxide levels, and alleviation of breathing difficulties. Long-term health benefits are significant, as quitting improves the individual's overall longevity and reduces the likelihood of stroke and coronary heart disease. Quitting smoking also has a positive impact on the health of others due to reduced exposure to second-hand smoke, and the ex-smoker will experience improved social acceptance.[15]

The individual reasons smokers want to quit vary considerably. One promising approach to help smokers quit is the stages of change model, which can be used to build upon the smoker's motivation to cease smoking.[15] Within this model, the smoker is guided, using a person-centered approach, through the various change stages. These include the stage of precontemplation (i.e., the smoker does not have the mind set to quit at this point); contemplation (i.e., the smoker is thinking about quitting at this point); preparation (i.e., the smoker is ready for action, that is quitting); and action stages (i.e., the smoker quits smoking on a designated date). This approach can increase the likelihood of smoking cessation because it puts the smoker in control of the process, rather than the treatment provider. A variety of techniques is available to assist treatment providers in guiding the smoker through the stages of change toward the goal of smoking cessation.[5]

Quitting smoking can be an overwhelming process for many. Everett Koop, the former U.S. Surgeon General reported that "The pharmacological and behavioral processes that determine tobacco addiction are similar to those that determine addiction to drugs such as heroin and cocaine."[59,p. 9] Even armed with knowledge of the dangers of smoking, the smoker will continue to "use." For treatment providers, understanding the addiction process is important when working with the smoking client. According to Shaffer,[48] three conditions must be present to diagnose a drug or alcohol addiction: compulsion/craving, loss of control, and continued use despite adverse consequences. All three criteria come into play when individuals are addicted to smoking, as illustrated in the examples below:

◊ *Compulsion/Craving*: the smoker has "tunnel vision" toward locating, securing, and using the addictive chemical. A smoker will be preoccupied thinking about smoking the next cigarette. For example, in the morning, if the smoker is out of cigarettes, all that is imagined is "When will I get my next cigarette?" Securing this cigarette becomes an uncontrollable drive that makes the smoker go to great lengths to satisfy the craving, even traveling miles through a snowstorm to buy a pack of cigarettes.

◊ *Loss of Control*: Addiction causes the user to ingest large amounts of the drug, more than was planned. For example, instead of having the three cigarettes at the bar, the user smokes two packs. Reducing the amount of drug use is not possible. A two-pack-a-day smoker is unable to cut down to a half- pack. The smoker is unable to quit or stop using the drug, lighting up a cigarette first thing in the morning.

◊ *Consequences*: Even when health becomes threatened, the smoker continues using the drug. For example, smokers with COPD may remove the oxygen mask in order to breathe the cigarette into their damaged lungs. Other consequences, such as vocational, social/familial, and legal or financial difficulties may have minimal impact on smoking behavior. The user will light the cigarette at all costs, despite its impact on health, family, or work.

Nicotine addiction involves symptoms of tolerance to and withdrawal from the drug, making it a challenging disease to channel into remission. Successful quitting requires that both smokers and treatment providers understand the nature of relapse, as well as other addiction principles.[49] In particular, the urge or craving to smoke has been identified as the strongest predictor of relapse.[50] The power of both the cigarette craving and the smoker's coping strategies are vital contributors in determining whether the smoker will either relapse or resist the urge to pick up that next cigarette. The treatment team should make clients aware that they have a choice and that the withdrawal symptoms, despite their enormous power, do not force them to smoke. They need to learn how to overcome these withdrawal symptoms and cravings through the use of coping strategies. In addition, they must recognize the power of autonomy and self-efficacy and realize they are the driving force determining their smoking behavior. Novice "ex-smokers" must be aware that if they resume smoking, they are extremely vulnerable to relapse and likely to consume cigarettes at the same pace as prior to quitting. That is, if they previously smoked two packs per day before quitting, this rate of smoking may resume after smoking only one cigarette.[6] Relapse most often occurs within the first few weeks after quitting, and the treatment team should notify smokers of this risk as they begin a smoking cessation program.[56] A smoker's guard should remain strong because smoking behavior may be resumed weeks or months later, long after the task to control their withdrawal symptoms.

Even after an extended period of abstinence from smoking, environmental cues may trigger smoking behavior through the process of Classical Conditioning. Classical Conditioning is a strong form of conditioning in which a stimulus elicits a respondent behavior (i.e., reflex).[26] For example, environmental stimuli may provide behavioral prompts to smoking in a bar that was a previous smoker's gathering place. In this case, the smell of cigarette smoke may cause a physiological arousal in the ex-smoker and create a powerful urge to resume smoking. Continued abstinence requires ex-smokers to recognize the role of environmental stimuli, which may produce strong reactions toward smoking. Due to Classical Conditioning, the sight and smell of smoke in a bar may stimulate a physiological arousal in the ex-smoker long after the nicotine withdrawal symptoms have ceased.

In addition to environmental cues, stress can have a critical impact on smoking behavior. When the "urge" to smoke occurs, some strategy is needed and quickly. Taylor and Katomeri[57] found that a 15-minute brisk walk reduced cigarette craving and withdrawal symptoms and increased the time interval between each cigarette. Since weight gain has been linked to cigarette relapse, a smoking cessation program should incorporate some type of exercise regime coupled with a nutritional component. Such an approach can replace the negative addiction to cigarettes with a positive addiction to exercise.[50] By keeping weight gain in check, the ex-smoker will stay trim and fit while also avoiding relapse.

Effective coping strategies are a key to helping ex-smokers resist the temptation to smoke "just one." Once the cigarette is consumed, the addiction process begins and regular smoking patterns will resume.[7,16] Ex-smokers must develop coping skills to help inhibit the initial craving and to decrease any environmental cues that may occur months after the last cigarette. Coping strategies may be either behavioral (e.g., chewing gum, sitting in nonsmoking sections) or cognitive (e.g., using self-talk such as "I can quit, I will not give in to these dangerous lies.")[50] When trying to quit, the smoker will be bombarded with an array of cognitions and excuses to smoke, such as "I will have just one cigarette; it's the weekend and I deserve a cigarette, one will not hurt." Amazingly, the mind will make up many rationalizations and falsehoods to justify smoking. Effective coping strategies involve either immediate (i.e., escape from high-risk smoking situations) or avoidance techniques. For example, assertively refusing a cigarette during a social interaction is an example of an immediate coping response to a high-risk situation. Likewise, avoiding a bar where smoking and alcohol are present is an anticipatory technique. One approach to addressing coping skills is using a "brainstorming" technique that helps smokers identify strategies they can use in potential relapse or high-risk situations.[37]

O'Connell et al.[37] found that within the first ten days of quitting, smokers most often used the following cognitive and behavioral coping strategies.

Behavioral strategies included:
◊ Stimulus control (e.g., avoid activities associated with smoking, such as drinking alcohol, playing softball, driving with music playing, and going to nightclubs);
◊ Oral (e.g., lick hard-candy, chew gum, keep pencil or toothpick in mouth);
◊ Drink and food (e.g., drink fruit juice, consume a piece of candy or potato chips);
◊ Breathing exercises (e.g., take six deep breaths, pretend to puff a cigarette);
◊ Informal exercise (e.g., leave desk and walk up and down the steps);
◊ Behavioral distraction (e.g., visit on the telephone, become consumed with work).

Common cognitive strategies included:
◊ Cognitive distraction (e.g., think about what needs to be done at work);

◊ Self-encouragement (e.g., perceives self as non-smoker; think "I can quit!");

◊ Psychologically dwell on smoking's negative implications (e.g., thoughts of lung cancer and COPD; think how nice it would be for children to have clean air).

Considering the essential role of coping skills, individuals who are trying to quit should be armed with a variety of coping strategies to avoid relapse when they confront the urge to smoke.[38] These techniques have been shown to lower the smoking urge in a high risk situation, but no one strategy worked best. This is a very personalized situation, as what works well for one smoker may not work for another. Treatment requires having a thorough understanding of the smoker and his or her coping deficits to determine which coping skills training strategies will be most effective. In addition to coping strategies, so called "rescue medications," such as nicotine gum, have been demonstrated to alleviate the urge to smoke. Social support from a partner, smoking cessation group, or a network of friends is another strategy that will help the individual resist cigarettes.[49]

An array of pharmacological approaches is now available in the form of nicotine replacement therapies (NRT) and medications such as bupropian (Zyban), varenicline (Chantix) and clonidine, which may be used in conjunction with behavioral therapies to combat the powerful nicotine addiction process. NRT reduces the withdrawal symptoms and aids in successful smoking cessation programs.[15,16,49] Commonly used NRTs include: Nicotine gum, nicotine transdermal patches, nicotine nasal spray, nicotine lozenges, and nicotine inhalers. In general, a combination of behavioral approaches and NRTs are used in smoking cessation.[4] Smoking cessation outcomes tend to be positive when the user is able to choose the specific NRT product (e.g., nicotine gum). Given that failure to take medication at all and/or using less than the recommended dose (e.g., insufficient amount of NRT) are the chief causes of unsuccessful smoking cessation regimes,[49] active participation of smokers in their own treatment may be critical. Current research suggests that a combination of both pharmacological and non-pharmacological approaches, such as individual and group counseling, are most effective, rather than a single approach.[36,58]

NICOTINE GUM

Fast-acting nicotine gum's strength is 2-4 milligrams and comes in a variety of flavors. Chewing the gum releases nicotine into the mouth's mucous membranes, enabling nicotine levels to peak in the bloodstream within 20 to 30 minutes.[49] Once the gum's flavor is gone, it is parked in the user's upper cheek.[15] When smokers experience withdrawal symptoms, they chew the gum, which relieves craving for approximately 30 minutes. The majority of individuals will chew one to two pieces of gum per hour to dampen withdrawal symptoms. It is recommended to avoid chewing over 20 pieces within a 24-hour period.

Individuals who smoke over one pack a day should begin with a 4-milligram piece of gum within 30 minutes of awakening.[2] Side effects of nicotine gum include mouth sores, nausea, racing heartbeat, hiccups, jaw ache, awkward taste in mouth, and a sore throat. It is also recommended that the user stop using this NRT within six months. Since the gum is safer than smoking, some ex-smokers may choose to use gum if a sudden urge arises or relapse occurs. Another disadvantage is that between 15-20 percent of users become addicted to the gum. Armed with this knowledge, the treatment provider and user can prevent overuse of this nicotine product.

NICOTINE PATCHES

Nicotine transthermal patches release a gradual nicotine dose through the skin over a period of 16 or 24 hours, depending on the type of patch. The user applies the patch to a non-sensitive skin area, avoiding body hair. Advantages of the patch include patient compliance and a constant flow of nicotine from the patch to the user.[16] The 16-hour patch may be ideal for light smokers because nicotine is not released during sleeping hours. For moderate to heavy smokers who require a constant release of nicotine, a 24-hour patch is recommended.[15] A major advantage of the 24-hour patch is that it reduces early morning craving by releasing nicotine during sleep periods. Unfortunately, negative implications of this patch include nightmares, sleep disturbances, and unpleasant dreams. The user should be aware that sleep disturbances typically occur early in the cessation process. Other disadvantages of both patches include skin irritations, dizziness, heartbeat (racing), headache, vomiting, nausea, muscle stiffness, and pain.[2]

NICOTINE NASAL SPRAY

Like cigarettes, nicotine nasal sprays release nicotine to the brain rapidly, addressing cravings almost immediately.[16] This rapid delivery of nicotine can combat withdrawal very effectively. Unfortunately, the user may easily take excessive doses if a strict regime is not followed. Other negative side effects include throat irritation, coughing, sneezing, runny nose, and watery eyes.[15]

NICOTINE LOZENGES

Nicotine lozenges gradually release nicotine into the mouth's mucous membranes and are available in either a two or 4-milligram dose. The lozenge's impact will last between 20-30 minutes following intake. The product should not be used for more than 12 weeks.[15] Possible side effects include sleep disturbances, gas, headache, coughing, hiccups, nausea, and heartburn.[2] Nicotine is delivered in a similar manner as gum, but the lozenge provides more nicotine than the gum at comparable dosage levels.[49]

NICOTINE INHALER

The nicotine inhaler provides the quickest reduction in craving symptoms.[16] This device is similar to a cigarette holder; when the user breathes through it, air is pulled through a nicotine-filled sponge. Nicotine inhalers resemble the cigarette, which can be helpful for some smokers. The user should stay within the recommended dose guidelines of six to 16 nasal spray cartridges per 24-hour period, for up to six months. Common side effects of the inhaler include coughing and irritation of the throat and stomach.[2]

MEDICATIONS

Initially used to treat depression, bupropion has been successful in reducing the urge to smoke and was approved by the FDA for smoking cessation treatment.[15] Bupropion blocks reuptake of dopamine and norepinephrine, and also has some ability to block nicotine receptors. It raises the levels of dopamine and norepinephrine in the brain, mimicking nicotine's effects on those neurotransmitters.[11] Varenicline is another medication used to combat both withdrawal and cravings. Varenicline appears to affect the subtype of the nicotinic receptor discussed earlier ($\alpha4\beta2$); it has less of an impact on these receptors than nicotine, but does help block nicotine's effects. Stimulation of the nicotinic receptor subtypes results in some dopamine release and helps lessen craving and withdrawal symptoms. Although varenicline has been shown to be one of the most effective of the FDA- approved medications, concerns have been raised about its rare but serious side effects. The medication clonidine may also assist with smoking cessation due to helping diminish feelings of anxiety and having a calming effect.[11]

CONCLUSION

Nicotine is a highly addictive psychoactive substance, possibly more addictive than many other drugs of abuse, and it creates physiological dependence. Nicotine dependence usually develops through using tobacco products, especially cigarettes. Similar to other drugs, nicotine's reinforcing properties are associated with activation of the reward pathways of the brain. Recent research suggests that dependence begins to develop rapidly as the brain adapts to nicotine, resulting in physiological changes associated with tolerance and withdrawal that may be permanent. Behavioral conditioning also plays an important role in reinforcing and maintaining smoking behavior. Although smoking has declined by half in the United States, it continues to be a widespread health problem in the U.S. and internationally. According to recent survey data, approximately 71 million Americans currently use tobacco products, and 60 million, almost one quarter of the population, smoke cigarettes. The impact of cigarette smoking on health is staggering, causing about one in five deaths in the U.S. each year and an economic cost to society of almost $158 billion per year. Because of nicotine's powerful addictive properties, most smokers have great difficulty quitting, despite a desire to do so. On average, smokers need to make four or more attempts to quit before they are successful. Smoking cessation programs that use a combination of pharmacological (e.g., nicotine replacement therapy and medications) and non-pharmacological types of treatment, such as group and individual counseling, are more effective than either approach used alone. Smokers can also benefit from learning effective coping strategies to help them resist the temptation to smoke and prevent relapse.

REFERENCES

[1]American Psychiatric Association (2000). *Diagnostic and Statistical Manual of Mental Disorders* (4th ed., text revision). Washington, DC: Author.

[2]Bellenir, K. (2007). *Tobacco Information for teens: Health tips about the hazards of using cigarettes, smokeless tobacco, and other nicotine products.* Detroit, MI: Omnigraphics.

[3]Benowitz, N. L. (2008). Neurobiology of nicotine addiction: Implications for smoking cessation treatment. *American Journal of Medicine, 121,* S3-S10.

[4]Bolinger, C. T. (2000). Practical experiences in smoking reduction and cessation. *Addiction, 95,* 19-24.

[4]Connors, G. J., Donovan, D. M., & DiClemente, C.C. (2001). *Substance abuse treatment and the stages of change: Selecting and planning interventions.* New York, NY: Guildford.

[6]DiFranza, J. R., & Wellman, R. J. (2005). A sensitization-homeostasis model of nicotine craving, withdrawal, and tolerance: Integrating the clinical and basic science literature. *Nicotine & Tobacco Research, 7*(1), 9-26.

[7]DiFranza, J. R. (2008). Hooked from the first cigarette. *Scientific American, 298* (5), 82-87.

[8]DiFranza, J. (2010). A new approach to the diagnosis of tobacco addiction. *Addiction, 105,* 381-382.

[9]Doherty, E. W., & Doherty, W. J. (1998). Smoke gets in your eyes: Cigarette smoking and   Divorce in a national sample of American adults. *Families, Systems, & Health, 16,* 393-400.

[10]Falvo, D. R. (1991). *Medical and Psychosocial Aspects of Chronic Illness and Disability.* Gaithersburg, MD: Aspen.

[11]Gardner, P. D., Tapper, A. R., King, J. A., DiFranza, J. R., & Ziedonis, D. M. (2009, Spring). The neurobiology of nicotine addiction: Clinical and public policy implications. *Journal of Drug Issues.* 417-442.

[12]Gilbert, G. R., Hannan, E. L., & Lowe, K. B. (1998). Is smoking stigma clouding the objectivity of employee performance appraisal? *Public Personnel Management, 27* (3), 285-300.

[13]Heatherton T. F., Kozlowski L. T., Frecker R. C., & Fagerström K. O. (1991). The Fagerström test for nicotine dependence: a revision of the Fagerström Tolerance Questionnaire. *British Journal of Addiction, 86,* 1119-1127.

[14]Henningfield, J. E. & Fant, R. V. (1999). Tobacco use as drug addiction: The scientific foundation. *Nicotine & Tobacco Research, 1,* S31-S35.

[15]Huber, G. L. & Mahajan, V. K. (2008). Successful smoking cessation. *Disease Management and Health Outcomes. 16,* 335-343.

[16]Inaba, D. S., & Cohen, W. E. (2007). *Uppers, downers, and all arounders: Physical and mental effects of psychoactive drugs* (6th ed.). Ashland, OR: CNS.

[17]Jarvis, M. J. (2004). Why people smoke. *British Medical Journal, 328,* 277-279.

[18]Johnson, J. L., Campbell, A. C., Bowers, M., & Nichol, A. M. (2007). Understanding the social consequences of chronic obstructive pulmonary disease: The effects of stigma on gender. *Proceedings of American Thoracic Society, 4,* 680-682.

[19]*Journal of Family Practice* (April, 2006). Critical insights into the nature of nicotine addiction: a summary of key learnings to date. *55*(4), 286-287.

[20]Kalman, D. (2002). The subjective effects of nicotine: Methodological issues, a review of experimental studies, and recommendations for future research. *Nicotine & Tobacco Research, 4,* 25-70.

[20]Kim, S. & Shanahan, J. (2003). Stigmatizing smokers: Public sentiment toward cigarette smoking and its relationship to smoking behaviors. *Journal of Health Communication, 8,* 343-367.

[21]Koblitz, A. R. , Magnan, R. E., McCaul, K. D., O'Neill, H. K., Crosby, R., & Dillard, A. J. (2009). Smokers' thoughts and worries: A study using ecological momentary assessment. *Health Psychology 28*(1), 484-492.

[22]Koh, J. S., Kang, H., Choi, S. W., & Kim, H. O. (2002). Cigarette smoking associated with premature facial wrinkling: Image analysis of facial skin replicas. *International Journal of Dermatology, 41,* 21-27.

[23]Kuhn, C., Swartzwelder, S., & Wilson, W. (2003). *Buzzed: the straight facts about the most used and abused drugs from alcohol to ecstasy.* New York, NY: W.W. Norton.

[24]Levinthal, C. F. (2008). *Drugs, behavior and modern society,* (5th ed.), Boston, MA: Allyn and Bacon.

[25]Martin, T. (2009). *The dangers of cigarette smoking.* Retrieved from http://quitsmoking.about.com/od/cigarspipesand smokeless/a/cigarfacts.htm

[26]Martin, G., & Pear, J. (2007). *Behavior modification: What it is and how to do it.* Upper Saddle River, NJ: Prentice.

[27]Mayo Clinic (2010). *Chewing tobacco: Not a safe alternative to cigarettes.* Retrieved from http://www.mayoclinic.com/health/chewing-tobacco/CA00019

[28]Moxham, J. (2000). Nicotine addiction. *British Medical Journal, 320,* 391-392.

[29]National Cancer Institute (2003). Factsheet. Smokeless tobacco and cancer: Questions and answers. Retrieved from http://www.cancer.gov/cancertopics/factsheet/Tobacco/smokeless

[30]National Cancer Institute (2004). *The truth about light cigarettes: Questions and answers. Fact Sheet.* Office on Smoking and Health at the Centers for Disease Control and Prevention and the NationalCancer Institute. Retrieved from http://www.cancer.gov/cancertopics/factsheet/Tobacco/light-cigarettes

[31]National Cancer Institute (2009). *Cigar smoking and cancer.* Retrieved from http://www.cancer.gov/cancertopics/factsheet/Tobacco/cigars

[32]National Institute on Drug Abuse (2006). *Tobacco Addiction.* NIDA Research Report Series.

[33]National Institute on Drug Abuse (2008a). Imaging studies elucidate neurobiology of cigarette craving. 22(2). *NIDA Notes.* 22(2). Retrieved from http://www.drugabuse.gov/NIDA_notes/NNvol22N2/Imaging.html

[34]National Institute on Drug Abuse (2008b). Cigarettes and other Tobacco Products. *Info Facts.* Retrieved from http://www.nida.nih.gov/pdf/infofacts/Tobacco09.pdf

[35]National Institute on Drug Abuse (2009). Tobacco Addiction. *Research Report Series.* U.S. Department of Health and Human Services. Retrieved from http://www.drugabuse.gov/PDF/TobaccoRRS_v16.pdf.

[36]Niaura, R. (2008). Nonpharmacologic therapy for smoking cessation: characteristics and efficacy of current approaches. *American Journal of Medicine, 121* (4A), S11-S19.

[37]O'Connell, K. A., Gerkovich, M. M., Cook, M. R., Shiffman, S., Hickcox, M., & Kakolewski, K. E. (1998). Coping in real time: Using ecological momentary assessment techniques to assess coping with the urge to smoke. *Research in Nursing and Health, 21,* 487-497.

[38]O'Connell, K. A., Hosein, V. L., Schwartz, J. E., & Leibowitz, R. Q. (2007). How does coping help people resist lapses during smoking cessation? *Health Psychology, 26,* 77-84.

[39]Pechmann, C., & Ratneshwar, S. (1994). The effects of antismoking and cigarette advertising on young adolescents' perceptions of peers who smoke. *Journal of Consumer Research, 21,* 236-251.

[40]Perkins, K. A. (1999). Nicotine self-administration. *Nicotine & Tobacco Research, 1,* S133-S137.

[41]Perkins, K. A. (2002). Chronic tolerance to nicotine in humans and its relationship to tobacco dependence. *Nicotine & Tobacco Research, 4,* 405-422.

[42]Piper, M. E., McCarthy, D. E., & Baker, T. B. (2006). Assessing tobacco dependence: A guide to measure evaluation and selection. *Nicotine & Tobacco Research, 8*(3), 339-351.

[43]Pollard, M. S., Tucker, J. S., Green, H. D., Kennedy, D., & Go, M. (2010). Friendship networks and trajectories of adolescent tobacco use. *Addictive Behaviors, 35,* 678-685.

[44]Rose, J. S., & Dierker, L. C. (2010). DSM-IV nicotine dependence symptom characteristics for recent-onset smokers. *Nicotine & Tobacco Research, 12*(3), 278-286.

[45]Rubin, S. E., & Roessler, R. T. (2008). *Foundations of the Vocational Rehabilitation Process*, (6th Ed.). Austin, TX: Pro-Ed. 4

[46]Ryan, J., Zwerling, C., & Orav, E.J. (1992). Occupational risks associated with cigarette smoking: A prospective study. *American Journal of Public Health, 82*(1), 29-32.

[47]Sargent, J. D., Tickle, J. J., Beach, M. L., Dalton, M. A., Ahrens, M. B., & Heatherton, T. F. (2001). Brand appearances in contemporary cinema films and contribution to global marketing of cigarettes. *Lancet, 357*, 29-32.

[48]Shaffer, H. L. (2001). *What is addiction and does it matter?* Symposium presented to the Department of Psychiatry of the Cambridge Hospital, Boston, MA, March 2.

[49]Shiffmann, S., Kassel, J., Gwalney, C., & McChargus, D. (2005). Relapse prevention for smoking. In G. A. Marlatt & D. M. Donovan (Eds.), *Relapse Prevention: Maintenance Strategies in the Treatment of Addictive Behaviors,* (2 ed., pp. 92-129). New York: The Guilford Press.

[50]Shiffman, S., Paty, J. A., Gwaltney, C. J., & Dang, Q. (2004). Immediate antecedents of cigarette smoking: An analysis of unrestricted smoking patterns. *Journal of Abnormal Psychology, 113*, 166-171.

[51]Sims, T.H. (2009). Technical Report – Tobacco as a substance of abuse. *Pediatrics, 124*(5), 1045-1053.

[52]Stuber, J., Galea, S., & Link, B. G. (2008). Smoking and the emergence of a stigmatized social status, *Social Science & Medicine, 67*, 420-430.

[53]Substance Abuse and Mental Health Services Administration, Office of Applied Studies. (2008). *The NSDUH Report: Nicotine Dependence: 2006.* Rockville, MD.

[54]Substance Abuse and Mental Health Services Administration (2009a). *Results from the 2008 National Survey on Drug Use and Health: National Findings* (Office of Applied Studies, NSDUH Series H-36, HHS Publication No. SMA 09-4434). Rockville, MD.

[55]Substance Abuse and Mental Health Services Administration, Office of Applied Studies (2009b). *The NSDUH Report: Smokeless Tobacco Use, Initiation, and Relationship to Cigarette Smoking: 2002 to 2007.* Rockville, MD.

[56]Swan, G. E., Ward, M. N., Carmelli, D., & Jack. L. M. (1993). Differential rates of relapse in subgroups of male and female smokers. *Journal of Clinical Epidemiology, 46*, 1041-1053.

[57]Taylor, A. & Katomeri, M. (2007). Walking reduces cue-elicited cigarette cravings and withdrawal symptoms, and delays ad libitum smoking. *Nicotine & Tobacco Research, 9*(11), 1183-1190.

[58]U.S. Department of Health and Human Services (2008). *Clinical Practice Guideline. Treating tobacco use and dependence: 2008 update.* Retrieved from http://www.surgeongeneral.gov/tobacco/treating_tobacco_use08.pdf

[59]U.S. Surgeon General (1988). *The health consequences of smoking: Nicotine addiction.* U.S. Department of Health and Human Services. U.S. Government Printing Office: Washington, D.C.

[60]U.S. Surgeon General (2000). *Reducing Tobacco Use: A Report of the Surgeon General.* U.S. Department of Health and Human Services, Centers for Disease Control and Prevention, National Center for Chronic Disease Prevention and Health Promotion, Office on Smoking and Health, 2000. Retrieved from http://www.cdc.gov/tobacco/data_statistics/sgr/2000/complete_report/pdfs/fullreport.pdf

[61]U.S. Surgeon General (2004). *The health consequences of smoking: a report of the Surgeon General.* Department of Health and Human Services, Centers for Disease Control and Prevention, National Center for Chronic Disease Prevention and Health Promotion, Office on Smoking and Health. Retrieved from http://www.cdc.gov/tobacco/data_statistics/sgr/2004/complete_report/index.htm

[62]Van Volkom, M. (2008). Attitudes toward cigarette smoking among college students. *CollegeStudentJournal, 42,* 294-304.

[63]Waltenbaugh, A. W., & Zagummy, M. J. (2004). Optimistic bias and perceived control among smokers. *Journal of Alcohol and Drug Education, 47,* 20-33.

[64]Watkins, S. S., Koob, G. F., & Markou, A. (2000). Neural mechanisms underlying nicotine addiction: acute positive reinforcement and withdrawal. *Nicotine & Tobacco Research, 2,* 19-37.

[65]WHO Report on the Global Tobacco Epidemic, 2008: *The MPOWER package (2008).* Geneva, World Health Organization.

Chapter Eleven

STEROID ABUSE

BY **KATIE SELL**

JAMIE GHIGIARELLI
HOFSTRA UNIVERSITY

Chapter Topics

INTRODUCTION

*A*nabolic steroids are one of the most highly trafficked drugs worldwide. Within the last decade, illicit use of steroids has become one of the most controversial topics in professional sports, but this abuse is not limited to elite athletes.[83,87]

Much of the information portrayed today in the media concerns androgenic (*development of male characteristics*), anabolic (*muscle building*) steroids (AAS).[48,58] However, the practice of abusing androgenic anabolic steroids (AAS) is not a new development. Testosterone (T) was originally identified in the 1930's and subsequently used for medical purposes from the 1940's onward. Steroids used for performance enhancement dates back to the early 1950's, when athletes realized the potential for increased muscularity above and beyond what was attainable naturally. The first documented use of AAS in competitive professional sports was by Russian weightlifters in the 1954 Olympic Games in Vienna.[48] AAS use grew through the 1960's, 70's and 80's as the bodybuilding culture became more popular e.g., competitions, "action man" toys along with the appearance of underground guides to the use of AAS e.g., Daniel Duchaine's *Original Underground Steroid Handbook* of 1981.

It was not until 1975 that detection methods for several AAS became available which enabled the International Olympic Committee (IOC) to place them on the IOC banned substance list. Presently, most AAS are considered an illegal narcotic and are currently listed under schedule III, II or I, depending on severity of complications documented with use, of the Controlled Substances Act, Title II of the *Comprehensive Drug Abuse Prevention and Control Act of 1970*, which prohibits their use as a sports performance aid.[48,52] Most recently steroid abuse has been associated with various professional sport scandals, such as the BALCO investigations and the Mitchell Report revelations.[25,60] These recent events have revolutionized anti-doping practices in sports.

The issue of AAS use and abuse is multifaceted and diverse. The purposes of this chapter are to discuss:

◊   The physiological effects of anabolic steroids on the cardiovascular, neuroendocrine, other vital organ systems;
◊   the more popular steroids used within the last decade;
◊   the psychological dependence and altered mood behaviors associated with AAS abuse;

◊   the various testing methods for AAS detection;
◊   the watchdog agencies which enforce the distribution laws and
     testing penalties;
◊   examples of contemporary scandals surrounding steroid abuse.

PREVALENCE AND CHARACTERISTICS OF AAS USERS

Current research suggests several populations tend to display a higher prevalence of AAS abuse, specifically professional athletes, and adolescents or youth (minor) populations. However, AAS use is also prevalent in the general population among individuals using for non-medical, personal improvement purposes.

Estimates indicate there may be as many as 3 million AAS non-medical users in the United States (US).[63] Typically, these users are noncompetitive body builders or recreational athletes who use AAS for cosmetic purposes or to improve self-esteem.[66] An online survey of 1,955 men based in the US found that the typical AAS user was Caucasian, 30 years of age, highly educated, and not actively participating in organized sports. The typical user in the aforementioned study was not motivated to take AAS for athletic performance, but for reasons related to physical appearance and improvements in skeletal muscle size and strength, that included taking AAS as part of a structured regime i.e., including proper diet and exercise.[16]

Research has estimated 1% of AAS male users will begin in the 9-12 grades (ages 14-19), with this rate increasing after age 20.[66] Among youth populations primary users are young male adolescents most of whom do not engage in organized levels of competition.[46,64] Steroid use increased among 12th graders from 2000-2004 but significantly decreased in 2005,[63] however more recent estimates of AAS use were between 1-5% among high school boys in the US,[46] and approximately the same prevalence in high school students (boys and girls) across Europe.[87] Adolescents use AAS primarily to improve physical attractiveness, enhance their "social appeal," level of peer acceptance, and increase self-security e.g., decrease risk of bullying.[64] Over the last few decades fitness magazines, action movies, and the popular media have portrayed an advanced muscular male physique as the cultural ideal, which may still be one of the largest promoters of AAS use in youth populations.[54] Additionally, AAS use may be validated further by non-medical AAS users, as they do not feel that their actions are unethical or illegal, given that they are not competitive athletes using substances to out-perform opponents.

    In athletes, research has reported relatively higher levels of AAS abuse in individuals participating in strength and power sports such as track/field and weightlifting, as well as competitive bodybuilders.[37] The most common reason why athletes would begin a cycle of steroids is to render the documented effects of increases in muscle size, maximum strength, protein synthesis, and lean body mass[10] especially when coupling steroid use (supraphysiological doses of T) with the proper strength training program.[23,48] Elite athletes may also choose to take steroids to quicken recovery following an injury, as well as improve physical performance in response to peer pressure.

    High salaries, large endorsements, and a pressure to win may further influence competitors to do whatever is necessary to maintain that competitive edge. If this requires the use of performance enhancing substances to gain a minor increase, some feel this is an acceptable gamble even knowing the legal ramifications.[52] A minor improvement in performance at a highly competitive level can have a dramatic impact. For example, the better the athlete performs in the National Football League (NFL) combine, the greater potential one can improve their NFL draft position. The sensitivity of marginal cost of the draft particularly in the first round of the first five picks is dramatic. Research reports a $700,000 drop from each pick when solely analyzing the first five picks of the first round. This potentially could be a difference of $400,000-$800,000 signing bonus when selected by their respective team.[90]

CASE STUDY

THE BALCO (BAY AREA LABORATORY CO-OPERATIVE) SCANDAL
    In 2002, the Bay Area Laboratory Co-operative (BALCO) investigation resulted in steroid abuse allegations against several high profile athletes including Marion Jones (track and field), Jason Giambi (baseball), and Bill Romanowski (football). The BALCO organization began in 1984 as a vitamin store called "Millbrae Holistic", but morphed into BALCO in 1985 as a sport supplement business run by Victor Conte in San Francisco, California. Conte's primary objective was the treatment of mineral deficiencies in athletes using herbal remedies. In the mid-1990's, supplemental steroids were added to the treatment program with the recruitment of Patrick Arnold (chemist)

and *Gregory Anderson (personal trainer) to the company.*

The primary steroid generated and distributed by BALCO was Tetrahydrogestrinone (THG or "The Clear"), but hGH, modafinil, and T cream were also incorporated into the BALCO drug treatment process from the late 1980's to 2002. With growing evidence and concern regarding steroid abuse among athletes, an investigation of BALCO's illegal distribution of banned substances was initiated in 2002. In 2003 the MLB drug tested 1200 major league baseball players. In the same year, the US Anti-Doping Agency (USADA) conducted an independent investigation. The results for 104 of the 1200 players tested came back positive for performance enhancing substances, and the names of these players were given to the federal investigators.[25]

The investigation developed further when Trevor Graham, sprint coach to Marion Jones and Tim Montgomery, anonymously mailed the USADA a syringe of THG. This lead to the development of a detection test for THG. Professional athletes as well as BALCO personnel i.e., distributors, strength and conditioning coaches, were asked to testify in front of a grand jury on a number of issues related to BALCO production and distribution practices, as well as AAS use and abuse on a personal level. Many BALCO personnel refused to support or confirm allegations against former athletes affiliated with BALCO e.g., Anderson refusing to testify against baseball players Barry Bonds and Gary Sheffield, even in front of a federal grand jury, and were subsequently punished. Victor Conte served a four-month prison sentence in 2005 for distributing AAS. The BALCO scandal was documented in a book, "Game of Shadows: Barry Bonds, BALCO, and the Steroids Scandal that Rocked Professional Sports."[25] The BALCO investigations lead the way for important incentives to reduce AAS abuse in professional baseball. Since the BALCO investigations, MLB introduced mandatory drug testing, a 50 game suspension for first offence, a 100 game ban for second offence, and a lifetime ban for a third offence.

CASE STUDY

MITCHELL REPORT

The Mitchell Report, published on December 13, 2007, is officially known as the "Report to the Commissioner of Baseball of an

Independent Investigation into the Illegal Use of Steroids and Other Performance Enhancing Substances by Players in Major League Baseball."[60] *In 2006, the Commissioner of Baseball, Bud Selig appointed former US Senator George J. Mitchell to investigate the history and prevalence of illegal ergogenic aids and the effectiveness of current drug testing practices in Major League Baseball (MBL). This investigation began following the revelations of the BALCO scandal and various accusations from members of the US Congress on the state of the MLB's drug testing policies. Over 700 people – including former and current players, coaches, managers, personal trainers, physicians, athletic trainers, and security personnel – were interviewed during the course of the investigation. Of the 500 contacted, 68 former players agreed to an interview and two were arraigned. Only two active players were interviewed - Toronto Blue Jays designated hitter, Frank Thomas, and Oakland Athletics (formally New York Yankees) first baseman, Jason Giambi. Based on random mandatory drug testing in MLB initiated in 2004, the report concluded that steroid use in MLB since 2002 was still prevalent, at least one player from each MLB team was suspected of involvement in steroid abuse violations. Overall, the Mitchell Report named 89 MLB players suspected of taking banned substances.*

The results of the Mitchell Report generated substantial recommendations for improving current MLB drug testing practices and penalties for violations of drug-related policy. These included the use of an independent drug-testing administrator in the MLB, and the implementation of advanced testing protocols to enhance the accuracy of current drug detection tests administered as part of the MLB Joint Drug Prevention and Treatment Program. Additionally the report called for an increase in educational efforts for players and club personnel e.g., coaches, trainers, managers, on the health and punitive repercussions of steroid abuse.

PHYSIOLOGICAL AND PSYCHOLOGICAL RESPONSES TO STEROID USE AND ABUSE

CARDIOVASCULAR RESPONSES

In the early 1990's the literature on the cardiovascular effects of AAS consisted of mostly case studies.[30] Potential adverse side effects from chronic abuse are increased platelet aggregation (clumping), high blood pressure (hypertension), arterial fibrillation, left ventricular hypertrophy, and arterial structural damage.[26] Many precede more serious cardiac complications such as atherosclerosis, myocardial infarction, thrombosis, and cardiac arrest.[9]

Those who abuse AAS for non-medical use have a higher risk of developing cardiac problems, but direct evidence linking to these pathophysiology conditions is unclear. Furthermore, the "side effects" of AAS are multi-factorial and additional confounding factors i.e., dosage amount and type of steroid being used, make it difficult for researchers to accurately assess the pathophysiology of abuse.[86]

ALTERED CHOLESTEROL PROFILE

One of the more consistent negative cardiovascular responses to AAS abuse is an altered cholesterol and lipid profile.[52] A large meta-analysis conducted by Glazer[34] reported attenuated levels of high-density lipoproteins (HDL) along with concomitant elevated levels of low density lipoproteins (LDL). HDL ("good cholesterol") positively affects the cardiovascular system by binding to cholesterol causing it to become inactive.[91] Reduced HDL levels coupled with increased LDL levels are associated with atherosclerosis and a predisposition for thrombotic plaque leading to coronary vasospasm.[9,39,85,86]

However, not all studies have found significant arterial damage from persistent AAS use. Sader[75] found no significant change in arterial function between bodybuilders using AAS and non-AAS bodybuilders. It remains to be clarified that AAS is not per se detrimental to cardiac function, especially if administered in low doses.

VENTRICULAR HYPERTROPHY

AAS use may also be associated with an increase in left ventricular (LV) size also known as cardiac hypertrophy.[75,86] Resistance training programs stimulate cardiac hypertrophy of the left ventricle wall without steroid use. However, steroid use combined with heavy resistance training will have a magnified effect on abnormal growth of the left ventricle leading to impaired diastolic function and possible abnormal arrhythmias.[86] Research has documented prominent differences in left ventricular mass, interventricular septal thickness, and internal diameter of the left ventricle between steroid users and non-users.[59] Many case studies in athletes who abuse AAS (supraphysiological doses) have documented grossly hypertrophied hearts at autopsy.[61]

NEUROENDOCRINE RESPONSES
Steroids with anabolic-androgenic properties exert their effects by binding
with androgen receptors located throughout the body i.e., reproductive
tissues, skeletal muscle, skin, and brain tissue.[49] While AAS may bind to
these receptors in the cytoplasm, when bound to receptors in the nucleus,
AAS will alter or mediate hormone function. Provided the stimulus is
sufficient this can lead to masculinising and anabolic effects that result in
an increase in muscle size and strength. This trend has been demonstrated
through supraphysiological doses of T across different age groups (young
and old), even in the absence of exercise.[6]

However, the impact of AAS use on the endocrine system, especially
when taken in supraphysiological doses, is not without potential side
effects. The detrimental effects of AAS abuse on the neuroendocrine
system may include testicular atrophy (hypogonadism), sterility or absence
of sperm (azoospermia), and abnormally large breast tissue development
in men (gynecomastra). Gynaecomastia is a paradoxical relationship of the
body that converts T to estrogen, which leads to the development of
mammary tissue.[1] In women, AAS abuse may lead to the development of
male physical characteristics e.g., deepened voice, hirsutism or abnormal
facial hair, decreased breast size, amenorrhea, and abnormal reproductive
tissue developments e.g., clitoral enlargement, ovarian cysts.[23,71] These
effects tend to be more prevalent in tissues more sensitive to the presence
of androgens, such as the prostate. Several early case studies, late 1980's
and early 1990's, suggested that potential side-effects may include prostate
hypertrophy and prostate cancer,[48] but this remains unsubstantiated.

HEPATIC RESPONSES
The relationship between liver function and AAS is widely documented in
the literature.[39,47,67] Hepatic carcinoma, jaundice, and the fatal degenerative
liver condition, petiocis hepatic, are some adverse side effects.[75] Most of
the evidence linking hepatic dysfunction to AAS use is based on elevated
liver enzymes (aminotransferase) indicative of liver function.[67] Alanine
transaminase (ALT) and aspartate transaminase (AST) are specific
enzymes commonly examined. Liver function tests exhibiting high levels
suggest the existence of other medical problems such as hepatitis and
hepatic lesions. Furthermore ALT and AST are shown to be higher in

steroid users as compared to non-users, however potential confounding factors i.e., dose, type, length of use, limit the ability to draw a direct relationship between AAS and these detrimental effects.[67]

The ability of steroids to induce hepatic toxicity however, is possibly questionable.[18] Higher enzymatic activity in the liver does not always result in significant hepatic enlargement.[79] The exercise programs of steroid users may also mask the effect of AAS abuse on hepatic function. Most AAS users partake in high intensity weightlifting programs resulting in large amounts of muscle damage, which would elevate ALT and AST levels. This makes it difficult to assume high liver enzymes are purely the cause of steroid administration[18,67] Additionally, AAS is known as a gateway drug and users may also abuse other substances including alcohol and recreational drugs.[72] Due to this multiple drug (polypharmacy) abuse, it becomes hard to conclude whether the steroid causes the degenerative hepatic effects or could it be from the abuse of other drugs.

ORAL VS. INJECTABLE STEROIDS

Findings linking liver damage with AAS use are seen in orally active agents (*type B modification*). Athletes who abuse orally administered steroids such as oxandrolone and stanozolol, appear to have higher elevations of ALT and AST because type B agents exhibit a higher first pass effect in the liver and are less resistant to hepatic degradation.[76]

Intramuscular injected steroids have a different effect. Type A modification steroids such as testosterone cypionate and enthanate are less likely to produce liver problems potentially due to type A's increased lipid solubility and slow release into the blood stream reducing the potency for hepatic damage.[37,76]

Despite being a class III substance, AAS may still cause hepatoxicity. The underlying reasoning for this is the additional stress the metabolism of steroids places on the liver, especially oral active agents. However, similar to the other side effects such as cardiovascular and neurological, many of the negative effects appear to happen when administering supraphysiological doses.[76] Therefore, it would be incorrect to conclude that the use of AAS has a direct detrimental effect on liver function. One has to consider factors such as dose, type, and length of time on the steroid before any valid assumptions can be made.

PSYCHOLOGICAL EFFECTS

An extensive review by Clark and Henderson[15] documented aggressive and violent behavior with AAS abuse in animal models. In humans, the psychotic effects linked to AAS users are anxiety, depression, hostility, paranoia, and depression.[83] A more serious side effect has been the linking of those who abuse AAS to violent criminal behavior.[45] Pronounced levels of aggression may preclude the proverbial "roid rage" episode, which may further lead to impulsive acts of violence, murder, and even suicide[65,68]

Suicidal tendencies and states of depression among AAS users are an additional concern, specifically in former users. Even though the association of hypomanic behavior and AAS users is inconsistent,[78] reason for speculation is viable. Following discontinuance or pauses in a cycle, AAS users typically have decrements in muscle mass, vascularity, and self esteem,[48] from which they suffer from a prominent male body-image disorder called muscle dsymorphia (*reverse anorexia nervosa*). In this case, individuals become preoccupied with self-image believing that their muscle development is not sufficient. Males with body image concerns will become dependent on AS because of the fear of losing muscle mass when they come off them. It is this concept that triggers a growing anxiety and may lead to AAS dependence.[12]

Although the use of AAS has been linked to aggressive behavior, limitations within the current literature limit the conclusions that can be drawn. Some of the alterations regarding the psychotic state of the subjects were insignificant. In addition, the studies which do report negative findings had subjects with a positive psychiatric history including personality disorder and tenable mood changes.[37,88] Therefore, before a strong correlation can be established, confounding psychosocial factors such as previous psychiatric history, effect size of behavior change, and as with the physiological systems previously described, AAS dosage, have to be considered. In some research trials, the participants were not exposed to a large enough dosage to elicit a significant change.

OTHER POTENTIAL SIDE EFFECTS OF ASS ABUSE
In addition to the side-effects of supraphysiological AAS doses already mentioned, men may experience alopecia, acne, water retention, loss of libido, and nose bleeds.[23,37] Many of these side-effects are highlighted by dermatological symptoms. Cutaneous striae marks (stretch marks), oily skin, acne, and male pattern baldness are commonly noted.[23,66] Supraphysiological doses increase skin surface lipids and cutaneous population of propionibacteria acnes, fundamental causes of acne.[81]

Stretch marks also occur from the rapid gains in body mass and skin's inability to accommodate the rate of stretch. In children, AAS abuse has been associated with premature closing of epiphyseal (growth) plates and subsequent reduction of final adult height.[80]

Other generally underreported effects of chronic AAS abuse include cases of ruptured tendons due to altered collagen structures and is suggested they predispose athletes to injury.[31] This may be due to the rapid strength adaptations that occur in skeletal muscles that are not matched by the slower less vascular tendon structures.[24] Although a large number of reports associate steroid abuse in healthy young athletes with the occurrence of a broad spectrum of (sometimes dramatic) side effects, this may not always reflect a causal relationship with AAS, therefore such reports must be interpreted with caution.[39]

STEROID PROFILES

The current World Anti-Doping Agency (WADA) prohibited substances list [94] contains numerous AAS, hormones, hormone antagonists, diuretics and masking agents. While many prohibited AAS are currently available through illegal commercial means, the following drugs are AAS that have received notable attention in the research arena and the media in recent years.

TESTOSTERONE
Most anabolic steroids will function in a similar manner to T, known as the chief male hormone.[58] T, secreted from the Leydid cells of the testes is a catalyst for numerous anabolic reactions. If administered properly, the skeletal muscle alterations in animal and human models are increased muscle protein synthesis, bone metabolism, increased muscle mass, increased nitrogen retention, and decreased muscle degradation.[23] Each are applicable to competitors because they can lead to faster recovery times between workouts and increases in exercise intensity; especially when coupled with a well executed strength and conditioning program.

Physiologically, T is such a powerful AAS due to the genetic alterations that occur to intracellular protein in target tissue (i.e. skeletal muscle) upon T's arrival.[2] Higher doses of T are associated with a greater increase in anabolic effects, but may be accompanied by a precipitous decrease in cardiovascular function as well as a decrease in HDL levels.[5,82]

In its common form, T will bind to adrenergic receptors of skeletal muscle tissue promoting DNA transcription resulting in fractional protein synthesis and a positive nitrogen balance, which are required for muscle growth.[38] T use is also attractive to the geriatric population or those who have deficient levels (*hypogonadal*) due to a drop in production associated with age.[10,35] Some literature suggests replacement therapy can be prescribed for hypogonadal men to promote anabolism of skeletal muscle as well as to decrease fat mass and enhance sexual function.[11] T's use in muscle wasting diseases and myopathies has been very beneficial to medical science.[50]

T, in its classic form, is relatively ineffective because of its susceptibility to rapid break down by the liver. Therefore, pharmacologists have altered the chemical structure leading to an artificial form of synthesized T designed to have a longer half-life. The objective was for researchers to:

◊ Increase T's rate of activation,
◊ enhance potency,
◊ slower absorption rate,
◊ change the pattern of metabolism,
◊ make it difficult to detect by blood or urine testing,
◊ allow for other viable methods of administration, such as gels, creams, pills, and intramuscular injection.[2,23]

T has multiple forms, which alters the way it is administered, and how T is administered to the body will depend on how the steroid is prepared.[37] The three common classes of T are class 1 (A), II (B), and III (C) modifications. Class 1(A) compounds are typically injected with a slow rate of absorption, higher potency factor, and slower rate of liver metabolism. Class II (B) is administered orally accompanied by a weaker potency factor and reduced hepatic degradation. Class III (C) modifications have been used to create both oral and injectable forms.[38]

Dosages. Dosages ranging from 250-3200 mg/wk can be administered through intramuscular injection, orally (pill form), trans-dermal patch, and in topical gel form.[10,23] In some studies doses may reach up to 3200mg/wk raising blood serum levels for free T 1000 ng/dl.[5] Such supraphysiological doses are typically taken in cycles over a 10-20 week period to induce dramatic strength increases and accelerated gains in muscle hypertrophy.

PROHORMONES

Two "supplements" which received much attention in the late 1990's and early into the recent decade were the popular pro-hormones such as androstenedione (Andro) and dehydroepiandrosterone (DHEA). These substances were over-the-counters substances sold in nutrition stores and supplement companies. Andro received a large amount of notoriety in Mark McGuire and Sammy Sosa's home run record breaking year of 1998. Shortly after, both admitted to taking Andro, but at the time it was a legal substance. Currently MLB has placed both these supplements on their banned list. These are considered a class II (B) modification because of their oral administration. The rationale is that once metabolized, an active form of T would be released, thus raising the overall serum concentrations in the blood.[2] However, research shows a lack of evidence to support the use of Andro and its use has declined sharply since 2001.[46] Andro also tends to show a very weak affinity for androgen receptors on skeletal muscle, which may have contributed to its decreased prevalence.[2]

GROWTH HORMONE

Another competitor in the steroid market used as an ergrogenic aid since the late 1980's, but currently prohibited by WADA (class E substance), is recombinant human growth hormone (rhGH or hGH), also known as somatotropin.[28] Over recent years the multiple arrests of athletes and celebrities possessing hGH, has brought greater attention to hGH as an ergogenic aid and as an increasing problem in professional sports.[19] The use of hGH is typically reported as a problem in sports such as track, swimming, and cycling[42] but more recently its anabolic benefits have enticed strength athletes, sprinters, body builders, and baseball players.[22,56]

Growth hormone is produced naturally in the body from the anterior pituitary gland. Its secretion is regulated by a growth releasing hormone and inhibited by somatostatin.[22,77] The major component of hGH is made up of 191 amino acid residue with a molecular weight of 22 kDa.[77] The complicated task of detecting exogenous hGH is due to its physiochemical and physiological properties, exogenous hGH and endogenous hGH have identical amino acid sequences.[7] Most commercially available preparations cannot be differentiated from pituitary derived hGH, thus once injected it is impossible to distinguish.[7,41]

Although it is difficult to detect the standard predominant form of hGH (22kDa), natural hGH does have approximately 100 different forms currently in circulation, each of which has a subtle variation.[28,] Consequently, when one of these hGH forms is injected, the 22kDa form will be significantly greater than the other circulating forms for a short period, 24-36 hours, making it easier to detect.[77] The pusatile release and short half life, about 20 minutes, of hGH means that it has a tendency to fluctuate within the day and is influenced by a number of different factors such as sleep, exercise, stress, and food intake.[19] It has been reported that acute exhaustive exercise > 70% VO$_{2max}$ accompanied by lactic acid accumulation is optimal intensity for hGH release.[77] Most athletes use hGH for its potency to increase muscle mass, contractile protein synthesis, and decrease fat mass. Supraphysiolgoical doses of hGH report a positive effect on collagen synthesis, which lowers the risk for tendon rupture and faster healing time between workouts.[19,74] hGH may also be helpful to endurance athletes,[42] but this is debatable.4

As with T, hGH is very popular with the geriatric population. hGH is at its highest peak at puberty but secretion will decrease with age, with about a 14% rate per decade.[44] Referred to as the "fountain of youth" drug, hGH replacement therapy takes place particularly in those who have deficient levels due to aging or bone deficiencies.[51] It has been prescribed for both childhood, Turner syndrome, and adult deficiencies and has also been used for those with excessive burns or trauma injuries.[19]

A potential side effect of excessive hGH use is acromegaly, which is characterized by the thickening of the bones in the forehead and jaw, in addition to swelling of the hands and feet.[28] The swelling of the extremities is underscored by hGH's anit-natriuretic effect and fluid retention properties from which long term abusers may suffer from disease such as diabetes mellitus and hypertension. Additionally, hGH abuse is expensive, the cost may range from $3,000 to $4,000 per month with daily doses estimated to run $75-$150 per day.[22,28]

Dosage. Typical dosages of hGH range between 10-25 IU/day three to four times a week (0.56 IU/kg/week to 63 IU/kg/week) with daily dose around 4 IU/day.[22,36] A combination of hGH taken with other anabolic substances has been a reoccurring trend in many power-based sports, and has been combined with erythropoietin, typically considered an endurance drug, to enhance aerobic performance and shorten recovery time.

TETRAHYDROGESTRINONE
Tetrahydrogestrinone (THG) is a highly potent anabolic androgenic steroid banned by the Food and Drug Administration (FDA) in 2003. Patrick Arnold developed THG specifically for the BALCO Company.

THG is considered a designer drug, a revised version of a previously existing or new substance developed to avoid detection under existing drug testing processes. THG was marketed to athletes as an ergogenic aid intended to enhance performance in sports dependent on explosive, high intensity effort, as well as in endurance-based sports to reduce recovery time. Research conducted since the BALCO investigation has shown THG works by promoting the growth of muscle tissue, and consequently muscle strength and hypertrophy.[17] However, in 2004 the FDA categorized THG as a Schedule I controlled substance, a drug that is potentially subject to abuse, has no accepted medical use in the US, and for which safe use is questionable. This and other designer AAS do offer the possibility of tissue-specific effects enhancing the beneficial medical effects of androgens but more research is warranted in using these drugs for medicinal purposes.[1]

When first developed in the mid- 1990's, THG was more potent than the anabolic steroids nandrolone and trenbolone. At the time, THG was undetectable in any standard drug testing procedures e.g., chromatography, mass spectrometry, and was consequently given the nickname, "The Clear". With the BALCO investigation initiated in 2002 and the subsequent development of a detection test via urine analysis by Dr. Don Caitlin in 2003, the prevalence of THG abuse in professional sports has received much attention, both in the public and on a research front.[14,55] The BALCO investigation initiated in 2002 lead to several highly publicized cases of THG abuse, two of the most notable being that of track athletes Marion Jones and Dwain Chambers.

Recent research has highlighted several potential side effects associated with THG abuse. In men, possible side effects include decreased sperm production, testicular atrophy, and infertility,[29,53] as well as hypomania, significant mood swings, when taken in high doses. In women, THG abuse has been shown to interfere with reproductive system function, infertility, ammenorhea and other menstrual cycle dysfunction.[17] Additional side effects may include weight loss and immunosuppression due to the binding affinity displayed by THG in laboratory-based studies.[29] However, these potential side effects are largely based on results drawn from short-term, animal-based studies. Further research is needed to verify these conclusions.

Dosage. At the time of its development, THG was the strongest anabolic steroid available, based on a milligram by milligram comparison. For example, it is ten times more potent than other commercially available prohibited substances, nandrolone and trenbolone.[53] Much information is still unknown about the potential toxicity of THG and the risk for human use given the proprietary nature of many THG production methods currently being used.[17,53] Given the potency of THG, a lower dose is needed relative to T, hGH, and DHEA,[29,53] with anecdotal reports suggesting only a small sample, several drops taken orally, is needed per dose.[20]

TRENBOLONE

Trenbolone (*Finaplix*) is a synthetic anabolic steroid previously used by veterinarians to promote animal husbandry in livestock.[73] Typically administered in the form of trenbolone acetate with doses ranging from 200-1000 mg/wk, it is commonly used by bodybuilders to promote increases in muscle mass and strength.[3] With properties similar to that of T, trenbolone is used as a stacking drug within a standard cycle. Stacking occurs when users combine suprahphysiological dosages of multiple steroids in both oral and injectable form while progressively increasing drug dosage (*pyramiding*) during the cycle.[58] Some of the anabolic effects of trenbolone are increases in nitrogen uptake in skeletal muscle leading to increased protein synthesis, as well as stimulated appetite, reduction in the amount of fat being deposited in the body, and decreased rate of catabolism.[3]

STANOZOLOL

Stanozolol (*Winstrol*) is classified as a controlled III substance in the US. Like trenbolone, stanozolol is also used by veterinarians to promote animal husbandry.[73] Due to its anabolic properties, stanozolol is often abused by athletes and bodybuilders to further increase muscle size and strength.[3] The chemical structure of stanozolol causes it to be one of the more destructive steroids to the body. Commonly administered orally, giving it a type B classification, stanozolol exerts a proliferative effect on liver cells altering liver capacity indicating moderate inflammatory damage.[8] If administered in high doses, stanozolol has also been shown to cause genotoxic damage to human lymphocyte cells.[3] However, stanozolol can also be used in treating muscle wasting diseases and forms of anemia.[32]

Stanozolol established a large amount of notoriety in the 1988 Olympic Games when the IOC stripped the gold medal from Canadian sprinter Ben Sprinter after testing positive in the 100 m sprint event.

Other popular athletes who are allegedly accused of its use are former professional baseball players Barry Bonds, Roger Clemens, and Rafael Palmeiro.

NANDROLONE

Nandrolone (*Deca-Durabolin*) is another common steroid used by athletes and in medical practice. Some of the anabolic effects include increases in lean body mass, bone mineral density, and enhanced weightlifting performance.[40] An injectable derivative of T, nandrolone is approved by the FDA as a treatment for anemia in men and women with chronic renal failure. It has also been used to combat muscle mass loss in HIV-infected patients, treat hepatic disorders, and decrease bone fractures in elderly osteoporotic women. Due to its weak androgenic activity, minimal changes have been reported in voice, body hair, or facial hair (*hirsutism*) in females who received low doses of 50 mg every three weeks. This gives it an attractive appeal to steroid users, particularly females. Nandrolone is also relatively inexpensive. Treatment typically costs approximately $87 per year, compared to hGH which costs approximately $27,500 per year.[39]

CLENBUTEROL

Clenbuterol, classified as a beta (β) adrenergic agonist, has been investigated at doses ranging from one to five mg/kg day in sedentary laboratory and livestock animals.[13] In some animals, it has been shown to be very effective in decreasing protein breakdown and increasing protein synthesis. Due to clenbuterol's stimulation of receptors in the cardiovascular system, it has been proposed as a treatment for horses with symptoms of inflammatory airway diseases.[57]

In humans, clenbuterol is effective in its responsiveness to circulating epinephrine and norepinephrine leading to enhanced fat breakdown (lipolysis). Its popularity among bodybuilders developed because of its purported tissue building and fat reducing benefits. Furthermore, AAS users have been known to substitute clenbuterol after discontinued initial steroid use to lessen further loss of muscle mass and facilitate fat burning. It also has a particular appeal to female athletes because of its reduced androgenic side effects.[58] Recent studies report chronic administration of therapeutic doses having a negative effect on aerobic capacity, cardiac function, and ability to tolerate high-intensity exercise. It has been speculated that one of the underlying mechanisms causing this to occur is an altered cardiac remodeling (*enlarged left ventricle*) that accompany chronic use of a β agonist.[84]

STEROID DETECTION METHODS AND TESTING PROTOCOLS

Anti-doping efforts over the last 50 years have focused on the development of drug testing, education and research, and legislative action. In 1967, the Union Cycliste Internationale put forth a battery of rules concerning illegal drug use for cyclists, but it was not until the 1970's that drug testing for steroids was initiated at the Olympic Games. The International Olympic Committee-Medical Commission (IOC-MC) was charged with two tasks, the first being to develop and distribute a list of banned substances for Olympic competition, and secondly to initiate and implement an accreditation protocol for laboratories testing samples for illegal substances. Initially, the banned substance list contained only drugs for which detection tests had already been developed, but by the mid 1980's, the list had grown to include drugs and doping approaches for which no established analyses was currently available. The IAAF was the first governing body to ban AAS use in 1974, but it was not until the Olympic Games in Montreal (1976) that not just one, but eight professional athletes tested positive.[14] Additional banned substance lists for professionals not under the governance of the IOC, also prominently feature steroid-based substances e.g., World Natural Bodybuilding Federation, NCAA.

The mid 1980's was also accompanied by improvements in the quality and integrity of laboratory accreditation programs, with on-site visits becoming commonplace and the mandatory adoption of standardized testing protocols and procedures. The growth in AAS use through the 1980s prompted the IAAF to expand testing practices further, making "out-of-competition" drug testing mandatory in 1991. This is now standard practice for all professional sports under the World Anti-Doping Code.[14]

WORLD ANTI-DOPING AGENCY (WADA)
The WADA was formed in 1999, financed by the IOC and the governments of participating countries, and was publically endorsed in 2007 at the United Nations Educational, Scientific, and Cultural Organization (UNESCO) Convention. WADA was developed to help

standardize anti-doping rules across national and international
organizations and to provide a central governing body to promote anti-
doping practices e.g., testing, research, and to address doping concerns,
especially AAS, in both the sports and public health domain.[14,86]
WADA is responsible for the accreditation of IOC drug testing
laboratories, 33 current sites worldwide, and updating the World Anti-
Doping Code,[92] adopted by WADA in 2003. The Code functions in
accordance with the World Anti-Doping Program to promote a healthy
and fair sporting environment for all athletes, and standardize the anti-
doping program approach at the national and international level. The
Code is currently adopted by 283 International Federations, 117
governmental-funded organizations, and numerous organizations outside
of the Olympic movement e.g., International Sports Federations for
Athletes with a Disability.[93] WADA also took over from the IOC Medical
Commission in updating the IOC prohibited substances list on a yearly
basis.[94] On the prohibited substance list, AAS fall into the category
prohibited both in and out of competition i.e., at all times, but does
incorporate criteria that allows for AAS use for therapeutic or health
reasons.

STEROID DETECTION METHODS
One of the earliest steroid detection tests focused on the most popular
AAS in the mid 1970's, T and methandrostenolone (Dianabol®). The
immunoassay (IA) approach was able to distinguish exogenous, synthetic
AAS due the difference in chemical structure (methyl group) between T
and Dianabol®, but was limited in its ability to accurately distinguish
synthetic AAS unless the difference in chemical makeup was substantial.
Consequently, early testing implementation efforts e.g., European
Athletics Championships in 1974, consisted of IA with additional, albeit
delayed, testing via gas-chromatography-mass spectrometry (GC-MS).[37]
Further advancements lead to testing processes that separated the
chemicals in a urine sample without using heat e.g., Liquid
chromatrography), thus reducing the number of compounds destroyed
during more aggressive approaches such as GC. These methods can
accurately test for the majority of banned substances, but not for specific
AAS or T-based substances produced naturally by the body e.g., hGH.[14,37]
    Currently, detection methods used to identify exogenous AAS consist
of a series of tests comparing urinary T to urinary epitestosterone, EPIT; a
T-isomer found in the body, but with no physiological function, followed

by a process called isotope ratio mass spectrometry (IRMS). An adverse result is defined as a urine sample with a ratio of T to EPIT ratio greater than four. To overcome the problem of a naturally elevated ratio in drug free athletes, IRMS was introduced in the late 1990's. IRMS, otherwise known as carbon isotope ratio (CIR) testing, involves comparing the relative carbon contents of compound in a urine sample, the CIR will differ for natural and artificial steroids. More recently, a high resolution MS (HRMS) protocol has been developed to detect minute levels of AAS and steroid mixtures in urine, however, this process is costly and not widely available[14]

Several prevalent steroids, such as hGH, present ongoing challenges to WADA detection test experts. Currently, no validated detection test for hGH exists, although researchers are working on several options that involve testing for markers of exogenous hGH use and monitoring immune system activity and alterations that may accompany hGH injection.[70] Tracking bone turnover markers such as osteocalcin may be a viable indirect method to detect exogenous hGH administration.[77] However, accurate detections tests have recently been developed for markers of hGH and other AAS recuperation or enhancement e.g., human chorionic gonadotrophin.

CASE STUDY

MANNY RAMIREZ

In 2009, current Major League Baseball player for the Los Angeles Dodgers, Manny Ramirez, tested positive for human chorionic gonadotrophin (hCG), which in accordance with WADA, is banned by the IOC, NCAA, and MLB. Known as the woman's fertility drug, hCG is reported to be a natural promoter of endogenous T production. Supplementing HCG is a common strategy by users who just came off a T cycle. The reason for this is the body's natural ability to produce T is decreased because of the already elevated levels from prolonged exogenous sources. Once off a cycle the body's natural production must begin again and athletes will attempt to kick start this process with hCG supplementation.[1] Manny received a 50 game suspension in accordance with MBL policy.

TESTING PROTOCOLS

Mandatory testing for AAS and other banned substances may occur in- or out-of-competition for all Olympic athletes and for athletes involved in sports under the purview of WADA e.g., IAAF, NBA, NFL, NBL, ITF, NHL, WNBF, INBF. In an effort to promote fair testing principles, WADA determines the athletes to be tested and the frequency of testing based on several key factors, including, but not limited to: athletes' recent performance, drug abuse history, and their "... vulnerability to the temptation to take performance- enhancing substances."[37] p. 522 Samples of urine and blood are primarily screened and tested further if testing returns positive for abnormal substances e.g., T/E ratio detection followed by CIR testing.[14]

An athlete must urinate into two coded, tamper-proof, clear-glass bottles when urinalysis is conducted for a drug test, one designated "A-Sample" (~70 mL) for primary analysis, and a "B-Sample" (30 mL) for confirmatory analysis. The urine pH (acid-base balance) and specific gravity is also measured at this time. If the A-Sample generates a positive result, the second sample is tested using the same analysis, at which time the athlete is permitted to observe the test procedure with legal representation and an independent analyst also present. Strict guidelines must be adhered to regarding transportation, storage, and duration between collection and analysis, in order to minimize potential degradation of various compounds or compromising the sample in any way, shape, or form. At the NCAA level, athletes may also be called upon during any NCAA competition with or without prior notification to provide a urine sample under the observation of a drug-testing official. All sample collections are monitored and the chain-of-custody documentation must not be broken, otherwise any evidence of improper practice becomes questionable in a court of law.[37]

CASE STUDY

DON CATLIN, MD

Don Catlin, MD has been a prominent figure in promoting anti-doping measures and enhancing modern drug testing practices. Between 1982 and 1997, Catlin served as the Laboratory Director for the UCLA Olympic Analytical Laboratory – the first of its kind in the US. In the 1980s, Catlin developed the urine carbon isotope ratio - CIR test to differentiate between T made naturally by the body or introduced artificially. Catlin is credited with identifying the first three reported designer anabolic steroids used by athletes, norbolethone in 2002, THG in 2003, and madol (DMT) in 2004. Furthermore, he designed the detection test for THG within weeks of identifying its composition, which assisted the federal prosecutors in the BALCO investigation.[14,55]

Since 2004, Catlin and his research team have identified and developed tests to detect several other designer steroids e.g., 6-OXO. Catlin has supervised the drug-testing procedures for the US Olympic Committee, the National Football League, the Major League Baseball's minor league system, and the National Collegiate Athletic Association. Catlin currently serves as a member of the International Olympic Committee Medical Commission, and as President and CEO of Anti-Doping Research, Inc., an organization that promotes anti-doping education and practice.[55]

EDUCATION AND RESEARCH

Ongoing research has shown to be of paramount importance in detecting future potential designer steroids, T derivatives and non-androgenic compounds designed to induce anabolic effects without the detrimental side effects of AAS. Research has suggested that changes in physiological profile such as parameters in urine and blood, can indicate doping and steroid abuse. This approach has been used in several sports e.g., cycling, in the form of a biological passport whereby an athletes' blood or urine markers are measured pre-competition to monitor variations in parameters indicative of AAS abuse.[14] Research has also enhanced the quality and efficiency of analytical equipment for use in drug detection testing. These developments have made drug testing more feasible at events such as the Olympic Games. For example, over 3,500 blood and urine samples were taken for testing during the Beijing Olympic Games in 2008, which reflected an increase of 22% in testing quantity over the 2004 Olympics.[27]

With the development of more accurate testing procedures and an increase in punitive punishments for individuals involved with AAS use or distribution, the governing bodies of many professional sports have implemented educational programs for athletes. However, educational programs and strategies are also growing in prevalence, and are targeting individuals across an increasing number of sports, and levels of involvement with AAS use. A government monitored hotline to answer questions and concerns regarding AAS use has been established in Norway, Denmark, and Holland, following the popularity of the initial incentive in Sweden in the early 1990's.[83] Similar internet-based hotlines have since been implemented in other countries, such as the Resource Exchange Center, REC; http://www.drugfreesport.com/rec/, established in the US for NCAA-based and professional athletes e.g., LPGA, NFL, MLB.

Policy makers and researchers are also pushing for better educational and reporting practices on the part of physicians who encounter individuals displaying the side effects of AAS abuse. Improvements in communicating the detrimental side effects of AAS abuse, as opposed to denying that AAS have any physiological benefit, is an emphasis in educational programs targeting medical professionals. Research has suggested that medical practitioners underreport the side effects of illegal AAS abuse to the relevant authorities.[83]

Multiple educational incentives and interventions targeting pediatric and youth populations have been developed over the last decade. These include the NCAA Drug Prevention Educational Program for collegiate athletes, the *Steroids: Play Safe, Play Fair* program implemented by the American Academy of Pediatrics, the *Youth Anti-doping Education Program* developed by the USADA, and the *Win With Integrity* youth outreach program, an anti-doping incentive through USA Track and Field.

LEGISLATION AND POLICY DEVELOPMENT
The USADA and WADA have been driving forces behind legislation and policy attempting to reduce steroid abuse in amateur and professional athletes, young and old. Many countries worldwide have strengthened laws e.g., 2004 Anabolic Steroid Control Act, 1989 Steroid Trafficking Act, against not only AAS use, but also possession and distribution. These policies are backed by both politicians and specific sport governing bodies. Legislative changes have been significantly influenced by official investigations e.g., BALCO investigation, Mitchell Report, into AAS practice in amateur and professional sports, as well as a growing demand for action to reduce AAS use as an unethical sports performance aid. Legislative and policy modifications have also lead to changes in punitive repercussions and penalties for players and personnel involved, and for sporting bodies and individual organizations for non-compliance with

national and international anti-doping policies such as the Drug Free Sports Act of 2005 and the USATF's "Zero Tolerance" Anti-Doping Action Plan.

CASE STUDY

THE ANABOLIC STEROID CONTROL ACT OF 2004

The Anabolic Steroid Control Act of 2004[21] *became federal law on October 22, 2004. It was an amendment to the Anabolic Steroid Control Act of 1990 and contained several notable changes. These revisions included an increase in the penalties, imposed by the US Sentencing Commission, for the manufacture, distribution, or possession with intent to circulate an AAS within 1,000 feet of a sports facility to twice the maximum imposed for a controlled substance violation elsewhere. THG and Andro were also included in the list of chemical substances defined as AAS for the first time. Moreover, the Attorney General was granted authorization, on the recommendation of the Secretary of Health and Human Services, to deregulate any substance containing an AAS that is unlikely to be abused as a performance enhancing agent. Furthermore, an increase in available grants for educational programs in elementary and secondary-school settings that emphasize the detrimental impact of AAS and the concerns regarding the use of such drugs.*[89]

CONCLUSION

Despite the legal repercussions, precarious health risks, and the potential for leading to other drug use, the prevalence of steroid use worldwide is steadfast.[37] In 2007, the DEA seized 11.4 million dosage units of AAS during Operation Raw Deal, which was the biggest seizure in the US to date. In the first 3 months of 2008, Australian customs officers had a record 300 AAS seizures.[48] Obtaining accurate gages of AAS use is an ongoing challenge due primarily to a lack of reliability in responses to questions on AAS use, the legal ramifications that can potentially come with disclosing AAS use, and the subsequent wariness regarding anonymity.[16]

Many feel that poor methodology regarding AAS detection systems and the previously minimal penalties for AAS possession in the U.S., have promoted the proliferation of AAS users from the domain of the elite athlete and into the general community.[69] Today's society is inundated with a plethora of information about steroid use but unfortunately, much of this is dramatized and often based on non-scientific information. However, research that documents the long-term detrimental side effects of supraphysiological doses of AAS use, populations at risk for AAS abuse, and effective interventions to target the changing AAS use demographic, is currently ongoing. The therapeutic effect that steroids have on treating muscle-wasting diseases and slowing the aging process is another major area of ongoing study.[23,51] While the therapeutic and medicinal uses of AAS are well accepted, the debate over the validity of drug testing and AAS use continues.

REFERENCES

[1]Antonio, J., Kalman, D., Stout, J.R., Greenwood, M., Willoughby, D.S., & Haff, G.D. (2008). Essentials of sports nutrition and supplements. Totowa, NJ: Human Press.

[2]Bahrke, M., & Yesalis, C. (2004). Abuse of anabolic androgenic steroids and related substances in sport and exercise. *Current Opinion in Pharmacology, 4,* 614-620.

[3]Beg, T., Siddique, H., & Afzal, M. (2007). Chromosomal damage induced by androgenic anabolic steroids, stanzolol and trenbolone, in human lymphocytes. *Advances in Environmental Biology, 1,* 39-43.

[4]Berggren, A., Ehrnborg, C., Rosen, T., Ellegard, L., Bengtsson, B., & Caidahl, K. (2005). Short-term administration of supraphysiological recombinant human growth hormone (GH) does not increase maximum endurance exercise capacity in healthy, active young men and women with normal GH-insulin-like growth factor I axes. *Journal of Clinical Endocrinology and Metabolism, 90,* 3268-3273.

[5]Bhasin, S., Woodhouse, L., Casaburi, R., Singh, A., Bhasin, D., Berman, N., et al. (2001). Testosterone dose-response relationships in healthy young men. *American Journal of Physiology, Endocrinology, and Metabolism, 281,* E1172- E1181.

[6]Bhasin, S., Woodhouse, L., Casaburi, R., Singh, A., Mac, R.P, Lee, M., et al. (2005). Older men are as responsive as young men to the anabolic effects of graded doses of testosterone on the skeletal muscle. *Journal of Clinical Endocrinology and Metabolism, 90,* 678-688.

[7]Bidlingmaier, M., Wu, Z., & Strasburger, C. (2000). Test method: GH. *Baillere Clinical Endocrinology and Metabolism, 14,* 99-109.

[8]Boada, L., Zumbado, M., Torres, S., Lopez, A., Chico-Diaz, B., Cabrera, J., et al. (1999). Evaluation of acute and chronic hepatotoxic effects by anabolic-androgenic steroid stanzolol in adult male rats. *Archives of Toxicology, 73,* 465-472.

[9]Bonetti, A., Tirelli, F., Catapano, A., Dazzi, D., Dei Cas, A., Solito, F., et al. (2007). Side effects of anabolic androgenic steroids abuse. *International Journal of Sports Medicine,* November 14, epub ahead of print.

[10]Brill, K., Weltman, A., Gentili, A., Patrie, J., Fryburg, D., Hanks, J., et al. (2002). Single and combined effect of growth hormone and testosterone administration on measures of body composition, physical performance, mood, sexual function, bone turnover, and muscle gene expression in healthy older men. *Journal of Clinical Endocrinology and Metabolism, 87,* 5649-5657.

[11]Brodsky, I., Balagopal, P., & Nair, K. (1996). Effects of testosterone replacement on muscle mass and muscle protein synthesis in hyogonadal men: A clinical research study. *Journal of Clinical Endocrinology and Metabolism, 81,* 3469-3475.

[12]Brower, K. (2002). Anabolic steroid abuse and dependence. *Current Psychiatry Reports, 4,* 377-387.

[13]Burniston, J., Tan, L., & Goldspink, D. (2003). Is the anabolic adrenergic agonist clenbuterol safe? *Journal of Sport Sciences, 21,* 312-313.

[14]Caitlin, D.H., Fitch, K.D., & Ljungqvist, A. (2008). Medicine and the science in the fight against doping in sport. *Journal of Internal Medicine, 264,* 99-114.

[15]Clark, A., & Henderson, L. (2003). Behavioral and physiological responses to anabolic-androgenic steroids. *Neuroscience and Biobehavioral Reviews, 27,* 413-436.

[16]Cohen, J., Collins, R., Darkes, J., & Gwartney, D. (2007). A league of their own: Demographics, motivations and patterns of use of 1,955 male adult non-medical anabolic steroid users in the United States. *Journal of the International Society of Sports Nutrition, 4*, 1-12.

[17]Death, A.K., McGrath, K.C.Y., Kazlauskas, R., & Handelsman, D.J. (2004). Tetrahydrogestrinone is a potent androgen and progestin. *Journal of Clinical Endocrinology and Metabolism, 89*, 2498-2500.

[18]Dickerman, R., Pertusi, R., Zachariah, N., & Dufour, R. (1999). Anabolic steroid-induced hepatotoxicity: Is it overstated? *Clinical Journal of Sport Medicine, 9*, 34-39.

[19]Doessing, S., & Kjaer, M. (2005). Growth hormone and connective tissue in exercise. *Scandinavian Journal of Medicine and Science in Sports, 15*, 202-210.

[20]Dohrmann, G. (2006). Is this Dr. Evil? *Sports Illustrated, 105*.

[21]Drug Enforcement Administration (DEA) (2004). *Anabolic steroid control act of 2004* (Public Law No. 108-358, 118 Stat. 1661). Washington, DC: U.S. Government Printing Office.

[22]Ehrnborg, C. (2000). Growth hormone abuse. *Baillere Clinical Endocrinology and Metabolism, 14*, 71-77.

[23]Evans, N. (2004). Current concepts in anabolic-androgenic steroids. *American Journal of Sports Medicine, 32*, 534-542

[24]Evans, N. (1998). Anabolic steroids and the orthopaedic surgeon. *Journal of Bone and Joint Surgery, 80*, 49.

[25]Fainaru-Wada, M. & Williams, L. (2006). *Game of shadows: Barry Bonds, BALCO, and the steroids scandal that rocked professional sports.* New York, NY: Gotham Books.

[26]Ferenchick, G., Hirokawa, S., Mammen, E., & Schwartz, K. (2006). Anabolic-androgenic steroid abuse in weight lifters: Evidence for activation of the hemostatic system. *American Journal of Hematology, 49*, 282-288.

[27]Fitch, K.D. (2008). Androgenic-anabolic steroids and the Olympic games. *Asian Journal of Andrology, 10*, 384-390.

[28]Fragala, M. (2006). Growth hormone: Understanding the endocrinology and ergogenics. *NSCA Hot Topics Series, 1*-5.

[29]Friedel, A., Geyer, H., Kamber, M., Laudenbach-Leschowsky, U., Schänzer, W., Thevis, M., et al. (2006). Tetrahydrogestrinone is a potent but unselective binding steroid and affects glucocorticoid signaling in the liver. *Toxicology Letters, 164*, 16-23.

[30]Fisher, M., Appleby, M., Rittoo, D., & Cotter, L. (1996). Myocardial infarction with extensive intracoronary thrombus induced by anabolic steroids. *British Journal of Clinical Practice, 50,* 222-223.

[31]Freeman, B. & Rooker, G. (1995). Spontaneous rupture of the anterior cruciate ligament after anabolic steroids. *British Journal of Sports Medicine, 29,* 274-275.

[32]Gannon, T. (1994). Dermatologic emergencies when early recognition can be lifesaving. *Postgraduate Medicine, 96,* 28-30.

[33]Gennari, C., Agnusdei, D., & Gonnelli, S. (1989). Effects of nandrolone decanoate therapy on bone mass and calcium metabolism in women with established post-menopausal osteoporosis: A double blind placebo controlled study. *Maturitas, 11,* 187-197.

[34]Glazer, G. (1991). Atherogenic effects of anabolic steroids on serum lipid levels: A literature review. *Archives of Internal Medicine, 151,* 1925-1933.

[35]Gooren, L. (2003). Testosterone supplementation: Why and for whom? *The Aging Male, 6,* 184-199.

[36]Graham, M., Baker, J., Evans, P., Kicman, A., Cowan, D., Hullin, D., et al. (2008a). Physical effects of short-term recombinant human growth hormone administration in abstinent steroid dependency. *Hormone Research, 69,* 343-354.

[37]Graham, M., Davies, B., Fergal, G., Kicman, A., & Baker, J. (2008b). Anabolic steroid use. *Sports Medicine, 38,* 505-525.

[38]Hall, R., & Hall, R. (2005). Abuse of supraphysiological doses of anabolic steroids. *Southern Medical Journal, 98,* 550-555.

[39]Hartgens, F., Rietjens, G., Kuipers, H., & Wolffenbuttel, B. (2004). Effects of androgenic-anabolic steroids on apolipoproteins and lipoprotein. *British Journal of Sports Medicine, 38,* 253-259.

[40]Hartgens, F., Van Marken Lichtenbelt, W., Ebbing, S., Vollaard, N., Rietjens, G., & Kuipers, H. (2001). Body composition and anthropometry in bodybuilders: Regional changes due to nandrolone decanoate administration. *International Journal of Sports Medicine, 22,* 235-241.

[41]Healy, L., Dall, R., Gibney, J., Bassett, E., Ehrnborg, C., Pentecost, C., et al. (2005). Toward the development of a test for growth hormone abuse: A study of extreme physiological ranges of GH-dependent markers in 813 elite athletes in the postcompetition setting. *Journal of Clinical Endocrinology and Metabolism, 90,* 641-649.

[42]Healy, M., Gibney, J., Pentecost, C., Croos, P., Russell-Jones, D., Sonksen, P., & Umpleby, A. (2006). Effects of high-dose growth hormone on glucose and glycerol metabolism at rest and during exercise in endurance trained athletes. *Journal of Clinical Endocrinology and Metabolism, 91,* 320-327.

[43]Huie, M. (1994). An acute myocardial infarction occurring in an anabolic steroid user. *Medicine and Science in Sports and Exercise, 26,* 408-413.

[44]Iranmanesh, A., Lizarralde, G., & Veldhuis, J. (1991). Age and relative adiposity are specific negative determinants of frequency and amplitude of growth hormone secretory bursts and the half-life of endogenous GH in healthy men. *Journal of Clinical Endocrinology and Metabolism, 73,* 1081-1088.

[45]Isacsson. G., Garle, M., Ljung, E., Asgard, U., & Bergman, U. (1998). Anabolic steroids and violent crime-an epidemiological study at a jail in Stockholm, Sweden. *Comprehensive Psychiatry, 39,* 203-205.

[46]Johnston, L., O'Malley, P., Bachman, J., & Schulenberg, J. (2008). Monitoring the future national results on adolescent drug use: Overview of key findings. (DHHS Publication No. 09-7401). Bethesda, MD: National Institute on Drug Abuse.

[47]Kafrouni, M., Anders, R., & Verma, S. (2007). Hepatotoxicity with dietary supplements containing anabolic steroids. *Clinical Gastroenterology Hepatology, 5,* 809-812.

[48]Kanayama, G., Hudson, J., & Pope, H. (2008). Long-term psychiatric and medical consequences of anabolic-androgenic steroid abuse: A looming public health concern? *Drug and Alcohol Dependence, 98,* 1-12.

[49]Keller, E.T., Ershler, W.B., & Chang, C. (1996). The androgen receptor: A mediator of diverse responses. *Frontiers in Bioscience, 1,* 59-71.

[50]Knapp, P., Storer, T., Herbst, K., Singh, A., Dzekov, C., Dzekov, J., et al. (2008). Effects of a supraphysiological dose of testosterone on physical function, muscle performance, mood, and fatigue in men with HIV-associated weight loss. *American Journal of Endocrinology and Metabolism, 294,* E1135-E1143.

[51]Kroft, S. (2006, April 23). *Aging in the 21ˢᵗ Century (60 minutes)* [Television broadcast]. New York, NY: Columbia Broadcasting System.

[52]Kutscher, E., Lund, B., & Perry, P. (2002). Anabolic steroids: A review for the clinician. *Sports Medicine, 32,* 285-296.

[53]Labrie, F., Luu-The, V., Calvo, E., Martel, C., Cloutier, J., Gauthier, S., et al. (2005). Tetrahydrogestrinone induces a genomic signature typical of a potent anabolic steroid. *Journal of Endocrinology, 184,* 427-433.

[54]Leit, R., Gray, J., & Pope, H. (2001). The media's representation for the ideal male body: A cause for muscle dysmorphia? *International Journal of Eating Disorders, 31,* 334-338.

[55]Lieber Steeg, J. (2007). *Catlin: The doping detective.* Retrieved April 2, 2009, from http://www.usatoday.com/sports/olympics/2007-02-28-catlin_x.htm

[56]Liu, H., Bravata, D., Olkin, I., Friedlander, A., Liu, V., Roberts, B., et al. (2008). Systematic review: The effects of growth hormone on athletic performance. *Annals of Internal Medicine, 148,* 747-758.

[57]Malinowski, K., Kerns, C., Guirnalda, P., & McKeever, K. (2004). Effect of chronic clenbuterol administration and exercise training on immune function in horses. *Journal of Animal Science, 82,* 3500-3507.

[58]McArdle, W., Katch, F., & Katch, V. (2005). *Sports and exercise nutrition.* Philadelphia, PA: Lippincott, Williams & Wilkins.

[59]Melchert, R., & Weider, A. (1995). Cardiovascular effects of androgenic-anabolic steroids. *Medicine and Science in Sports and Exercise, 27,* 1252-1262.

[60]Mitchell, G.J. (2007, December 13). Report to the commissioner of baseball of an independent investigation into the illegal use of steroids and other performance enhancing substances by players in major league baseball. Retrieved April 2, 2009, from http://files.mlb.com/mitchrpt.pdf.

[61]Mochizuki, R., & Richter, K. (1988). Cardiomyopathy and cerebrovascular accident associated with anabolic androgenic steroid use. *The Physician & Sports Medicine, 16,* 109-114.

[62]Mulligan, K., Zachin, R., & Clark, R. (2005). Effect of nandrolone decanoate therapy on weight and lean body mass in HIV-infected women with weight loss: a randomized, double blind, placebo-controlled, multicenter trial. *Archives of Internal Medicine, 165,* 578-585.

[63]National Institute on Drug Abuse (NIDA) (2006). *National Institute on Drug Abuse Research Report Series: Anabolic steroid abuse* (DHHS Publication No. 06-3721). Washington, DC: U.S. Government Printing Office.

[64]Nilsson, S., Baigi, A., Marklund, B., & Fridlund, B. (2001). The prevalence of the use of androgenic steroids by adolescents in a county of Sweden. *European Journal of Public Health, 11,* 195-197.

[65]Papazisis, G., Kouvelas, D., Mastrogianni, A., & Karastergiou, A. (2007). Anabolic androgenic steroid abuse mood disorder: A case report. *International Journal of Neuropsychopharmacology, 10,* 291-293.

[66]Parkinson, A., & Evans, N. (2006). Anabolic androgenic steroids: A survey of 500 users. *Medicine and Science in Sports and Exercise, 38,* 644-651.

[67]Pertusi, R., Dickerman, R., & McConathy, W. (2001). Evaluation of aminotransferase elevations in a bodybuilder using anabolic steroids: Hepatitis or rhabdomyolysis? *Journal of American Osteopathic Association, 101,* 391-394.

[68]Petersson, A., Garle, M., Holmgren, P., Druid, H., Krantz, P., & Thiblin, I. (2006). Toxicological findings and manner of death in autopsied users of anabolic androgenic steroids. *Drug and Alcohol Dependence, 81,* 241-249.

[69]Pope, J., Kouri, E., & Hudson, J. (2000). Effects of supraphysiologic doses of testosterone on mood and aggression in normal men: A randomized controlled trial. *Archives of General Psychiatry, 57,* 133-140.

[70]Powrie, J.K., Bassett, E.E., Rosen, T., Jørgensen, O., Napoli, R., Sacca, L., et al. (2007). Detection of growth hormone abuse in sport. *Growth Hormone and IGF Research, 17,* 220-226.

[71]Prendergast, H.M., Bannon, T., Erickson, T.B., & Honore, K.R. (2003). The toxic torch of the modern Olympic Games. *Veterinary and Human Toxicology, 45,* 97-102.

[72]Rashid, H., Ormerod, S., & Day, E. (2007). Anabolic androgenic steroids: What the psychiatrist needs to know. *Advances in Psychiatric Treatment, 13,* 203-211.

[73]Richold, M. (1988). The genotoxicity of trenbolone, a synthetic steroid. *Archives of Toxicology, 61,* 249-258.

[74]Rosen, T. (2006). Supraphysiological doses of growth hormone: Effects on muscles and collagen in healthy active young adults. *Hormone Research, 66,* 98-104.

[75]Sader, M., Griffiths, K., McCredie, R., Handelsman, D., & Celermajer, D. (2001). Androgenic anabolic steroids and arterial structure and function in male bodybuilders. *Journal of the American College of Cardiology, 37,* 224-230.

[76]Sanchez-Osorio, M., Duarte-Rojo, A., Martinez-Benitez, B., Torre, A., & Misael, U. (2007). Anabolic-androgenic steroids and liver injury. *Liver International, 28,* 278-282.

[77]Saugy, M., Robinson, N., Saudan, C., Avois, L., & Mangin, P. (2006). Human growth hormone doping in sport. *British Journal of Sports Medicine, 40,* i35-i39.

[78]Schmidt, P., Berlin, K., Danaceau, M., Neeren, A., Haq, N., Roca, C., et al. (2004). The effects of pharmacologically induced hypogonadism on mood in healthy men. *Archives General Psychiatry, 61,* 997-1004.

[79]Schroeder, E., Singh, A., Bhasin, A., Storrer, T., Azen, C., Davidson, et al. (2003). Effects of an oral androgen on muscle and metabolism in older, community-dwelling men. *American Journal of Physiology Endocrinology & Metabolism, 284,* E120-E128.

[80]Schuckit, M.A. (1988). Weightlifters folly: The abuse of anabolic steroids. *Drug Abuse and Alcohol Newsletter, 17.*

[81]Scott, M. & Scott, A. (1992). Effects of anabolic-androgenic steroids on the pilosebaceous unit. *Cutis,* 50, 113-116.

[82]Sinha-Hikim, I., Artaza, J., Woodhouse, L., Gonzalez-Cadavid, N., Singh, A., Lee, M., et al. (2002). Testosterone-induced increase in muscle size in healthy young men associated with muscle fiber hypertrophy. *American Journal of Endocrinology and Metabolism, 283,* E154-E164.

[83]Sjoqvist, F., Garle, M., & Rane, A. (2008). Use of doping agents, particularly anabolic steroids, in sports and society. *Lancet, 371,* 1872-1882.

[84]Sleeper, M., Kearns, C., & McKeever, K. (2002). Chronic clenbuterol administration negatively alters cardiac function in the horse. *Medicine and Science in Sports and Exercise, 34,* 643-650.

[85]Steinberg, D. (2008). The LDL modification hypothesis of artherogenesis: An update. *Journal of Lipid Research, 50,* S376-S381.

[86]Sullivan, M., Martinez, C., Gennis, P., & Gallagher, E. (1998). The cardiac toxicity of anabolic steroids. *Progress in Cardiovascular Diseases, 41,* 1-15.

[87]Thiblin, I. & Petersson, A. (2005). Pharmacoepidemiology of anabolic androgenic steroids: A review. *Fundamental & Clinical Pharmacology, 19,* 27-44.

[88]Tricker, R., Casburi, R., Storer, T., Clevenger, B., Berman, N., Shirazi, A., et al. (1996). The effects of supraphysiological doses of testosterone on angry behavior in healthy eugonadal men-A clinical research center study. *Journal of Clinical Endocrinology and Metabolism, 81,* 3754-3758.

[89]United States Sentencing Commission - Drug Working Group (USSC-DWG) (2006). *2006 steroids report.* Retrieved April 2, 2009, from www.ussc.gov/USSCsteroidsreport-0306.pdf.

[90]Van Riper, T. (2009). *Fixing Football's Pay Scale.* Retrieved May, 19, 2009, from http://www.forbes.com/2009/03/04/nfl-pay-scale-sports-business_pay_scale.html.

[91]Wardlaw, H.J. (2007). *Perspectives in nutrition.* New York, NY: McGraw Hill.

[92]World Anti-Doping Agency (WADA) (2009a). *WADA Code.* Montreal: WADA. Retrieved May 26, 2009, from http://www.wada-ama.org.

[93]World Anti-Doping Agency (WADA) (2009b). http://www.wada-ama.org.

[94]World Anti-Doping Agency (WADA) (2009c). *The 2009 prohibited list: International standard.* Montreal: WADA. Retrieved May 25, 2009, from http://www.wada-ama.org/en/prohibitedlist.ch2.

Chapter Twelve

PATHOLOGICAL GAMBLING

BY ERICA L. WONDOLOWSKI

JOSEPH F. STANO

SPRINGFIELD COLLEGE

KATHERINE STANO

ARGOSY UNIVERSITY

Chapter Topics

◊ Introduction

◊ Brief History of Gambling in America

◊ What People Gamble On

◊ Gambling Among Various Demographic Groups

◊ Comorbidity

INTRODUCTION

As of 2008, 2% of adults and 4% - 6% of adolescents meet the diagnostic criteria, as set forth by the Diagnostic Statistical Manual, 4th edition, for pathological gambling. An additional 4% of adults and 8% of adolescents have manifest problematic gambling issues.[20] Pathological gambling is an impulse-control disorder characterized by the inability to cease gambling despite adverse social, psychological, financial, and legal consequences. These consequences include, but are not limited to, depression, suicide, divorce, unemployment, and homelessness. The present chapter seeks to quantify pathological gambling while also identifying risk factors within several sub-populations (e.g., gender, age, and ethnicity).

DIAGNOSTIC CRITERIA

The diagnostic criteria for pathological gambling are defined under the umbrella diagnosis of impulse-control disorder. Also found in this family of diagnoses are kleptomania (impulsive stealing of objects), pyromania (impulsive setting of fires), trichotillomania (impulsive pulling and removal of hair), and intermittent explosive disorder (impulsive destruction and aggression towards persons or property). Pathological gambling, the impulsive engagement in gambling behaviors despite negative consequences, is identified by qualified clinical staff after having met five or more of the following criteria:

◊   Is preoccupied with gambling (e.g., preoccupied with reliving past gambling experiences, handicapping or planning the next venture, or thinking of ways to get money with which to gamble).

◊   Needs to gamble with increasing amounts of money in order to achieve the desired excitement.

◊   Has repeated unsuccessful efforts to control, cut back, or stop gambling.

◊   Is restless or irritable when attempting to cut down or stop gambling.

◊   Gambles as a way of escaping from problems or of relieving a dysphoric mood (e.g., feelings of helplessness, guilt, anxiety, and depression).

◊   After losing money gambling, often returns another day to get even ("chasing" one's losses.)

◊   Lies to family members, therapist, or others to conceal the extent of involvement with gambling.

◊   Has committed illegal acts such as forgery, fraud, theft, or embezzlement to finance gambling.

◊   Has jeopardized or lost a significant relationship, job, educational or career opportunity because of gambling.

◊   Relies on others to provide money to relieve a desperate financial situation caused by gambling.

Additionally, the gambling behavior cannot be executed as a direct result of a Manic Episode.[1]

The diagnostic criteria noted above are reliable indicators of pathological gambling. In their 2007 study, however, Lakey, Goodie, Lance, Stinchfield, and Winters[15] report that meeting four, rather than five, of the ten DSM-IV criteria was more indicative of pathological gambling and proposes that the criteria may one day be transitioned from a requirement of five to four.

BRIEF HISTORY OF GAMBLING IN AMERICA

Beginning as early as 50,000 B.C., gambling has been documented among Indigenous populations in the Western Hemisphere as they gambled on the results of contests. For the next several thousand years, gambling has developed to what it is now through a series of growths, prohibitions, and legalizations. The following is a listing of significant dates as they apply to this development in America:[18,21,24]

1620	Twenty horses were shipped from England to the Virginia Colony. Horse racing with private wagering ensued.
1621	Restrictions are placed on gambling within the Plymouth Colony and opposition to forms of card playing and gambling where instituted in the early Massachusetts Bay Colony.
1665	The first oval horseracing track is laid in Long Island, New York Colony, catalyzing the commercial racing industry in North America.
1682	The Quaker government of the Colony of Pennsylvania passes antigambling laws.
1780s-1830s	Lotteries are used to finance civic projects such as building the Nation's capital, buildings for colleges (i.e., Yale, Harvard, Columbia, and Rutgers), and churches.

1812	The first steamboat begins operation on the Mississippi River. This is the beginning for riverboat gambling.
1815	Casino gaming was licensed in New Orleans.
1827	The first complete casino is open in New Orleans by John Davis.
1833-1840	Twelve states banned lotteries during a time of governmental reform. By the time of the Civil War, all legal lotteries have been banned.
1835	John Davis's casino closes, but underground gambling continues illegally.
1864	The Travers Stakes horse race, the first stakes race in the United States, is run at Saratoga, New York.
1868	The Louisiana Lottery began what would become a thirty-year reign of abuse and corruption. Although it was created to generate revenue for the state, it eventually led to the bribery of state officials.
1876	Congress bans the use of mails for lottery propaganda.
1887	Charles Fey invents the slot machine in San Francisco, CA.
1890	Congress bans the sale of lottery tickets via mail and also prohibits the advertising of lottery in newspapers.
1891	New York begins licensing jockeys and trainers through a private board of control so that horseracing is now regulated.
1894	The Jockey Club of New York is established.
1895	The Louisiana Lottery ends when Congress bans the transportation of lottery tickets.
1906	Kentucky establishes the first government-run state racing commission.

1907	Arizona and New Mexico outlaw gambling in order to remain candidates for statehood.
1910	With the exception of horse racing at specific tracks, gambling is illegalized within the United States.
1920s	Dog racing becomes popular.
1931	Nevada legalizes wide-open casino gambling.
1935	New horse-race betting legislation is approved in Illinois, New Hampshire, Louisiana, Florida, West Virginia, Michigan, Ohio, Massachusetts, Rhode Island, and Delaware.
1937	Bill Harrah opens the first of what would become one of the largest casino empires.
1940	Pari-mutuel horse race betting is legalized in New York.
1941	The Las Vegas Strip begins to establish itself as the primary destination for casino gambling.
1945	The state of Nevada begins licensing casinos.
1949	Congress passes the Gambling Ship Act of 1949. The Act prohibits flagships from operating casinos onboard.
1951	The Johnson Act, which states that gambling machines cannot be transported unless they are moving to areas where they are legal, was passed.
1955	The Gaming Control Board is created by the state of Nevada and a process of professionalizing gaming regulation begins.
1959	The Nevada Gaming Commission is created to oversee the Gaming Control Board.
1961	The Wire Act, Travel Act, and Waging Paraphernalia Act are passed in response to the investigation of organized crime and its relation to gambling activity.

1962	The Johnson Act is amended to include all devices used for gambling.
	Edward Thorpe's, *Beat the Dealer*, which described card counting in the game of Blackjack, is sold. Blackjack becomes the most popular card game in Las Vegas.
1964	New Hampshire sells its first lottery ticket.
1969	Nevada permits ownership of casinos by public corporations.
	The World Series of Poker is established in Las Vegas.
	New Jersey authorizes a lottery. Due to its success, other states begin to follow suit.
1970	New York City creates the Knapp Commission, which investigates police corruption as it relates to illegal gambling.
1971	New York authorizes off-track betting.
1974	Massachusetts becomes the first state in North America to have an instant lottery game.
1975	New Jersey begins the first numbers game where patrons will select their own three numbers on which to bet.
1976	New Jersey authorizes gambling in Atlantic City.
1977	The legislature of New Jersey develops a regulatory structure for casino gambling.
1978	The Interstate Horse Racing Act is passed. This Act provides standards by which patrons can participate in both off-track and inter-track better.
1979	High-stakes bingo games begin on the Seminole Indian reservation in Florida. This begins the focus on unregulated gambling within reservations.

1981	Legislation in New York rejects casino gambling.
	North Dakota votes against lotteries.
1984	California voters authorize a state lottery.
1986	The Money Laundering Act is passed by Congress, which states that all large gambling transactions are to be recorded.
1987	The U.S. Supreme Court upholds the rights of Indian tribes to offer unregulated gambling as long as operations do not violate state criminal policies.
1988	The Indian Gaming Regulatory Act is passed by Congress. This Act allows for federal and tribal regulation of bingo games and mutually negotiated Indian-state government schemes.
1989	Limited casino gambling begins in South Dakota.
	The legislature of Iowa allows for riverboat casino gaming with a limited wager.
	Oregon begins the first sports-based lottery.
1990	Ohio voters refuse to authorize casino gambling.
	Colorado voters approve for limited casino gambling in select historic towns.
	West Virginia allows slot machines at racetracks.
1991	Riverboats are approved by Mississippi legislature.
	Keno is introduced in Oregon and Colorado as a lottery game.
1992	Louisiana legislature approves riverboat casinos and a land-based casino in New Orleans.
	Sports betting is prohibited beyond the states of Nevada, Oregon, Montana, and Delaware.

1992	U.S. flagships are allowed by Congress to have casino gambling.
	Rhode Island and Louisiana allow for slot machines at racetracks.
1993	Boat casinos are approved by Indiana legislature.
	Georgia establishes a lottery.
	Florida voters vote down a proposal for limited casino gambling.
1994	Congress passes the Money Laundering and Suppression Act.
1995	Delaware and Iowa allow for slot machines in racetracks.
	Internet gambling sites are made available.
1996	Part of the Indian Gaming Regulatory Act of 1988 is ruled unconstitutional by the U.S. Supreme Court. A tribe's ability to sue states over compact negotiations is found to violate the 11th Amendment.
1996	Congress approves gambling on cruise ships which travel from state to international waters unless otherwise determined by the state in which the cruise ship docks.
1998	Voters in California pass Proposition 5, which states that Native American casinos can operate without limits.
1999	South Carolina Supreme Court orders that all slot machines be shut down.
	Voters made Alabama the second state to vote down lotteries.
	The California Supreme Court finds that allowing Native American casinos to operate without limits is unconstitutional. (Proposition 5)
2000	California voters approve Native American casinos with certain limits.

The gambling industry, since its inception, has seen tremendous growth and fluctuation as it struggled to become an establishment within mainstream America.[16,18,22,24] It is to be expected that this tumultuous advent continues for several more years until legislation can be reconciled nationwide.

WHAT PEOPLE GAMBLE ON

Gambling can occur at any point when more than one outcome is possible. Often, unregulated wagers are placed between friends and/or co-workers as people anticipate certain outcomes rather than others. More commercialized forms of gambling, however, often revolve around sports, the lottery, horse racing, casino games (e.g., craps, roulette, slots), bingo, and card-playing.[4] Individuals who engaged in more than one form of commercialized gambling on a daily basis were more likely to have a manifestation of pathological gambling later in life.[6,17] Although lottery tickets are reported to be the most common form of gambling across all ages, both adolescents and older adults report a strong preference for electronic gaming machines.[5,28] Because of individuals' preference for electronic gaming machines, the use of the Internet as a medium by which to gamble has surged.

INTERNET GAMBLING

By the mid-1990s, Internet gambling had become established within the World Wide Web as an alternative to other forms of gambling. This process allowed for gamblers to maintain anonymity while retaining the comfort and security of gambling within an area in which they felt unthreatened. By the end of 1998 there were approximately 76 million Web sites that allow individuals to gamble in this guarded manner.[24] This prevalence throughout the Internet allows for those individuals who would otherwise have limited access to gambling facilities to now have them within their own households.[14] In order to participate, each gambler must set up a financial account and grant access to the account for the Web site and its Web masters to withdraw the money lost and deposit any money earned.

As of 2008, approximately $2.3 billion per year was spent on online gambling across approximately 1,400 Internet gambling sites.[16] These gambling sites are able to reach any individual across the world who has access to the Internet and a valid account with which to fund the user's online gambling. It is important to note that during a 2008 study, Khazaal et al.[12] found that of the online gambling Web sites that were studied, none offered online treatment for pathological gambling. The lack of Website quality as it applies to health-related education for the individual consumer can only serve to benefit the gambling Web sites and those individuals in charge of them. Failure to address the needs of the pathological gambler only helps to retain their client base.

GAMBLING AMONG
VARIOUS DEMOGRAPHIC GROUPS

Age. Adolescence is a developmental stage during which individuals are beginning to exhibit and experiment with a newfound sense of independence in which they are capable of making their own decisions. During this time, adolescents are also beginning to hold employment and manage the money they earn. Frequent gambling within this cohort is reported to be significantly more common among males, older adolescents, and those who work ten or more hours a week.[9,27] Those adolescents who engaged in gambling behaviors were also more likely to engage in other risky and/or thrill seeking behaviors, such as the use of drugs and alcohol or involvement in delinquent behaviors. This illustrates a common presence of unhealthy coping strategies that, at this age, can have a strong detrimental effect on the development of the individual.[25]

Those adolescents who exhibited impulsiveness in early adolescence were more likely to engage in excessive gambling in later adolescence and into adulthood. As the frequency and amount of the betting wager increases, so do the risk of problem and pathological gambling in later life. Problematic gambling is defined as the period of time during which individuals can either begin to regulate their gambling behavior or continue to progress into pathological gambling. More difficulty with academic studies is often seen in adolescents with a problematic gambling history. However, as individuals progresses from problematic to pathological gambling, their rationale for engaging in such behaviors changes from desiring money and having fun, to feeling invincible and otherwise dissociating from everyday life.[21,25] It has been posited that there are lower rates of problem and pathological gambling within adolescents when compared to adults, although there is a strong correlation between gambling-related issues and the transition to adulthood.

Traditional college-aged students often find themselves in a developmental stage that is "marked by heightened risk-taking, identity exploration, instability, self-focus, and self-exploration without the parental and social controls imposed during adolescence."[2,p.181] Although these individuals are more likely to gamble if they are working full-time, live independently, and not enrolled in college, their enrolled peers also have difficulty managing their gambling behaviors.[27] Specifically, approximately 12 percent of males and four percent of females between the ages of 18 and 24 meet the criteria for pathological gambling.

Students overestimate how their cohort perceives, and whether they approve of, gambling behaviors. This perception of acceptance and high prevalence often results in an increase in individual gambling frequency and an increase in wagers. It should also be noted that reports indicate that six percent of males and one percent of females within this age range utilize a bookmaker or "bookie" to place and manage their betting activities.[26]

The National Collegiate Athletic Association (NCAA) stipulates that no student-athlete is to engage in any sports wagering activity that involves college sports or professional athletics. Despite this, student-athletes have been reported to be approximately 1.5 times more likely to engage in gambling activities than non-athlete students.[26] Gambling behaviors by student-athletes and non-athlete students differ with regard to the secrecy that is maintained by the student-athlete in order to maintain eligibility to play their collegiate sport. Both student-athletes and non-athletic students report having experienced some type of negative consequence related to their gambling behaviors.

Within the older adult population, ages 65 and older, pathological gambling is seen to manifest itself differently. Older adults who develop problem or pathological gambling issues often initiated their gambling habits later in life and, with a larger percentage no longer in the workforce (e.g., retired, unemployed), older adults have an increased amount of free time within their day. Those with gambling issues, and some without, often fill this time engaging in gambling behaviors. These behaviors, however, differ from younger cohorts in that the older population gamble more often, but wager less.[5,20] In both studies, it was reported that many older adults with and without pathological gambling issues do not gamble to win but as a means to occupy time. Bingo and slots are often the primary forms of gambling which put older adults at risk for becoming a problem or pathological gambler, as they allow the individual player to continuously play and remain engaged. This effect is seen specifically in women.

Gender. Of both genders, males tend to develop gambling-related problems and subsequent pathologies earlier in life. Males are also three times as likely to be problem gamblers, as well as having a propensity towards gambling more. This group, however, is also at a greater risk for negative consequences such as psychological difficulties, substance abuse, and the manifestation of gambling-related issues and/or disordered gambling.[2,27]

Female gamblers resemble their male counterparts in risk for gambling problems and pathology. In terms of behavior, however, women often engage in a higher frequency of betting within smaller time periods and place larger bets.[5,14] For women, a "telescoping" effect has been identified which illustrates the effect by which women move more rapidly than men from initial gambling exposure to fitting the criteria for gambling pathology.[20] Overall, females are more likely than their male counterparts to experience negative consequences as a result of their gambling behaviors.

Both males and females reported similar gambling-related etiology, negative consequences, and/or risk factors. Additionally, 84% of both men and women have gambled at least once in their lives. Each gender is reported to equally experience difficulties found in the general adult population when they also experience gambling-related issues or pathology.[8] Finally, both men and women prefer similar types of gambling (i.e., card playing).

Ethnicity. It has been posited that cultural and ethnic factors provide a great amount of influence over gambling and problematic/pathological gambling rates. Individuals who identify as being a cultural and ethnic minority remain at the greatest risk for developing gambling-related issues. Minorities are reported to experience higher rates of problem gambling than Caucasians. More specifically, Caucasian and Asian students gambled less frequently than Black, Hispanic, and American-Indian individuals.[7,27] Although Black individuals were less likely to gamble, those that affiliate with this group and participate in gambling behaviors are more likely to do so frequently. Individuals who are a part of the first generation to live away from their native country and also experience acculturation difficulties are at least three times more likely to experience gambling-related issues.

Individuals who affiliate with Asian ethnicities are the least likely to have gambling-related issues; however, they do not abstain. The acknowledgement of "least" is relative to the level at which other ethnicities gamble. For Chinese societies, gambling is a way of life and although problematic behaviors surrounding gambling are met with social disapproval, these behaviors are not indicative of a psychiatric illness within the specific culture.[23] Chinese gamblers report severe financial, familial, and employment-related consequences and both men and women within this culture identify an inability to control gambling.

Male gamblers within this culture prefer sports gambling (e.g., horse races, soccer) to those activities that require less thinking, such as Mahjongg or slot machines. Conversely, Chinese female gamblers prefer these activities as they require fewer skills.[23] These female populations began gambling at an older age, have a shorter duration of overall gambling involvement, and are troubled by similar interpersonal and financial problems as males. Given that approximately 65% of Chinese females are either unemployed or homemakers, they often run into many more financial problems (e.g., credit card debt, owing money to bookies) than their male counterparts.

Socioeconomic Status. Socioeconomic status can also serve as a determinant as to which groups are more likely to engage in gambling behaviors. Individuals who belong to a lower socioeconomic status, regardless of ethnicity or race, are more likely to have abstained from gambling. Individuals belonging to this group who did participate in these behaviors, however, were more likely to be problem gamblers within their status.[27] Individuals who fall within a higher socioeconomic status are at a greater risk for frequent gambling involvement and higher wagers being placed. This escalation in involvement also puts many of the individuals who fall within this status at risk for developing a gambling-related problem and/or pathology.

COMORBIDITY

Psychiatric. Problematic and pathological gambling is highly correlated with difficulties with work, school, family, and finances. Those afflicted with gambling-related issues are also faced with mental health disorders such as anxiety, depression, and drug/alcohol addiction.[16,20]

Individuals with a history of problematic and/or pathological gambling often experience an accompanying co-morbid psychiatric disorder, or the existence of a mental disorder that is accompanied by an additional mental disorder.[3] Specifically, persons afflicted with problematic and/or pathological gambling issues often also experience depression, alcohol dependence, panic disorder, and generalized anxiety disorder, in addition to obsessive-compulsive and avoidant personality disorders.[11]

Clinical depression and/or anxiety are more prevalent in females than males. More than half of women with problematic gambling-related issues have sought help with depressive and anxiety symptoms, respectively.[3,11] Men, on the other hand, are more likely to acknowledge physiological and psychological signs of a chemical addiction than a psychological/psychiatric disorder. Regardless of gender, approximately eight out of 10 individuals within the older adult population, 65 years old and older, with a history of gambling-related issues and/or pathology report having dealt with major depression during the time they were engaging in gambling behaviors. Adolescents of both genders also report experiencing low self-esteem and depressive symptoms.[25] Due to the potential for considerable financial loss from problematic gambling behaviors, access to and/or ability to afford mental health care may be considerably reduced and may possibly affect the recovery rate within this population.

Problematic and pathological gamblers are six times more likely to experience prolonged suicidal ideation or to attempt suicide than those in the general population.[3,20] For older adults, this inclination toward suicide is three to four times more likely to result in seeking help. Almost half of women pathological and problematic gamblers report having had suicidal ideations at some point within the time span that they have been gambling, and 29% of this group report having a history of suicide attempts.

Substance Abuse. It is very rare that psychiatric conditions such as depression and anxiety manifest themselves without the accompaniment of some type of substance use. For both men and women, the rate at which they experience depression, substance use, and weekly gambling behaviors is very similar. Adolescents who experience gambling-related problems are also more likely than their non-gambling peers to report a high rate of weekly drug use, school-related problems, and clinical depression.

Problematic gambling is highly correlated with substance use, with reports indicating as many as 53% of problematic gamblers self-identifying.[19] Within non-problematic gambling groups, women are less likely to use substances than their male counterparts. However, when both genders engage in problematic/pathological gambling, they are both highly likely to use and/or abuse alcohol, cigarettes, marijuana, and hard drugs including cocaine, LSD, and ecstasy.[7]

Partner Violence. In their 2008 study, Korman et al.[13] reported that having gambling-related issues can lead to having clinically significant anger problems and subsequently an increased risk of being both the perpetrator and victim of intimate partner violence. Of the sample studied, approximately 63% of those involved reported perpetrating violence, being a victim, or some combination of both. Of that 63%, 53% report having committed physical assault, injury, and/or sexual coercion with their partner. Men and women equally experienced being victims of intimate partner violence. Both perpetration and victimization of problematic gamblers was reported to be significantly higher than the general population.

TREATMENT

Similar to other addictions and pathologies, treatment for pathological gambling is more successful when an individual struggling with addiction has a strong support system. This support system is primarily comprised of family, friends, and/or mentors. Research has reported that the participation of a significant other in treatment can significantly influence the gamblers' length of stay in treatment,[10] but age, ethnicity, and gambling debt can also mitigate successful treatment outcomes. Those with less than a high school diploma, younger than 25 years old, and with excessive debt are less likely to engage in an adequate length of treatment for pathological gambling and, subsequently, are less likely to abstain from gambling behaviors.

CASE STUDY

Ivan Cebula is a 28 year old man with an associate's degree in Heating, Ventilation, and Air Conditioning (HVAC) Technology. His annual income in 2009 was $63,000. He works for Acme HVAC as a senior technician. He is unmarried and resides with his parents Stan and Linda Cebula. He has no steady romantic relationship. His prized possession is a 2008 H3 Hummer.

Ivan began sports gambling with friends while in high school; in addition, he also partook in weekly "card games" with his friends. He considers himself an average guy but someone who is naturally "lucky." By the time he was 17 he was gambling approximately $50 per week on illicit sports gambling. He states that most times his card game winnings easily financed his sports betting; he felt that he won often in sports betting since he was a lifelong fan of various sports and "he really knew what was going on." He does admit to occasionally having to "borrow" money from his parents without their knowledge to cover his gambling shortages. He insists that he always promptly replaced the money.

Ivan's gambling markedly increased when he turned 21. He and a group of friends went to the Connecticut casinos to celebrate his birthday and, as he said, "it seems like he died and went to heaven" when he was legally able to enter the casinos. Since that time he has gone from 1-2 times per month visits to the casinos to his currently 1-2 times per week. His game of choice is Blackjack; he believes that this is a game of skill and *he is very good at it. He states that he frequently wins as much as $5000 per night. Due to the level of his gambling, he frequently gets a room at the casino hotel "comped," so his Friday after work trip lasts until late on Saturday.*

In spite of his perceptions, there are some "disconnects" in Ivan's life. Currently, Ivan has seven credit cards; the total charged exceeds $50,000 and each card is charged to the maximum credit limit. Over 95% of the charges are cash advanced received at the casinos. His current monthly payments exceed $3000. In addition, several months ago, he skipped two automobile payments, repossession was threatened, and he asked his parents for temporary assistance. He was told by his parents that they would not assist again and he has failed to repay them for the two payments.

Ivan feels that he is just one "lucky break" away from making a big hit; then he will pay off all of his bills and everything will be fine. Lately, he has started to go to the casinos two evenings per week in addition to the weekend. He knows that a change of luck is right around the corner.

CASE STUDY

Gloria Winston is a 67 year old retired woman. Prior to her retirement, she was a secretary in the History department of the local college. She and her life partner, Francine, own their home and there is no mortgage.

Gloria's main sources of income are a private pension via the college, Social Security benefits, and some interest on investments that are managed by her life partner. Francine is eight years younger than Gloria, she works as a nurse manager at the local medical center and she intends to retire in approximately three years.

Gloria has played the state-run lottery since its inception. Originally, she would take her change from a purchase at a local convenience store in a lottery ticket or two. As time has gone on her focus has shifted to playing the lottery more and more and the time spent on lottery tickets has increased dramatically. Since she is retired and Francine is not, Gloria has much unsupervised free time on the days that she is alone. Buying lottery tickets at one convenience store has progressed to buying multiple tickets at several stores per day. It is typical for Gloria to spend $60 per day on lottery tickets; she has spent in excess of $100 in a day upon occasion. In addition, on two days a week she has lunch at a local establishment where Keno games are broadcast over closed-circuit television. Gloria may stay there until mid-afternoon.

Gloria's gambling behavior has begun to have an affect upon her relationship with Francine. She frequently has to dip into the household expenses envelope; she states that she always returns the money. Gloria takes her lottery winnings in the form of new tickets. She is always expecting that "one big hit" so that she and Francine will have no money problems the remainder of their lives.

REFERENCES

[1]American Psychiatric Association: *Diagnostic and Statistical Manual of Mental Disorders*, Fourth Edition, Text Revision. Washington, DC, American Psychiatric Association, 2000.

[2]Blinn-Pike, L., Worthy, S. L., & Jokman, J. N. (2007). Disordered gambling among college students: A meta-analytic synthesis. *Journal of Gambling Studies, 23*, 175-183. doi: 10.1007/s10899-006-9036-2

[3]Boughton, R., & Falenchuk, O. (2007). Vulnerability and comorbidity factors of female problem gambling. *Journal of Gambling Studies, 23*, 323-334. doi: 10.1007/s10899-007-9056-6

[4]Ciarrocchi, J. W. (2002). *Counseling problem gamblers: A self-regulation manual for individual and family therapy.* San Diego, California: Academic Press.

[5]Clark, D. (2008). Older adults' gambling motivation and problem gambling: A comparative study. *Journal of Gambling Studies, 24*, 175-192. doi: 10.1007/s10899-008-9090-z

[6]Cronce, J. M., Corbin, W. R., Steinberg, M. A., & Potenza, M. N. (2007). Self-perception of gambling problems among adolescents identified as at-risk or problem gamblers. *Journal of Gambling Studies, 23*, 363-375. doi: 10.1007/s10899-006-9053-1

[7]Ellenbogen, S., Derevensky, J., & Gupta, R. (2007). Gender differences among adolescents with gambling-related problems. *Journal of Gambling Studies, 23*, 133-143. doi: 10.1007/s10899-006-9048-y

[8]Ellenbogan, S., Gupta, R., & Derevensky, J. (2007). A cross-cultural study of gambling behaviour among adolescents. *Journal of Gambling Studies, 23*, 25-39. doi: 10.1007/s10899-006-9044-2

[9]Hansen, M., & Rossow, I. (2008). Adolescent gambling and problem gambling: Does the total consumption model apply? *Journal of Gambling Studies, 24*, 135-149. doi: 10.1007/s10899-007-9082-4

[10]Ingle, P. J., Marotta, J., McMillan, G., & Wisdom, J. P. (2008). Significant others and gambling treatment outcomes. *Journal of Gambling Studies, 24*, 381-392. doi: 10.1007/s10899-008-9092-x

[11]Kerber, C. S., Black, D. W., & Buckwalter, K. (2008). Comorbid psychiatric disorders among older adult recovering pathological gamblers. *Issues in Mental Health Nursing, 29*, 1018-1028. doi: 10.1080/01612840802274933

[12]Khazaal, Y., Chatton, A., Cochand, S., Jermann, F., Osiek, C., Bondolfi, G., & Zullino, D. (2008). Quality of web-based information on pathological gambling. *Journal of Gambling Studies, 24,* 357-366. doi: 10.1007/s10899-008-9095-7

[13]Korman, L. M., Collins, J., Dutton, D., Dhayananthan, B., Littman-Sharp, N., & Skinner, W. (2008). Problem gambling and intimate partner violence. *Journal of Gambling Studies, 24,* 13-23. doi: 10.1007/s10899-007-9077-1

[14]LaBrie, R. A., LaPlante, D. A., Nelson, S. E., Schumann, A., & Shaffer, H. J. (2007). Assessing the playing field: A prospective longitudinal study of Internet sports gambling behavior. *Journal of Gambling Studies, 23,* 347-362. doi: 10.1007/s10899-007-9067-3

[15]Lakey, C. E., Goodie, A. S., Lance, C. E., Stinchfield, R., & Winters, K. C. (2007). Examining DSM-IV criteria for pathological gambling: Psychometric properties and evidence from cognitive biases. Journal of Gambling Studies, 23(4), 479-498. doi: 10.1007/s10899-007-9063-7

[16]Lee, H., Lemanski, J. L., & Jun, J. W. (2008). Role of gambling media exposure in influencing trajectories among college students. *Journal of Gambling Studies, 24,* 25-37. doi: 10.1007/s10899-007-9078-0

[17]Lund, I. (2007). Lessons from the grey area: A closer inspection of at-risk gamblers. *Journal of Gambling Studies, 23,* 409-419. doi: 10.1007/s10899-007-9058-4

[18]McGurrin, M. (1992). *Pathological gambling: Conceptual, diagnostic, and treatment issues.* Sarasota, Florida: Professional Resource Press.

[19]Nordin, C., & Nylander, P. (2007). Temperament and character in pathological gambling. *Journal of Gambling Studies, 23,* 113-120. doi: 10.1007/s10899-006-9049-x

[20]Nower, L., & Blaszczynski, A. (2008). Characteristics of problem gamblers 56 years of age or older: A statewide study of casino self-excluders. *Psychology and Aging, 23(3),* 577-584. doi: 10.1037/a0013233

[21]Stinchfield, R. (2004). Demographic, psychosocial, and behavioral factors associated with youth gambling and problem gambling. In J. L. Derevensky & R. Gupta (Eds.), *Gambling problems in youth: Theoretical and applied perspectives* (pp 27-40). New York, New York: Plenum Publishers.

[22]Stucki, S., & Rihs-Middel, M. (2007). Prevalence of adult problem and pathological gambling between 2000 and 2005: An update. *Journal of Gambling Studies, 23,* 245-257. doi: 10.1007/s10899-006-9031-7

[23]Tang, C. S., Wu, A. M. S., & Tang, J. Y. C. (2007). Gender differences in characteristics of chinese treatment-seeking problem gamblers. *Journal of Gambling Studies, 23,* 145-156. doi: 10.1007/s10899-006-9054-0

[24]Thompson, W. N. (2001). *Gambling in america: An encyclopedia of history, issues, and society.* Santa Barbara, California: ABC-CLIO.

[25]van Hamel, A., Derevensky, J., Takane, Y., Dickson, L., & Gupta, R. (2007). Adolescent gambling and coping within a generalized high-risk behavior framework. *Journal of Gambling Studies, 23*, 377-393. doi: 10.1007/s10899-007-9066-4

[26]Weinstock, J., Whelan, J. P., Meyers, A. W., & Watson, J. M. (2007). Gambling behavior of student-athletes and a student cohort: What are the odds? *Journal of Gambling Studies, 23*, 13-24. doi: 10.1007/s10899-006-9043-3

[27]Welte, J. W., Barnes, G. M., Tidwell, M. O., & Hoffman, J. H. (2008). The prevalence of problem gambling among U.S. adolescents and young adults: Results from a national survey. *Journal of Gambling Studies, 24*, 119-133. doi: 10.1007/s10899-007-9086-0

[28]Wickwire Jr., E. M., Whelan, J. P., West, R., Meyers, A., McCausland, C., & Leullen, J. (2007). Perceived availability, risks, and benefits of gambling among college students. *Journal of Gambling Studies, 23*, 395-408. doi: 10.1007/s10899-007-9057-5

Chapter Thirteen

SEXUAL ADDICTION:

CLINICAL COMPONENTS

BY **ANDREA PERKINS**

HOFSTRA UNIVERSITY

JOSHUA L. CARPENTER

CLUBHOUSE OF SUFFOLK

Chapter Topics

◊ Theoretical Perspectives

◊ DSM Criteria

◊ Factors Impacting Sexual Addiction

◊ Treatment

◊ Implications for Counseling

The nomenclature "addict" has been used widely to explain any repetitive behavior, such as shopping, gambling, and smoking. Sexual behavior being described as a clinical "addiction" is a fairly recent phenomenon. Patrick Carnes[5] has been credited with naming the disorder "sexual addiction" in the early 1980's. The Society for the Advancement of Sexual Health[19] currently defines sexual addiction as "a persistent or escalating pattern or patterns of sexual behavior acted out despite increasingly negative consequences to self and others." However, in common vernacular, "sex addict" has been used to describe anyone from a spouse who asks for sex too frequently, to a celebrity caught having frequent extramarital affairs, to a repeat offending pedophile, despite differences in the perceived severity of these actions. The term might result in a chuckle, a raised eyebrow, or even bit of wicked curiosity, adding to the stigma associated with sexual addiction and the barriers to seeking necessary treatment. It is estimated that approximately three to six percent of the population live with sexual addiction, although estimating the true prevalence of the disorder is difficult because many do not seek treatment due to feelings of shame and remorse.[13]

Sexual addiction has only recently begun to be understood and discussed as a legitimate condition warranting attention by mental health professionals. More and more individuals who are seeking mental health and addiction treatment are presenting with problems related to out of control, obsessive, compulsive, or impulsive sexual behaviors that are causing significant distress in their lives. It is important to understand:

◊   How sexual addiction affects the individual,
◊   how it impacts those close to the person, and
◊   what behaviors and symptoms constitute a true sexual addiction in need of treatment.

Sexual addiction is unique when compared to other addictions in that there is little empirical evidence supporting a unified diagnosis and effective treatment methods. Consequently, many mental health professionals are not skilled in recognizing and treating individuals who may struggle with issues related to sexual addiction. This chapter will explore the clinical disorder of sexual addiction, its presentation, and its treatment.

THEORETICAL PERSPECTIVES

Those who have studied the disorder of hypersexuality have been at odds in terms of the way that they conceptualize the cause or origins of the disorder.[14] Some view the disorder as a sexual addiction in which sex can be viewed as a "drug of choice" that produces a change in mood states and produces psychosocial consequences. Others view the disorder as sexual compulsivity, where sexual behaviors are driven by anxiety reduction, and not necessarily sexual desire. A third perspective views hypersexual behavior as a result of sexual desire dysregulation. The foundation of this viewpoint is impairment in the voluntary control over sexual desires. While this appears to be similar to compulsivity, the driving force here is purely psychosexual and not for anxiety reduction.[14] Individuals continue to give into their arousal despite the presence of negative consequences.[17]

Despite these early theoretical differences, there has recently been more consensus toward conceptualizing the disorder as sexual compulsivity/addiction, as certain criteria and concepts are shared among the perspectives.[14] To begin, they recognize that the disorder results in significant psychosocial impairment, with the possibility of comorbidity with other psychiatric conditions. The behaviors and activities in which the individual engages are the same, despite varying terms used to identify the disorder. Familial and developmental factors are seen as playing a role in the disorder. Neurobiology is also seen as a prominent component in the etiology of this disorder. Finally, the condition can be mitigated by treatment and counseling modalities. It is generally considered, however, that an addiction model of treatment (e.g., self-help and 12-step programs) is the central method of treatment for those who hold an addiction perspective, while those who hold a compulsivity view would lean more toward incorporating psychopharmacology and psychotherapeutic approaches for treatment. Treatment options will be discussed further in a later section of this chapter.

DSM CRITERIA

There is no set of specific diagnostic criteria for sexual addiction in the current edition of the Diagnostic and Statistical Manual for Mental Disorders (DSM-IV-TR),[1] the primary manual for the classification of psychiatric disorders. However, there is a history of inclusion of similar disorders in earlier editions of the DSM. Kafka[14] contends that hypersexuality and sexual addiction have been marginalized in the most recent diagnostic manuals because of a lack of empirical research to support diagnostic criteria.

The second edition of the DSM, the DSM-II, recognized sexual deviations as personality disorders. The DSM-III subclassified paraphilic disorders as distinct pathologies, with disorders such as nymphomania being classified as psychosexual disorders not otherwise specified. Paraphilias are conditions characterized by recurrent, intense sexual urges, fantasies, or behaviors involving unusual objects, activities, or situations causing distress and impairment in functioning. Examples of paraphilias include voyeurism and sexual sadism. The term "sexual addiction" was mentioned in two places in the DSM-III-R, but these references were removed in the subsequent DSM-IV, as were all terms related to addiction.[8] The DSM-IV-TR does not specifically discuss addictions or addictive disorders, but rather portrays them as part of, or related to, substance-related disorders, mood disorders (such as bipolar disorder), anxiety disorders (such as obsessive-compulsive disorder), or impulse-control disorders. In terms of general addiction, the DSM-IV-TR primarily focuses on issues related to substance use and abuse, in which addiction is largely characterized by dependence and tolerance. Sexual addiction may not always have dependence and tolerance; if present, the addiction is usually overshadowed by sexual obsession, impulsivity, and/or compulsion.

Interestingly, the DSM-IV-TR does have a Sexual and Gender Identity Disorder category, but neglects to discuss sexual addiction or hypersexuality in this category. Arousal and desire disorders are discussed, but only in the context of lack of arousal or desire, such as with hypoactive sexual desire disorder and sexual aversion disorder. No adequate diagnoses exist for individuals who experience excessive desire or engage in excessive sexual activity that occurs at distressing levels. In this category, sexual addiction can only be diagnosed under Sexual Disorder Not Otherwise Specified (NOS), which provides no specific criteria and is a "catch-all" for all other sexual disorders not discussed in the manual. If impulsivity is a main theme in an individual's experience of sexual addiction, a diagnosis of Impulse Control Disorder NOS can also be given, though again, no specific diagnostic criteria are provided.

The next iteration of the DSM, the fifth edition, is anticipated in 2012. There has been some effort on the part of the American Psychiatric Association (APA) and other researchers in the field of sexual compulsivity/addiction to have a further clarification of this disorder in order to represent its salience in current society. Goodman[12] described provisional diagnostic criteria for sexual addiction derived from DSM-IV-TR criteria for substance dependence:

Sexual addiction is a maladaptive pattern of sexual behavior that leads to clinically significant impairment or distress, as manifested by at least three of the following that occur at any time in the same 12-month period:

◊ Markedly increased amount or intensity of the sexual behavior or markedly diminished mood with continued involvement in the sexual behavior at the same level of intensity.

◊ Characteristic withdrawal syndrome of physiologically or psychologically described changes upon discontinuation of the sexual behavior or engaging in the same or closely related sexual behavior to relieve or avoid withdrawal symptoms (dependence).

◊ The sexual behavior is often engaged in over a longer period, in greater quantity, or at a higher level of intensity than was intended (tolerance).

◊ Persistent desire and efforts to cut down or control the sexual behavior are not successful.

◊ A great deal of time is spent on activities necessary to prepare for, engage in, or recover from the sexual behavior.

◊   Important social, occupational, or recreational activities are given up or reduced because of the sexual behavior. The sexual behavior continues despite knowledge of having a persistent or recurrent physical or psychological problem that is likely to have been caused by or exacerbated by the behavior (e.g., sexually transmitted diseases, marital or relationship discord, mania).[pp. 1-2]

To explore inclusion of diagnostic criteria that capture this disorder, the APA convened the Sexual and Gender Identity Disorders Working Group to investigate current and proposed disorders in this category. One current proposal recommends the inclusion of *hypersexual disorder*. Acknowledging that differing perspectives contribute to the research literature—the compulsivity model, the addiction model, and the sexual desire dysregulation model—consensus seems to lie in the fact that this clinical phenomenon exists.[15] Table 1 contains the criteria the APA currently has up for opinion. The most current criteria defining hypersexual disorder and future decisions regarding its inclusion in the manual can be found online at the American Psychiatric Association's DSM-5 website.[2]

Table 1

HYPERSEXUAL DISORDER[2]

A. Over a period of at least six months, recurrent and intense sexual fantasies, sexual urges, and sexual behavior in association with four or more of the following five criteria:
   (1) Excessive time is consumed by sexual fantasies, urges, and by planning for and engaging in sexual behavior.
   (2) Repetitively engaging in these sexual fantasies, urges, and behavior in response to dysphoric mood states (e.g., anxiety, depression, boredom, irritability).
   (3) Repetitively engaging in sexual fantasies, urges, and behavior in response to stressful life events.
   (4) Repetitive, but unsuccessful efforts to control or significantly reduce these sexual fantasies, urges, and behavior.
   (5) Repetitively engaging in sexual behavior while disregarding the risk for psychical or emotional harm to self or others.
B. There is clinically significant personal distress or impairment in social, occupational, or other important areas of functioning associated with the frequency and intensity of these sexual fantasies, urges, and behavior.

C. These sexual fantasies, urges, and behavior are not due to direct physiological effects of exogenous substances (e.g., drugs or medications) or to Manic Episodes.

D. This person is at least 18 years of age.

Specify if:

Masturbation

Pornography

Sexual Behavior with Consenting Adults

Cybersex

Telephone Sex

Strip Clubs

Other:

Specify if:

In Remission (During the Past Six Months, No Signs or Symptoms of the Disorder Were Present)

In a Controlled Environment

Differential Diagnosis and Comorbidity

With lack of guidance in the DSM-IV-TR and typically little experience with its clinical presentation, counselors may be at a loss to accurately diagnose sexual addiction. Clients may present with sexual histories that appears to be "against the norm" or undesirable within their current relationship. Yet, a finding of sexual compulsion/addiction may be incorrect, despite the presence of defining characteristics and behaviors consistent with how the disorder is currently understood.

An accurate diagnosis of sexual addiction begins with understanding two key features of any addictive behavior:

◊   Recurrent failure to control the behavior, and

◊   continuation of the behavior despite harmful or negative consequences.

Often underlying these two features is difficulty with controlling impulses, obsessing over sexual behaviors, and compulsion to keep engaging in sexual behaviors in the face of adverse effects. It should be noted that no form of sexual behavior in itself constitutes sexual addiction, as it is not determined by the type of behavior, but rather by the relationship between the behavior and its effect on individual's life.[11]

The features of a presumed sexual addiction need to be examined closely to be sure that what presents as behaviors related to sexual addiction are not another, similar disorder. For example, sexual addiction can involve or revolve around a paraphilia. Some sex addicts, however, are not parahiliacs, and some paraphiliacs are not sex addicts. Kafka[14] made the distinction that paraphilic behaviors are viewed as socially deviant, while those of a sexual addict are typically within the social norms, albeit to excess. A similar distinction can be made between sexual addiction and pedophilia, where the area of overlap between the two is considerably smaller (i.e., sex offenders are typically not sex addicts or vice versa, despite some similarities in symptomology).

The behaviors that characterize sexual addiction can also occur as manifestations of underlying pathology (e.g., brain lesion/injury, side effect of medication, or endocrine abnormality) or psychiatric condition.[11] Clues that may indicate underlying medical or organic causes include onset in middle age or later, regression from previously normal sexuality, excessive aggression, report of auras or seizure-like symptoms prior to or during the sexual behavior, and presence of soft neurological signs (e.g. poor motor coordination, perceptual sensory difficulties). Sexual addiction needs to be distinguished from non-addictive patterns of exploitive or aggressive sexual behavior that can occur with antisocial personality disorder, as well as the obsessions and compulsions with sexual content that can occur in obsessive-compulsive disorder (OCD). Although fairly common, the content of these obsessions typically centers around fears of acting on sexual impulses or being labeled a pervert, and not on sexual fantasies. Symptoms of sexual addiction may differ from those of obsessive and compulsive disorders in that addiction is more typically associated with arousal and pleasure, whereas obsessions and compulsions are not.

It is useful also to understand the high level of co-occurrence between sexual addiction and other disorders, such as mental illness and substance abuse. This co-occurrence masks the sexual addiction and makes it difficult to ascertain the full scope of problems a person is currently experiencing. It is critical, therefore, to understand the interplay and complexity of this potential cyclical relationship in order to more fully understand the individual experiencing these problems.

An individual may choose to self-medicate with substances to numb or diminish thoughts, urges, or problem related sexual addiction or a psychiatric disorder. Conversely, individuals may also use substances as a disinhibitor to make it easier to engage in behaviors they know are unhealthy and problematic. As a result, sexual addiction can exacerbate any ongoing substance or mental health problems. Worsening psychiatric problems (e.g., increased anxiety, depressive or manic episode, increased substance use) can, in turn, exacerbate any underlying sexual addiction. When sexual activity and substance abuse occur together, there is increased likelihood of engaging in risky sexual behaviors (e.g., unprotected sex) due to disinhibition, which increases the risk of abuse or contracting sexually transmitted infections.

Estimates point to a high-level of co-occurrence existing among sexual addiction and other psychiatric disorders, especially substance use disorder (64%), anxiety disorder (50%), and mood disorders, where those with bipolar disorder may exhibit hypersexuality or promiscuity as components of a manic episode (39%).[4] Syndromes that meet Goodman's[12] provisional criteria for sexual addiction can also occur in the context of other psychiatric disorders, such as bipolar disorder, schizophrenia, personality disorders, and substance abuse/dependence. When the criteria for both sexual addiction and another psychiatric disorder are present, both diagnoses are valid, regardless of whether the sexual addiction is secondary to the other psychiatric disorder. Including a diagnosis of sexual addiction along with another disorder provides a description of how sexual behavior relates to and affects an individual's life. Symptoms and behaviors characteristic of sexual addiction can vary widely among individuals since the behavior itself does not define sexual addiction, but rather its impact on the individual's life and functioning.

FACTORS IMPACTING SEXUAL ADDICTION

As mentioned earlier, those who contribute to the theoretical and empirical research regarding sexual compulsivity/addiction have reached some consensus on the common characteristics among their perspectives. It is important to delve a bit deeper into some of these factors before exploring treatment modalities, as this knowledge will contribute to a more appropriate assessment and clinical history. Some of the common factors influencing the experience of sexual addiction include family of origin characteristics, psychosocial impact, sexual orientation, and sexual activities of choice.

FAMILY OF ORIGIN CHARACTERISTICS

Much of the sexual addiction literature points to deficits in the capacity for intimacy as a key component in developing the disorder. Salisbury[17] reported that her clinical experience has led her to believe that childhood attachment issues and/or trauma interfere with the individual's capacity for intimacy. As many as two-thirds of individuals engaging in problematic or sexually addictive behaviors were sexually abused, which could exacerbate the shame and secrecy surrounding these behaviors, especially if the behaviors serve to relive the abusive experience.[18] The wives of men with sexual addiction are also more likely to have experienced some type of abuse, abandonment, punishment, or depression in their family of origin.[16] Individuals with sexual addiction will not be able to achieve basic levels of well-being in their adult relationships without addressing these attachment deficits.

PSYCHOSOCIAL IMPACT

By definition, sexual addiction causes social and psychological impairment. This can translate to difficulties with employment, independent living, and socialization. An individual's sexual addiction may interfere with maintaining employment if the individual is spending excessive amounts of time planning or engaging in problematic sexual behaviors. This distraction can lead to decreased productivity and accuracy in job performance. It can cause further complications if an individual is using company resources to facilitate sexual behaviors, such as looking at pornography on an office computer or using a business credit card to rent a hotel room. If an individual's sexual addiction has especially obsessive or compulsive components (e.g., compulsive cybersex), it can even interfere with normal socialization and one's ability to maintain activities of daily living, as in neglected housework or personal grooming and hygiene.

SEXUAL ORIENTATION

Another interrelationship to consider is the role sexual orientation and identity may play in the presentation of an individual with sexual addiction. A significant number of individuals with sexual addiction identify as homosexual or bisexual, whereas even more individuals who identify as heterosexual also engage in sexually addictive behaviors with members of the same sex. Homosexual sex is still viewed by many in society as culturally taboo, immoral, and not to be flaunted. As a result, if an individual experiences homosexual desires, he or she may attempt to deny or resist them, and eventually engage in these behaviors in secrecy while maintaining a heterosexual lifestyle. Some of these individuals may come to identify as homosexual, while many others continue to lead heterosexual lives. Again, engaging in such behavior is not a criterion for sexual addiction unless it causes significant distress and impairment. Homosexual behavior can be a part of normal development and experimentation in forming a sexual identity; however, due to the stigma surrounding homosexuality that persists even today, many individuals may internalize this stigma, possibly contributing to or exacerbating any sexual problems or addiction.

ACTIVITIES OF CHOICE

While it is not the activity, but its intensity and effect on relationships that is at issue in sexual addiction, a number of activities and behaviors are typical within sexual addiction. These include compulsive masturbation, heightened promiscuity, pornography dependence, telephone sex dependence, cybersex, and severe sexual desire incompatibility (i.e., the excessive sexual desire in one partner produces sexual demands on the other partner).[14] The proliferation of the Internet in recent years has had an interesting impact on the experience and incidence of sexual addiction.[13] The Internet provides an opportunity to explore sexual fantasies and discuss similar interests with others while remaining anonymous, impersonal, easy to access, and private. This results in a heightened and intensified secrecy around sexual addiction. The Internet can be a safe way to explore one's sexuality, but can also lead to damaging behaviors associated with sexual addiction related to compulsive cybersex and Internet pornography addiction.

TREATMENT

A number of different approaches can be explored and utilized in the treatment of an individual with sexual addiction, including cognitive-behavioral therapy, individual and group counseling, self-help, and family therapy. It is critical to point out that, because sexual addiction has no official diagnostic criteria and remains somewhat controversial, many mental health professionals do not have the experience or training to adequately address issues related to this disorder. Kafka[14] has proffered a model of the central issues that need to be addressed when treating someone with sexual addiction. The three domains he identified are:

- Gaining control over the troublesome sexual behaviors;
- dealing with here and now issues, such as triggers to behaviors and changing response patterns; and
- addressing developmental factors, such as childhood abuse or early attachment issues.

Although the treatment approaches presented in this section are commonly used as therapeutic modalities, counselors need to become versed in the implications for using them with this population.

PSYCHODYNAMIC APPROACHES
The goals of psychodynamic psychotherapy in treating sexual addiction are to enhance self-regulation of moods and thoughts, and to facilitate a person's ability to form and maintain interpersonal relationships. According to Goodman,[11] psychodynamic psychotherapy is comprised of three main components: understanding, integration, and internalization.

Understanding refers to the relationship between the problematic sexual behaviors and difficulty in regulating mood.

Integration refers to the individual's personality and facilitating a greater awareness of one's moods, needs, wishes, fears, conflicts, beliefs, and defense mechanisms. If dissociation is present within an individual's sexual addiction, integration can be important for the individual to understand these different urges and beliefs and integrate these into a more functional, whole self. The function of

Internalization in psychotherapy is to develop a means of self-regulating moods. For example, one purpose of internalization is to provide new opportunities to resolve and internalize self-regulatory functions that were impaired during childhood and adolescent development.

COGNITIVE-BEHAVIORAL APPROACHES
The goals of cognitive-behavioral approaches are to stop/control the behaviors and find new ways of viewing the self and relating to others.[13] Relapse prevention

strategies aim to help individuals with sexual addiction recognize triggers to problematic sexual thoughts and behaviors, cope more effectively with sexual urges, and recover more rapidly from the effects of problematic behavior. These strategies facilitate people to learn more about how to improve their recovery. With sexual addiction, relapse prevention addresses urges to engage in problematic behaviors as a sign of a disruption in healthy mood, which can only be improved through better awareness and coping skills.

Cognitive-behavioral techniques other than relapse prevention focus not on specific problematic behaviors, but on what causes the person to rely on these unhealthy behaviors as a means of coping with distress and unmet needs.[14] One technique may include skills training, which helps individuals learn and practice thoughts and behaviors that will help them more effectively manage their moods and needs (e.g., anger management, assertiveness training). Another technique could include lifestyle regeneration, which helps individuals learn aspects of how to achieve and maintain a healthy, balanced lifestyle.

GROUP THERAPY APPROACHES

Therapeutic groups can facilitate the development of abilities to make and keep meaningful connections with others and use support in times of crisis instead of turning to destructive behavior. The most prominent model for this in the addictions community is the Twelve-step program. The Twelve-step approach begins with the person acknowledging that they are powerless over addictive sexual behaviors and can only make change with outside help and sponsorship, along with a commitment to abstinence from addictive behaviors, belief in a higher power, and participation in service. This approach is prevalent because of the many advantages it offers as a treatment choice. These advantages include:

◊   A readily accessible service, especially in metropolitan areas;

◊   no financial investment in the service;

◊   a lessening of the secrecy associated with the condition because it is being publically acknowledged;

◊   a healing community to provide support and crisis management; and

◊   a format that mirrors a relapse prevention program, which has been shown to have some efficacy with sex offender populations.[14]

This approach does involve a long-term membership and frequent participation, which can be problematic to maintain for some.

PSYCHOPHARMACOLOGY

Psychiatric pharmacotherapy (e.g., psychotropic medication) can be used to treat mood instability and anxiety issues as well as other symptoms related to co-occurring psychiatric disorders. Anti-depressant medications, most notably the selective serotonin reuptake inhibitors (SSRIs), can reduce the frequency of addictive sexual behavior and the intensity of the urges to engage in problematic sexual behavior, even when the individual is not experiencing significant depression. One common side effect reported by individuals with depression treated with SSRIs is a reduction in libido and pleasure in sexual activities; therefore, it makes sense that this side effect could, in fact, be helpful to individuals struggling with an obsessive or compulsive need for sex. Some case studies have also indicated that the drugs Lithium and Depakote may be helpful in treating hypersexuality associated with manic or depressive episodes, such as in bipolar disorder.[11]

MOTIVATIONAL INTERVIEWING

Adopted from the treatment of substance dependence, motivational interviewing has been an emerging practice in the treatment of sexual addiction. The crux of motivational interviewing is the welcoming and accepting environment created by the counselor. Motivational interviewing relies on a collaborative partnership between the counselor and client, established within healthy, supportive boundaries, that clients can use as a model for other relationships in their lives.[7] This therapeutic technique focuses on the individual over the disease, uses the unconditional acceptance of the client as the centerpiece, avoids judgmental statements, and emphasizes self-efficacy and internal locus of control. Four major principles that underlie this approach are:

◊   Expressing empathy;
◊   developing discrepancy;
◊   rolling with resistance and avoiding argumentation; and
◊   supporting self-efficacy.[3]

Del Giudice and Kutinsky[7] advocate for this treatment approach because it promotes an internal locus of control, whereas other approaches mandate adherence to predetermined guidelines (e.g., twelve-step approaches) or elicit client dependence on the therapist (e.g., psychodynamic approaches). Motivational interviewing is also better equipped to foster the therapeutic alliance than other competing techniques because it emphasizes rapport development and change movement from the very beginning of treatment. This approach is also easily understood so they can be readily taught to treatment staff and clinicians as an adjunct to more traditional treatment approaches.

SEXUAL ADDICTION AS A FAMILY ISSUE

Sexual addiction has been conceptualized as a systemic disorder because of its impact upon the family system. In conjunction with individual counseling and pharmacological treatment, family or couples therapy may also be helpful in treating sexual addiction, mostly for resolving any interpersonal or dysfunctional relationship patterns associated with the sexual addiction. As noted earlier, one of the proposed causes of sexual addiction is deficits in the capacity for intimacy, originating in the family of origin and perpetuating into adult relationships.[16] Couples and family therapy is typically most beneficial after the individual's sexual addiction has been mostly stabilized and recovery is in progress. It is useful at this juncture because the behaviors have decreased but the root or motivation for the development of the condition may persist, opening the door for relapse.

The main foci of couples or family therapy are rebuilding trust, lack of intimacy, problems setting limits or boundaries, problems resolving conflict, issues of forgiveness, and financial problems.[16] One of the first tasks of this process may be disclosure of the condition to the family and containing the effects of that news. A spouse or significant other can feel betrayed, shamed, isolated, jealous, angry, and experience decreased self-esteem when the sexually addictive behaviors are revealed or discovered. Spouses/significant others may also experience shock and disbelief that this "secret life" was occurring without their knowledge, and they may have difficulty fully grasping the situation. Arguments, separation, and divorce are common after a sexual addiction is revealed, especially if it involved adultery or infidelity. The therapeutic environment presents a forum to address and process these feelings.

Kafka[14] advocates assessing the strength of the commitment of the couple, the impact of the disclosure, and how the addictive behavior relates to the underlying issues in the relationship (e.g., spouse not interested in sex, not feeling validated or loved) as a starting point for couples or family therapy. Based on this information, treatment goals and the need for individual therapy for the client and spouse/significant other, can be determined. Salisbury[17] supports the use of a co-therapist model for counseling couples. Under this model, the individual therapists form a team to treat the couple as a collective, but can separate to address individual resistance or concerns as needed without the perception of "taking sides" that would occur if a single therapist were to provide the treatment.

The impact on children in the family need also be addressed, as well as their appropriateness for engaging in the therapy process. Children as young as eight can be aware when there are problems in the parental relationship, and can internalize the lack of attention and increased tension as something they may have caused. The timing of disclosure to children is also delicate. Phillips[16] concluded that it was best to tell children when they are in their teenage years, when the parents have a definitive decision regarding divorce, or when they are likely to hear it from other sources. She reported a study of children over the age of thirteen to whom a parent disclosed a sexual addiction and nearly two-thirds of the respondents already knew of the addiction prior to disclosure. This finding would point to earlier individual or family intervention for children of parents with a sexual addiction.

RESEARCH ON THE EFFECTIVENESS OF TREATMENT

Most of the evaluations of effectiveness of sexual addiction treatment rely upon case studies and anecdotal evidence. There is currently limited empirical evidence on the effectiveness of these types of treatment, specifically for individuals with sexual addiction. Even less is available related to the systemic and family treatment of the disorder.[16] Most types of treatment for sexual addiction have been developed based on what is known about the treatment of addiction in general, or treatment of the specific psychosocial factors related to sexual addiction. Wholesale adoption of treatment methods effective for those living with substance abuse would be shortsighted, as sex is a more complex experience than the mere ingestion of a drug.[9]

Salisbury[17] suggests that it is too early for the field to work toward a definitive treatment model for sexual addition or hyper-sexuality until there is better clarification of manifestations of the disorder and etiological factors underlying it, and deficits in the client's capacity for intimacy are addressed. She suggested a comprehensive treatment model that utilizes multiple modalities. Further research is needed regarding the effectiveness of various interventions specifically for sexual addiction before a comprehensive, validated, and scientifically accepted method of treatment can be utilized. Until that time, it is generally agreed that treatment for sexual addiction is most likely to be effective when it:

◊ Uses an integrated approach employing a variety of therapeutic methods,

◊ is personalized to the individual, and

◊ is adjusted as the individual progresses.

IMPLICATIONS FOR COUNSELING

As noted above, the realm of sexual addiction and out-of-control sexual behavior is not one that is frequently encountered by many mental health professionals. This does not let counselors "off the hook" for being knowledgeable about the population and interventions that would be successful. Several issues are of critical importance for the treatment of individuals with sexual addition:

◊ Barriers to seeking treatment;

◊ proper assessment;

◊ decreasing bias and creating an environment of acceptance; and

◊ ethical counseling practices.

BARRIERS TO SEEKING TREATMENT

Sexual addiction is a complex disorder that can have far-reaching affects on an individual's life and functioning as far as it concerns relationships, children, education, employment, social stigma, abuse/trauma, and spirituality, as well as mental health and physical health. When working with an individual who may have a sexual addiction, counselors should be aware of barriers to treatment that may be present stemming from interpersonal conflict and societal pressures.

Within the individual, it is paramount to explore and be aware of the sensitivity around discussing problematic sexual behaviors. Individuals may be reluctant to seek treatment or fully disclose their problems and behaviors, as they may feel ashamed of their behavior or be fearful of isolation and humiliation if they share their true feelings and experiences. Many individuals are also reluctant to disclose because of the negative social stigma around being viewed as sexually deviant or abnormal. Because of the shame and humiliation an individual may face, many individuals with sexual addiction keep these behaviors well hidden from their everyday lives and may act highly secretive as a result.

As another confound to the situation, an individual may experience spiritual or religious conflict if the sexual behaviors that are problematic are also against one's prescribed faith. This can lead to great internal distress as the desire to follow the tenets of one's faith conflict with the strong sexual urges and desires that may be considered sinful or immoral by religious leaders. Social stigma and spiritual conflict may create the conditions for the person to become trapped in an addiction cycle. Having indulged in their addictive activities, persons are remorseful and anxious about their behaviors. They feel powerless against the disorder but too ashamed to seek the treatment they need, so they are unable to maintain healthy relationships and must continue with their "drug of choice" (i.e., sex) for intimacy and fulfillment.[13]

PROPER ASSESSMENT

The assessment of sexual addiction must seek to identify those who are at-risk or living with the condition. This can be done though a combination of psychometric instruments and clinical interviewing. It has been established earlier in the chapter that there are characteristics and factors that are common to the sexual compulsivity/addiction phenomenon. These characteristics also need to be considered within the context of the person and the impact that they have on the person's life and functioning.

The most well established tool for the exploration of sexual addition is *The Sexual Addiction Screening Test* (SAST)[5] The SAST is a 25-item questionnaire designed to screen for the presence of sexually addictive behaviors. Scores on the instrument can range from 0 to 25; individuals with a scale score of 10 or more should receive further assessment for sexual addiction and scores of 13 or more indicated the probable presence of a sexual addiction. Other tools developed by Carnes are available online to assist those considering seeking treatment to explore their behaviors, including the *Sexual Addiction Risk Assessment Test* and the *Internet Sex Screening Test.* Other available assessment instruments include the *Sexual Compulsivity Scale*, the *Sex Addicts Anonymous Questionnaire*, and the *Compulsive Sexual Behavior Inventory.*[12]

Goodman[12] cautioned that the criterion or construct validity of these instruments is hard to evaluate based on the absence of a standard set of diagnostic criteria. Many contain questions that are not diagnostically relevant (i.e., provide no information as to whether a criteria was met or not). The one instrument that is most likely to be useful is the *Sexual Compulsivity Scale* because it addresses the key features of impaired control and harmful consequences. In general, these yes/no questionnaires can be useful for screening or self-assessment, but are not meant to replace clinical interviews using open-ended questions. Kafka[14] offered a number of questions to serve as a screening tool for further exploration of sexual addiction:

◊ Have you ever had persistent, repetitive trouble controlling your sexual behavior?

◊ Has your sexual behavior ever caused you significant personal distress or caused significant personal consequences to you such as loss of a relationship, legal problems, job-related problems, or medical problems including sexually transmitted disease or unwanted pregnancy?

◊ Have you ever had repetitive sexual activities that you felt needed to be kept secret or that you felt very ashamed of?

◊ Have you ever been troubled by feelings that you spend too much time engaging in sexual fantasy, masturbation, or other sexual behavior?

◊ Have you ever felt that you have a high sex drive? For example, if we include both partnered sex and masturbation, have you ever been sexual seven or more times a week during at least a 6-month period since adolescence?

In structuring a more in-depth clinical interview, it is best to start with discussing the behaviors in which individuals with sex addiction engage that are problematic in their life, since these may be part of the presenting problem. To increase the likelihood of disclosure, the initial exploration of behaviors and history should occur without a spouse or a significant other present.[14] An individual with sexual addiction may engage in high-risk sexual behavior (e.g., unprotected sex, anonymous sex); use substances (e.g., drugs, alcohol) before, during, or after sex; have a negative self-image and low self-esteem; spend a considerable amount of time fantasizing about the behavior; attempt to resist sexual urges; engage in problematic sexual behaviors (e.g., adultery resulting in divorce or hiring a prostitute and getting arrested); and/or identify with paraphilias, such as exhibitionism, fetishism, or transvestism. Keep in mind that not all of these behaviors need to be present for an individual to be considered to have a sexual addiction, but that those behaviors that are present cause significant distress and impairment in the individual's life. If engaging in the behavior is not problematic or distressing for the individual, then it cannot be considered as part of sexual addiction, such as a wife who is comfortable with her husband's cross-dressing desires, supporting him.

Next, the motivation for engaging in the behavior should be explored. Guigliano[9] proposed several factors that possibly underlie the reasons for engaging in the sexually addictive behaviors:

◊ meeting sexual needs (e.g., hyperactive libido);

◊ fulfillment of narcissistic needs (e.g., need to be desired);

◊ desire for human connection;

◊ compensation for low self-esteem;

◊   need for control;
◊   reenactment of childhood trauma or abuse;
◊   distraction/avoidance of disturbing feelings; and/or
◊   coping with sexual orientation/identity issues (e.g., married man engaging in secretive homosexual acts).

The reason behind the behavior, and not necessarily the behavior itself, is the true target of treatment.

For example, many individuals who experience sexual addiction report that they engage in problematic sexual behaviors as a means of mood regulation. Among some individuals, a paradoxical relationship exists between negative mood and sexuality. In other words, for these individuals, as depression or anxiety increases so can sexual desire, impulsivity, obsession, or compulsion to engage in problematic behaviors.[4] This seems counterintuitive, as one would suspect that the more depressed or anxious an individual, the less likely that individual would be interested in sexual activity. This increased interest in sexual activity in the presence of distressing depression or anxiety is a strong characteristic of sexual addiction.

Lastly, the psychosocial impact of the behavior should be assessed. This will serve as a compass for treatment, as goals may be developed to address relational issues, resolve financial issues, reconnect with alienated friends and family, or improve decision-making abilities. The end result in treatment is to address the underlying issue and replace the behavior with a more appropriate means for satisfying the motivation, in order to reduce the impact on one's life situation. Structuring a clinical interview based on these guiding elements will elicit the information necessary for plan development to achieve this result.

DECREASING BIAS AND CREATING AN ENVIRONMENT OF ACCEPTANCE

Gaining competence in working with any diverse group lies in the counselor developing awareness, knowledge, and skills related to the group.[30] Prior to engaging in the treatment of these individuals, counselors must first be aware of any biases or prejudices in their beliefs about sexual addiction. This can include examining how the disorder has affected them in their personal life and relationship, the influence the media has had on sensationalizing or stigmatizing the condition for them, and identifying any value-based or moral objections they might have to treating certain individuals (e.g., could not treat a client who has a history of sexual offenses against children).

Next, the person should seek additional knowledge or training in the area of sexual addiction in order to more effectively treat and address this disorder. For example, this might include having a working knowledge of the aforementioned factors that influence sexual addiction and the typical motivational patterns behind sexually addictive behaviors. The counselor should also become versed in the community-based services and educational resources that are available for clients.

Finally, the individual should seek guidance from knowledgeable practitioners on the application of integrated therapies for the treatment of sexual addiction. This may include learning motivational interviewing techniques or entering into a co-therapy relationship for the treatment of a family dealing with the disclosure of a sexual addiction.

A strong body of research has shown that the most salient feature of counseling is the strength of the therapeutic alliance, not necessarily the specific techniques chosen. Entering into the counseling relationship with this awareness, knowledge, and skills will better create the therapeutic conditions necessary for engaging the client. Much of the difficulty in treating and making progress with individuals with sexual addition is that they feel ashamed, stigmatized, or rejected as a result of their behaviors. Individuals fear their counselor will not understand the power of their sexual experiences. Clients living with sexual addiction have voiced their desire to have counselors who are better trained to meet their specific needs.[9] Demonstrating the understanding, openness, and skills to assist clients from the moment they walk in the door will go a long way in allaying their fears and forming strong alliances.

ETHICAL COUNSELING PRACTICES

Despite slight differences in clinical orientation, those who provide services to individuals with sexual addictions (e.g., marriage and family therapists, mental health counselors, clinical social workers) subscribe to a code of professional ethics that exemplify parallel principles. These codes set out the standards for competence and conduct. Although bound by law in many aspects of clinical life, ethical codes embody the aspirational or "gold" standard for quality counseling and service.

Counselors are called upon to keep the dignity, welfare, and safety of their clients at the forefront; this safety also extends to those whom they may be putting in imminent danger, based on their actions. Boundaries of the relationship should be solidly established and reiterated so that clients will openly disclose and receive proper treatment when dangerous situations are present. Given that family and couples therapy is a prominent feature in the treatment of sexual addiction, boundaries of these interrelationships should also be firmly established to maximize rapport with all participants.

Not only is being competent in the knowledge and skills related to the treatment of sexual addiction a hallmark of effective practice, it is also an ethical imperative should you treat clients from this group.[13] This includes seeking out evidenced-based practices and empirically validated instruments for inclusion in treatment. With the field of sexual addiction gaining more clinical prominence, it is incumbent on the professional to seek out more appropriate and effective methods, as they emerge. Additionally, counselors should choose to make referrals when a situation beyond their scope of knowledge, or relating to a personal bias, presents itself.

REFERENCES

[1]American Psychiatric Association. (2000). *Diagnostic and statistical manual of mental disorders* (4ᵗʰ ed., treatment revision). Washington, DC: Author.

[2]American Psychiatric Association. (2010). *American Psychiatric Association DSM-5 Development: Hypersexual disorder.* Retrieved July 1, 2010, from http://www.dsm5.org/ProposedRevisions/Pages/proposedrevision.aspx?rid=415

[3]Antick, J. R., & Goodale, K. R. (2007). Motivational interviewing. In M. Hersen & J. C. Thomas (Eds.)., *Handbook of clinical interviewing with adults* (pp. 38-48). Thousand Oaks, CA: Sage Publications.

[4]Bancroft, J., & Vukadinovic, Z. (2004). Sexual addiction, sexual compulsivity, sexual impulsivity, or what? Toward a theoretical model. *The Journal of Sex Research, 41*(3), 225-234.

[5]Carnes, P. J. (1989). *Contrary to love: Helping the sexual addict.* Minneapolis, MN: CompCare Publishers.

[6]Carnes, P. J. (2010). *Online addictions tests.* Retrieved on July 1, 2010 from http://www.sexhelp.com/addiction_tests.cfm

[7]Del Giudice, M. J., & Kutinsky, J. (2007). Applying motivational interviewing to the treatment of sexual compulsivity and addiction. *Sexual Addiction & Compulsivity, 14,* 303-319.

[8]Giugliano, J. (2004). A sociohistorical perspective of sexual health: The clinician's role. *Sexual Addiction & Compulsivity, 11,* 43-55.

[9]Giugliano, J. (2006). Out of control sexual behavior: A qualitative investigation. *Sexual Addiction & Compulsivity, 13,* 361-375.

[10]Giugliano, J. R. (2008). Sexual impulsivity, compulsivity, or dependence: An investigative inquiry. *Sexual Addiction & Compulsivity, 15,* 139-157.

[11]Goodman, A. (1998). Sexual addiction: Diagnosis and treatment. *Psychiatric Times, 15*(10), 1-9.

[12]Goodman, A. (2009). Sexual addiction update: Assessment, diagnosis, and treatment. *Psychiatric Times, 26*(6), 1-11.

[13]Hall, P. (2006). Understanding sexual addiction. *Therapy Today, 17*(2), 30-34.

[14]Kafka, M. P. (2000). The paraphilia-related disorders: Nonparaphilic hypersexuality and sexual compulsivity/addiction. In S. R. Leiblum & R. C. Rosen (Eds.), *Principles & practice of sex therapy* (3ʳᵈ ed.) (pp. 471-503). New York, NY: Guilford Press.

[15]Kafka, M. P. (2010). "What is sexual addiction?" A response to Stephen Levine. *Journal of Sex & Marital Therapy, 36,* 276-281.

[16]Phillips, L. A. (2006). Literature review of research in family systems treatment of sexual addiction. *Sexual Addiction & Compulsivity, 13,* 241-246.

[17]Salisbury, R. M. (2008). Out of control sexual behaviors: A developing practice model. *Sexual and Relationship Therapy, 23*(2), 131-139.

[18]Schwartz, M. F., & Southern, S. (2000). Compulsive cybersex: The new tea room. *Sexual Addiction & Compulsivity, 7,* 127-144.

[19]Society for the Advancement of Sexual Health (2010). *Sexual addiction.* Retrieved on July 1, 2010 from http://sash.net/sexual-addiction.html

[20]Stone, J. H. (Ed.). (2005). *Culture and disability: Providing culturally competent services.* Thousand Oaks, CA: SAGE Publications.

Chapter Fourteen

INTERNET

ADDICTION

BY **ROBERT L. HEWES**

SPRINGFIELD COLLEGE

Chapter Topics

◊ Causes of Internet Addiction

◊ Signs and Symptoms

◊ Risk Factors

◊ Steps Toward Recovery and Treatment

*T*hrough a constant flow of information and as a source of entertainment, the Internet has changed the way the world moves and relates. From Twitter and RSS feeds, information is delivered in real-time, updated daily, and sometimes hourly. Add to this mix the fact that people are now connected to thousands of other people on social networking sites, chat rooms, email, message boards, et cetera, the Internet has significantly broaden our field for potential problematic behaviors. Through rapid and extensive growth and accessibility, the Internet has also changed communication patterns, business transactions, vocational interests and employment, sexual health and behavior, interpersonal skills, and relationships. Unfortunately, with most modern technology and advancement, there are great successes and conveniences, coupled with problems and maladaptive behavior concerns.

Chief among these concerns involving the Internet is a new arena for addictive behavior. With computers becoming more and more affordable, there are a growing number of people worldwide accessing the Internet. People who use the Internet spend on average 9.6 hours per week visiting more than 200 million web sites.[5] From the outside looking in, there is great debate (American Medical Association; American Psychiatric Association; American Society of Addiction Medicine). This debate focuses squarely on the inclusion of "Internet Addiction" or "Internet Disorder" within the next edition of the Diagnostic and Statistical Manual of Mental Disorders (DSM). The debate is complex, but appears to center on the definitions of the terms "overuse" versus "obsession" versus "compulsion." The purpose of this chapter is to give clarity to the issue of Internet addiction by addressing causes, signs and symptoms, risk factors, online behaviors, sexual activity and the Internet, and providing resources and steps toward treatment and recovery.

CAUSES OF
INTERNET ADDICTION

Currently there is no consensus on a definition or defined causes of Internet addiction. This can be explained by the fact that the internet is a rather new communications media. That being true, there appears to be a lack of precedents and explanations on the origin of problematic Internet activity. However, our understanding of addiction in general provides a logical starting point. Three plausible causes for Internet addiction follow.

Social Causes
People often become addicted to the Internet because of the social connections they make online. Online relationship activity can be useful for business, school, and staying in touch with friends and family. Online forums for advice and support have developed in nearly every hobby, interest area, and recreational

activity. Many people use chat rooms for relaxation, fun, entertainment, and excitement. Unfortunately, when people isolate themselves from real life personal relationships, problematic behavior can develop. Emotional attachment, escape, fantasy, pseudo-lives/personas, and alter egos can develop that can be emotionally dangerous for people with other mental health conditions. These behaviors could potentially exacerbate preexisting conditions. This can lead to increased symptoms of depression and feelings of inadequacy that may draw people into online social networks and communication activities.

ENVIRONMENT AND TRAUMA

Considering what we know about the origins of other addictions, it seems likely that some people may be predisposed to online addictions, as one can be predisposed to alcoholism due to the "alcoholic home." Trauma, life stressors, and poor emotional health from one's family of origin could significantly affect relational coping skills, leaving one more vulnerable to Internet addiction.

BEHAVIORAL CAUSES

Skinner's work on operant conditioning may provide additional understanding. Reward or punishments are believed to influence behavior. To avoid the negative effects of trauma, stress, and anxiety, one may attempt to escape from the negative feelings. At the same time, when one finds relief (reward), this often serves as a positive reinforcement for continuing such activity. Persons desiring the positive effect and discovering that the Internet will provide escape and comfort, will likely return to the Internet time-after-time. Thus, the cycle of addiction begins.

Whether or not we view the origin as social, environmental, or behavioral, one issue remains clear. If the Internet provides escape, relief, comfort, positive reinforcement, excitement, social connectivity, entertainment, and the promise of "love," the powerful grip and stronghold of the Internet has the potential to develop in one's life.

SIGNS AND SYMPTOMS

As with other addictions (e.g., alcohol, drugs, gambling), overuse, compulsion, and consequences that interfere with daily life as a result of problematic behavior are the primary concerns. For example, a person who is involved with Internet addiction is likely to experience one or more of the following:

◊ An extreme sense of pleasure/comfort and or guilt/shame during computer use.

◊ Unsuccessful attempts to cut down, control, limit, or quit computer use.

◊ Loss of time, i.e., not realizing one has stayed on-line for hours.

◊ Neglect/avoidance of friends, family, and/or responsibilities in order to be online.
◊ Downplaying, dismissing, or disregarding the amount of time spent on the computer to others.
◊ Feeling agitated, anxious, or upset if computer time is delayed or interrupted.
◊ The computer becomes an outlet to combat trials, sadness, or depression.
◊ The computer becomes an outlet for sexual pleasure and gratification.
◊ Problems at home, school, and or work begin to develop as a result of time spent on the computer.
◊ Compulsive thoughts and feelings begin to develop about computer use when away from the computer.
◊ Excitement builds just prior to going on-line, gaming, social networking, or other computer activities.

RISK FACTORS

The search for antecedents to problematic behavior is ongoing and complex. While the Internet is fairly new, there are some risk factors that appear to have some validity:

◊ Coexisting addictions or psychiatric problems/behaviors.
◊ People with depression or high anxiety may use the Internet for social connections or reaching out; comfort and release of loneliness; distractions from fear/worry.
◊ Social isolation and intense anxiety or fear of others.
◊ Feeling rejected or not fitting into a peer group. The Internet becomes a safe outlet for interaction and entertainment.
◊ Exposure to pornography and sexually explicit material at a young age.
◊ Sexual compulsivity and risk taking behavior.
◊ Psychological vulnerabilities that may lead to compulsive behavior patterns.
◊ Compulsive behavior disorders (e.g., OCD) may contribute to excessive problematic checking of emails, chat rooms, FaceBook, MySpace, stock markets, sports updates, et ceteria.
◊ The Internet is used for sexual gratification and pleasure.
◊ Poor interpersonal skills or lack of family/social support. Chat rooms, social networks, instant messaging, or online gaming become a new way of forming relationships and relating to others.

ONLINE COMPULSIVE COMPUTER USAGE

The numbers and types of activities on the Internet are wide ranging. A few unique types of online compulsive computer behaviors have been identified:

◊ Cybersexual Addiction - viewing, downloading, and trading online pornography or engaging in adult fantasy role-play, e.g., Simms.

◊ Cyber-Relational Addiction - Individuals excessively involved in chat rooms, instant messaging, or social networking sites often become over involved in online relationships.

◊ Net Compulsions - Excessive online gaming, online gambling, stock marketing watching, online auctions, are a new area of problematic compulsive computer behaviors.

◊ Information Overload - Excessive web surfing and database searching for news, information, trivia, film, videos, and clips, out of the ordinary sound bites, tidbits, and facts to absorb or share within a social network.

SEXUAL ACTIVITY AND THE INTERNET

Woody Allen once said, "Sex without love is an empty experience, but as empty experiences go it's one of the best." Not surprisingly, the rapid rise in Internet usage is positively correlated with the increasing availability of online pornography. Sexually explicit websites are one of the fastest growing sites on the Internet. According to Goldberg,[4] the five most frequently visited adult web sites receive over nine million visitors per month with nearly one-third of the online population visiting an adult website at least once. Accessibility, affordability, and anonymity[2] are three reasons why Internet use and Internet addiction are rising.

Online sexual activity is defined as the use of the Internet for any activity that involves sexuality for recreation, entertainment, education, or support. Cybersex is a subcategory of online sexual activity and can be defined in three forms:[3]

◊ Online exchange of pornography. e.g., email, FaceBook, personal homepages.

◊ Live modes of communication of sexually explicit material, e.g., web cam, chat rooms, audio, and video.

◊ Online sexual activity, e.g., online exchanging of pornographic material that leads to mutual masturbation, or luring, coercing and or arranging an offline sexual encounter.

There appears to be an inverse progression of addiction to sexually explicit material when compared to progression of addiction to other substances. For example, a typical progression of addiction to alcohol might follow this pattern: use, misuse, abuse, and dependency. However, Dr. Victor B. Cline[1] reporting on "Pornography's effects on adults and children" pointed out that addiction (i.e., compulsion and dependency) to sexually explicit material is almost immediate. The "addiction-effect" occurs once the person begins to consume pornographic material. With further involvement and increased exposure, the individual will often keep coming back for more. Cline[1] noted that the progression continues through four stages:

Addiction. Initial exposure to sexual stimuli that produces an aphrodisiac effect, followed by sexual release such as masturbation.

Escalation. Over time, individuals require more sexually explicit material; rougher, more deviant, out of the norm, "kinkier" material to get their "high" or sexual release or sexual satisfaction.

Desensitization. Sexually explicit material that once appeared shocking and stimulating, illegal, taboo or immoral becomes normalized.

Acting out sexually. Some individuals begin to act out sexually the behaviors viewed in the pornographic material, e.g., compulsive promiscuity, voyeurism, group sex, having sex with minors, rape.

STEPS TOWARD RECOVERY AND TREATMENT

Treatment for Internet addiction is somewhat new. Steps to modify Internet use, uncover cues, triggers, and antecedents, and provide proper treatment planning seems to parallel other addiction treatment models. For example, counselors will often ask clients to monitor their internet use through journals and logs. Careful attention is given to cues and triggers, feelings and excitement prior to computer use, the time of day one uses the computer, frequency and duration, and specific online activities.

Clients are encouraged to replace Internet usage with alternative activities especially when bored, tired, lonely, and feeling anxious or depressed. Plans and schedules are created to limit and oversee time spent on the computer. Goals are established for time-on and for time-off the computer. Accountability groups are suggested for problems with cybersex and pornography. Support groups to work on social and coping skills such as for anxiety or depression are also possible. Therapy (individual and group counseling) can provide support in stopping excessive and compulsive Internet behaviors and working through unhealthy emotions.

Other countries have treated compulsive Internet usage or "cyber junkies" as a public health danger. There are several residential clinics in China, South Korea, and Taiwan where internet addiction has been treated through government-sponsored boot camps.[6] In addition, Amsterdam has developed detoxification centers to combat other Internet concerns such as video gaming.[7]

To date, very few treatment centers across the United States specialize in treating Internet addiction. At the same time, day-by-day millions of adolescents, teens, young adults, and the elderly will continue to discover the power, influence, and speed of the Internet–a superhighway of potential addiction and maladaptive behavior problems that remains highly affordable, accessible, and anonymous.

RESOURCES

Center for Online Addiction - Dr. Kimberly Young
www.netaddiction.com
The Center for Internet Studies - Dr. David Greenfield
www.virtual-addiction.com
Pure Intimacy - www.pureintimacy.org
Caught in the Net, by Dr. Kimberly Young, New York: John Wiley & Sons, Inc. 1998
Center for Online Addiction on Gambling -
www.netaddiction.com/net_compulsions.htm
Focus on the Family -
www.focusonthefamily.com/socialissues/gambling/gambling.aspx
Pathological Gambling: The Making of a Medical Problem, by Brian Castellani, New York: University of New York Press, 2000
The Centerfold Syndrome: How Men Can Overcome Objectification and Achieve Intimacy with Women, by Dr. Gary Brooks, San Francisco: Jossey-Bass, 1995
Don't Call it Love: Recovery from Sex Addiction, by Patrick Carnes, New York: Bantam Books, 1992
Real Solutions for Overcoming Internet Addictions, by Stephen O. Watters, Ann Arbor, MI: Servant Publications, 2001
Protecting Your Child in an X-Rated World: What You Need to Know to Make a Difference, by Frank York and Jan LaRue, Wheaton, IL: Tyndale Publishers, 2002
Center for Online Addiction on Daytrading
www.netaddiction.com/daytrading.htm
Every Man's Battle: Winning the War on Sexual Temptation One Victory at a Time, by Stephen Arterburn and Fred Stoker with Mike Yorkey, Colorado Springs: WaterBooks Press, 2000
National Coalition for the Protection of Children and Families
www.nationalcoalition.org
Stone Gate Resources - www.stonegateresources.org
False Intimacy: Understanding the Struggle of Sexual Addiction, by Dr. Harry W. Schaumburg, Colorado Springs: NavPress, 1997
The Silent War: Ministering to those Trapped in the Deception of Pornography, by Henry J. Rogers, Green Forest, AK: New Leaf Press, 1999
Pornography's Effects on Adults and Children, by Dr. Victor B. Cline, New York: Morality in the Media, 1999

REFERENCES

Cline, V. B. (1999). *Pornography's Effects on Adults and Children,* Retrieved from http://www.sif.org.au/forum-drvictorcline.html

Cooper, A. (1998). Sexuality and the Internet: Surfing into the new millennium. *CyberPsychology and Behavior, 1(2),* 187-193.

Delmonico, D. L. (1997). Cybersex: High tech sex addiction. *Sexual Addiction and Compulsivity, 4,* 159-167.

Goldberg, A. (1998). *Monthly users report on adult sexually oriented sites for April 1998.* Washington, D.C.: Relevant Knowledge.

Greenspan, R. (2002). *The web continues to spread. Trends and statistics: The web's richest source* [Online]. Retrieved December 2004, from http://www.clickz.com /stats/sectors/geographics/article.phpr/1556641

Harvey, M. (2009). *CyberJunkies Weaned off the Web,* Retrieved from http://www.theaustralian.com.au/news/world/cyber-junkies-weaned-off-the-web/story-e6frg6so-1225776520576

Horaczek, S. (2006). *Rehab center for video game addicts opens in Amsterdam,* Retrieved from http://www.engadget.com/2006/07/15/rehab-center-for-video-game-addicts-opens-in-amsterdam/

Chapter Fifteen

THE SPECTRUM OF TREATMENT OPTIONS & THEIR COMPONENTS

BY   GENEVIEVE WEBER GILMORE

HOLLY SEIRUP

REBECCA RUBINSTEIN

HOFSTRA UNIVERSITY

Chapter Topics

◊ Treatment Options

◊ Treatment Components

TREATMENT OPTIONS

It is essential that mental health professionals in various settings (e.g., community agencies, colleges, and schools) understand the spectrum of treatment options and their components in order to match unique client clinical needs to a treatment setting[3]. There are many aspects associated with treatment, and each client who presents to counseling has unique clinical concerns that require an individualized treatment approach. Although the common clinical issue presented is that of substance use or abuse, treatment frequency and intensity will vary depending on the severity of the client's symptoms, whether they are related to substance use, mental health, or both. Identifying where clients are on the continuum of use is also crucial in the planning of treatment options. The authors' experience in substance abuse treatment settings supports the application of the continuum of use in conceptualizing the severity of one's abuse or dependency. The continuum of use can often be seen as a progression from experimentation, continued use, abuse, and dependency. This subjective proposal is supported by Budney, Sigmon, and Higgins[5] in their note, "drug use is considered a normal learned behavior that falls along a continuum ranging from patterns of little use and few problems to excessive use and dependence." [p. 249] An advantage of such a continuum is that it allows for the classification of various intensities and patterns of alcohol and drug use and abuse. Intervention at any point during the continuum of use can be beneficial, but intervention is of particular importance and benefit during the latter stages of abuse and dependency. It is essential, however, to refer to the criteria articulated in the *Diagnostic and Statistical Manual of Mental Disorders* (DSM IV TR, American Psychiatric Association, 2000) for diagnosing substance related disorders (i.e., substance abuse, substance dependence) and the American Society for Addiction Medicine's *Patient Placement Criteria*[2] for treatment planning. DSM IV TR provides definitions and criteria for determining substance related disorders. The classification of a substance related disorder based on the DSM IV TR is crucial as it often impacts the type of treatment that medical insurance will cover.

The patient placement criteria introduced by ASAM is a commonly used guide for determining the most appropriate level of care for the client's substance abuse needs.[2] It includes two sets of guidelines for treatment of adolescents and adults, as well as five broad levels of care for each group.

Levels of Care

    Level 0.5: Early Intervention

    Level I: Outpatient Treatment

    Level II: Intensive Outpatient Treatment/Partial Hospitalization

    Level III: Medically Monitored Inpatient Treatment/Residential
        Treatment

Level IV: Medically-Managed Intensive Inpatient Treatment

A brief overview of treatment components for each level of care is provided. For example, services relevant to a range of addiction severities and their associated problems are presented, along with a comprehensive description of settings, staff, services, and admission criteria for the following six dimensions:

Dimensions of Severity

◊   Acute Intoxication/Withdrawal Potential
◊   Biomedical Conditions and Complications
◊   Emotional, Behavioral, or Cognitive Conditions and Complications
◊   Readiness to Change
◊   Relapse/Continued Use/Continued Problem Potential
◊   Recovery Environment

Both the DSM IV TR and ASAM PPC-2R are critical in diagnosing a substance-related disorder and identifying an appropriate treatment setting.

According to Brookes and McHenry,[3] substance abuse treatment is designed to provide structure and boundaries; peer and professional feedback; individual, group, family or couples counseling; and relapse prevention comprised of coping skills training. Abstinence from all mood-altering substances is very important throughout treatment as it allows for the resolution of ambivalence and the internalization and understanding of the psycho-educational material provided and insight gained through corrective emotional experiences. This internalization allows each client to develop a personal recovery program that consists of a treatment plan inclusive of relevant goals and objectives that will help the client maintain sobriety and experience relational change. Not all clients will stop using alcohol and drugs entirely during treatment; although not ideal, a reduction in alcohol and drug use might still allow for the planting of "seeds for both current and future growth."[3, p.115]

Substance abuse treatment is usually delivered in two basic settings: inpatient and outpatient, and is often conceptualized as detoxification, intensive treatment, residential programs, outpatient services, and aftercare services.[29] According to the Center for Substance Abuse Treatment[8], the general goal of treatment, regardless of the setting, is to place clients "in the least restrictive environment that is still safe and effective. The person is then move them along a continuum of care as they demonstrate the capacity and motivation to cooperate with treatment and no longer need a more structured setting or the types of services offered only in that environment." Progress through treatment, however, does not always move in the direction from most to least intense; rather, a relapse, either substance and or mental health related, might require moving to a more intensive treatment than the previous treatment setting. This chapter will present the spectrum of treatment options for clients who present with substance abuse or dependency.

DETOXIFICATION

The primary purpose of detoxification is to help the client become medically stabilized as he or she experiences withdrawal symptoms that could otherwise be fatal without medical supervision.[29] Over the past 15 years, outpatient ambulatory detoxification has also become a practical alternative to inpatient detoxification for some clients (e.g., those at low-risk for medical complications.[30] The determination for one to participate in inpatient or outpatient detoxification should be made after a thorough examination by a physician.

Commonly referred to as "detox," detoxification services are often delivered in hospital settings or in community centers. A multidisciplinary treatment staff usually includes a physician and nurse, as well as various other mental health professionals such as licensed professional counselors, social workers, rehabilitation counselors, or counselors certified in the area of substance abuse. Medical staff focus on medical supervision (e.g., blood pressure, respiration, pulse), while clinical staff help the client with other immediate needs, particularly those of the psycho-social nature (e.g., discharge planning, housing, financial assistance).[30]

Detoxification is an opportunity for the client to take important steps toward recovery. First, physicians can intervene during the client's withdrawal with medical means that lessen the effects of the withdrawal syndrome. These interventions may include continuous fluids, aspirin, phenobarbital, Buprenix, or Librium.[29] While clients are experiencing detoxification, the medications work in the body to prevent seizures, delirium tremens (DTs), and other high risk side effects from withdrawal. As the withdrawal symptoms lessen in severity with time, the clients are slowly taken off the medications before being discharged from the detoxification setting.[29] Second, detoxification is an important step in treatment as it provides mental health professionals with an opportunity to assess and motivate clients towards continued treatment post-discharge, if appropriate (i.e., inpatient or outpatient treatment). During the client's stay in detoxification treatment, a full evaluation is conducted through an initial psychological assessment as well through participation in group and individual counseling. Detoxification alone will not address the multitude of complex issues in addition to the substance abuse or dependence such as employment, relationship, and other psycho-social concerns.[12] Thus, detoxification is often considered the first step in the process of recovery.[29]

INPATIENT HOSPITALIZATION

Originally a defining characteristic of the Minnesota Model of Treatment, inpatient treatment includes a thorough and ongoing assessment of a client. The assessment is followed by a comprehensive treatment program comprised of group, individual, family, and couples therapy, which is provided by a multidisciplinary team of professionals.[26] Inpatient treatment is usually found in hospital-based or community settings that specialize in substance abuse treatment. Inpatient treatment often begins with detoxification, thus offering continuous 24 hour care as well as providing a means of removing a client from his or her environment that might be detrimental to long-term recovery.[17, 29] Such detrimental recovery environments might include limited financial resources; issues with housing; alcohol or drug using peers; places or things that might be triggers; and, concurrent mental health issues. The length of stay for an client in inpatient treatment will vary depending on factors such as motivation, support network, and other variables that the multidisciplinary team considers to be important for recovery.[12] A sample daily schedule for inpatient treatment might include two counseling groups for one hour each; one individual counseling session for 50 minutes; urine analysis; support group meeting (e.g., Alcoholics Anonymous, Marijuana Anonymous); social activity(ies) such as arts and crafts or an outside nature walk; exercise such as yoga; "free time" for reading and reflecting; breakfast, lunch, and dinner. Psychiatric evaluations and psychopharmacological management might be scheduled for once a week or on an as-needed basis.

RESIDENTIAL TREATMENT
Residential treatment is usually found in a nonhospital or "freestanding facility."[17] It often includes halfway houses and therapeutic communities. Halfway houses were originally developed to "serve alcoholics," and therapeutic communities were originally designed to "serve drug addicts."[29, p.112] Both residential settings provide a safe and sober environment where clients can move further towards recovery with the support and camaraderie of other community members. Halfway houses are an option for those who want to continue with structured support in a sober living environment. This house or residence is run by professional staff but occupied by clients who are in recovery. Reasons for entering a halfway house might vary from individual to individual, but usually those with housing needs benefit from such structure. Clients in a halfway house may have the option to work in or out of the residence, and are expected to maintain abstinence and participate in weekly individual or group counseling sessions.[3] The therapeutic community has moved away from its initial controversial treatment paradigm which was "harsh" and confrontational,"[12, p354] and more towards an integrated program that utilizes the community (i.e., sober support network). Other characteristics include a structured living environment where rewards and punishments follow behaviors, social and physical isolation, and a focus on self-examination and past unhealthy behaviors. The length of treatment for clients in a therapeutic community ranges from six months to three years, depending on the client's situation (i.e., self-admitted versus mandated by the criminal justice system.[12] The overarching goal for both the halfway house and therapeutic community is for the client to transition successfully back into the community and society. A sample residential treatment schedule might resemble

that of inpatient treatment, with an increased focus on connecting the client to his or her community through employment or attendance at support groups.

OUTPATIENT TREATMENT

Outpatient treatment for substance abuse varies in structure, time, and services provided ranging upon a continuum from intensive outpatient, through partial hospitalization, to day treatment. Traditionally, outpatient treatment followed a 28 day inpatient treatment program where a client underwent detoxification, along with intensive individual and group counseling. Outpatient treatment assists clients maintain sobriety/abstinence while transitioning back into the community, their jobs, and relationships. The main goals for outpatient treatment are to promote abstinence and a substance free lifestyle; identify the underpinning of the unhealthy behaviors (e.g. issues within the family, coping, stress, anxiety); and prevent relapse. To meet these goals, clients usually participate in individual, group, and family counseling, Twelve step self-help groups (such as Alcoholics/Narcotics Anonymous) are recommended as adjuncts to treatment.[28] Outpatient treatment staff usually consists of a substance abuse counselor (e.g., social worker, mental health counselor, certified substance abuse counselor), a psychiatrist, and a consulting psychologist for psychological testing, if necessary.[3]

The growth of managed health care has led to some restrictions in insurance coverage for the traditional 28 day inpatient care.[22, 19] In fact, McLellan, et al.,[26] reported a decrease nationally in inpatient facilities along with significant increases in outpatient programs. Fisher[13] noted that at times even detoxification is occurring in outpatient settings. There have been many studies comparing the outcomes of residential versus non-residential treatment.[31, 15, 16] Most have concluded that both treatment modalities can be equally effective and outcome depends upon the severity of addiction and the client's overall mental health (e.g., dual diagnosis), motivation, and willingness to cooperate and participate in treatment. Optimally, clients should be placed in a treatment environment where the client can be successful, that is safe and provides the least restrictions.[9]

Intensive outpatient care (IOP). Stevens & Smith[28] wrote, "intensive outpatient treatment (IOP) programs consist of abstinence-based treatment that can range in intensity from daily all-day activities to weekly meetings." (p.179) Intensive outpatient care can consist of partial hospitalization and/or day treatments. Intensive outpatient treatment is recommended when clients are in need of structure, have some support, and are transitioning from inpatient hospitalization care or a residential treatment facility. The client participates in treatment throughout the day and may go to their home in the evenings. Treatment consists of five to seven days or evenings per week for three to eight hours each day.[8] This allows the client to attend treatment part of the day, evening, and weekends and at the same time reintegrate into their home and community. Family interaction and dysfunction may be a part of the issue supporting the addiction, therefore re-integration into home, work, and the community gives the client an opportunity to practice the skills learned in treatment to real life situations. A sample intensive outpatient treatment schedule might include group counseling three times per week on Mondays, Wednesdays, and Fridays for three hours; individual counseling one to two times per week on Tuesdays or Thursdays for 50 minutes; urine analyses (if applicable) two days per week (to be decided by counselor); family counseling one time per week for 50 minutes (if applicable); and, support groups (e.g., Alcoholics Anonymous, Marijuana Anonymous) one time per week at the treatment center as well as two times per week outside of the treatment center.

Outpatient care. Less intensive outpatient treatment may be recommended based upon client needs. This would include meeting less frequently (1 to 2 times per week). These programs work best with motivated clients with strong support systems, including appropriate living arrangements and available transportation in place.[8] A sample outpatient group schedule might include group counseling two times per week on Tuesday and Thursday evenings for one hour; individual counseling one time per week on Wednesday for 50 minutes; urine analyses (if applicable) two days per week (to be decided by counselor); and, support groups (e.g., Alcoholics Anonymous, Marijuana Anonymous) two times per week.

Relapse. Relapse and program retention continue to be a problem in outpatient treatment. McLellan, et al.[25] note, "In outpatient settings it cannot be assumed that patients are abstinent or even making progress during treatment, and a significant number of patients drop out from outpatient treatment prior to a planned completion point."A study by Laudet, et al.,[21] identified a number of reasons why clients choose to leave treatment. Many clients indicated that they did not like the program, or had other activities which interfered with participation in treatment. Some clients reported that they had returned to using substances, while others identified personal reasons as why they discontinued treatment, particularly lack of finances. Finally, some reported that they did not find the program to be helpful.

To prevent clients from dropping out of treatment, it is important to engage them in the program and try to get their commitment early. Providing the ongoing support as well as complimentary services such as career development, job placement, and stress management may also prove to retain clients and assist them on their road to recovery.

AFTER CARE TREATMENT

Once a client completes their outpatient treatment program, it is helpful to continue with a formal aftercare treatment plan. Aftercare is considered the least structured and least restrictive treatment option. During aftercare, the client may continue to attend counseling sessions (individual, family and/or group) but with less frequency (i.e., once or twice each week),[4] and it is expected that they continue to attend a peer support group (e.g., Alcoholics Anonymous, Narcotics Anonymous). Treatment goals developed during the aftercare treatment process are to prevent relapse and to assist and support a client in the life-long recovery process).[12] This is particularly important as many clients relapse after completing intensive outpatient treatment. Lash and Blosser[20] found that participation in after-care treatment increases positive treatment outcomes. A sample aftercare treatment schedule might include group counseling one time per week on Wednesdays for one hour; individual counseling one time per week on Mondays for 50 minutes; urine analyses (if applicable) one day per week (to be decided by counselor); and, support groups (e.g., Alcoholics Anonymous, Marijuana Anonymous) one time per week outside of the treatment center.

TREATMENT COMPONENTS

Individual, group, and family counseling are common to all treatment options, and beneficial to the client's personalized recovery plan.

INDIVIDUAL COUNSELING

Individual counseling has been found to be successful with clients to explore the difficulties they encounter in their daily lives and how these issues may disrupt their healthy functioning.[10] Issues such as limit setting, coping, decision making, problem solving, and stress management are often discussed. The individual counselor can also be a major source of support and offer possible resources as the client moves through the treatment process.

GROUP COUNSELING

Psycho-educational and peer support group interventions are often used in all modalities of substance abuse treatment. Groups give clients an opportunity to share and communicate their feelings as well as listen and offer support to others as it relates to the struggles of substance abuse and maintaining abstinence. There is no overall consensus on the specifics of the development and structure of a group (e.g. frequency of meetings, open or close membership, confrontational or supportive in nature) but it is the most common and effective treatment modality when working with clients with addictions.[9] See chapter 20 for a more in-depth discussion of group counseling.

Family counseling. Difficulties and dysfunctions among families may impact a client's addiction and subsequent recovery.[10] Families play an important role in getting a client into treatment and providing support and encouragement during and after the completion of treatment. Learning to communicate among the family is often an important goal of family therapy. Family members can also benefit from psycho-educational programs that might take place in the form of workshops offered by the treatment setting. See chapter 19 for a more in-depth discussion of family counseling.

Cognitive behavioral therapy. Cognitive behavioral therapy (CBT) is often utilized in individual, group, and family counseling to assist clients to confront their irrational thoughts which may lead to addictive behavior. It assists the client to develop new skills and behavior changes to support their road to recovery.[22] CBT strategies often include behavioral contracting, contingency management, self monitoring, stress management social skills training.[8]

Dual-diagnosis issues. It is very common for clients to experience mental health and substance abuse disorders concurrently. Treating more than one issue or disorder at the same time has been identified as a barrier to successful treatment.[30] According to the Center for Substance Abuse Treatment,[7] if a client has a substance abuse disorder, they are at risk for developing a mental illness; if they have a mental illness, they are at risk for developing a substance disorder. Clients who are diagnosed with a dual-diagnosis (i.e., alcohol dependence and Major Depressive Disorder) are often prescribed medications, participate in group counseling, and attend twelve-step groups[7]. *MICA*, or mentally ill chemical abusers, is the acronym designated for treatment settings where services are provided to clients with dual-diagnoses.

For clients with a dual-diagnosis, asking for help and entering treatment is often a struggle. Therefore, initial assessment and screening are very important in determining psychological functioning and severity of the dual diagnosis, as well as in constructing a treatment plan or making decisions regarding treatment.[9] Dual-diagnosis programs are programs that identify and treat all of the disorders a person has with equal emphasis and which has mental health professionals who are trained to counsel clients with a variety of mental disorders. A dual-diagnosis treatment center should also provide a range of services such as detoxification, psychiatric evaluation, and psychopharmacological management. Factors that are likely to enhance treatment for clients with dual-diagnosis include long term treatment focused on rehabilitation and recovery as well as individual case management and group counseling.[8]

ADOLESCENT TREATMENT

Adolescence can be a difficult time when many psychological and physical changes take place. Adolescents are experiencing a developmental transition and may feel the need to conform to peer pressure or expectations of those around them. Adolescents face many challenges including new found independence, more relationships with peers, planning for the future and their career, and whether or not to use substances. It is often during adolescence when mental health and substance abuse problems begin to emerge.[18] At times, symptoms of substance abuse and dependence may be overlooked and seen as typical developmental issues of adolescence rather than indicative of more serious problems.[18]

Adolescents who have an earlier start to substance abuse are more likely to continue using in the future and are at a greater risk of developing substance dependence as adults. Furthermore, youth who have co-occurring behavioral and substance abuse issues may have higher rates of using multiple substances, engage in delinquent activities, experience academic difficulties, attempt suicide, and drop out of treatment and have poorer outcomes. If adolescence substance abuse and other mental health concerns are left untreated, these problems can continue into adulthood, placing the client at risk for unemployment, serious medical problems, victimization, legal issues, homelessness, and increased emergency room care.[18]

Adolescents may not feel comfortable discussing their substance abuse with counselors[6]. For counselors, it is important to work with the adolescent client, and not against them. Counselors working with adolescents should be aware of the developmental events that occur during this time to more accurately understand the client's presenting concerns. The treatment setting should be equipped to offer a variety of services to address the adolescent's educational, recreational, social, and psychiatric needs.[12] Treatment programs tailored to adolescents should include a family component where focus is placed on improving communication; a treatment approach that is appropriate to the adolescent's level of development; innovative and engaging interventions; and, a sufficient duration that allows for substantial change in the coping skills of the adolescent and his or her family.[12, 22]

WOMEN IN TREATMENT

The concept of gender may pose unique barriers to entering and receiving treatment.[14] When women enter treatment, they often have different needs than their male counterparts. For example, mothers may struggle with whether or not to discuss issues regarding their children in treatment, fearing that their disclosure may lead to negative effects such as losing custody of their children. There is also the emotional component including feelings of shame, guilt, and the fear that their support system will not be there for them during the treatment process. Because of these issues, women may feel more comfortable in an all-female group and treatment environment.

Trauma is also a risk factor for substance abuse among women. Women who have substance use disorders are at an increased risk of trauma and abuse, and for many, being exposed to trauma and abuse came before the use of substances.[27] Women survivors of abuse may have also had problems in school and, thus, began to use alcohol or drugs, which also makes them more likely to have experienced homelessness and victimization. According to Sacks, McKendrick, & Banks,[27] women who need trauma related services are not receiving them adequately, and due to their traumatic experiences, women may have had poorer treatment outcomes. Treatment outcomes could be improved when the counseling process integrates a focus on the trauma, substance abuse, and related mental health issues.[27]

LESBIAN, GAY, BISEXUAL, AND TRANSGENDER ISSUES

The lack of possible opportunities for LGBT individuals to socialize may give reason as to why many go to bars, and thus increase their risk for substance abuse and misuse.[11] Stress that results from discrimination can lead to increased substance use due to feelings of shame and guilt. Furthermore, LGBT individuals who experienced victimization in childhood may be at increased risk for domestic violence and may have partners who abuse substances.[11] LGBT individuals typically have a greater frequency of substance use, use more mental health services, are at higher risk for being victims of domestic violence and homelessness, and have been treated for more physical health issues.[11] Therefore, the unique stressors for LGBT individuals must be considered in substance abuse treatment programs.

Treatment programs that are most effective for LGBT clients are those that are free of homophobic bias.[11] It is also necessary that counselors receive training in working with LGBT clients and their specific needs. Counselors should be aware of their own thoughts regarding homophobia and heterosexism and attitudes and biases towards LGBT clients. Counselors should also consider the intersections between substance abuse, and gender identity or sexual identity. It is important, however, not to attribute substance abuse issues to gender identity or sexual identity if no connection has been made. Participating in programs that reference the connection between substance use and the societal stigma towards LGBT clients is helpful for LGBT clients. Programs that are sensitive to LGBT clients and focus on psychological stressors and problems unique to LGBT clients, are needed.[11]

REFERENCES

[1]American Psychiatric Association. (2000). *Diagnostic and statistical manual of mental disorders* (4th ed., text revision). Washington, DC: Author.

[2]American Society of Addiction Medicine. (2001). *ASAM PPC-2R*. Chevy Chase, MD: Author.

[3]Brooks, F. & McHenry, B. (2009). *A contemporary approach to substance abuse and addiction counseling.* Alexandria: VA, American Counseling Association.

[4]Brown, T.G., Seraganian, P., & Annis, H. (2002). Matching substance abuse aftercare treatments to client characteristics. *Addictive Behaviors, 27,* 586-604.

[5]Budney, A. J., Sigmon, S. C., & Higgins, S. T. (2003). Contingency management in the substance abuse treatment clinic. In *Treating substance abuse: Theory and technique* (2nd ed.) (Rotgers, F., Morgenstern, J., & Walters, S. T., Eds.). New York: Guilford.

[6]Burrow-Sanchez, J.J. (2006). Understanding adolescent substance
abuse: prevalence, risk factors, and clinical implications. *Journal of
Counseling and Development, 84,* 283-290 .

[7]Center for Substance Abuse Treatment. *Assessment and Treatment of
Patients with Coexisting Mental Illness and Alcohol and Other Drug Abuse.*
Treatment Improvement Protocol (TIP) Series 9. Rockville, MD: Substance
Abuse & Mental Health Services Administration; 1995. Available at:
http://www.ncbi.nlm.nih.gov/bookshelf/br.fcgi?book=hssamhsatip&part=A29
713.

[8]Center for Substance Abuse Treatment. *A Guide to Substance Abuse
Services for Primary Care Clinicians.* Treatment Improvement Protocol
(TIP) Series 24. Rockville, Md: Substance Abuse & Mental Health Services
Administration; 1997. Available at: http://www.ncbi.nlm.nih.gov/bookshelf/
br.fcgi?book=hssamhsatip&part=A45293

[9]Center for Substance Abuse Treatment. *Substance Abuse Treatment for
Persons With Co-Occurring Disorders.* Treatment Improvement Protocol
(TIP) Series 42. Rockville, Md: Substance Abuse & Mental Health Services
Administration; 2004. Available at: http://www.ncbi.nlm.nih.gov/bookshelf/

[10]Center for Substance Abuse Treatment. *Substance Abuse: Critical
Issues in Intensive Outpatient Treatment.* Treatment Improvement Protocol
(TIP) Series 47. Rockville, Md: Substance Abuse & Mental Health Services
Administration; 2006. Available at: http://www.ncbi.nlm.nih.gov/bookshelf/
br.fcgi?book=hssamhsatip&part=A88658

[11]Cochran, B. N. And Cauce, A. M. (2006). Characteristics of lesbian,
gay, bisexual, and transgender individuals entering substance abuse
treatment. *Journal of Substance Abuse Treatment, 30,* 135-146.

[12]Doweiko, H.E. (2009). *Concepts of chemical dependency* (7th ed.).
Belmont, California: Brooks/Cole.

[13]Fisher, G.L., & Harrison, T.C. (2009). Substance abuse information for
school counselors, social workers, therapists, and counselor (4th ed). Boston,
Pearson.

[14]Greenfield, S. F., Trucco, E. M., McHugh, K., Lincoln, M., and Gallop,
R. J. (2007). The women's recovery group study: A stage I trial of women-
focused group therapy for substance use disorders versus mixed-gender
group drug counseling. *Drug Alcohol and Dependence, 90,* 39-47.

[15]Guydish, J., Sorenson, J., Chan, M., Werdegar, D., Bostrom, A., &
Acompora, A. (1999). Drug abuse day treatment: A Randomized clinical trial
comparing day treatment and day programs 18 month outcomes. *Journal of
Consulting and Clinical Psychology, 67*(3) 428-434.

[16]Guydish, J., Werdegar, D., Sorenson, J., Clark, W., & Acompora, A.
(1998). Drug abuse day treatment: A randomized clinical trial comparing day
treatment and day programs. *Journal of Consulting and Clinical Psychology,
66*(2) 280-284.

[17]Harrison, P.A., & Asche, S.E., (1999). Comparison of substance abuse treatment outcomes for inpatient and outpatients. *Journal of Substance Abuse Treatment, 17*(3) 207-220.

[18]Hawkins, E.H. (2009). A Tale of two systems: co-occurring mental health and substance abuse disorders treatment for adolescents. *Annual Review of Psychology, 60,* 197-227.

[19]Jason, L. A., Olson, B. D., Ferrari, J. R., & LoSasso, A.T. (2006). Communal housing settings enhance abuse recovery. *American Journal of Public Health, 96*(10), 1727-1729.

[20]Lash, S. J. & Blosser, S .L. (1999). Increasing adherence to substance abuse aftercare group therapy. *Journal of Substance Abuse Treatment,* 16(1) 55-60.

[21]Laudet, A. B., Stanick, V., & Sands, B. (2009). What could the program have done differently? A qualitative examination of reasons for leaving outpatient treatment. *Journal of Substance Abuse Treatment 37,* 182-190.

[22]Mark, T. L., Song, X., Vandivort, R., Duffy, S., Butler, J., Coffey, R., and Schabert, V. F. (2006). Characterizing substance abuse programs that treat adolescents. *Journal of Substance Abuse Treatment, 31,* 59-65.

[23]McKay, J. R., Alterman, A. I., Cacciola, J. C., Rutherford, M. J., O'Brien, C. P., & Koppenhaver, J. (1997). Group counseling versus individualized relapse prevention aftercare following intensive outpatient treatment for cocaine dependence: Initial results. *Journal of Consulting and Clinical Psychology, 65*(5) 778-788.

[24]McLellan, A. T., Carise, D., & Kleber, H. D. (2003). Can the national addiction treatment infrastructure support the public's demand for quality health care? *Journal of Substance Abuse Treatment, 25,* 117-121.

[25]McLellan, A. T., McKay, J. R., Forman, R., Cacciola, J., & Kemp, J. (2005). Reconsidering the evaluation of addiction treatment from retrospective follow up to concurrent recovery monitoring. *Addiction, 100* 447-458.

[26]National Institute of Drug Abuse. (2010). Minnesota Model: Description of Counseling Approach. Available at http://archives.drugabuse.gov/adac/ADAC11.html.

[27]Sacks, J. Y., McKendrick, K., & Banks, S. (2008). The Impact of early trauma and abuse on residential substance abuse treatment outcomes for women. *Journal of Substance Abuse Treatment, 34,* 90-100.

[28]Stevens, P., & Smith, R. L. (2005). Substance Abuse Counseling Theory and practice (3rd.) Upper Saddle River, NJ, Pearson.

[29]van Wormer, K. & Davis, D. R. 2008: Addiction treatment: A strengths perspective (2nd ed.). Belmont, CA: Wadsworth Watkins.

[30]Watkins, K. E., Burman, A., Kung, F. Y., Paddock, S. (2001). A national survey of care for persons with co-occurring mental & substance use disorders. *Psyiatric Services, 52,* 1062-1068.

[31]Witbrodt, J., Bond, J., Kaskutas, L., Weisner, C., Jaeger, G., Pating, D., & Moore, C. (2007). Day hospital and residential addiction treatment: Randomized and non randomized managed care clients. *Journal of Consulting and Clinical Psychology, 75*(6) 947-959.

Chapter Sixteen

DIAGNOSTIC

& SCREENING

TESTS

BY **ARNOLD WOLF**

HUNTER COLLEGE
CITY UNIVERSITY OF NEW YORK

JOSEPH KEFERL

WRIGHT STATE UNIVERSITY

Chapter Topics

◊ Overview

◊ Assessment Techniques

◊ Closing Remarks

OVERVIEW

*T*he need for early identification of substance abuse, coupled with many different belief systems that attempt to define why people abuse various chemicals such as drugs and alcohol, lead to numerous assessment and testing techniques. It is beyond the purpose of this chapter to explore all of the reasons relative to early identification and various theories that are significant to an understanding of substance abuse. A few concepts must be presented, however, to understand better why multiple assessment techniques are needed.

Critical to making sound clinical judgments of how best to help a person is knowing whether or not a person is using or abusing substances. A person who is abusing substances should be treated for substance abuse, while a person who is not abusing any chemicals, but who exhibits unusual or changed patterns of behavior, should be seen by a physician, psychiatrist, counselor, or other trained behavioral health professional for further assessment and diagnosis since the person may actually have a medical or mental health problem that mimics abuse behavior.

CASE STUDY

John, age 17 and a high school senior, falls asleep during class, drools on his work assignments, and no longer achieves in school at the levels he did in previous years. His parents report that he seems lethargic, and lacks interest in hobbies, sports, and friends that he had enjoyed for years. John's behavior changes have occurred rather quickly, and seem to be getting worse. Although no tangible signs of drug use have been found, his parents are very concerned, and come to an assumption that it may be due to drug use. His teacher, who has also been witnessing his behavior changes in class, also assumes that John is abusing drugs. Despite numerous attempts by his family to question John about his apparent drug use, he continues to deny any involvement with drugs. In an effort to gain the "truth," John's parents request several medical tests including urine analysis and blood work. Results indicate that John's plea of innocence was truthful and is indeed drug-free. However, slight anomalies discovered by the blood tests warranted further medical testing, which indicated that John has developed a brain tumor that is operable, but has been interfering with his ability to learn and function on a daily basis. The brain tumor caused significant behavior and emotional changes, which mimicked substance abuse behaviors, and would not have been identified until much later in the progression of the tumor had John's parents and teacher not assumed that he was abusing drugs and pushed for such testing.

In the final analysis, either a person is or is not a substance abuser.[7] Yet, a simple statement of yes or no provides little insight into the problems presented by an individual who is a substance abuser. The challenge to arriving at this decision accurately is that substance abuse is part of a broad continuum of use that can change over time, evolve to include new drug or alcohol use, and, to an extent, can be hidden from others. The goal of any assessment should be to capture enough accurate information to allow us to recognize the extent to which persons may be experiencing difficulties with their relationship with alcohol and drugs, so that they can access the appropriate support services/interventions. A detailed assessment of the presenting problem should address not only the basic diagnosis of substance abuse, but help create a treatment plan that includes all of the various life components relative to the individual and the reasons for substance abuse.[5]

THEORIES AND ASSESSMENT
A brief overview of some of the key theories is provided only to help clarify the reasons why so many different approaches are used to assess substance use and abuse.

The previous example of "John," relates well to the disease model of addiction. The medical model often tests parts of the body, such as urine,[19] blood, and more recently, hair, to search for biochemical evidence of chemical abuse. This approach to investigating the person's history with using alcohol or drugs also lends itself to learning whether a genetic predisposition toward substance or chemical abuse may be present. Using medical research to unlock the biological keys to understand both the effects of chemicals on the body as well as identifying potential genetic predispositions to use, has made significant progress. Many biological and behavioral mysteries remain to be discovered, however. As new discoveries are made, we are continually reminded that the relationship of chemicals and the mind/body is highly complex, incorporating not only the physical realm, but also psychological, cultural, social, spiritual, and behavioral.

The disease model, similar to the medical model, states that addiction is a progressive pattern of abuse similar perhaps to that of some physical disabilities or disease processes like cancer, that would worsen with time, thus making it very difficult for the person to withdraw from abuse of the identified chemical.[23] In addition to the concept of substance abuse being progressive in nature, this model also supports an understanding that the disease of alcoholism or substance abuse will not stop unless an appropriate intervention occurs without which, the disease, like many other chronic physical diseases, will ultimately culminate in death.

This model of understanding the physical and mental processes accompanying alcohol or drug abuse became popularized as a result of E.M. Jellinek's initially published results of his studies on alcoholism in 1947. His initial works provided a plausible explanation of how alcoholism occurs and progresses. The medical community, who had struggled with understanding alcoholism, latched on to this new understanding, and the disease model quickly became the model of choice in the helping professions. By 1956, the disease concept of alcoholism was officially recognized by the American Medical Association (AMA). Soon after his original study results were published, E.M. Jellinek amended his original research findings on alcoholism to recognize that not every alcohol abuser was necessarily an alcoholic. Jellinek proposed that alcohol abuse actually belonged on a continuum, and introduced the concept of alcohol typologies to help define a range of alcohol use patterns. The timing of the establishment of the disease model, and the rise in worldwide popularity of Alcoholics Anonymous (AA) and other 12-step models, provided a new foothold for understanding the nature of, and approach to helping someone with abuse problems.

Learning theory approaches[3] postulate that addiction develops as a result of faulty learning. The notion of "people use drugs because they *work*" is supported by this theory. Within learning theory, substance use is rewarding both physically and socially since the person tends to feel "good" while abusing drugs, and friends who abuse chemicals together also socially reinforce the person. Under this theory, drug abuse can only stop if the person perceives drug use as negative reinforcement, and the person no longer socializes with other persons who abuse drugs. It is the point at which a person realizes that the negative consequences associated with using outweigh the "benefits" of their habit. Getting to this realization can prove to be very challenging, as the person's defense mechanisms (denial, rationalization, minimization), combined with biological changes in the brain due to the abuse, begin to erode the person's ability to make logical, rational decisions.

On a similar note, the relapse prevention model assumes that addiction is an acquired habit that can only be changed through learning (and using) new behaviors. This model involves a three-step approach to living drug free that includes:

- A readiness to make change in behavior by stopping the use of a drug,
- Making change through treatment or through self-help, and
- Becoming aware that the person can become drug-involved again, called relapse prevention, and that it will take time for the person to develop the appropriate coping skills needed to remain drug free.[27]

Perhaps the most comprehensive model is the biopsychosocial model that includes biological, psychological, and social components to drug addiction. This model suggests that all three components interact differently within each person.[13] The biopsychosocial model attempts to offer a more holistic perspective of a person's abuse behavior. Understanding the concept that abuse and addiction influences the person in multiple, often confounding ways, helps us to consider the person's motivations and potential for use in greater depth, and sets the stage for developing an intervention/treatment strategy that more aptly addresses the range of needs.

CASE STUDY

Let's assume that John from our first case study tested positive for drugs and did not have a brain tumor. The biological proof (urine and blood tests), would fit well (medical model). Knowing that John has been socializing with people who use drugs, and that he does not want to feel left-out of his peer group (psychosocial model), and that a feeling of inadequacy without peer support would likely reinforce a psychological component to John's problems. The ability to acquire physical, interpersonal, and psychological information about John is paramount to fully understanding him. Acquiring such multi-dimensional information can be a daunting task since it means that a school setting, counselors, family and others, such as John's friends, must each provide some data to form a comprehensive picture of John's presenting problems. Treatment would include medical testing to monitor John's body for proof that he was not using chemicals, while John would undergo counseling to develop appropriate skills to cope with life's problems and bolster his sense of self without turning to drugs, and he would learn to modify his lifestyle by avoiding people who abused drugs.

Approaching a person from a biopsychosocial perspective can be challenging, but is probably the most appropriate lens from which to view a person's abuse behaviors. Clearly, it may seem easier simply to require John to submit to random drug testing, but it is important to consider that using only one measure to determine a person's drug using potential is likely limiting in itself in terms of the range and complexities of the person's use behaviors. No single theory or approach has developed dominance within the substance abuse profession. Each practitioner will need to develop his or her own approach to identification, assessment, and treatment of substance abuse.

To add to the various concerns raised by many theories and different approaches to the identification of substance abuse, it should be noted that treatment of substance abuse is carried out in a variety of medical, in-patient, out-patient, mental health, non-medical, ideologically-driven settings, therapeutic communities, free-standing drug treatment centers, and religious organizations, to name a few. Each different type of setting provides different services with staff that possess different training, experiences, and belief systems about the nature and identification of substance abuse. In this regard, matching the person to the appropriate level, style, and delivery method of treatment makes good sense, and typically leads to better outcomes.

There are numerous screening and testing procedures used by various organizations to identify substance use, and to assess why the person abuses drugs. The remainder of this chapter will provide some of the more relevant assessment techniques used.

ASSESSMENT TECHNIQUES

OBSERVATIONAL, MEDICAL, AND BEHAVIORAL APPROACHES

A common place to begin is with an observation of an individual and noting the person's behavior. For example, slurred speech, poor coordination, memory or recall problems, bloodshot eyes, bruising, burns, rashes, being overly excited, animated, or agitated; or conversely, withdrawn, listless, or tired, or the smell of such substances of abuse as alcohol or marijuana exuding from the person would be behaviors likely associated with active substance use. Factors such as disruption in regular daily routine, changes in mood over a given day or days, unexplained injuries or frequent/prolonged illness, problems with work or school, failure to attend school or show-up to work, financial problems, family problems, legal problems, changes in social behavior, style of dress, and loss of valuable personal items are indicators of acute or culminating consequences of substance use. It should be clear to even a novice in the field of substance abuse that such behavior changes could well indicate a substance abuse problem, and the best way to verify the problem is through a medical analysis of blood, breath, hair, or urine to determine the presence or absence of a substance within the human body. These types of assessments are very useful when the person is either unwilling or unable to provide the information since they either are intoxicated and cannot respond, or they do not want to answer because of a fear of potential legal, work, relationship, or other life concerns.[38]

CASE STUDY

Mary is a female, 38 years of age, who is quickly moving up the ranks within a banking firm. She is so committed to her career that she no longer dates anyone, and has long since given up her hopes of having children. She attends a banquet for a retiring member of her bank and has several martinis more than would be appropriate to drive a car. Despite her drinking, she decides to drive herself home. Mary is stopped by a police officer for erratic driving. When questioned by the officer, Mary slurs her speech, appears half awake, has poor coordination, cannot recall what the police officer asked, cannot remember where she was prior to being pulled over by the police officer, and smells of alcohol. The police officer asks Mary to take a breath test to verify either sobriety or the presence of excessive alcohol. Although Mary may indeed be intoxicated, her survival instincts take control and she refuses the breath test since she knows that she could not pass the physical examination. A part of her brain is also aware that a drunken driving charge could threaten to ruin her career. It is apparent that Mary has no interest in admitting to the officer that she drank far more alcohol than appropriate or safe. In addition, without knowing more about Mary and her life, it is equally possible that Mary may frequently drink too much, and possibly be defined as someone with a substance abuse problem.

In yet another example, behavioral observation can be useful in determining both "misuse" and abuse.

"Joe" is a twenty-four year old male who is involved in a rehabilitation program to help him return to work after he sustained a significant brain injury. Since his injury, Joe had been experiencing periodic seizures. His doctor prescribed anti-seizure medication, and told Joe that it was important "not to drink alcohol when he was taking his medication." Rehabilitation staff started noticing that Joe was not coming to his rehab on Mondays, and was having a tough time with tasks on Tuesday mornings when he did come into the center. He seemed tired, distracted, and often despondent to others in the clinic. Upon further investigation, it was discovered that Joe was heeding his doctor's advice exactly...he was NOT drinking when he took his medication. Instead, he would stop taking his seizure medication on Friday so that he could drink on Saturday and Sunday, then would restart his medication on Monday or Tuesday. Although technically, he was being compliant with his doctor's advice, his interpretation of the information was problematic. NOT taking his seizure medication created disruptions in the required medication schedule to control his seizures (misuse of how the medication was intended/prescribed). Coupled with binge drinking on the weekends, Joe's ability to be effective in his rehabilitation program and become employed was significantly jeopardized (abuse).

Advancements in medical technology offer techniques to assess antibodies that compete with many substances for binding sites to human fluid samples, including marijuana, amphetamines, barbiturates, cocaine, alcohol, and opiates that bind with certain chemicals. These techniques look at how antibodies bind with chemical substances in human fluids.[38] As another example, various serum levels, such as glycoprotein, increase with greater alcohol use, and can readily identify alcohol abuse.[31]

Medical practice and research have known for a relatively long period of time that substance abuse and dependence are often associated with a range of related physical conditions, such as gastrointestinal disturbances, hypertension, heart disease, liver disease, and neurological changes.[19,30] Physicians often ask patients who present with such ailments if they use alcohol or other substances.

Interestingly, it appears that even physicians may frequently "miss" signs of alcohol abuse. Reports of studies suggest a lack of adequate training to recognize abuse symptoms has resulted in significant rates of under diagnosing among child, adult, and elderly populations.[1,34,39]

With proper physician training, modern medicine is capable of identifying substance abuse through related ailments and medical tests that clearly identify the presence of substances associated with illegal drugs, abuse of prescription medications, and/or alcohol abuse. Medical procedures have improved the potentiality for diagnosing substance use and abuse, but in and of itself, it only defines the existence of a problem, but not the cause of the problem.

PSYCHOMETRIC INSTRUMENTS

Non-medical instruments have been developed that detect substance use by the way a person answers specific questions. Psychometric instruments, or written tests, aid in the specific diagnosis of substance abuse, and help in the development of formal diagnoses. Many psychometric instruments exist, and they are designed for various populations.

For the most part, two types of assessment instruments exist; structured and semi-structured instruments.[36] The fully structured instrument follows a specific script in which the trained professional person asks specific questions that use the same wording at all times, and the respondent is limited to a choice of responses. A semi-structured assessment also uses a list of specific questions, but the trained professional is allowed to conduct independent follow-up to clarify or further identify a response given by a person

The *Addiction Severity Index* (*ASI*) is an instrument designed as a clinical interview between a trained instructor who knows how to ask all of the questions within the instrument (structured), and a person who potentially has a substance abuse problem. The *ASI* assesses both alcohol and drug abuse and develops feedback on five life domains, including work, family and social supports, medical, psychological, and legal concerns.[25] Overall, the *ASI* can review and identify substance use occurring from within the last thirty days, to a year. In a somewhat modified format, researchers have identified that the *ASI* can assess client progress during treatment.[22,29,35] The *ASI* develops a comprehensive picture of an individual on multiple levels so that abuse is identified along with other variables that may interplay with abuse.

CASE STUDY

George, a 27 year-old male lost his job last year. His marriage failed due to little to no income and his wife's belief that he was abusing drugs. George used marijuana intermittently, but more frequently after losing his job. He then started using cocaine as a means of escaping the real problems interfacing his life, including his inability to hold a job and a failed marriage. George agreed to an assessment of his current condition. ASI findings pointed to treatment that would include elimination of cocaine use, seeking employment, and interpersonal counseling to either help George re-connect with his wife, or to at least realize why the marriage failed so that he could move forward with life knowing what caused the marriage to end. It would appear that George was addicted to various illegal drugs, and was insecure within interpersonal relationships.

While the *ASI* is a comprehensive instrument requiring about one hour to administer, and which collects considerable data across multiple aspects of life, The *CAGE* is a very short screening tool that assesses alcohol abuse. It is a self-reporting instrument in which the person answers four basic questions including:

◊   Have you ever felt the need to Cut down?
◊   Do you feel Annoyed by people complaining about drinking?
◊   Do you ever feel Guilty about your drinking?
◊   Do you ever drink an Eye opener in the morning to relieve the shakes?

Two or more positive responses to the four questions indicate a potential drinking problem. The *CAGE* is a quick, superficial screening device that is most effective in busy, crisis environments such as emergency rooms.[2] Its main function is to provide some initial feedback to an alcohol user in a setting where intensive treatment cannot be provided, but is completed in the hope that the person will seek treatment once discharged from the acute or crisis setting. Although the instrument does not exhibit consistent outcomes in all settings, it does help identify alcohol symptomology as a general rule, in many settings.[10,11]

A somewhat more detailed screening device is the *Michigan Alcoholism Screening Test (MAST)*. It was developed to identify alcohol use by having people respond to 25 questions requiring a "yes" or "no" response. A rating of 0 to 5 is assigned to each "yes" response, depending on the severity of the presenting problem. The questions focus on physical symptoms associated with alcohol dependence, marital problems resulting from drinking, previous hospitalizations caused by alcohol use, legal problems that resulted from drinking, and psychological problems caused by the use of alcohol. As per previous discussion, the *MAST* uses a biopsychosocial approach to exploring alcoholism. Research on the *MAST* indicates that a combined score of 4 or below on all questions probably indicates no alcohol problem, while scores ranging between 5 to 7 across all questions indicates a potential problem, and combined scores of 8 or better strongly suggest alcoholism.[18]

Two shorter versions of the *MAST* exist, and they have been used extensively in various settings over several decades because of their smaller size. The two are the *Short MAST* (SMAST) that uses only 13 items from the original *MAST*,[37] and the *Brief MAST (B-MAST)* that only uses 10 of the original items.[33]

Self-report instruments such as the *CAGE, MAST* and the variations of the *MAST (SMAST)* and *(B-MAST)* have internal problems since some people will deny use of alcohol, and will under-report symptoms, while others may choose to exaggerate the problem to seek attention.[17] People who under report use may be exhibiting denial of the problem, or are aware of the problem, but are afraid that public exposure will lead to such things as job loss, or a jail sentence. People who over report abuse may be seeking attention, and could suffer from psychiatric problems, or exhibit dual diagnoses. An additional concern related to the various versions of the *MAST* is that it can lead to false positive responses. Asking someone if they ever attended an AA meeting will automatically lead to a positive interpretation, while the person may have attended the meeting for other reasons than their own actual use of alcohol.[26]

CASE STUDY

Wilma has been a police officer for fifteen years with an excellent record. Last year she was involved in a shootout with two men who held up a bank. Wilma shot and killed one of the suspects. Since the shooting, the police captain noticed a change in Wilma's behavior. Wilma had started drinking alcohol at lunch, and often went out for drinks with some of the other officers at night. Rumor had it that Wilma was becoming an alcoholic. The captain decided to send Wilma to see the police department's employee assistance program (EAP), because he was aware that Wilma exhibited behavior changes within the last year, and appeared to be drinking heavily. Wilma told him that she does not have a drinking problem and she just enjoys having a few beers with her fellow police officers. Yet, Wilma knows that she has a drinking problem. She was told that the employee assistance program does not share their findings with the police department. However, Wilma is fearful that they will find out, so she attempts to lie about the problem by failing to answer all of the questions on the MAST honestly. She presents her problem as a marital issue, and reports that her marriage is failing, but it has little or nothing to do with alcohol.

In isolation, the use of a single instrument to detect Wilma's alcohol problems may not be adequate. Despite the problems presented by the *MAST* and its other versions, it and the *CAGE* are used extensively within the field of substance abuse, often in conjunction with other screening/assessment tools. The practice of using a battery of various assessment measures helps to provide corrobative information to accurately detect the extent and nature of the person's use.

THE STAGES OF CHANGE READINESS AND TREATMENT EAGERNESS
SCALE (SOCRATES) assesses people's ability to make changes in their lives by
stopping the use of alcohol and drugs.[28] The scale looks at the relationship
between the person's motivational readiness to stop using drugs and/or alcohol,
and compares that readiness to various interventions provided through outpatient
or in-patient treatment programs. There are three sub-scales that include:

◊   Recognition or admitting that a problem exists,
◊   Taking steps or making changes in their life, and
◊   Ambivalence or openness to change.

Each of the three sub-scales can provide potential direction, such as a specific
program, that would be helpful to the person with an alcohol or drug abuse
problem. The scale differs from many other types of psychometric instruments
by looking for relationships between a person's readiness for treatment and
various treatment options. The concept of matching treatment to readiness has
been explored,[14] and researchers have noted that persons with addiction
problems need to be matched to appropriate and safe programs that will help
them before they can do greater harm to themselves. It may be appropriate, for
example, to start a person with a harm reduction model that allows the person to
continue using, if that is the only place where you can interact with the individual,
but the treatment team needs to move the person up to an abstinence oriented
treatment program as quickly as possible to insure safety and keep the person
alive. *SOCRATES* authors' report that the scale is an experimental instrument,
and still needs development of concurrent and predictive validity scales, or
outcome relationships between readiness and treatment modality.

The *MacAndrew Alcoholism Scale (MAC)* uses 49 items based on
components of the *Minnesota Multiphase Personality Inventory (MMPI)* to
identify substance abuse.[16] The questions do not focus directly on alcohol or
substance use, but relate to personality variables associated with substance abuse.
The scale is reported to be more resistant to faking than other psychometric
instruments since it does not focus directly on the topic of abuse. The *MAC* has
been found quite useful when working with people who are in denial, or are
defensive about their drinking behavior.[2] Research indicates that the *MAC* helps
distinguish between people who have an alcohol problem and persons with
psychiatric problems who do not have a substance abuse issue.[24]

CASE STUDY

The case of Wilma (a police officer with an alcohol problem
discussed earlier) is an example of a person who might provide more
honest feedback about her drinking problem by using the MAC versus
SOCRATES since Wilma might not recognize the questions as related
to alcohol on the MAC, but would clearly see the relationship with

SOCRATES. It should be noted that most people who want to deny or avoid admitting a problem would be cautious with all instruments that might expose the truth. Hence, it is still possible that Wilma might answer the questions in such a way that she avoids or minimizes exposure.

Another scale designed to reduce bias against the instrument for fear of exposure and faking answers is the *Substance Abuse Subtle Screening Instrument (SASSI).*[27,4] The instrument is designed to identify substance abuse and alcoholism problems. Although several versions are currently available, the *SASSI* has two distinct parts, the subtle items that ask true and false questions that appear unrelated to substance abuse, and a second section called the Risk Prediction Scales that contain 12 alcohol and 14 other drug-related items that query the individual about chemical abuse but, as before, they assume honest responses from the individual taking the test. The authors developed scales to assess men and women separately, and it can distinguish between individuals who abuse substances and persons who do not exhibit addiction patterns. The SASSI lineup of screening instruments includes both paper/pencil tests, Internet versions, tests in different languages, and their latest addition, the Substance Abuse in Vocational Rehabilitation Screener or SAVR-S. The SAVR-S is specifically designed and normed for use with people who have disabilities and substance use disorders.

The *Alcohol Use Disorders Identification Test (AUDIT)* is another self-report instrument that is used to identify alcohol abuse among adults in medical settings,[6] and is somewhat similar to the *CAGE* since it is designed to work in medical settings. It is a ten-item survey that explores the frequency of alcohol consumption, dependence on alcohol, and experiences of negative consequences relative to alcohol. It may be used as a stand-alone instrument, or in conjunction with other more in-depth instruments. People who respond to the *AUDIT* use a four-point rating scale with a range of responses from zero, indicating no problems in that defined area, through 4, a high frequency of problems in that area. The instrument has been an effective tool that identifies substance abuse when working with a population of either adults or adolescents.[6,12,15,21,32]

Numerous psychometric assessment techniques exist that work in conjunction with other tools to identify substance abuse and related concerns such as mental illness. The World Health Organization (WHO) developed the *Composite International Diagnostic Interview (CIDI)* to assess mood, anxiety, and substance abuse disorders, while the *Alcohol Use Disorder and Associated Disabilities Interview Schedule (AUDADIS)* can assess current substance abuse, and develop a relationship with major diagnostic criteria of the *DSM-IV* such as major mood disorder, anxiety, and personality disorders.[36] The purpose of such assessment tools is to make sure that all aspects of the person's problems are addressed simultaneously rather than being treated separately. For example, treating mental health and substance abuse problems in isolation might lead to relapse of a substance abuse issue while the person is receiving treatment for major depression, or the opposite can be equally destructive in helping the person remain drug free while receiving on-going mental health treatment.

CASE STUDY

William, age 25, is paroled from prison after serving 3 years of a seven- year sentence for narcotics sales and use. He enters a housing program for substance abusers, and reports that he wants to remain drug free, complete his GED, and find a job in the construction industry. He attends required individual and group sessions, and all urine screens indicate that he is not using drugs. His case manager reports that he appears to be responding to the various components of the program, but he also seems lethargic and lacks genuine enthusiasm. After two weeks, he is allowed a trip outside of the program. He does not report back to his housing unit that evening, and he does not have any contact with the program for three days. The program receives a telephone call from the local police who advise that he was found wandering the streets in what appeared to be a drug-induced stupor. They could not find any drugs on him, and they decide that it might be best to return him to his housing program for further treatment. He returns to the program and seems very depressed and embarrassed over his behavior. His case manager makes it clear that continued inappropriate behavior will lead to dismissal from the program, and a potential return to jail. The case manager presents William at the next staff meeting, and it is unanimously agreed that he should receive a complete medical and psychiatric assessment to make sure that he does not have a medical or psychiatric problem that went unnoticed when discharged from the prison setting. The psychiatric assessment indicates that he is diagnosed with substance abuse and depression.

William spends a month in an in-patient psychiatric unit where he is stabilized on anti-depressant medication and returned to his program for continued substance abuse treatment. As a component of discharge from the hospital unit, William must meet with a psychiatrist once a week at a local mental health clinic while undergoing substance abuse treatment. The case manager accompanies William to all of his psychiatric sessions. Within two months, William presents as more enthusiastic, motivated, and wants to enter a high school equivalency diploma program so that he can erase the embarrassment of not possessing a high school diploma. Within six months, William is defined as drug free, and his psychiatric diagnosis appears stable since he is taking his medications in a timely manner. After one year, William is ready for independent living with the understanding that he must continue to see a psychiatrist monthly to evaluate his medication regimen and depressive symptoms, while attending community-based support groups for substance abuse. William is a somewhat typical case of an individual who presents as a substance abuser but, in fact, he is dually diagnosed with substance abuse and depression. The depressive component of his illness would not have been identified unless someone decided to have William assessed medically for potential problems such as depression.

CLOSING REMARKS

The chapter provided an overview of medical, biological, and psychometric instruments that help assess substance abuse and drug abuse disorders. None of the instruments presented in this chapter should be used to diagnose a substance abuse disorder. Only the most recent edition of the *Diagnostic and Statistical Manual of Mental Disorders* should be used by an appropriately trained and licensed professional for the purposes of diagnosis.

One study[20] found that assessment tools are not used very often in the substance abuse field. This may be attributed to the fact that some professionals believe that they possess enough clinical skills that they can diagnose without an instrument, or they lack training in the use of such tools. Professionals are often more concerned with psychiatric disorders that are apparent, rather than substance abuse disorders. Yet, there is a genuine need to develop skills in the use of instruments that identify substance abuse disorders, and to identify tools that are superior to other instruments for use on a consistent basis in the profession of substance abuse identification and treatment.[9] In a somewhat related study, 75% of rehabilitation psychologists reported working with persons who abuse alcohol and other drugs, but they report that their training in substance abuse treatment was inadequate.[8] Among the feedback provided by persons interviewed for the study was a recommendation to improve graduate training coursework in the substance abuse field.

Despite some of the problems presented, such as faking, early identification, and the ability to target special needs, treatment programs can help reduce the time a person remains a substance abuser, and can help the person avoid problems in other spheres of living including legal issues, marital problems, employment concerns, and medical issues.

REFERENCES

[1]Alexander, D. E., & Gwyther, R. E. (1995). Alcoholism in adolescents and their families. *Pediatric Clinics of North America, 42*, 217-234.

[2]Allen, J. P., Eckardt, M. J., & Wallen, J. (1988). Screening for alcoholism: Techniques and issues. *Public Health Reports, 103,* 586-592.

[3]Bandura, A. (1977). Self-efficacy: Toward a unifying theory of behavior change. *Psychological Review, 84,* 191-215.

[4]Benshoff, J. J. & Janikowski, T. P. (2000). *The rehabilitation model of substance abuse counseling.* Belmont, CA: Brooks/Cole.

[5]Blume, S. (1983). *The disease concept today.* Minneapolis: The Johnson Institute.

[6]Bohn, M. J., Babor, T. F., & Kranzler, H. R. (1995). Alcohol Use Disorder Test (AUDIT): Validation of a screening instrument for use in medical settings. *Journal of Studies on Alcohol, 56,* 423-432.

[7]Budziack, T. J. (1993). Evaluating treatment services. In, A. W. Heinemann (Ed.), *Substance abuse and physical disability* (pp.239-255). Binghamton, New York: The Haworth Press.

[8]Cardoso, E., Pruett, S., Chan, F., & Tansey,T. (2006). Substance abuse assessment and training. The current training and practice of APA Division 22 members. *Rehabilitation Psychologist, 51*(2).

[9]Carrol, K. & Rounsaville, B. (2002). On beyond urine: Clinically useful assessment instruments in the treatment of drug dependence. *Behavior Research and Therapy, 40*(11).

[10]Chan, A. W., Pristach, E. A., Welte, J. W., & Russell, M. (1993). Use of the TWEAK test in screening for alcoholism/heavy drinking in three populations. *Alcoholism Clinical and Experimental Research, 17,* 1188-1192.

[11]Cherpitel, C J. (1995). Analysis of cut points for screening instruments for alcohol problems in the emergency room. *Journal of Studies on Alcohol, 56,* 695-700.

[12]Conigrave, K. M., Hall, W. D., & Saunders, J. B. (1995). The AUDIT questionnaire: Choosing a cut-off score. *Addiction, 90,* 1349-1356.

[13]Donovan, D. M. & Marlatt, G. A. (Eds.). (1988). *Assessment of addictive behaviors.* New York: Guilford.

[14]Finney, J. & Moos, R. (2006). Matching clients' treatment goals with treatment oriented toward abstinence, moderation, or harm reduction. Editorial. *Society for the study of addiction, 101,* 1540-1542.

[15]Fleming, M. F., Barry, K. L., & MacDonald, R. (1991). The Alcohol Use Disorders. Identification Test (AUDIT) in a college sample. *International Journal of the Addictions, 26,* 1173-1185.

[16]Graham, J. R. (1990). *MMPI-2 Assessing personality and psychopathology.* New York: Oxford University Press.

[17]Gruber, J., Gardner, W. J., & Chan, F., & Wang, M. H. (1995). *Substance abuse rehabilitation.* [computer software]. Madison, WI: Department of Rehabilitation and Special Education, University of Wisconsin-Madison.

[18]Ingraham, K., Kaplan, S., & Chan, F. (1992). Rehabilitation counselors' awareness of client alcohol abuse patterns. *Journal Applied Rehabilitation Counseling, 23* (3), 18-22.

[19]Jellinek, E. M. (1945). The problem of alcohol. In Yale Studies on Alcohol (Ed.), *Alcohol, science, and society* (pp. 13-30). Westport, CT: Greenwood Press.

[20]Juhnke, G., Vacc, N., Curtis, R., Coll, K., and Paredes, D. (2003). Assessment instruments used by addiction counselors. *Journal of Addictions and offender Counseling, 23,* 66-72.

[21]Larsen, S. (1994). Alcohol use in the service industry. *Addiction, 89,* 733-741.

[22]Leonhard, C., Mulvey, K., Gastfriend, D.R., & Shwartz, M. (2000). Addiction Severity Index: A field study of internal consistency and validity. *Journal of Substance Abuse Treatment, 18,* 129-135.

[23]Marlatt, G. A. (1992). Substance abuse: Implications of a biopsychosocial model for prevention, treatment, and relapse prevention. In, J. Graboswki & G. R. Vandenbos (Eds.), *Psychopharmacology: Basic mechanisms and applied interventions* (pp. 127-162). Washington, DC: American Psychological Association.

[24]MacAndrew, C. (1965). The differentiation of male alcoholic outpatients from nonalcoholic psychiatric outpatients by means of the MMPI. *Quarterly Journal of Studies on Alcohol, 26,* 238-246.

[25]McLellan, A. T., Luborsky, L., O'Brien, C. P. & Woody, G. E. (1980). An improved diagnostic instrument for substance abuse patients: The Addiction Severity Index. *Journal of Nervous & Mental Diseases, 168,* 26-33.

[26]McNeese, C. A., & DiNitto, D. M. (2005). *Chemical dependency: A systems approach.* NY: Person Press.

[27]Miller, G. A. (1985). *The Substance Abuse Subtle Screening Inventory manual.* Bloomington, IN: Addiction Research & Consultation.

[28]Mitchell, D., Francis, J. & Tafrate, R. (2005). The psychometric properties of the Stages of Change Readiness and Treatment Eagerness Scale (SOCRATES) in a clinical sample of active military service members. *Military medicine, 170*(11).

[29]Moos, R. H., Finney, J.W., Ferderman, E. B., & Suchinsky, R. (2000). Specialty mental health care improves patients' outcomes: Findings from nationwide program to monitor the quality of care for patients with substance use disorders. *Journal of Studies on Alcohol, 61,* 704-713.

[30]National Institute on Drug Abuse (1999). Principles of drug addiction treatment. NIH Publication No. 99-4180, Washington, DC. Government Printing Office.

[31]Niemlä, O. (2007). Biomarkers in alcoholism. *Clinica Chemic Acta, 377,* 39-49.

[32]O'Hare, T. (1997). Measuring problem drinking in first time offenders: Development and validation of the College Alcohol Problem Scale. *Journal of Substance Abuse Treatment, 14,* 383-387.

[33]Pokorny, A. D., Miller, B. A., & Kaplan, H. B. (1972). The Brief MAST: A shortened version of the Michigan Alcoholism Screening Test (MAST). *American Journal of Psychiatry, 129,* 342-345.

[34]Reid, M. C., Tinetti, M. E., Brown, C. J. & Concato, J. (1998). Physician awareness of Alcohol Use Disorders among older patients. *Journal of General Internal Medicine, 13*(11), 729-734.

[35]Rosen, C. S., Henson, B. R., Finney, J. W. & Moos, R. H. (2000). Consistency of self-administered and interview-based Addiction Severity Index composite scores. *Addiction, 95,* 419-425.

[36]Samet, S., Waxman, R., Hatzenbuehlor, M., Hasin, D. (2007). Assessing addiction: Concepts and instruments. *Addiction screening and clinical practice,* December, 19-31.

[37]Selzer, M. L., Vinokur, A., & van Rooijen, L. (1975). A self-administered short verions of the Michigan Alcoholism Screening Test (MAST). *Journal of Studies on Alcohol, 36,* 117-126.

[38]Verebey, K., Buchan, B. J., & Turner, C. E. (1998). Laboratory testing. In, *Clinical Textbook of Addictive Disorders* (2nd Ed.), R. J. Frances and S. I. Miller (Eds.). NY: The Guilford Press.

[39]Wing, D.M. (1995). Transcending alcoholic denial. *Imagine, 27,* 121-126.

Chapter Seventeen

DETOXIFICATION & PRIMARY TREATMENT

BY **ANDREA PERKINS**
HOFSTRA UNIVERSITY

CINDY ROBINSON
SOUTH OAKS HOSPITAL

Chapter Topics

*T*he benefits of substance abuse treatment have been well documented. The client benefits to seeking treatment include improved health, self-concept, and personal goal attainment.[7] Recovery from addictions is related to reduction in crime, general healthcare costs, and expensive medical treatment for acute conditions related to untreated substance abuse.[5] Nonetheless, access to and participation in treatment lags far behind the number of individuals who need treatment. In a survey of treatment usage, SAMHSA[19] reported only 1.2 million people were being served in nearly 14,000 treatment facilities that responded to the survey (94.1% response rate). Approximately 21.1 million of the 23.6 million people who needed treatment for alcohol and drug addiction in 2006 did not receive the treatment.[18]

One issue that has influenced success in treatment has been the philosophy that detoxification has been viewed as a stand-alone, viable option for recovery by providers, funders, and patients.[20] Individuals physically recover from a substance and believe that they are "better" and can tackle their addiction without additional supports or lifestyle changes. This lack of continuity of care results in a relapse.[14] A "revolving door" of treatment results.[4] A paradigm shift is necessary to understand the continuum of services that are needed to facilitate the road to recovery for a person with substance addictions. The following chapter describes the elements of initial treatment, options, personnel, factors related to positive outcomes, and implications for counseling in these settings.

OVERVIEW OF DETOXIFICATION AND PRIMARY TREATMENT

When referring to substance abuse treatment, one may use the terms "detoxification" and "substance abuse treatment/rehabilitation" synonymously, but they are distinct concepts. The treatment or rehabilitation of substance abuse refers to "a constellation of ongoing therapeutic services ultimately intended to promote recovery for substance abuse patients."[5,p. 4] This represents the broader umbrella or spectrum of services that are available, one of which may be a detoxification program. Detoxification is related to the initial steps of ridding the body of addictive substances. The Center on Substance Abuse Treatment[5] defines detoxification in the following way:

Detoxification is a set of interventions aimed at managing acute intoxication and withdrawal. Supervised detoxification may prevent potentially life-threatening complications that might appear if the patient was left untreated. At the same time, detoxification is a form of palliative care (reducing the intensity of a disorder) for those who want to become abstinent or who must observe mandatory abstinence as a result of hospitalization or legal involvement. Finally, for some patients it represents a point of first contact with the treatment system and the first step to recovery.[p. 4]

Detoxification is achieved through a process of evaluation, stabilization, and fostering the patient's entry into treatment. This treatment may occur in a number of facilities within the community, each with their own unique characteristics. Aftercare plans and case management are vehicles for moving clients from acute treatment phases to longer term treatment options. The primary goals of treatment following detoxification are relapse prevention, the development of a healthy support network, and the development of social and independent living goals.

LEVELS OF CARE

Determining the proper level of care for an individual, based on an assessment of the severity of his/her addiction, is a key factor in ensuring the fit of a program to an individual. The goal of efficient treatment is to provide services in the least restrictive environment in the most cost-effective manner possible.[5] The American Society of Addiction Medicine (ASAM)[1] identified six dimensions for assessment when making treatment admission decisions:

◊ Acute intoxication and/or withdrawal potential;
◊ biomedical conditions and complications;
◊ emotional, behavioral, and psychological conditions/complications;
◊ readiness to change;
◊ relapse, continued use, or continued problem potential; and
◊ recovery/living environment.[5]

These speak to the severity of symptoms and issues with which the person presents. Five levels of services are available to treat individuals once this assessment has been made. These include early intervention services; outpatient treatment; intensive outpatient (IOP)/partial hospitalization program (PHP); residential/inpatient services; and medically managed inpatient treatment services.[1] These levels should not be considered discrete, but rather part of that larger continuum of services available for treatment/rehabilitation, as their provision is complimentary to one another. Later sections of this chapter will discuss the facilities and staff who provide these services, but we first will explore the initial reactions to ceasing the use of substances.

WITHDRAWAL

When a person stops using an addictive substance, they may or may not experience a series of physical and psychological side effects. It is difficult to predict the severity of withdrawal symptoms that one will experience, since many factors play a part in determining this, such as body composition, frequency and length of use, and type of substance used. It has been shown that people with a longer history of heavy substance use (namely alcohol) are more likely to have more severe withdrawal effects and, therefore, are more likely to require professional assistance in detoxification.[18]

PHYSICAL WITHDRAWAL

Detoxification from a specific subset of addictive substances will result in physical withdrawal symptoms. These substances include alcohol, opiates, barbiturates, and benzodiazepines. Physical withdrawal symptoms include tremors, seizures, sweating, tachycardia (rapid heartbeat), hypertension, nausea, vomiting, and diarrhea.

Physical withdrawal symptoms typically begin to occur within 24-48 hours of a person's last use of drugs or alcohol. They may begin gradually or abruptly with variable periods of duration. For example, physical withdrawal from alcohol may take only three to four days, but the duration of physical withdrawal symptoms from benzodiazepines lasts approximately two weeks. Physical withdrawal symptoms are overt, meaning they can be observed by others or measured by medical tests. These symptoms can be treated in a medically focused facility; there presence is a requirement for admission for medical detoxification units.

PSYCHOLOGICAL WITHDRAWAL

Physical withdrawal symptoms tend to exhibit for only a finite amount of time, usually no longer than two weeks. Psychological withdrawal symptoms can last much longer. Some people report psychological side effects of withdrawal for months after stopping substance use. Psychological withdrawal is much less substance-specific. While physical detoxification symptoms only occur when stopping use of a few specific substances, psychological symptoms occur for these and other substances, such as cocaine, marijuana, nicotine, and hallucinogens.

A wide range of psychological effects is possible. One of the most common effects is cravings. When one's brain is accustomed to certain chemical levels, changing those levels causes the brain to want (crave) the higher level again. People can experience cravings during the day or at night. When cravings occur while a person is sleeping, they are commonly known as "drug dreams," where a person dreams they are engaging in drug activity and experience the positive euphoria of their past addiction.

Other psychological withdrawal symptoms include hallucinations, delirium tremens (DTs), sleep disturbance, depression, and anxiety. Hallucinations can be tactile, visual, or auditory. Delirium tremens are both physical and psychological in nature; this syndrome is characterized by visual hallucinations and profound confusion.[7] Physical and psychological withdrawal symptoms are very specific to the person and the detoxification episode they are experiencing. The presence of physical withdrawal symptoms will trigger a referral for detoxification treatment for the safety of the individual. Therefore, careful assessment of these symptoms is necessary, as evidenced in the following conversation between a client and counselor:

COUNSELOR: "What brings you in to see me today, Ashley?"
ASHLEY: "Well, I have been told before that I have an 'addictive personality'. I think I'm starting to believe it. I've been

drinking more often lately and gambling all of my money away. I just tried to stop both of them cold-turkey, but I feel so uncomfortable and unhappy, I don't know what to do."

COUNSELOR: "When did you stop drinking and gambling?"

ASHLEY: "I haven't gambled in a week, but the last time I drank alcohol was two days ago."

COUNSELOR: "And how do you feel physically today?"

ASHLEY: "I couldn't sleep last night; I just kept tossing and turning. I woke up shaking this morning, and it doesn't seem to go away. I tried to eat, but it made me feel more nauseous. But the gambling makes me feel even worse. I have no money to pay back my mom for the money she lent me. I even stole money from her! I can't believe I stole from my mother! I mean, what kind of daughter am I? I'm so scared that I'll lose her."

COUNSELOR: "Ashley, I'm hearing that you're dealing with a lot of things all at once with stopping gambling and drinking. But the first thing we need to make sure of is that you're physically healthy. Do you know what withdrawal is?"

ASHLEY: "No."

COUNSELOR: "This is what your body goes through when you stop using a substance or doing something that you do repeatedly. Sometimes withdrawal symptoms are physical, and sometimes they are psychological. It sounds like the symptoms you're having from the alcohol right now are physical."

ASHLEY: "Yeah, like the shaking and nausea."

COUNSELOR: "Exactly. We have to be concerned first with the physical withdrawals, to make sure that you are safe and healthy. Then we can focus more on discussing your emotions and the issues that you're currently facing."

OTHER MEDICAL CONCERNS DURING DETOXIFICATION

During the process of detoxification, a person's body experiences a great deal of change, namely the alteration of the internal chemical balance. Within and immediately following this stage, it is important to be medically assessed, whether it is while a client is in an inpatient detoxification program or by a primary care physician, once the withdrawal effects have ceased.

Drug and alcohol use can mask other medical concerns that may be undiagnosed. These medical problems can be issues that began prior to substance use, or have been caused (directly or indirectly) by substance use. Having been engaged in drug activity for a number of years, the person may have neglected self-care and routine medical check-ups, resulting in lingering issues. For example, heavy use of alcohol is associated with medical issues such as cirrhosis, neuropathy, and liver disease. Those with a history of cocaine abuse may have cardiac complications. Other medical concerns may result from the disinhibition that often occurs when using substances or taking part in an addictive activity. Infectious diseases, including HIV and Sexually Transmitted Infections (STIs), can be spread through sharing of needles or sexual encounters with infected persons.

Another common concern is malnutrition.[5] When a person is abusing substances, they often fail to take in essential nutrients the body needs to thrive. In many cases, substance use becomes more necessary to a person than eating and exercising. The detoxification process itself also takes a toll on vitamin and hydration levels in the body. Part of the detoxification process should include a nutritional evaluation, monitoring, and planning for a return to a healthy diet regimen. Now that we have explored some of the effects of substance abuse on the body, we will discuss options for treating the condition.

OPTIONS FOR INITIAL TREATMENT

A person's first step into treatment is often the most difficult step to take. There are many options a person has in terms of the treatment in which they choose to enroll initially. Placement options are carefully considered based on an assessment of the six dimensions outlined by ASAM[1] above. The presence of a co-occurring disorder creates the need for a program that can address the dual issues presented. Those with other cognitive and medical conditions, such as pregnancy, infectious diseases, or mental retardation, may need extended/specific services available at the treatment facility. Family and social issues (e.g., dependent children, domestic violence, and isolation in the community) need to be carefully considered when determining the duration and location/facility for treatment. Diversity factors, such as gender, sexual orientation, age, and race/language of origin, must be considered to provide the most culturally responsive services. Below are descriptions of the types of initial treatment people may utilize, as well as the positive and negative aspects of each.

MEDICALLY MANAGED INPATIENT TREATMENT
Medically managed inpatient treatment (MMIT) removes the person from their environment and places them in a hospital setting. The purpose of an MMIT program is to use medications and/or continuous fluids to treat the withdrawal symptoms that occur when stopping the use of a substance.[4] These hospital units are only for people who are experiencing physical withdrawal symptoms.

Therefore, people going through detoxification from alcohol, opiates, benzodiazepines, and barbiturates would have the opportunity to utilize this type of initial treatment.

Medically managed inpatient treatment is beneficial in that it removes the client from people, places, and things that trigger the use of substances in their daily environment. It also increases a client's comfort level by medically decreasing the intensity of withdrawal symptoms. A client is able to start to build a sober support network with other patients on the unit. When a client is discharged from an inpatient detoxification unit, an aftercare plan is developed, which often includes further long-term treatment and relapse prevention.

There are some limitations to MMIT programs. The main focus of this type of treatment is based in the medical model. Therefore, counseling is not a primary focus. Minimal therapy is provided during this program; however, the discharge plan helps to refer people to treatment that is more therapeutic in nature. Another downside to this type of program is that the time period for treatment is very short-term. On average, a person is a client in this program for three to six days. Since the purpose of the unit is to medically manage the withdrawal of a substance, once physical withdrawal symptoms have subsided the client is discharged.

COMMUNITY DETOXIFICATION

The purpose of a community detoxification facility is similar to that of an MMIT in that it removes the person from their environment in favor of an inpatient setting and is designed for people encountering physical withdrawal symptoms. However, the stark difference between the two settings is that a community detoxification facility is not medically managed. Therefore, the client experiences withdrawal symptoms as they occur, without any pharmacological treatment. This type of program is based in the social model, which rejects the use of medication and relies on a supportive environment to assist the person.[5]

While experiencing the full effects of withdrawal symptoms would not appear to be a desirable choice, there are a variety of reasons why individuals would choose this treatment route. There are several positive aspects to community detoxification facilities. For example, financial situation may play a role in treatment choices; medical treatment is much more expensive than non-medical treatment. Also, individuals might not feel comfortable in a "hospital" although they may need medical monitoring. In this type of facility, there are medical personnel on staff in case of an emergency. Therefore, if a client were to experience severe withdrawal, they would be assessed and transported to a medical hospital if necessary.

INPATIENT REHABILITATION

Inpatient rehabilitation programs are residential programs for individuals who are typically beyond the physical withdrawal from substances. Clients are admitted to this type of treatment initially if they are addicted to substances that do not cause physical withdrawal symptoms. They may also enter this type of treatment program once they have already experienced physical withdrawal symptoms (on their own or in managed detoxification) or have not used the substance long enough to encounter physical withdrawal symptoms when use is discontinued. If, at admission, they are determined to require a detoxification protocol, they will be provided these medically monitored services first.

Inpatient rehabilitation programs also differ from detoxification programs in that a client is involved for a longer period of time. Although not all rehabilitation programs are 28-day programs, as had been typical in the past, the client is removed from their daily environment for more than a few days. Due to the longer term of treatment, more services that are therapeutic are available in an inpatient rehabilitation program than an inpatient detoxification program. While a client's medical health is assessed and addressed, the main focus of the treatment is psychological and therapy-based. Clients can discuss deeper issues in groups and with counselors, as well as work on important daily living tasks in groups and workshops. An interdisciplinary treatment team approach is used and individual/group therapy, education, community meetings, and leisure activities are components of the programming.

MAINTENANCE/OUTPATIENT PROGRAMS

Some people choose to avoid inpatient programs when initiating treatment for addictions because they prefer or need to remain in their homes. Several factors may play a role in this. The person may have a job and not want to take time off from work, so they attend the program during evening hours. The person may have children and is not able to arrange/afford extended childcare. The person may also be unwilling to be away for an extended period for fear that others discover the reason for their absence. In these cases, a person may choose to begin their treatment through an outpatient program and/or maintenance program.

Outpatient programs can occur at different levels of intensity. Many outpatient programs require weekly individual sessions and multiple group sessions over the course of the week, in addition to self-help groups. A person would typically attend 90-minute group sessions twice a week, with 60 minutes of individual counseling and attendance at self-help meetings on non-program days. Intensive outpatient (IOP) treatment occurs at a greater frequency (groups three times/week) and duration (3 hour sessions), in addition to individual, family, and self-help sessions.[4] Individuals who require a higher level of structure would engage in an IOP program, with careful assessment to determine the intensity of their treatment.

Maintenance programs are outpatient in nature, as well. People with addictions to opiates often initiate treatment in this type of program. The program physician prescribes medications that work like opiates or conflict with opiates in order to prevent patients from using their substance of choice. A methadone maintenance program, for example, will schedule the client to attend the program daily to receive their dose of methadone. Methadone is a synthetic opiate that blocks the effects of withdrawal from heroin.[4] Over time, the amount of methadone that a client is given is scheduled to decrease, with eventual weaning of the client completely off opiates. Individuals may be on methadone from months to years as a substitute drug, which enables them to lead a productive life. Suboxone maintenance is similar although it is less intensive than a methadone program. Suboxone is the first drug to be approved for office-based treatment, meaning a client's private doctor would prescribe a daily dose to be taken at home. The dose would be lowered over time, and eventually be discontinued. The use of methadone and Suboxone in maintenance programs must be closely monitored, as they are addictive substances and have the potential to be abused.

The length of time that a client participates in a maintenance program is determined by the doctor or facility and depends on the client's progress during the program. A requirement of most programs is routine urine screening for the presence of other illicit drugs. Maintenance programs often include counseling or require that the client engage in individual/group counseling at another facility. The inclusion of counseling in maintenance programs has demonstrated fewer positive opiate urine tests.[11]

Beginning treatment at an outpatient level can be positive in that it does not remove a client from their daily life. It also can be negative in that it allows clients to remain in situations that may trigger them to continue their addiction. Frequent appointments, whether for medication, group counseling, or individual counseling, help to provide structure for the client and promote the formation of a daily routine. Many outpatient programs utilize drug and alcohol screens (i.e., breathalyzers and urine screens) as a way to promote honesty between the counselor and client. Outpatient programs also allow for a client to concurrently become actively involved in self-help programs.

SELF-HELP MEETINGS

Self-help meetings are not a mode of treatment for addictions, but are mentioned here because of their prevalence in complimenting primary treatment options. Self-help meetings are voluntary gatherings in the community that bring together people with a commonality amongst them. Some of these meetings include Alcoholics Anonymous (AA), Narcotics Anonymous (NA), and Gamblers Anonymous (GA). In the case of addictions, people with a common addiction meet during planned times as a support group, in support of one another's recovery and abstinence.

These meetings are beneficial in that they connect a person to a large support network. Self-help meetings often work along the Twelve Steps philosophy (see Chapter 18 for more on this topic). Self-help meetings embrace the concept of sponsorship, in which a person who is new to recovery pairs up with someone as a guide who has been in recovery for a longer period of time. A sponsor agrees to be contacted at any time, day or night, in the event that the person is having a difficult time or needs support.

Another beneficial aspect of self-help meetings is that there is no cost to the person attending. The meetings are run for the community, by the community. The positive aspect of this is that one can come and go as they please from these meetings. The down side to this, as an initial mode of treatment, is that a structured schedule is not enforced or monitored and attrition could result. Some people do utilize this as a primary modality for abstinence from substances, although not recognized as a treatment on its own.

PSYCHOLOGICALLY-BASED PROGRAMS
Psychologically-based treatment programs are a newer addition to the treatment of addictions. Since it is a newer program philosophy, interventions have not yet been thoroughly tested.[9] Due to the current trend of increasing co-morbidity (the diagnosis of clients with both substance abuse and mental health issues), there is an increased need for programs that address both issues simultaneously.

Drapkin and colleagues[9] investigated the differential effects of integrated Cognitive Behavioral Therapy (CBT) and a Twelve-step focused program on abstinence, attendance in a program, and symptoms of depression of clients that have both a substance abuse diagnosis and depressive disorder diagnosis. The study found that there was no significant difference between groups on any of the three factors measured. Further research would be beneficial in this area to determine if psychologically-based programs are more beneficial than more traditional substance abuse programs.

PRIMARY PERSONNEL INVOLVED IN INITIAL TREATMENT

The staff composition at the different facilities depends on the type of services they provides. For example, if a client begins treatment in a medically managed inpatient treatment unit, the staff working with them will differ from those who work with someone beginning treatment in an outpatient program. The following discussion describes various staff involved in initial treatment and the types of facilities in which they may be employed.

MEDICAL STAFF
Medical staff consists of nurses, medical doctors, psychiatrists, and nurse practitioners. They are involved in any type of facility that provides medical care to patients, administers or prescribes medications, or medically manages physical withdrawal symptoms. Some medical staff would also be employed at a community detoxification facility in order to assess and transport a person in need of medical care. Medical staff, namely psychiatrists and psychiatric nurse practitioners, may be employed in a psychologically-based program if psychiatric

medications are being prescribed or administered to clients as part of their treatment of mental health issues.

Medical doctors and nurse practitioners have the role of overseeing the medical treatment of clients being treated at a facility. They often sign off on charts, create a medical treatment plan, and review the treatment plan created by counselors and nurses. Doctors and nurse practitioners assess the need for and prescribe medications to help manage withdrawal symptoms, both physical and psychological. They also order toxicology labs to test for addictive drugs in the system, as well as levels of the medications they are prescribing for the client.

Medical doctors and nurse practitioners may not only be responsible for treating the client's physical and psychological symptoms directly related to withdrawal, but also other health related conditions. Complications of both short- and long-term medical issues that have gone undiagnosed or untreated may become apparent during initial treatment, and should be addressed by the doctor.

Screening for mental health issues is an important consideration for medically managed inpatient treatment units. A recent study found that over 80% of clients in an inpatient alcohol detoxification unit met a diagnosis for a mental health condition, which was significantly higher than those that were not in treatment at the time.[10] Psychiatrists, as well as nurse practitioners who specialize in psychiatry, would provide these services. These medical professionals may assist by assessing clients for mental health issues and prescribing psychotropic medications, in addition to their medical duties.

Nurses work with medical doctors and nurse practitioners to carry out the medical treatment plan. They take the client's vital signs to measure physical withdrawal symptoms and the effects of the medications prescribed. Nurses and doctors work together to perform physical exams on clients to determine their general physical health at the time of admission to a program. This helps in creating an appropriate treatment plan, as well as assessing a client for any health conditions not previously known.

COUNSELORS

Counselors are involved in each type of initial treatment, with the exception of self-help meetings. A counselor plays several roles in working with clients who are beginning treatment. Counselors who provide services may be rehabilitation counselors, drug and alcohol counselors, mental health counselors, social workers, occupational therapists, recreation therapists, and creative art therapists, depending on the nature of the activity. Counselors facilitate group and family sessions, as well as provide individual counseling. They may provide educational classes related to employment and life skills issues. Leisure and creative programming is also coordinated by the counseling staff.

As a person nears the completion of treatment, the counselor will serve as a case manager to assist in the development and coordination of an aftercare plan. They may have to be a liaison with the insurance company to ensure that services are funded or coordinate with outside agencies to gain admission to programs. They are also instrumental in the transition back to the individual's community or further inpatient treatment. Specific implications for counseling will be addressed at the end of the chapter.

NUTRITIONIST

Some facilities employ nutritionists or dieticians to work with clients in identifying diet problems that may be caused by both medical conditions and substance use. Among people with substance addictions, malnutrition is common because drug use replaces healthy eating habits. Clients who have active eating disorders will also be dealing with nutritional issues. Furthermore, if a client is involved in an inpatient program or program that involves serving meals, it is important that the facility cater the meals to the needs of the client. This can best be done with the help of a nutritionist or dietician.

FACTORS RELATED
TO POSITIVE OUTCOMES

Positive outcomes in initial treatment can be measured in a variety ways. Completion of treatment, defined as continuing with treatment until staff and the client agree that meaningful goals have been accomplished, is one way that positive results are measured. Positive outcomes can also be measured by number of positive urine screens, follow-up with the aftercare plan, attendance at self-help meetings, or reported days abstinent from substances. A number of factors within the person, program, and system contribute to greater likelihood of achieving positive outcomes and recovery.

CLIENT CHARACTERISTICS

A number of research studies have investigated the characteristics of those who seek and complete treatment more often. Individuals who are older tend to seek out and complete treatment more often than their younger counterparts, although this may be a function of length of time with an addiction rather than age, per se.[8] Higher number of symptoms and greater levels of drinking were associated with seeking treatment, indicating that problem severity correlates highly with help seeking. In terms of gender, studies show that men may seek help more often,[8] although females may have higher completion rates for detoxification programs.[22]

Domestic situation and marital status were strong predictors of relapse one-year following a detoxification program.[21] Those who were single, left a partner, or were living alone prior to admission demonstrated poorer outcomes, indicating the protective factors of personal support in recovery. Other factors predictive of entry into treatment included higher levels of education, full-time employment, and dependent children.[8] This possibly indicates that those with more access to resources and responsibility have greater pressure to commit to recovery. Studies of this type are helpful to programs and facilities because they can focus on ways to improve the outcomes of those who are less likely to complete or benefit from treatment.

PROGRAM CHARACTERISTICS

Aside from program elements being tailored to the needs of the client (i.e., needs medical management while undergoing physical withdrawal), there are a number of program characteristics that are indicative of more positive outcomes. The first of these is family-focused counseling. Primary treatment facilities may offer group and individual counseling to a client; some programs may offer family counseling, as well. Addictions frequently cause family and marital discord and impact more than the client. Treatment that involves the family can be beneficial to the client, building stronger supports and educating the family on the disease concept of addiction. It can also help build up the client's hope, as they will use their family's desire for sobriety as a motivator to remain in treatment. In a study related to inpatient detoxification, O'Farrell and colleagues[16] found that having a meeting with the client and an adult family member increased the chances that the client would continue with substance abuse treatment after discharge. Having an in-person family meeting was also correlated with fewer days of drug and alcohol use following discharge.

Peer counseling within primary treatment programs has also been correlated with positive outcomes. This method involves volunteers who have been in recovery for a long period of time serving as peer counselors to those that have entered initial treatment. It has been shown to promote positive outcomes in treatment, including increased self-help attendance, continuing substance abuse treatment, and abstinence from drugs and alcohol.[3] Peers can help clients work through some of their fears about treatment by sharing their past experiences and troubles in recovery. With proper rules, training, and guidelines for confidentiality in place, peer counseling can be very beneficial to patients entering treatment.

The practices of peer counseling and family therapy all build on the concept of support systems. A strong positive sober support system is important for a person who is initially entering treatment for an addiction. The support helps to promote hope and motivation for the person attempting to remain abstinent. A client's support network can consist of many types of individuals. A person's family and close friends may compose their support system. Some people may find their support in self-help meetings and group therapy. A support network can also consist of an array of professionals, including the doctors, nurses, and counselors who work with them in the program.

Finally, discharge planning that leads to a strong continuum of care is a benchmark for positive treatment outcomes. As stated earlier, detoxification alone is not sufficient to promote lasting change; substance abuse treatment must address the psychological, social, and behavioral aspects of substance abuse.[2]

When a client is being prepared to complete their initial treatment program, a continuing treatment plan is written to address their full range of biopsychosocial needs, including addiction treatment, mental health, physical health, and daily living concerns. Some of the aftercare services desired most by clients exiting programs included access to self-help meetings, job seeking assistance, and individual counseling.[20] Aftercare plans are person-and context-specific. Consider the following scenario. A client returns to the inpatient medically managed detoxification program at which you work and you engage in conversation with him:

COUNSELOR: "John, I understand that you have been a client of ours quite a few times. Tell me about that."

JOHN: "I don't know. I come in motivated to stop using heroin, clean up for a few days, and then go back to using within a week of being discharged."

COUNSELOR: "Well, John, you are usually only involved in our care for a few days while you're withdrawing. What do you typically do to continue your treatment once you are discharged from here?"

JOHN: "You guys always set me up with an appointment at an outpatient program, but I don't think I've ever made it to the evaluation appointment. I always seem to relapse before getting there and then decide to not go. When they call wondering where I am, I just ignore the phone call."

COUNSELOR: "Do you think that putting yourself back into your daily environment so quickly after being clean is a stumbling block for you?"

JOHN: "Oh, definitely. My friends know just where to find me."

COUNSELOR: "Do you think that you would benefit from avoiding that environment for a longer time so you can engage in treatment more fully? Maybe something on an inpatient basis?"

JOHN: "I think that would be very helpful! I can become more level-headed and process more of my concerns. Then maybe I can prevent relapsing!"

COUNSELOR: "Glad to hear that. We can work on discharging you directly to an inpatient rehabilitation program now that you are done with your detoxification."

Each program should gear discharge plans to the specific needs of the clients with whom they work. Some programs may treat clients who are not working, prompting referrals to vocational services. Some inpatient programs may deal more frequently with housing and basic needs issues as a part of the discharge plan because of the socioeconomic status of their clientele. It is important that programs periodically survey clients to understand their needs, create a greater network of referral resources, and train staff in counseling/planning for these needs in order to increase the rate of positive outcomes.

SYSTEM CHARACTERISTICS

There are a couple of global, systems factors that impact on the outcomes of individuals in recovery. The availability of health insurance either grants or restricts access to a number of programs. Utilization of a full range of treatment options is correlated to recovery and abstinence. Some funding sources support treatment in detoxification facilities, but not the adjunct services that are typically recommended in a discharge plan.[14] Third-party payers may treat treatment services as isolated events ("unbundling" treatment) and require separate authorization for services, creating lag time in the continuation of treatment.[5] When individuals do not receive the duration and intensity of services they need to stabilize, they may relapse and find themselves seeking detoxification at a later time. Insurance companies also might not allow for repeated admissions to the same type of program in a certain timeframe.

A trend to shorten the length of treatment has also persisted in the field of substance abuse due to policy directives and budget constraints. Those who have not had adequate time to address their full range of personal, medical, and psychological issues will find themselves reentering treatment. Luckily, there are a number of funding sources and options available for clients of various circumstances to access services. These include Access to Recovery vouchers; Medicaid and Medicare; TRICARE and the Veteran's Affairs for military personnel and veterans; State Children's Health Insurance Program; social service programs such as state Vocational Rehabilitation; and private insurance. Lifting of financial barriers for services helps ensure access to the services that enable recovery.

COUNSELING CONSIDERATIONS DURING PRIMARY TREATMENT

Programs designed for detoxification and primary treatment must embrace the characteristics that will lead to outcomes that are more successful. Some of these factors were outlined above, but other specific philosophical and programmatic characteristics should be considered, as they create the conditions/environment for program retention and completion. These include assessing client readiness; using strategies to engage and motivate clients; using an holistic approach to treatment; and bridging the gap between programs to allow for the continuity of care.

ASSESSING CLIENT READINESS

Prochaska, DiClemente, and Norcross[17] delineated the stages of change as pre-contemplation, contemplation, preparation, action, and maintenance, where a person moves from a state of not considering change to a place of actively incorporating their desired behaviors. Readiness to change is comprised of two components: psychological openness and psychosocial/physical freedom. Those who developmentally are not ready to make a change (either have not considered change or are thinking about it only in terms of the future) may not capture the benefits of current treatment. There are several instruments that have been developed to assess these psychological factors (see the National Institute on Alcoholism and Alcohol Abuse for a comprehensive list).[15] It has been found that once individuals have established the psychological readiness to change and seek initial help, they have an increased likelihood of recovery, even with fewer services.[8] Beyond mindset, however, a person must not be hampered by personal and social barriers that prevent their full participation in a program. The basic needs for childcare, transportation, shelter, and food must also be addressed before a person is going to be open to the higher order need of surmounting their addiction.

ENGAGING AND MOTIVATING CLIENTS

As established earlier, there is a phenomenon of a "revolving door" when it comes to treatment for substance abuse because individuals are not linked with proper aftercare services or they too quickly return to their original environments, which are fraught with triggers to relapse. Detoxification and primary treatment programs represent only the first step on the road to recovery. Strategies for retaining clients in treatment and sustaining their recovery effort include:

◊ Educating the client about the withdrawal process, including the longer acting impact of psychological withdrawal and cravings.

◊ Using support systems to coach the client along the path to recovery and intervene in crisis.

◊ Maintaining a drug-free environment.

◊ Considering alternative approaches, including acupuncture detoxification and complementary treatments that may be more culturally appropriate.[5]

Motivational counseling has been implemented as an effective technique in addictions counseling because of its goal-directed, strengths-based approach. It emphasizes a therapeutic partnership with the counselor in the change process. Establishing a collaborative relationship with staff early on allows clients to take ownership of their recovery so that treatment is not something that is done "to" them. Other program factors that enhance motivation to engage and continue in treatment include identifying barriers to continued participation, matching clients to the least intensive and restrictive treatment for their presenting issues, and developing individualized plans for services.[6] Knowing the client's treatment history and being flexible in your approach to treatment planning will ensure that you are not continuing with ineffective strategies.

UTILIZING A HOLISTIC APPROACH TO TREATMENT
With an understanding of a person's readiness to change and their engagement in the treatment process, a counselor must employ a holistic approach to treatment and planning. A biopsychosocial approach should address medical and psychological/psychiatric issues; employment/support; patterns of use; criminal history and legal status; and family and social relationships (including history of trauma and abuse). While sometimes overlooked, assessment and counseling should also address sexuality, self-concept, recreation and leisure, spirituality, and values.[4] Knowledge of the whole person, especially contextual knowledge (i.e., how the person is going to interact in their life environments following treatment), was the best predictor of better outcomes in a study of addiction services.[12] More in-depth knowledge of a person, gained through reflective counseling, fosters the therapeutic alliance necessary for effective treatment.

BRIDGING THE GAP BETWEEN PROGRAMS
Patients are more likely to engage in treatment if they believe their full range of needs, in addition to recovery, are addressed.[5] Those who receive the "wrap around" services to address their holistic needs are more likely to remain in treatment longer than those who do not. Aftercare/discharge planning and clinical case management (CCM) coordinate these services. McLellan et al.[14] found that those receiving clinical case management as a bridge to supportive services showed a reduction in detoxification-only admissions (67% to 30%), increase in the use of rehabilitation services (30% to 70%), and increase in the average length of stay per treatment episode (6.4 to 27.6 days) over the course of a year of CCM intervention. Higher levels of client involvement in the planning process also enhance compliance with aftercare instructions. The average compliance with instructions for treatment following detoxification range between 10 and 40 percent.[20] A better match between the desires of the client and the goals/services listed in the aftercare plan greatly improves compliance. Greater engagement in the process and addressing holistic needs results in more lasting outcomes for those on the road to recovery.

REFERENCES

[1]American Society of Addiction Medicine. (2001). *Patient placement criteria for the treatment of substance-related disorders: ASAM PPC-2* (2nd ed., revised). Chevy Chase, MD: Author.

[2]Amodeo, M., Lundgren, L., Chassler, D., & Witas, J. (2008). High-frequency users of detoxification: Who are they? *Substance Use & Misuse, 43,* 839-849.

[3]Blondell, R. D., Behrens, T., Smith, S. J., Greene, B. J., & Servoss, T. J. (2008). Peer support during inpatient detoxification and aftercare outcomes. *Addictive Disorders & their Treatment, 7*(2), 77-86.

[4]Brooks, F., & McHenry, B. (2009). *A contemporary approach to substance abuse and addiction counseling: A counselor's guide to application and understanding.* Alexandria, VA: American Counseling Association.

[5]Center for Substance Abuse Treatment. (2006a). *Detoxification and substance abuse treatment.* Treatment Improvement Protocol (TIP) Series 45. Rockville, MD: Substance Abuse and Mental Health Services Administration.

[6]Center for Substance Abuse Treatment. (2006b). *Substance abuse: Clinical issues in intensive outpatient treatment.* Treatment Improvement Protocol (TIP) Series 47. Rockville, MD: Substance Abuse and Mental Health Services Administration.

[7]Craig, R. J. (2004). *Counseling the alcohol and drug dependent client: A practical approach.* Boston, MA: Pearson Education.

[8]Dawson, D. A., Grant, B. F., Stinson, F. S., & Chou, P. S. (2006). Estimating the effect of help-seeking on achieving recovery from alcohol dependence. *Addiction, 101*, 824-834.

[9]Drapkin, M. L., Tate, S. R., McQuaid, J.R., & Brown, S. A. (2008). Does initial treatment focus influence outcomes for depressed substance users? *Journal of Substance Abuse Treatment, 35*, 343-350.

[10]Griswold, K. S., Greene, B., Smith, S. J., Behrens, T., & Blondell, R. D. (2007). Linkage to primary medical care following inpatient detoxification. *The American Journal on Addictions, 16*, 183-186.

[11]Gruber, V. A., Delucchi, K. L., Kielstein, A., & Batki, S. L. (2008). A randomized trial of 6-month methadone maintenance with standard or minimal counseling versus 21-day methadone detoxification. *Drug and Alcohol Dependence, 94*, 199-206.

[12]Kim, T. W., Samet, J. H., Cheng, D. M., Winter, M. R., Safran, D. G., & Saitz, R. (2007). Primary care quality and addiction severity: A prospective cohort study. *Health Services Research, 42*, 755-772.

[13]McKeon, A., Frye, M. A., & Delanty, N. (2008). The alcohol withdrawal syndrome. *Journal of Neurology, Neurosurgery, & Psychiatry, 79*, 854-862.

[14]McLellan, A. T., Weinstein, R. L., Shen, Q., Kendig, C., & Levine, M. (2005). Improving continuity of care in a public addition treatment system with clinical case management. *The American Journal on Addiction, 14*, 426-440.

[15]National Institute on Alcoholism and Alcohol Abuse. *Quick reference instrument guide.* Retrieved on July 10, 2010 from http://pubs.niaaa.nih.gov/publications/Assesing%20Alcohol/quickref.htm

[16]O'Farrell, T. J., Muirphy, M., Alter, J., & Fals-Stewart, W. (2008). Brief family treatment intervention to promote continuing care among alcohol-dependent patients in inpatient detoxification: A randomized pilot study. *Journal of Substance Abuse Treatment, 34*, 363-369.

[17]Prochaska, J. O., DiClemente, C. C., & Norcross, J. C. (1992). In search of how people change: Applications to the addictive behaviors. *American Psychologist, 47*, 1102-1114.

[18]SAMHSA. (2007). *2007 ATR factsheet.* Retrieved on July 10, 2010 from http://atr.samhsa.gov/Factsheet07.aspx

[19]SAMHSA. (2008). *National survey of substance abuse treatment services. State profile—United States.* Retrieved on July 10, 2010 from http://wwwdasis.samhsa.gov/webt/state_data/US08.pdf

[20]Tuten, M., Jones, H. E., Lertch, E. W., & Stitzer, M. L. (2007). Aftercare plans of inpatients undergoing detoxification. *The American Journal of Drug and Alcohol Abuse, 33*, 547-555.

[21]Walter, M., Gerhard, U., Duersteler-MacFarland, K. M., Weijers, H., Boening, J., & Wiesbeck, G. A. (2006). Social factors but not stress-coping stypes predict relapse in detoxified alcoholics. *Neuropsychobiology, 54*, 100-106.

[22]Webb, L., Ryan, T., & Meier, P. (2008). Care pathways to in-patient alcohol detoxification and their effects on predictors of treatment completion. *Journal of Substance Use, 13*(4), 255-267.

ALCOHOLICS ANONYMOUS & THE SELF-HELP MOVEMENT

BY **SHARON SABIK**
WINSTON-SALEM STATE UNIVERSITY

Chapter Topics

Alcoholics Anonymous (AA) has been helping alcoholics and other drug abusers to recover for approximately 75 years. Although there is a scarcity of empirical research to support the success of AA, over these several years the success of the program has been spread from state to state and country to country. It is not a program for everyone; it does not claim to be everyone's solution to the problem of alcoholism. There is no doubt, however, that anecdotally there is a history of success in this self-help fellowship that is not comparable to other self-help or other types of programs. However, even with this success, the program has remained controversial. Strong views about AA remain an issue and criticism about the program continues to surface. Just as professionals have started to have a more favorable view of AA and accept it as a complementary approach in treatment, others still have difficulty with the AA focus on spirituality as a foundation of life transformation and attainment and maintenance of sobriety.

A BRIEF HISTORY OF AA

Alcoholics Anonymous (AA) was founded by two men who had trouble staying abstinent during a period of time when alcohol was thought to be evil and alcoholism was immoral.[5] The two desperate men met, talked, and thought that they could help each other to get and stay sober. One man was a financial advisor, Bill Wilson, who was from the Midwest. Dr. Bob Smith was a medical doctor from New York. They had very different personalities and seemed an odd pairing, but both wanted to find a solution to alcoholism. Thus began three-fourths of a century of AA. In fact, June 10, 1935 was the day that Bill W. had his last drink and is considered to be the birth of the AA program.

The two men started groups and held meetings in their own parts of the world but stayed in touch. From their discussions and their first trials, they determined that support and anonymity were the primary tools for sobriety. They borrowed some principles from the Oxford Group, a Christian Movement of the time, and added others as the process or program evolved. Eventually, they put the principles in a book called Alcoholics Anonymous, commonly called The Big Book or the AA Bible. These principles became the Twelve Steps of AA. They are 12 principles or guidelines for recovery from the disease of alcoholism. These 12 steps were designed not only for alcoholics to attain abstinence but to ultimately transform their lives and maintain sobriety for life.

THE 12 PRINCIPLES

These are the Twelve Steps of AA and the principles that are suggested as a method of recovery by the AA program:

1. We admitted that we were powerless over alcohol - that our life has become unmanageable.
2. Came to believe that a power greater than ourselves could restore us to sanity.
3. Made a decision to turn our will and our lives over to the care of God as we understood Him.
4. Made a searching and fearless moral inventory of ourselves.
5. Admitted to God, to ourselves, and to another human being the exact nature of our wrongs.
6. Were entirely ready to have God remove all these defects of character.
7. Humbly asked him to remove our shortcomings.
8. Made a list of all persons we had harmed, and became willing to make amends to them all.
9. Made direct amends to such people wherever possible, except when to do so would injure them or others.
10. Continued to take personal inventory and, when we were wrong, promptly admitted it.
11. Sought through prayer and meditation to improve our conscious contact with God, as we understood Him, praying only for knowledge of His will for us and the power to carry that out.
12. Having had a spiritual awakening as the result of these steps, we tried to carry this message to alcoholics, and to practice these principles in all our affairs.[1]

THE AA PROGRAM

There also evolved another set of 12 principles, the Twelve Traditions of AA, so that the program of AA would itself survive.[2,5] These traditions are guidelines within which the local groups operate so that the structure and function of the groups themselves are facilitated. These principles guide the function of the program and the different types of groups themselves. This is actually a delicate concept because AA prides itself on the non-organization and a lack of bureaucracy. Yet something has to keep things going and has for all these years. This something is a simple yet loose framework. There are no dues or fees; AA is self-supporting. The one requirement of membership is a desire to stop drinking. Notice that this is a *desire* to stop drinking. The person is seeking help to stop drinking; there is no requirement that says an alcoholic who is having a problem with stopping cannot attend meetings. In many in- or out-patient programs the requirement is to have stopped drinking for a certain amount of time. AA has no such rule. There is an understanding that relapse is part of the disease and that it may take a while for a person to attain and keep sobriety. Alcoholics feel free to keep coming until they understand the program, obtain, and maintain abstinence, and eventually long-term sobriety. Alcoholics have a distrust of authority and a defiant attitude that must be taken into account when planning the structure of a group. No lectures, rules, or requirements of membership are to be met. There are suggestions to follow certain ways and alcoholics look to models in the groups in order to attain sobriety.

Sharing, experiential learning, and self-reflection take the place of authority per se. Group members are always consulted; this is shared governance at its strongest and yet most simple. Members run the groups and the program. In the early days Bill W. was tempted by power and realized, with the help of others; that power, money, and too much organization could ruin the fellowship of AA. That is the basis of AA. It is a fellowship not simply an organization. Many self-help groups have started out humble only to succumb to the temptations of professionalization. AA adamantly stays the same year after year because it is understood that this is the only way that it can work.

The one primary purpose of the program is to spread the message and help others to stay sober. This is a very narrow focus but this has its advantages. Nothing gets in the way of the primary focus; nothing distracts. There are many to reach out to for this assistance on a 24-hour and 7-day a week basis. Psychotherapy or counseling cannot offer this level of support. AA does not prevent others from going out and getting any other support that they can get. The common and only goal in the meeting rooms and in the discussions revolves around not drinking. The narrow focus of AA also includes the fact that the groups are emphatically self-supporting. There are no fees for membership. Members pay what they can as a basket is passed around at meetings. Outside donations are not sought and are strictly capped at an amount when offered and given. There are no lobbyists at AA. Every effort is to remain low key; there is no political or social agenda. The program needs enough to survive and nothing more.

Bill W. and Dr. Bob, as they were called, were always co-leaders and gave much of the everyday functioning over to the members. They made this official in 1950 when the transfer of leadership to the groups themselves was made official. The structure of AA is decentralized, egalitarian, non-hierarchical, and non-bureaucratic. Membership is self-defined and power is at the base, with the groups not at the top. Groups are the organization. They are not incorporated; anyone can start a group anywhere at any time. They are neither affiliated nor endorsed by anyone or any entity. In fact, the court's use of AA as a referral source is a problem for many. There are some alcoholics and non-alcoholics who think that AA is affiliated with the government or the court system because of the practice of sending offenders to meetings. This is not the case at all. Offenders are supposed to get a signature from a group member and bring it back as proof of attendance. Many members refuse to sign; AA is not affiliated with the courts or any arm of enforcement. In addition, it is left up to the individual member if they wish to sign or not. This has been brought up at group conscience and business meetings time after time.

Overview of structure:
◊ Local groups with officers and representatives
◊ District offices
◊ Regional meetings
◊ State representatives
◊ National General Services Conference once a year

The Conference is the guardian of world services, the Twelve Steps, Twelve Traditions, and all of the publications.

Someone looking for a simple answer as to why AA works will be disappointed. There are many questions that may have to be tested and answered. This is not a program that lends itself to scientific examination. One question that comes to mind is whether it is the motivation to commit to the program that helps a person to attain sobriety. A person who seeks help and is ready to do whatever is necessary to get it may simply be ready to get better.[2] Is fellowship with other alcoholics the difference? These are people who can truly empathize with the alcoholic. There is a bonding that takes place like nowhere else. Friends are made for life. The support is 24/7; where else can you get that kind of help? AA saves money. The cost of going to AA meetings compared to inpatient or even outpatient rehabilitation is significant. Again, there are no dues or fees; a member pays whatever they can manage - which may be nothing at times.

Interdependence and cooperation are also defining characteristics of the AA program structure and the meetings themselves. There are no major authority figures; there are co-leaders. Leaders change frequently. Elections are held yearly and rotation is encouraged. Service is certainly encouraged, but there are many ways to accomplish this. Some groups elect officers and sometimes people volunteer. There many ways to give back from group service positions to group maintenance like making of the coffee for meetings and setting up chairs and tables. Giving back is not only a part of the primary therapeutic method of AA but is very practical. People who give of themselves tend to change.

Volunteering for even the smallest tasks promotes responsibility. This is something the active alcoholic has lost and given away. Alcoholism is a very self-centered disease. Transformation in the way of volunteering to do tasks and chores promotes selflessness and humility. No one is coerced or even solicited to do these things; the idea is look at us, this is how we got sober. If you want it, come and get it. People who are sober make suggestions to those who are not or who are in danger of losing sobriety. There is no status to doing, however; the person who makes coffee has just as much value as the person who acts as a group representative. They are all important tasks for group sustenance and everyone does what they can.

The core method of AA is in the sharing of experiences.[2] What does this sharing of experiences do? It offers support and hope to the once and often hopeless. Experiences are shared with peers who have had similar experiences.

Peers in AA cut across all classes, professions, income, and disability. A peer in AA means someone who has the same problem. This mutuality of assistance is extremely important. There is a built in reciprocity. What one shares one day may be needed and shared back again at some point in time. Sober alcoholics who speak at meetings or who share and sponsor become models for those trying to attain abstinence and sobriety.

No one is immune to relapse and or the effects of alcoholism like depression, financial problems, and relationship issues. These are all lived experiences and they are shared in real time. In other words, there are many opportunities to get the help you need when you need it. If an alcoholic has to wait for an appointment with a professional, it may be too late to stop the relapse.

THE FELLOWSHIP

The AA program is often called a fellowship.[5] Just what is a fellowship and why is the label so important? There are many self-help groups and organizations with some having the elements of fellowship. In a very general view, fellowship refers to sharing similar ideas and experiences with others. In AA, Fellowship is the cohesive factor that often is the difference between attaining and maintaining sobriety. It goes beyond sharing with individuals with similar interests. Fellowship in the AA program is a bond that often cannot be seen anywhere else. Members are there for each other, to offer friendship and assistance no matter what the circumstances. That bonding often outlasts attendance at meetings. The idea of Fellowship is so strong in AA that a member may not go to meetings for years, but still feels comfortable walking into a meeting. It could be a meeting far from home with strangers but that member always feels welcomed.

THE MEETINGS

Meetings are the primary way that members share their experiences and help other alcoholics to get and stay sober. Meetings have several different purposes and structures. The two overriding categories are that some meetings are closed and only alcoholics can attend. The other type of meeting is open and you do not have to be an avowed alcoholic to attend. Persons who are not sure of their status, families of alcoholics, and other interested parties can attend open meetings. A typical meeting does have a certain standardized format with some variation between meetings. The typical meeting begins with socialization between attendees, a chairperson is in charge of the meeting and has one or more speakers tell their stories. A speaker will usually focus on what it was like to be drinking, how he or she found sobriety, and what it is like now. If it is a one speaker meeting; discussion among attendees usually follows and the meeting comes to a close. If it is a two or more speaker meeting then the meeting generally closes after the speakers finish.

Meetings start with the chairperson calling the meeting to order, offering a moment of silence, and reading from the Big Book. Practices vary by groups and meetings. There may be announcements, celebrations of anniversaries (of sobriety); donations are accepted by passing a basket around the room. Sharing is neither required nor coerced. Meetings typically end with a prayer which can be the Serenity Prayer and/or The Lord's Prayer. The group holds hands and forms a loose circle reciting the chosen prayers together. There are many specialty groups and specialty formats as well. For instance, there are women's and men's groups, Hispanic and African American groups, groups for lesbians and gays. Different formats include discussion only, Step discussions, Big book Study, speaker/discussion, and Eleventh Step groups that focus on spirituality.

Diversity was a part of the program from the beginning because the two co-founders lived so far away from each other. The first groups started in different areas of the country and had members who were diverse spiritually as well as regionally. There were not many women in the first groups. That did take a while but eventually changed. While groups still tend to be predominantly male, more and more women and ethnic groupings are being represented. Class has never really been an issue since alcoholism spares no one. Money does not protect the alcoholic from his or her consequences. It is also no longer a hindrance to getting help, although this was not always the case. Unity of the members and the groups overrode any problems that surfaced within. In fact, there is a mechanism for dealing with conflict. Once a year, each group has what is called a special group conscience meeting in which conflict is aired and resolved.

CRITICISMS OF THE AA MODEL

The AA model has outlasted many other programs of treatment as well as become a template for other self-help groups.[4,5] Yet controversy and criticism still remain a strong issue. There are reasons for this. After 75 years it is still the most widely known treatment for alcohol and other drug addictions. The science of both addiction and AA is frequently under scrutiny. On the one hand, this can be explained by some of the very factors thought to make the group what it is. Like anonymity, distrust of research and professionals in general, self-selection. The former, the science of addiction itself, is rapidly supporting the disease model used by the program. However, there is still as much or more research on nonabstinence models as there is on the AA program.

Many of the critics, who criticize AA and warn about the dangers of a cult and other nonsense, have never been to a meeting. One meeting is certainly not enough to gain even a small understanding of this mighty but simple program. Most of the evidence is hearsay; for instance, that AA members coerce attendees to be compliant and to believe in a higher power. The opposite could be said to be true that those who do self-select have a tendency toward this way of thinking no matter what. Motivation is what makes someone want to stay abstinent, gain long-term sobriety, and do anything to obtain it (often called compliance). A belief in a higher power is not a requisite, especially a belief in a named God, but many people do believe in something out there that is more powerful than the individual is. Although there are atheists and agnostics in the program, there may be a self-selection factor that this is a comfortable and attractive element to many who join. Most critics completely miss the point. Many alcoholics succeed in the AA programs that have not succeeded in various other kinds of treatment. To AA, it is not a competition. The primary purpose of AA is to help the person who is suffering.

Here are some common criticisms with responses:

◊ AA takes power away from the individual and the groups. The opposite is true. The groups have all the power.

◊ AA supports the disease model of alcoholism. This is not a strengths model. Again, understanding the lived experience of the group, the opposite is actual y true. AA uses the disease model in a positive way by taking alcoholism away from the moral defect model. This way shame and doubt can be dealt with and the alcoholic can move forward. By atonement and giving back to society, the recovering alcoholic is at a place of strength.

◊ AA meetings are a substitute for addiction. First of all, if this were true - who cares? A sober life attending meetings with a valued fellowship and positive actions is so much better than living life as a guilt ridden and destructive alcoholic. However, the truth is that most people get better and cut down on meetings because they go back to living productive and normal lives.

◊ AA requires total abstinence. Yes, it does. Why is there something wrong with choosing not to put something noxious and poisonous in the body?

◊ AA is a cult or a religion and is predominantly white, male, and Christian. Certainly, this may have some truth but it is not a requirement. As the US and the world become more diverse, so does AA.

◊ It is degrading to identify self as an alcoholic at meetings. This is true only to outsiders who do not understand that they do so with pride. The label has become a positive one that reminds members of the life they have chosen and the defective aspect of the label has been reframed. I am an alcoholic and part of a wonderful fellowship of people who have chosen to do something about it. This is the underlying message every time a person introduces themselves as an alcoholic. This is yet another lived experience that persons outside the program have great difficulty in understanding.

◊ AA is run by a strictly nonprofit organization. This is very true. Why is this considered a problem? This is a good thing; as noted it keeps people focused and nonpolitical.

PROFESSIONALS AND AA

Professionals are taking more favorable notice of AA and other such groups in recent years.[7,8] People are referred to AA as an adjunctive therapy, and why not? Where else can you find assistance that is free of charge and operates on a 24 hour seven day a week schedule with a variety of locations, usually locally as well as more far flung, and several ad doc counselors willing to share their strength and hope? Another reason that professionals are taking more notice is that that to treat those with addictive disorders the professional must have more than a passing knowledge of how the disease operates. It is very helpful if the counselor/psychologist or group leader can speak the language of the drug dependent client. The counselor must also be aware of the pattern of the disease process and be mindful of the manipulative aspects of addiction. These are clients that are not above using anything, including the counselor's lack of knowledge about the disease and the program, to stay in denial, and keep an illusion of control.

SELECTED RESEARCH

Strong and controversial views about AA remain an issue but so does the anecdotal and research sponsored reports of positive outcomes related to AA attendance whether resulting in total abstinence or reduction in problem behaviors. Quality research is becoming more and more feasible. That research is tending to show comparable and randomized outcomes.

One of the problems of research, however, is the narrow criterion and protectiveness of those in the program. Still, quality research is possible, and AA and other self-help groups with the same challenges have proven to be successful for certain groups. The goal has been to identify what characteristics will predict success in self-help groups like AA and Narcotics Anonymous (NA). The problem with the research is multi-fold. Most research has been carried out with very small samples due to the problem of anonymity. Samples are self-selected due to anonymity and confidentiality and stigma issues. As previously noted, AA and other self-help groups are simply not for everyone so how does one define or predict success in AA?[8] People who do not make it may simply not be right for the AA program; rather than AA has failed them.

Kubicek, et al.[9] examined AA attendees and spontaneous remitters looking for attributes common to each in the outcome of success. All had supportive people around them, accepted help from a higher power, had a strong motivation for sobriety, were honest and trying to build self-confidence, and remembered the negative rather than the positive consequences of use. This latter point, remembering negative consequences, should be noted because it could be an important factor in the prevention of and protection for relapse. In sum, however, these study participants had the characteristics of people who wanted more than abstinence as a goal. They wanted to transform their lives. Moos, et al.[11] found gender differences when they examined 461 participants, half men and half women. They found that women were more likely to participate in AA and have better outcomes. Women participated more intensely, improved more than men, and demonstrated better problem-solving skills and had extended remission/recovery.

Several characteristics are associated with attendance in Twelve Step groups. This is a variable that is often studied. People who attend more frequently and who become more committed in the program are more likely to be more successful. However, focus on attendance is also problematic. What defines the correct amount of attendance is different for everyone as is the degree of drinking that causes problems. Research tends to be quantified and AA may not be readily quantifiable. However, Masudomi, et al.[10] examined a large group of AA attendees in Tokyo at 5-year follow-up and found that attendance at self-help groups was the key to success. They looked at several factors like age, sex, physical illness, employment status, health insurance, family background, and outpatient treatment. None of these factors was significant predictors of mortality, only attendance.

The number of AA meetings attended by persons over time has long been thought to be a predictor of sobriety.[14] Indeed, research relating success as abstinence and/or reduction in drinking or using substances has used correlation measures of meeting attendance and success or reduction. However, AA affiliation is not as simple as attendance or any other quantifiable measure. Often, people who are sober for many years only attend meetings sporadically because the reason for attendance has changed. They are no longer needy but attend in appreciation of the gift they have gotten, sobriety. Moreover, attendance that is more frequent does not seem to improve outcomes when compared with moderate or occasional attendance.[8] Attendance may mean different things to different people. Although the standard suggestion of a meeting a day for several months for initial sobriety is often voiced, in fact people's attendance varies substantially. What is high motivation for one person may be equal to one or two meetings a week. Another person may attend several meetings and join several groups to show commitment and attain sobriety. The type of meeting may also play a role.

However, can we study a program as subtle as AA using quantitative measures?[13] Many of the studies that have been conducted examined attendance as a measure of success. In addition, number of times attended categorized as successful or not was variable. One study considers twice a week meeting attendance as high. Most members of the fellowship would differ on this aspect alone since attendance, especially initially, is recommended to be seven meetings in seven days. Presence or attendance at meetings may be one factor of success but it is certainly not the only one. It may not even be the most important. The cohort effect and other group components may be more important to the success of AA with its members. Member modeling of behavior leading to sobriety may be an important element in attainment of abstinence and subsequent life transformation leading to long-term sobriety.

OTHER SELF-HELP GROUPS

Self-help groups have become a part of the culture. Mutual assistance type groups have sprung up through the last several decades that deal with various disease, problems, social groups and issues, and special populations.

A number of these groups are formed around the AA Twelve Step model, still the most popular and widely used. While others are almost anti-AA, or anti-spiritual, programs. There are other AA based model programs for spouses, teens, children of alcoholics, and co-dependent significant others as well as different groups for different problems.

NARCOTICS ANONYMOUS

Narcotics Anonymous (NA) is for drug abusers. NA is the second most widely used self-help group aimed at those persons who identify more with drug abuse than with alcohol abuse.[12] Both substances can be a factor but people either go to both types of groups, or choose the one with which they are most comfortable. The Twelve Steps are changed a bit to suit drug abuse. Members choose to use the phrase addiction rather than drug use. NA was first created in the 1940s and the structure is similar to the AA model but it is not as recognized as AA. Communication with members is still through the meeting structure but brochures are used in place of a descriptive book.

AL-ANON FAMILY GROUPS

This is a Twelve Step recovery program for friends and family. Al-Anon is specifically for spouses, friends, and other family members. Meetings tend to be small and not as easy to find as AA meetings. The focus of these meetings is on understanding the problem, sharing experiences, taking care of self, discussing problems common to those who deal with alcoholics (like enabling and abuse).

There are other self-helps groups (non-AA model) not so widely known but can be used as an alternative to AA and the AA models. Generally, these groups are for those persons who have a problem with the spiritual content of the Twelve Step programs. The following are three of the most well-known.

Save Our Selves (SOS). SOS is a securely based approach that makes the individual responsible for achieving and maintaining sobriety.[16] It is a secular approach that is totally held apart from religion or spirituality. There is no reliance on any kind of higher power. The support of others is crucial to achieving and maintaining sobriety. SOS is also non-profit and antonymous and strictly dedicated to one thing: sobriety.

Rational Recovery (RR). RR is another self-help group that is an alternative to the spiritually based Twelve Step Groups.[14,15] It is more widely known than

SOS and was founded by Jack Trimpey, a clinical social worker from California. RR, however, is also very anti-AA in its beliefs and criticisms. It has even developed *The Small Book*, as a counterpart to AA's Big Book. Contrary to RR members, AA members have no special issues with RR, and AA members are not threatened by RR. They feel it is a choice that the individual makes. RR is very loud in its criticism of AA as a religion or cult. RR no longer has meetings but periodically publishes brochures or flyers on pertinent RR issues and is available on the internet.

Women for Sobriety. This is also a non-profit program that was started by Jean Kirkpatrick in 1976 for those women who do not feel that AA and other programs focus on women's issues enough.[6] The focus of discussion and transformation is on women's issues such as self-esteem building and guilt reduction. In addition, this is a secular group; a higher power is not required to help the alcoholic woman. Instead of 12 steps, Women for Sobriety present 13 affirmations revolving around women's issues. Some women attend both AA and Women for Sobriety. It is not a radical or feminist group; it is simply more focused on women.

CASE STUDIES

THE CASE OF THOMAS

Thomas is a 32 year old investment broker. He has been drinking since the age of 14. He started with marijuana at the age of 11, and smoked with his peers. He and his friends soon graduated to drinking beer and whiskey. Thomas and his peers stole it from their parents or had an older boy who could get it for them. This behavior was considered a rite of passage for Thomas and his friends. It was part of being an adult and was risky behavior.

In Thomas' case it became more than just a rite of passage. He began drinking to deal with all kinds of stress such as what he experienced at school, in dating and relationships, and then at his job. In the beginning, Thomas only drank beer; but he was soon drinking it every night. At the young age of 22, Thomas started to realize that he was drinking too much. He talked to his friends who told him not to worry since he was only drinking beer. However, he was drinking every night and more on the weekends.

This went on for several years and Thomas finally graduated to drinking whiskey and other hard liquors. He started to have trouble at work and was in danger of losing his job. He was often irritated at work and was slowing down cognitively, which affected his productive abilities at work. He went to a local clinic and started outpatient therapy. He was introduced to AA meetings during this therapy.

Thomas was abstinent for three months when he had his first relapse. He continued with the AA meetings, joined a group, and got a sponsor. He became committed to the AA program and became a General services representative for his group. Today, Thomas has been sober for five years. He continues to go to a weekly group meeting and enjoys the social life and friends that AA has provided for him.

THE CASE OF DIANA

Diana is a 48-year-old stay-at-home mother of two children. Her husband is an insurance broker. Diana drinks wine every night, anywhere from 2 to 5 glasses a night. She only drinks hard liquor when she accompanies her husband to a party.

Diana's children, both girls, are in college now and she is at home alone and bored. Her husband works a varied schedule so she is often alone at night. She has tried taking night classes to keep her busy but finds that she is still drinking after class. Her husband has noticed this drinking and is not sure what to think. Diana is often tired or asleep when he comes home from work. He has broached the subject with her only to get a defensive reaction. She responds that she only drinks wine and she should certainly be allowed to do so as an adult. It is not a problem in her mind.

However, to prove to her husband that this is not a problem, Diana tries to stop drinking and experiences signs of withdrawal. Neither she nor her husband is aware of what is happening and she is rushed to the doctor.

The doctor suggests that Diana get a part-time job to keep busy and prescribes tranquilizers for her stress, loneliness, and sleep disturbance. He does not tell her to stop drinking. It never comes up. Diana goes home and now she is taking medication and drinking wine. She starts to experience intermittent blackouts but does not realize what is happening. She has a minor traffic accident; she hits a garbage can. A friend tells her about AA and she attends a meeting. Diana is not really a joiner, or so she assumes; the meeting with all the friendliness and gaiety makes her uncomfortable.

She decides this is not for her and returns to her routine of medications and drinking. Soon her life is spinning out of control. She does not leave the house. She stays home and drinks, watches television, and sleeps. Neither she nor her husband is happy with the situation. The daughters are starting to notice something is wrong with their mother. They talk to their father who, in turn, talks to the friend who brought her to her one and only AA meeting.

The father joins Al-Anon, a group for the spouses of people who have trouble with drinking so that he can understand and take care of his own needs. Eventually, Diana is talked into going to another meeting with her friend. She attends some open meetings, and then she eventually joins a women's discussion group. She has now been sober for six months and is *enjoying the fellowship of AA. She and her husband often go to meetings together.*

THE CASE OF CRYSTAL

Crystal is a 23-year-old college student who has been using drugs since she was 9 years old. As a child, she was painfully shy and did not have many friends. She quickly found that one of the ways to fit in at school was to use various types of drugs. Unfortunately, drugs at many schools are easy to get--much easier than parents would guess.

Eventually, Crystal settled on alcohol as her drug of choice and started to go around with a circle of friends who also used alcohol. They never got in trouble so no one ever found out about their use. Crystal found that alcohol made things easier for her. She could make friends more easily and her anxiety levels went down.

Crystal went to a different public high school than most of her friends so the circle broke up but her drug use did not stop. Crystal had found a way to make school and home tolerable for her through the use of alcohol. She made good grades all the way through high school. Again, her use of alcohol was manageable enough so it did not cause her problems.

Crystal went off to a college a few hundred miles away from home. She was smart so at first college was not difficult. She was away from her friends and her comfort zone so again her best friend was the bottle. She found friends who were a little older than she was so that took care of the source of supply. The problem was college got harder and there were more interpersonal relationships and problems to get through. Crystal started to rely on alcohol more and more heavily. It started to interfere with her work and her grades. She started to sleep through early morning classes and miss examinations.

The student counselor in her dormitory noticed that Crystal was having problems and she had a talk with her one night. After initial denial and a round of defensive measures on Crystal's part, the counselor eventually got through to her. She referred her to the school's drug counselor for an initial appointment. While it took several meetings to get Crystal to go to a meeting, she went one evening to an off-campus meeting with a volunteer. After a few off campus meetings, Crystal tried a lunchtime campus meeting.

Crystal was sober for three months only to relapse. She finds it difficult to understand how someone as young as she is could have a problem. She continues to go to both on and off campus meetings because she feels comfortable there. She is beginning to realize that she has a problem and there is a solution. The peers who share at these meetings are similar to her and her situation; this helps her to accept the fact that she is an alcoholic. She is also happier than she has been in some time. Crystal continues to work on her sobriety one day at a time.

REFERENCES

[1]AA World services (1976). *Alcoholics Anonymous.* NY: Author.
[2]Borkman, T. (2006). Sharing experience, conveying hope. *Nonprofit Management & Leadership, 17*(2), 145-161.
[3]Davey-Rothwell, M. A., Kuramoto, J. S., & Latkin, C. A. (2008). Social networks, norms, and 12-Step group participation. *American Journal of Drug & Alcohol abuse, 34*(2), 185-193.
[4]Davis, D. R., & Jansen, G. G. (1998). Making meaning of Alcoholics Anonymous for social workers: Myths, metaphors, and realities. *Social Work, 43*(2), 169-182.
[5]Flores, P. J. (1997). *Group psychotherapy with addicted populations: An integration of Twelve-Step and psychodynamic theory* (2nd ed.). NY: Haworth Press.
[6]Kirkpatrick, J. (1999). *Turnabout: New help for the woman alcoholic.* NY: Barricade Books.
[7]Knack, W. A. (2009). Psychotherapy and Alcoholics Anonymous: An integrated approach. *Journal of Psychotherapy Integration, 19, 86*-109.
[8]Krentzman, A. R. (2007). The evidence base for the effectiveness of Alcoholics Anonymous: Implications for social work practice. *Journal of Social Work Practice in the Addictions, 7*(4), 27-48.
[9]Kubicek, K. R., Morgan, O. J., & Morrison, N. C. (2002). Pathways to long-term recovery from alcohol dependence: Comparison of spontaneous remitters and AA members. *Alcoholism Treatment Quarterly, 20*(2), 71-81.
[10]Masudomi, I., Isse, K., & Uchiyama, M. (2004). Self-help groups reduce mortality risk: A 5-year follow-up study of alcoholics in the Tokyo metropolitan area. *Psychiatry and Clinical Neurosciences, 58,* 551-557.
[11]Moos, R. H., Moos, B. S., & Timko, C. (2006). Gender, treatment, and Self-help in remission from alcohol use disorders. *Clinical Medicine & Research,* 4(3), 163-174.
[12]Narcotic Anonymous World Services, Inc. (1986). *N. A. Booklet.* NY: Author.
[13]Terra, M. B., Barros, H. M. T., Stein, A. T., Figueira, I., Athayde, L. D., Ott, D. R., De Azambuja, R. D. S., & Da Silvereirs, D. X. (2008). Predictors of relapse in 300 Brazilian alcoholic patients: A 6-month follow-up study. *Substance Use & Misuse, 43,* 403-411
[14]Trimpey, J. (1995). *The Small Book: A revolutionary alternative for overcoming drug and alcohol abuse.* NY: Dell.
[15]Trimpey, J. (1996). *Rational Recovery: The new cure for substance addiction.* NY: Pocket Books.
[16]What is SOS (2009). *Save Our Selves.* Retrieved on May 25, 2009 from: http://www.sossobriety.org/whatissos.htm.

Chapter Nineteen

CHILDREN

OF

ALCOHOLICS

BY **ALLISON FLEMING**
MICHIGAN STATE UNIVERSITY

ROBERT L. HEWES

MICHAEL P. ACCORDINO
SPRINGFIELD COLLEGE

Chapter Topics

◊ Identifying Children of Alcoholics

◊ Alcoholism and the Family System

◊ Potential Risk Factors for Children of Alcoholics

◊ Adult Children of Alcoholics

◊ Effects of Ethnicity and Culture Among COAs

◊ Treatment

Alcoholism is widely recognized as both an individual and a family disease, and effects on the children of parents who have alcoholism have been the subject of heavy focus in recent years.[24] Much of what we know about children of alcoholics comes from clinical observations and more recent research efforts. In this chapter, we will use the term children of alcoholics, or COAs, to describe individuals who grew up in a home with one or more parents or major caregivers who experienced alcoholism. This chapter will serve as an overview of major issues that affect these children. COAs are often studied to determine affects of growing up in an alcoholic environment, especially in the areas of physical and emotional health, cognitive development, interpersonal development, relationships, and the risk of developing substance abuse disorders themselves. These issues, as well as an explanation of the family system, will be explored. Some case studies will also be presented to enhance your understanding of this subject.

Robinson & Rhoden[27] identified four types of family alcoholism:

◊ Active alcoholism in all generations.
◊ Active member has stopped drinking, but the family remains untreated. The dysfunction remains and is risk transmitted to future generations.
◊ Active drinking is removed for one generation or more, dysfunction continues and the family dynamics and increased risk for alcoholism is transmitted.
◊ No previous family history, but a parent develops alcoholism and the children will have adult issues to deal with and will be at risk.

What makes family alcoholism so insidious is that the presence or absence of active drinking is not what causes or cures the dysfunction in the family environment. It is the family dynamics that contributes to the potential negative experiences and development for children of alcoholics. Untreated families will continue to re-create negative dynamics in future generations. The impact on families can often be observed in the family environment, but is subtle and frequently is unknown to the family. For example, there may be a tendency not to openly address conflict; instead, resorting to sarcasm and other passive-aggressive responses. Alternatively, a family may impose various "shoulds," on children, such as one should be "other-oriented" and accommodating even when one may not want to, or one should be more of a "perfectionist". Both attempt to project an outward appearance of stability, thereby taking the focus off of the individual and or family system in crisis. The challenge to counselors treating children of alcoholics and their families is considerable.

Alcoholism treatment was historically focused on the individual. The counseling field has made great gains in understanding alcoholism as a disease, rather than a character flaw or a moral failing. A major discovery in the 1960s and 1970s revealed the family system as an important component in treatment.[31] As a result, family treatment has become a critical part of recovery for both the family members and the individual with alcoholism. Wegscheider-Cruse[31] aptly explained the impact of treating the whole family by stating, "since we are discovering that families who receive treatment do not develop new chemical dependencies, family treatment may be our best hope for preventing alcoholism and drug dependency in the next generation [sic]" (p. 31).

Estimates on the number of children of alcoholics (COAs) range from 8-27% of the population.[9] COAs are a group of individuals; therefore, no broad assumptions can be made about a person's likelihood for behavior, temperament, ability, interpersonal skills, or any other characteristics based solely on having one or more parents with alcoholism.[28] However, children growing up in an environment affected by alcoholism cannot help but be affected in some way by the experience. Alcoholism becomes an inseparable aspect of the family system, "...it generates family dynamics and influences family functioning through its interaction with and impact on each family member."[27, p. 1] Given all of the observed differences in the functioning of COAs and adult children of alcoholics (ACOAs), an understanding of family dynamics and other factors that impact future outcomes of these individuals is an important undertaking, since "it is likely that alcoholic families can be characterized on a continuum of dysfunction and that there are numerous within-group differences in their environments and experiences."[24, p. 441]

IDENTIFYING CHILDREN OF ALCOHOLICS

Identifying COAs in the non-clinical population can be a challenge, largely because of the likelihood that the family will try to hide the secret, and the fact that the signs and symptoms are often subtle. Cujipers[9] explained the lack of adequate measures to identify COAs, assess the severity of the situation, and involve the parents when they are contributing to the problem. Schools seem to be the best place to identify and intervene with COAs, as professionals have daily access to children and opportunities to observe behavioral cues. Intervention at an early age is important; pre-school has been identified as a key point in the child's development where a lack of appropriate care can influence the child's development through adulthood.

Clues that something is going on in the home can be related to behavior or cognitive performance. Younger COAs often display problems eating, sleeping, toileting, , handling transition, separation anxiety, insecure attachments, sudden changes in play or temperament, and in regression of behavior. Dramatic play is an activity that young children often engage in, and the theme of alcohol in dramatic play may be an indication that the child is exposed and aware of drinking behavior at a level that is above his or her development. School professionals need support and training to know how to respond to these subtle signs.

Often, the most observable clue is that the child displays symptoms of neglect or even abuse. Alcohol is a factor in many domestic violence and child protective issues. Observations of COAs three to five years of age, revealed increased incidence of hyperactive behavior, negative mood, and aggression, with impaired social relationships and cognitive functioning. Children also demonstrated more advanced recognition and cognition of alcoholic beverages, when compared with peers.[12] School aged and younger adolescent COAs have been found to have lower self-esteem than their peers.[22]

Teachers, counselors, and other helping professionals may notice issues with attentiveness, behavior, or developmental progress, and contact the family. As a result of observations and interactions, they may suspect that alcohol is a factor in dysfunctional family dynamics, but often this is outside the scope of practice of teachers and other school-based professionals. Younger children are more willing to talk honestly about their feelings with respect to alcohol in the home, while children nine and older have already been socialized to deny the problem.[27]

Identifying clues for older children are slightly different, as they are engaged in coping in a way that younger children are not capable of achieving. Absenteeism, difficulty concentrating, sudden behavior or mood changes, or signs of abuse or neglect are often displayed. COAs may also present as being extremely shy and easily embarrassed, overly confrontational, or experience frequent illness–such as headache, stomachache or other stress-related symptoms.

Screening tests and other instruments have been used successfully in identifying COAs who have reached a certain age and developmental level. Since these instruments are generally paper and pencil, the child must be old enough to read and understand the questions. One example is the Children of Alcoholics Screening Test (CAST),[20] developed as a way to identify individuals who have experienced or are currently experiencing difficulties as a result of living with a parent who has alcoholism.[7] The instrument is a 30-item questionnaire with questions about feelings, perceptions, attitudes, and experiences related to the drinking patterns of the parents of the test-takers. Questions are answered with a yes or a no only, for example:

◊ "Have you ever thought that one of your parents had a drinking problem?

◊ "Did you ever feel responsible for or guilty about a parent's drinking?"

◊ "Did you ever feel alone, scared, nervous, angry, or frustrated because a parent was not able to stop drinking?"

◊ "Did you ever take over any chores and duties at home that were usually done by a parent before he or she developed a drinking problem?"[20]

The CAST has been shown to have high internal validity and is often used to identify COAs in practice and research.[7]

Labeling children can be harmful to their self-image. COAs often feel intense shame and guilt regarding their home lives. They do not want others to know, or to treat them differently. Considering individual differences of COAs, it is dangerous to try to group them together as having the same experiences and emotions.

ALCOHOLISM AND
THE FAMILY SYSTEM

Alcoholism has long been considered a "family disease," and the effects on all of the family members have been studied and documented as early as 1969.[31] While all family members understand and cope with the disruption that an alcoholic member causes, no one goes untouched. Wegscheider-Cruse[31] provided a seminal piece on the rules and roles within the alcoholic family, and her work has provided us with a simple model for understanding how alcoholism can affect the family. In addition, many internal and external factors can moderate the potential harm to the children. This section will include an overview of alcoholism in the family, and protective factors that can affect family and individual functioning.

Alcoholism creates disruptions in the lives of both addicted individuals and those around them. Relationships are severely impacted, and the disordered behavior spreads among family members. Laybourn, Brown, and Hill[23] explained, "There is a constant interplay within a family between particular actions or events and the wider set of relationships. Any action or change by one person in the family has repercussions for everyone else."[(p. 62)] Some of the "interplay" can be observed by examining some common family "rules" and "roles" found within alcoholic family systems.

FAMILY "RULES"
Within an alcoholic family system, the chaos caused by the behavior of the dependent drinker has an effect on everyone. As a way for the others to process and deal with the unpredictability and mood swings of the alcoholic, the other family members learn to keep an unspoken set of family "rules" as an effort to maintain some stability. All families follow a set of rules in order to keep the family functioning and protect the members of the family from harm, but the unspoken rules of the alcoholic family are serving a different purpose. Rules in a healthy family system are consistent with demonstrated family values, are for the benefit of everyone, are flexible, and can be discussed openly. In an alcoholic family, rules often do not make sense, and do not keep people safe. They are also not discussed openly, and may or may not be consistent with values. The rules identified as most common, "don't trust, don't talk, don't feel" are designed to avoid conflict, deny the problem, and allow the family members to protect themselves and the family as a whole.[31]

Denial is the most common way that alcoholic families manage conflict and stress.[27] One of the family rules, "don't talk" speaks to denial as a way to deter attention away from the source of the problem–the dependent's drinking. The people closest to the person with alcoholism will often go to lengths to pretend that everything is "OK" and expect others to do the same. Children who try to talk about the alcohol-related problems within the family, or share their feelings about how the issue is affecting them will be met with invalidation. For example, the non-dependent parent may minimize the issue, explaining that it is not that their mother or father is drinking too much, he or she is just under a lot of pressure right now, or that the child is just overreacting.[27] This denial creates an unhealthy environment, where the issue is not addressed and instead everyone dances around it. The drinking can be conceptualized as the "elephant in the room" or a situation that everyone can see, but no one can talk about. This can be especially confusing for children, who learn quickly not to believe their eyes and ears. They may sense that something is not right, but since everyone else seems fine, they lose confidence in their own perceptions.

"Codependency" and "enabling" are two terms that are also closely associated with familial alcoholism. Codependency is defined by Wegsheider-Cruse[31] as, "a specific condition characterized by preoccupation with and extreme dependency on another person, group, idea, or substance" p. 243. This person is experiencing disorder much the same way that the dependent drinker is. Co-dependence is described as "emotional, social, and sometimes physical."[31] The most common person to be deemed "co-dependent" is the spouse, or closest person to the alcoholic. This person perceives that he or she is powerless to change the situation caused by the behavior of the dependent drinker, and is often fully entrenched in denial as to the cause of the family disturbance. This person may "enable" the dependent drinker to continue in his or her behavior with limited consequence. Enabling is an action that is often seen within the context of codependency and is defined as, "denial or making up of excuses for the excessive drinking of an alcohol addict to whom someone is close."[16, p. 211] Enabling can be conscious or unconscious, and is often done out of a sense of care or loyalty to the person with alcoholism. The "enabler" can be anyone, a spouse, a coworker, a parent, or a friend. There is usually one primary enabler, and that person's behavior will be discussed below within the context of family roles.

FAMILY "ROLES"
The following is a discussion of common "roles" found within an alcoholic family. It should be made clear that we are describing behavior, not people, and we are depicting one general version of the way these behaviors play out within a family system. These family roles were developed and are discussed in the literature as a basic way to understand how the family copes with the dysfunction that an alcoholic member brings.

The first family member that we will focus on is the person with alcoholism. This family member can be anyone in the family; a parent, grandparent, or child. For the purpose of this discussion, we will focus on the parent role, so that we can talk about the effects on the children. The issues surrounding alcoholism that are most pertinent to this discussion include the physical and psychological dependence on alcohol, and the loss of control regarding when and how much a person drinks. It is at this point in the person's disease development that they are incurring negative consequences (e.g., health, legal, social, work-related) associated with their drinking, but continue to engage in drinking behavior. In situations such as the one described, alcohol and alcoholism becomes a dominant issue affecting daily activities of all of the family members.[27,31]

The next family member to address is that of the "enabler." This person is usually the closest person to the alcoholic, is often the spouse, or if the alcoholic is unmarried, a friend, family member, or oldest child. This person plays the role of protecting the person from consequences related to drinking. The enabler may do things like call the boss and say the alcoholic is sick when he or she is unable to get up for work, make excuses about the person's behavior, get an extra job to try to make ends meet for the family, or take on extra responsibilities that the alcoholic is no longer able to fulfill. However, if you ask the enabler if he or she wishes the alcoholic would stop drinking, the answer is yes, of course, and they would do anything to help that happen. The motivation for the enabler is love, loyalty, fear, and sometimes shame. The actions are a misguided attempt at taking some control over a situation where they feel powerless. Inside, the enabler feels guilty, angry, helpless, afraid, inadequate, and stuck.[31]

The "hero" is the next family role to be discussed. In terms of childhood roles, the hero is usually filled by the oldest child in the family. Of all the family roles, this one is most strongly related to birth order.[31] The hero is characterized by drive, achievement, and success. This child is in constant search of positive attention, thinking that if he or she can perform then the family will be happier. Also, no one will know that there is a problem, because no child who can do so well would come from a dysfunctional family. This child is well regarded by teachers, coaches, and friends. Yet to the hero, there is a lingering feeling of inadequacy and fear. Heroes are prone to developing stomach ulcers, migraines, and Type A "workaholic personalities," as well as heart attacks and strokes as they grow older.

The "scapegoat" of the family is usually the second child. By the time this child arrives in the family the hero is already excelling. There is no way that this child can keep up with such an overachieving older sibling, so the second child quickly learns to do other things to gain attention. This child often acts up or acts out to mask the hurt and loneliness felt. This child is likely to be suspended or expelled from school, run away, experiment with drugs and alcohol, become delinquent, and engages in sexual activity at a young age. The Scapegoat feels like a family outsider, and seems to operate on a principle that negative attention is better than none at all.[31]

The third and fourth roles of "Lost Child" and "Mascot" are less closely tied to birth order, and may co-exist in the same child if there are only three in the family. The "Lost Child" arrives in the family in the thick of the dysfunction, and feels like an outsider much the same way the scapegoat does. Unlike the scapegoat who vies for attention, the lost child stays out of the way and does not try to get involved in the family dynamics. These children becomes loners, taking care of themselves, and try not to make waves. With all of the chaos in the family, it is somewhat of a relief to the alcoholic, the enabler, and the other family members to not have to worry about or pay attention to this child. Isolation contributes to the lack of self-worth that this child feels. These children do not understand what is going wrong with the family and no one else will explain it, so they retreat and stay in their own world and have no expectations of the family to live up to. This contributes to the low self-esteem and difficulty in finding success in social and other life situations as they grow older.[31]

The "Mascot" is also a latecomer to the family dynamics. This child, as the youngest, is protected by older members of the family. The child feels the tension and may experience anxiety as a result of knowing that something is wrong, but is too young to fully make sense of it. So instead, they try to make people laugh to bring positive attention and alleviate some of the stress. As mascots get older, they learn to joke around whenever things become uncomfortable, and are often the class clowns at school. Mascots are often kept as the "baby" and are more immature than are peers. The Mascot may get into trouble at school for being fidgety, clowning around, and causing disruption to the class. The mascot puts on a show to hide the feelings of hurt, confusion, and fear on the inside.[31]

POTENTIAL RISK FACTORS FOR CHILDREN OF ALCOHOLICS

Given that the views towards alcohol in the U.S. can generally be described as "ambivalent," it may be difficult to imagine that a drug that is legal can cause so many problems within the family. Considering that 88% of people who have ever had a substance use disorder have had an alcohol-related diagnosis, with or without the involvement of other drug dependence, "the problem of children of addiction in the United States is primarily one where alcohol is the parental drug of choice."[35, p. 111] Alcoholism in the family serves as an indirect risk for other family stress, as alcohol is often a factor in domestic disputes, separation, divorce, child abuse and neglect, work related problems, and financial strain. Fitzgerald,[12] identified adults with co-occurring antisocial personality disorder as being at high risk for experiencing downward social mobility as related to their families of origin. This is often a result of a compilation of the above named potential aspects of family stress. As we have mentioned, COAs are a heterogeneous group, so assumptions should not be made regarding the following potential risk factors based on family background alone. Clinical and empirical observations have been made regarding COAs with respect to physical, emotional, and developmental problems that differentially affect this population.

HEALTH-RELATED RISKS

A major health risk for COAs is Fetal Alcohol Syndrome (FAS) or Alcohol Related Birth Defects (ARBD). FAS is a developmental disorder caused by high levels of exposure to alcohol during pregnancy. FAS has been, "recognized as the leading known cause of mental retardation in the United States, surpassing Down Syndrome and spina bifida."[19, p. 69] Other associated symptoms include impeded intrauterine and post-natal growth, central nervous system impairments, and distinct facial abnormalities.[19] Children who are born with FAS experience delays in physical, mental, and emotional growth and development. The extent of the delays is a result of both the uterine environment and the situation in which the child is raised.[10] Other risks associated with prenatal alcohol use are low birth weight, small head circumference, and difficulty feeding.[10] As with other developmental disorders, the risk of delay continues along all developmental milestones and the child may struggle with many of these events. Investigators are still unclear regarding the level and duration of alcohol during pregnancy that is required for FAS and other risks to materialize, but there is no established "safe" level of alcohol use during pregnancy.

Other health risks common to COAs are best described as accumulated due to family environment. Connors[8] made several observations of health risks in a sample of children of primarily single mothers diagnosed with alcohol or other drug use disorders. Children were found to be at increased risk for living in an environment characterized by limited family financial resources, unstable housing, parental legal problems, physical and mental parental health issues, and a lack of social support. These issues affect the level of care that the parent is able to provide, access to nutritious food and healthcare, and family stability. Children in this sample had higher rates of asthma, and vision and hearing problems as compared to a national sample of similar-aged children, and were more likely to be exposed to cigarette smoke, alcohol, and other drugs.

EMOTIONAL AND DEVELOPMENTAL RISKS

Some experiences reported by COAs can seem relatively minor. For example, COAs often feel "guilt" or "worry" related to parent drinking. Others suffer the much more serious impact of violence in the home, fear, disruption of day-to-day and family activities, embarrassment, and isolation.[23] Young children may feel that they are responsible for parental drinking, feeling that if they were better behaved, or helped out at home more, their parents would not need to turn to alcohol to relieve stress or improve mood. Children may also take steps to try to stop their parent or parents from drinking, such as hiding or dumping out bottles, and older children may have learned to avoid the situation by spending time outside of the home or staying out of sight when they know that the parent is drinking.[23]

Clinical observations form the bulk of what we currently accept as "known" regarding COAs as a group, however, due to a host of reasons, characteristics that are commonly attributed to COAs have not been universally found after empirical investigation. Windle[33] explained that in the 1950s and 1960s, people believed that there was a single root of alcoholism, found within a gene or as a personality trait. Now it is accepted that multiple factors are related to the onset and the continuation of an alcohol use disorder. Moderating factors related to family environment that seem to make a difference in risk to children include co-occurring depression or anti-social personality disorder in the dependent parent, abuse, or having two parents with alcoholism.[11,14,18,]

Some affects of the alcoholic family can be characterized as immediate, describing the emotional impact (i.e., how the child feels), attitudes towards alcohol, and understanding of the affects of addiction. Emotional symptoms of COAs are most often classified as either "internalizing" or "externalizing" symptoms.[28] Internalizing symptoms include things like depression and anxiety, and these issues of adjustment are not proven as a link to COAs. Externalizing symptoms include examples of "acting out" behaviors such as rule breaking, defiance, inattention, aggression, and impulsivity. These symptoms correspond to behavior associated with Attention Deficit Hyperactivity Disorder (ADHD), conduct disorders, and Oppositional Defiant Disorder (ODD).[28] Children of Alcoholics also seem to be affected by other problems such as hyperactivity and inattention, emotional problems, conduct disorders during adolescence, and development of alcoholism in adulthood.[28]

In some family situations, problems arise due to ineffective or absent parenting, while in other situations, COAs may be filling roles in their families that are above their current developmental level. Prime examples of these situations are parentification of children and adolescents, and COAs who must serve as mediators or confidants to their parents.[23] Parentification is defined as a distorted relationship between parent and child where the child cares for the parent instead of being cared for. Care may include physical, emotional, or even financial.[5] Extra responsibility for children is not always harmful, for instance if it coincides with the child's current developmental ability, if proper support is provided, and if the child is recognized for his or her help. In large, single parent, and dual earner families children are often expected to help. Parentification is more common in family situations characterized by unpredictability, turmoil, and families that are non-intact. Burnett[5] found a relationship between parental alcoholism and parentification "over and above" family unpredictability, suggesting that there are additional factors at play. Authors explained their findings with the observations that parents who are overwhelmed, have poor coping and self-care skills, or experience psychopathology may be more likely to elicit help from children using inappropriate means.

Parentification in alcoholic families can turn harmful when, "parents are excessively and chronically dependent on the children for nurturance."[5, p. 182] Children who are taking on many important family responsibilities are not able to participate in age appropriate social activities and experience impeded social and emotional development. There is some evidence that parentification is used by children to bring a sense of control to what they perceive as a chaotic situation.[5]

ADULT CHILDREN OF ALCOHOLICS

Long-term effects are characterized by the impact on personality development, social functioning, and overall emotional health as children, adolescents, and adults. Observed effects that are classified as long term include higher levels of negative emotionality (i.e., tendency to experience negative mood, engage in self-blame, and over-sensitivity to criticism). Other ACOAs experiencing difficulties coping with life stressors and demonstrate increased difficulty related to adjustment when compared to their peers.[15] There is mixed support in the empirical literature for these observations.[28] Other long term effects suggested to be related to COA status include: Type A personality, difficulty recognizing and explaining emotions (alexithymia), locus of control issues, and self-consciousness. These characteristics were found to distinguish COAs from Non-COAs in at least one study. It is difficult to draw strong conclusions based on limited study, but these are areas to focus on in future research.[28]

Some specific adult outcomes of experiences during childhood have been linked to family unpredictability and parentification. The result of impeded social and emotional development is associated with a number of problems in affect and interpersonal relationships in adulthood, including depressive symptoms, difficulty recognizing and interpreting dependency needs, narcissistic or self-defeating personality styles, a sense of personal inauthenticity or "imposter phenomenon," and a tendency to use psychological defense mechanisms.[5]

Aside from those that are linked to parentification, effects on adult relationships have been observed in COAs. In a longitudinal study of marital relationships, Kearns-Bodkin & Leonard[21] identified some differences between COAs and non-COAs in a sample of 634 couples. Husbands and wives were less likely to have children if either the mother or both parents of one of the spouses experienced alcoholism. Wives with maternal alcoholism lived with their partner for a longer period of time before marriage. Significant effects on marital satisfaction and aggression were also observed with respect to alcoholism in the opposite gendered parent.[21]

There has been much discussion regarding the risk of COAs developing alcohol and other drug use disorders as adults.[9,11,28] Investigators have found that COAs are four to 10 times more likely than their peers to develop a disorder.[26] We must remember that COAs vary widely in their characteristics and levels of adaptive functioning, so it is important to recognize individual differences. Duncan[11] investigated genetic factors and environmental factors in an attempt to clarify the risk. Genetic factors were identified as explaining 40-60% of the variance in developing alcohol use disorders as adults, and other contributing factors included alcohol-specific (e.g., modeling of alcohol behavior, development of expectancies related to alcohol) and non-specific environmental factors (e.g., poor parenting, abuse, poverty).

Griffin and Amodeo[13] pointed out some more specific differences between COAs who develop an alcohol use disorder and COAs who do not. The authors explained that COAs are both more likely to engage in heavy drinking and abstain from drinking alcohol all together. Researchers found differences between pairs of sisters in experiences within the home (e.g., abuse, recollection of negative experiences, recollection of positive experiences as children, and outside support) and outcomes related to adult drinking.[13]

Trim and Chassin[30] investigated "drinking restraint" as a factor in alcohol use. Drinking restraint is defined as "cognitive preoccupation with control over drinking."[(p. 122)] In the larger population, high levels of drinking restraint is associated with initial successful regulation of alcohol consumption, but if the person is unable to meet their self-set requirements for control, then "failure" is associated with higher levels of consumption. Trim and Chassin[30] found that in COAs, this pattern did not hold true. The authors suggested that "aversive transmission" or the experience of witnessing the potential negative effects of overconsumption of alcohol is a motivator for abstinence in adult COAs. This finding is consistent with other observations that COAs may abstain from alcohol and will not necessarily develop alcoholism.

PROTECTIVE FACTORS

As we explained in the beginning of the chapter, not all Children of Alcoholics (COAs) will experience the same effects related to family background. Some characteristics of the family will put the child at increased risk, while other factors and childhood experiences will reduce the risk of the child continuing to experience physical or emotional effects into and through adulthood. Aspects of the family experience that impact the children include things like family environment, birth order, when their parent develops alcoholism, whether there are periods of recovery or sobriety, any co-occurring personality disorder or mood disorder, use of illicit drugs as well as alcohol, and whether one or two parents drink.[2,18,27]

Palmer[25] suggested a strengths perspective, citing the resilience of COAs due to the typical environment of the alcoholic family. Resilience, in this case, is used to explain the healthy adaptation to unhealthy circumstances. For example, children from alcoholic families often take over responsibilities of parents and learn to take care of themselves. Resilient children show lower degrees of internalizing symptoms of family dysfunction, and higher levels of positive affect and academic, social, and rule-abiding competence than children who are found to be less resilient.[6]

Werner and Johnson[32] investigated the role of caring adults in the lives of COAs (N=65) in a longitudinal study. In their sample of COAs, participants were divided into three groups determined by their level of coping. Individuals in the "Successful Coping" group (51%) were characterized by being satisfied with work or school, relationship with significant other, relationship with children (if had), relationships with peers, and overall life satisfaction. Individuals in the "Major Coping" group (21%) were experiencing difficulties in most of the above-mentioned areas, while participants grouped in the "Minor Coping" (28%) category were experiencing mixed success and difficulty in the life areas used to classify. Protective factors for the participants in the "Successful Coping" group included an adult or other caring person who took special care or attention with the child when he or she was growing up. The non-alcoholic parent, grandparents, aunts and uncles, older siblings, teacher and elder mentors, and friends and parents of friends all were identified as people who helped the child cope with, escape from, or put into a healthy perspective what was going on at home. In addition, individuals in the "Successful Coping" group described a process where they sought out or created environments where they could participate in activities they liked, felt supported for being "themselves," and rewarded for things that they were good at. Investigators also observed that children described as having an "easy temperament" had greater access to social support, demonstrated higher scholastic competence, and had more parental interaction as an infant and toddler. As adults, more of the "Successful Coping" group had moved away from their family and they chose not to become closely enmeshed with family problems. This seemed to be the most common adult coping strategy with family issues.[32] This research contributes to our knowledge that not all COAs have the same experiences as young children. There are many factors both within the child and within the environment that contribute to more effective coping or more difficulty as adolescents and adults.

EFFECTS OF ETHNICITY AND CULTURE AMONG COAs

Family dynamics and functioning must be considered within the context of the culture and ethnicity of the family. Much of the literature regarding alcohol and the family has been written from the dominant cultural perspective, and it should be applied with care to individuals of color. There is a need for more research on how alcoholism in families affects racial and ethnic minority groups. COAs of color may cope more effectively and display greater levels of resilience because of the care they receive within their communities, or less effectively because of the increased likelihood of living in a lower socioeconomic status and racism experienced by racial and ethnic minorities.[1]

Ramisetty-Mikler and Caetano[26] examined ethnic differences in the number of children exposed to parental problem drinking or alcohol dependence. Higher proportions of Black and Latino children than White children are being exposed to both problem use and alcohol dependence. This study only included three racial and ethnic groups and further investigation must be done to find proportions in other racial and ethnic communities.

The perception of what constitutes alcohol misuse and dependence often develops out of cultural norms. Families also exist within the context of culture, and norms may dictate the acceptable response to family stress and response to crisis situations. For professionals working with families, it is important to know and respect the cultural context and norms to which the family ascribes. It is especially important for the professional to respect the family dynamics and how past experiences with social service agencies may affect how the family receives services. It is well known that families of color are often misunderstood and poorly served by counselors who are not culturally competent. Families who are vulnerable as a result of dysfunction often do not seek services or terminate counseling relationships prematurely. Counselors need to understand the root of the trepidation that many families of color feel towards "outsiders."[17]

Hall[14] identified alcoholism as the "number one health problem within the African American community,"[(p. 259)] resulting in both medical and social problems. Harley[17] discussed cultural factors that influence the experiences of African American COAs. The development of the often-discussed family "roles" (e.g., hero, scapegoat, lost child) and functioning are impacted by African American culture. Harley[17] discussed the complexity for children developing a personal and family role identity at the same time that they are developing a racial identity as a result of their experiences within the African American community and dominant culture.

The presence of alcoholism in the family interacts with the experiences of oppression and racism and adds a layer of complication in how the roles within the family and the larger community are expressed and used for coping. Spirituality is a large part of the African American culture, and alcohol dependence may be seen as a weakness of morality, or may be ignored completely. The problem may be denied, or kept within the family as a result of these cultural influences. Harley[17] and Hall[14] both identified "kinship bond" or relationships with kin and fictive kin as a strength of the African American community. These relationships extend to friends, neighbors, and church and other neighborhood group members, and are a source of support and protection against long-term negative dynamics resulting from family alcoholism.[14,17]

Native Americans have been identified as another group differentially affected by alcoholism.[29] There are vast differences, both within and between tribes, with respect to norms and views towards alcohol use. There are many potential explanations of the enhanced incidence of alcohol-related problems within groups of Native Americans, including the degree to which the tribe has been disrupted by the dominant culture, levels of control and conformity, and oppression that Native Americans have experienced. Professionals must take care to understand the context of the specific tribe when working with a family affected by alcoholism. Native Americans have experienced differentially high consequences of alcohol-related deaths, including suicide, homicides, accidents, motor vehicle crashes, and alcohol-specific medical conditions.[29]

There has been significant interest in the increased incidence of FAS found in some Native American and Alaska Native communities. Research and intervention in recent years has resulted in a decrease of this phenomenon, but it remains higher than rates found across the US. There are also tribes where the rate is as low as or lower than the general US population.[29] Native American children who are abused or neglected are significantly more likely to come from a home where alcohol use is problematic. There are many cultural dynamics of tribes that may serve as risk or protective factors in the lives of Native American children, including cultural norms regarding alcohol use, family and extended family strength and involvement, poverty, domestic violence, family stress, and spiritual support.[29] Professionals working with Native American children and families need to be respectful of tribal customs, views towards "outsiders," and the role of spirituality in health, and will likely work in concert with tribal leaders in provision of services.

TREATMENT

Treatment for COAs must be personalized to individual characteristics, for example, the age and developmental level of child, temperament, family "role," and severity of family situation. The challenge in treating children is that often they are still living in the home environment, the cause of the problems that they are having. A major goal of treatment is to empower children to feel less like "victims" and teach them problem solving and coping skills. Many children feel a sense of guilt or responsibility for the problems at home. For example, if they were better behaved, then their parents would not need to drink. They may spend a lot of time and energy trying to prevent their parent or parents from drinking, hiding alcohol, dumping alcohol, keeping drinking friends away, and making sure that money gets spent on other things so that the parents will not be able to buy alcohol.[27]

For counselors treating children of alcoholics, including adult children, the most important thing to remember is to assess the person as an individual, and not indiscriminately assume that a person will have certain characteristics or emotional reactions as a result of their family experiences. Young COAs, who may still be living in the home, will have different needs than adult COAs, so treatment should be developmentally appropriate. Observations in clinical practice suggest that many COAs who come in for treatment will exhibit characteristics that fit the patterns of the family roles that we discussed earlier. In that event, counseling and treatment will be slightly different depending on the child. For example, for lost children, the focus may be on helping them feel like they fits in, and making positive comments to them and encouraging pursuit of an interest or potential talent. For a scapegoat, the focus may be on implementing positive behavioral change and encouraging the child to identify and express feelings in appropriate ways.[27]

Several treatment approaches have been developed for working with children. Many COAs have missed out on play experiences as a result of the neglect in the home. Play therapy and dramatic play have been identified as two methods for assisting children in developing social skills, limit setting, a sense of fairness, and negotiating conflict in developmentally appropriate ways. These skills have not been modeled for the children in the home, so often they are behind their peers in these key skills. Play therapy also helps children develop motor coordination, and is a fun diversion. Dramatic play and psychodrama are often used to help children express feelings and act out scenarios that are the source of frustration or confusion for the child. Art therapy is also used for these purposes, children can learn to express feelings through art, music, or dance.[27] Children may also engage in group therapy, where they can see that they are not alone and group provides another opportunity to practice healthy social interactions. A major problem for COAs is that they feel isolated, and that no one else's family is anything like theirs. By joining a group of children who have similar families and experiences, they can have a safe place to express feelings and confront denial, and give and receive peer support.

Adult COAs may present with some of the same issues as children; for example, difficulty identifying and expressing emotions, or engaging in self-sabotaging behavior. Given the differences in development and context, adult COAs may be more removed from the source of their pain. Early research[3] into the role and function of the alcoholic family system suggests that COAs will often appear to function well upon initial separation from their families of origin, they are "...coping with life's problems in ways that have been of great value to them; such as being responsible, adjusting or placating, as well as not talking, not feeling, and not trusting."[p. 49]

For adult COAs, helpful interventions include social skills training, such as limit setting, learning to ask for what they need, saying no, handling criticism, asking others to change their behavior, and dealing with conflict.[34] Adult COAs may also need support regarding interpersonal relationships, feelings of control, and fear of abandonment. Some adult COAs may need treatment for mental health disorders such as Post Traumatic Stress Disorder (PTSD), depression, or anxiety. They may also need treatment for substance abuse.[28,11,18]

CASE STUDY

Chad is a 34-year-old male licensed professional counselor with a master's degree in rehabilitation counseling specializing in psychiatric and substance abuse counseling. He has been married for 12 years and has three children. Chad's mother remains an active alcoholic. Chad works as a clinical director of a large outpatient substance abuse treatment facility. He is active in the community, his local church, coaches his son's tee-ball team, and he is currently looking to start a private, home-based counseling practice. Chad struggles with compulsive behavior. Specifically, Chad has attempted several times to cut back on his Internet usage. He spends hours each day playing fantasy football, instant messaging, online gaming, checking financial accounts, and so on. Chad tends to be an authoritarian parent demanding obedience and order with little room for error. His marriage is stable but not flourishing. He tends to stonewall and avoid concerns within the family, specifically from his wife. He lacks patients with others and has had ongoing sleeping problem for the past 15 years. While Chad earns a high income, supports his family, engages in the community and other interests, Chad was recently diagnosed with depression and insomnia.

CASE STUDY

Lisa is a 44-year-old female data processor with a high school education. She is unmarried and the fifth child in birth order out of five children. Her parents were divorced when she was 19. Her father was a compulsive gambler who went in-and-out of treatment for depression and addiction to narcotics. While Lisa has never been in treatment herself, she experienced a long history of physical and sexual abuse from her father and older brother. Lisa attempted suicide once at the age of 13 and was diagnosed with depression and bulimia at the age of 17. Lisa is quiet and unassuming. She is fearful of others and rarely goes out in social settings unless escorted by a group. She currently lives with her mother and older sister in a two-bedroom apartment. Lisa struggles with her sexual identity and has never been sexually active post sexual abuse and trauma. Lisa's outlet for her depression and anxiety is the computer. Lisa spends hours shopping online and interacting within a variety of social networks, chat rooms, and fantasy role-playing games. Her online shopping has contributed to over $76,000 of financial debt that Lisa tends to ignore and downplay. Her computer usage has also resulted in the loss of two jobs, one apartment, and the repossession of her car. Lisa began drinking at the age of 12. While she has never been in treatment *for problematic drinking or substance abuse, her drinking has escalated over the past 6 months.*

REFERENCES

[1]Amadeo, M., Griffin, M. L., Fassler, I., Clay, C., Ellis, M. A. (2007). Coping with stressful events: Influence of parental alcoholism and race in a community sample of women. Health and Social Work, *32*(4), 247-257.

[2]Bijttebier, P., Goethals, E., & Ansoms, S. (2006). Parental drinking as a risk factor for children's maladjustment: The mediating role of family environment. Psychology of Addictive Behavior, *20*(2), 126-130.

[3]Black, C. (1981). *It will never happen to me.* New York: Ballentine.

[4]Berkowitz, A., & Perkins, H.W. (1988). Personality characteristics of children of alcoholics. *Journal of Consulting and Clinical Psychology, 56,* 206-209.

[5]Burnett, G., Jones, R.A., Bliwise, N.G., Ross, L.T. (2006). Family unpredictability, parental alcoholism, and the development of parentification. The American Journal of Family Therapy, *34*(3), 181-189.

[6]Carle, A.C., & Chassin, L. (2004). Resilience in a community sample of children of alcoholics: its prevalence and relation to internalizing symptomatology and positive affect. Applied Developmental Psychology, *25,* 577-595.

[7]Chartland, H., & Cote, G. (1998). The children of alcoholics screening test (CAST): Test-retest reliability and concordance validity. *Journal of Consulting and Clinical Psychology, 54*(7), 995-1002.

[8]Connors, N.A, Bradley, R.H., Mansell, E.W., Liu, J.Y., Roberts, T.J., Burgdorf, K., & Herrell, J.M. (2004). Children of mothers with serious alcohol abuse problems: An accumulation of risks. The American Journal of Drug and Alcohol Abuse, *30*(1), 85-100.

[9]Cuijpers, P. (2005). Prevention programmes for children of problem drinkers: A review. Drugs: Prevention, Education, and Policy, *12*(6), 465-475.

[10]Day, N.L, & Richardson, G.A. (2000). The teratologic model of the effects of alcohol exposure. In H.E. Fitzgerald, B.M. Lester, & B.S. Zuckerman (Eds.), Children of addiction: Research, health, and policy issues (pp. 91-108). New York: Routledge Falmer Publishing.

[11]Duncan, A.E., Scherrer, J., Fu, Q, Bucholz, K.K., Heath, A.C., True, W.R., Haber, J.R., Howell, D., & Jacob, T. (2006). Exposure to paternal alcoholism does not predict development of alcohol-use disorders in offspring: Evidence from an offspring of twins study. Journal of Studies on Alcohol, *67*(5), 649-656.

[12]Fitzgerald, H.E., Puttler, L.I., Refior, S., & Zucker, R.A. (2007). Family response to children and alcohol. Alcoholism Treatment Quarterly, *25*(1), 11-25.

[13]Griffin, M., & Amadeo, M. (1998). Mixed psychosocial outcomes of sisters from families with alcoholic parents. American Journal of Drug and Alcohol Abuse, 24(1), 153-168.

[14]Hall, J.C. (2008). The impact of kin and fictive kin relationships on the mental health of Black adult children of alcoholics. Health and Social Work, 33(4), 259-266.

[15]Hall, C.W., & Webster, R.E. (2007). Multiple stressors and adjustment among adult children of alcoholics. Addiction Theory and Research, 15(4), 425-434.

[16]Hansom, G.R., Venturelli, P.J., & Fleckenstein, A.E. (2009). Drugs and society (10th Ed.). Sudbury, MA: Jones and Bartlett Publishing.

[17]Harley, D.A. (1995). African American adult children of alcoholics: The impact of cultural influences. The Journal of Rehabilitation, 61(4), 36.

[18]Hussong, A.M., Wirth, R.J., Curran, P.J., Edwards, M.C., Chassin, L.A., & Zucker, R.A. (2007). Externalizing symptoms among children of alcoholic parents: Entry points for an antisocial pathway to alcoholism. Journal of Abnormal Psychology, 116(3), 529-542.

[19]Jacobson, S.W., & Jacobson, J.L. (2000). Assessing vulnerability to moderate levels of prenatal alcohol exposure. In H.E. Fitzgerald, B.M. Lester, & B.S. Zuckerman (Eds.), Children of addiction: Research, health, and policy issues (pp. 69-90). New York: Routledge Falmer Publishing.

[20]Jones, J.W. (1983). The children of alcoholics screening test: Test manual. Chicago: Camelot Unlimited.

[21]Kearns-Bodkin, J.N., Leonard, K.E. (2008). Relationship functioning among adult children of alcoholics. Journal of Studies on Alcohol, 69(6), 941-950.

[22]Larkins, J.M., & Sher, K.J. (2006). Family history of alcoholism and the stability of personality in young adulthood. Psychology of Addictive Behaviors, 20(4), 471-477.

[23]Laybourn, A., Brown, J., & Hill, M. (1996). Hurting on the inside: Children's experiences of parental alcohol misuse. Brookfield, VT: Ashgate Publishing Company.

[24]Lease, S. (2002). A model of depression in adult children of alcoholics and non-alcoholics. Journal of Counseling and Development, 80, 441-451.

[25]Palmer, N. (1997). Resilience in adult children of alcoholics: A nonpathological approach to social work practice. Health and Social Work, 22(3), 201-210.

[26]Ramisetty-Mikler, S., & Caetano, R. (2004). Ethnic differences in the estimates of children exposed to alcohol problems and alcohol dependence in the United States. Journal of Studies on Alcohol, 65(5), 593-599.

[27]Robinson, B.E., & Rhoden, J.L. (1998). Working with children of alcoholics: The practitioners handbook (2nd Ed.). Thousand Oaks, CA: Sage Publications.

[28]Sher, K. (1997). Psychological characteristics of children of alcoholics, Alcohol Health and Research World, 21(3), 247-254.

[29]Spicer, P., & Fleming, C. (2000). American Indian children of alcoholics. In H.E. Fitzgerald, B.M. Lester, & B.S. Zuckerman (Eds.), Children of addiction: Research, health, and policy issues (pp. 143-164). New York: Routledge Falmer Publishing.

[30]Trim, R. & Chassin, L. (2004). Drinking restraint, alcohol consumption, and alcohol dependence among children of alcoholics. Journal of Studies on Alcohol, 65(1), 122-125.

[31]Wegscheider-Cruse, S. (1989). Another Chance: Second Edition. Palo Alto, CA: Science and Behavior Books.

[32]Werner, E.E., & Johnson, J.L. (2004). The role of caring adults in the lives of children of alcoholics. Substance Use and Misuse, 39(5), 699-720.

[33]Windle, M. (1997). Concepts and issues in COA research. Alcohol Health and Research World, 21(3), 185-191.

[34]Woititz, J. G., & Garner, A. (1990). Lifeskills for adult children. Deerfield Beach, FL: Health Communications, Inc.

[35]Zucker, R. A., Fitzgerald, H. E., Refior, S. K., Puttler, L. I., Pallas, D. M., & Ellis, D. A. (2000). The clinical and social etiology of childhood for children of alcoholics: Description of a study and implications for differentiated social policy. In H.E. Fitzgerald, B.M. Lester, & B.S. Zuckerman (Eds.), Children of addiction: Research, health, and policy issues (pp. 109-142). New York: Routledge Falmer Publishing.

Chapter Twenty

GROUP COUNSELING APPROACHES

BY **GENEVIEVE WEBER GILMORE**

ANDREA PERKINS
HOFSTRA UNIVERSITY

Chapter Topics

◊ Advantages of Group Counseling

◊ The Logistics of Group Therapy in Addictions

◊ The Group Experience

◊ Special Considerations for Group Therapy in Addictions

Group counseling is the most common intervention used in substance abuse treatment. It is also more advantageous both economically and clinically than other treatment modalities (e.g., individual counseling, partner counseling).[1,2,3] According to the Association for Specialists in Group Work (ASGW),[1] group counseling provides the platform where individuals can reach mutual goals which may be intrapersonal, interpersonal, or work-related. The goals of the group may be twofold: accomplish tasks related to work, education, personal development, personal and interpersonal problem solving, or, remediation of mental and emotional disorders.[1] Substance abuse group counseling brings together a group of diverse individuals who have the same focus of concern: the use and abuse of drugs and alcohol and its impact on their lives and their relationships.[2] Although most of the treatment provided by inpatient and outpatient substance abuse centers occurs in group counseling, not all counselors are prepared to provide this service. Training for counselors who will lead group counseling is, therefore, essential. This chapter addresses the advantages of group counseling, logistics of counseling groups, group experience, and special considerations for diverse and difficult clients.

ADVANTAGES OF GROUP COUNSELING

Recovery from alcohol and drug use can be considered a "we" process, meaning that clients enter and maintain sober living through the support of community and fellowship with others.[2, pg. 163] Group counseling provides the platform for this process. Advantages of group counseling include:

◊   A reduction in clients' sense of isolation;
◊   real-life examples of people in recovery;
◊   the development and practice of coping skills;
◊   feedback from peers and counselors;
◊   a substitute family that could correct the negative experiences of the client's family of origin;
◊   social skills training;
◊   structure and accountability often missing from the lives of people abusing substances; and
◊   social support that helps prevent the client's return to the use and abuse of alcohol and drugs.[3]

Group counseling is effective in helping clients move towards and maintain sober living, and is often the preferred modality of treatment of both counselors and clients. The base of group therapy is the foundation of therapeutic factors that facilitate change and set the climate for personal growth. The following section will review these factors in general, and in relation to substance abuse treatment.

THERAPEUTIC FACTORS

Group counseling is a powerful mechanism by which participants experience personal growth and change. According to Yalom and Leszcz,[14] eleven therapeutic factors help create therapeutic change in group. They referred to these factors as "an intricate interplay of various guided human experiences"[(p. 1)] that is the "actual mechanisms of effecting change"[(p. xiii)] in group counseling. The validity of these factors is based on extensive empirical research with participants of various counseling groups. Each of the eleven therapeutic factors is presented below with a definition, its relevance to substance abuse counseling, and an example of its mechanism in a substance abuse group.

The first therapeutic factor is *universality*. This occurs when group members learn they share similar feelings and experiences, and that these feelings and experience may be more common or more universal among others than originally thought. This helps clients feel less isolated, more validated, and more hopeful.

Universality and substance abuse treatment. Often individuals are ambivalent about entering treatment due to stigma and fear of rejection by members in their community. They feel they are unique in their struggles with substance abuse. Group counseling connects them with others who have similar issues, increasing comfort to self-disclose and motivation to work on personal goals.

Example. Jim discloses he stole money from his mother to buy heroin, which led to similar disclosures from Lynn and Todd and an overall feeling of connection and support.

The second therapeutic factor is *altruism*. Group members can help each other, which raises their self-esteem and purpose. Altruistic helping also strengthens coping styles and interpersonal skills.

Altruism and substance abuse treatment. Helping others in group often leads to camaraderie among individuals working on recovery. This fellowship is crucial to building a sense of community, a strong support network, and the prevention of a relapse.

Example. Natasha extended support to Bob after he disclosed his struggle with resentment. Bob later extended similar support to Betsy, which lifted his mood and feeling of connection to the group.

The third therapeutic factor is *instillation of hope.* Group members might feel inspired by others in the group, particularly those who are further ahead in their personal growth and have successfully overcome problems that other individuals are currently dealing with.

Instillation of hope and substance abuse treatment. Often clients feel hopeless as a result of a long downward spiral of substance abuse comprised of various kinds of loss (i.e., relationships, job, and home) and isolation. Connecting with others who have longer periods of sober time might give the client the hope he or she needs to manage challenging times during early recovery.

Example. Mohammad lost his job as a medical assistant due to multiple absences related to his alcohol use. After listening to another member who gained employment after nine months of recovery, Mohammad felt more optimistic that he will also return to work.

The fourth therapeutic factor is *imparting information.* Members find it helpful to learn factual information about their presenting concerns from both the counselor and other members in the group. This helps them develop insight into their thoughts, feelings, and behaviors.

Imparting information and substance abuse treatment. Education on the side effects of substance use; common co-occurring disorders and their symptoms; and other issues associated with the substance abuse often help clients understand their presenting issues.

Example. Utilizing a DVD that explains the role of neurotransmitters in the biological basis of addiction can help a client not only gain insight into the benefits of psychopharmacological treatments such as antidepressants, but also reduce feelings of guilt and shame related to the belief that one "chooses" to be an alcoholic or drug addicted.

The fifth therapeutic factor is *corrective recapitulation of the primary family experience.* Group members might unknowingly interact with the group counselor and group members as if they were family members. Through interpretations and feedback, members can learn how to avoid unhelpful interpersonal skills that are reinforced by the family system.

Corrective recapitulation of the primary family experience and substance abuse treatment. Oftentimes, clients have family members who may be codependent or enablers of their substance abuse, or who may be negative influences to their recovery. Through peer interactions, a client might experience these family patterns in the "here and now" of group, which provides an opportunity to learn more about family dynamics while practicing new behaviors.

Example. Through feedback from a group member, Javier learned his comments in group are said in sarcastic ways, often hurting the feelings of others. Javier disclosed this has been a problem for him before, particularly with his partner. This feedback and realization allowed for Javier to practice commentary to the group without sarcasm.

The sixth therapeutic factor is *development of socializing techniques.* The group setting provides a safe and supportive environment where members can take risks to improve their interpersonal and social skills.

Development of socializing techniques and substance abuse treatment. Many clients began using drugs in adolescence, which impacted their ability to learn effective ways to socialize. It is not uncommon for clients to share that they feel their emotional or social development stopped at the age they started using. Group counseling allows for the exploration of this arrested development, and practice of socialization with peers.

Example. Chuck is very shy and used cocaine to help him connect with others in social settings. Without cocaine, Chuck finds it hard to speak up and share his thoughts and feelings. After learning about this struggle in a written exercise, the counselor, with Chuck's consent, invited other group members to role play when Chuck shared his thoughts and feelings on a topic, and his peers provided feedback on how he did. As a result, Chuck felt more confident with his interpersonal style.

The seventh therapeutic factor is *imitative behavior.* Members can develop new social and life skills by imitating healthy behaviors of the counselor or other group members.

Imitative behavior and substance abuse treatment. With lost opportunities to learn positive behaviors as a result of isolation and drug or alcohol use, many clients turn to their counselor and peers in treatment for such lessons. These behaviors might include replacing addictive thoughts with sober thoughts; identifying people, places, and things who or which might be risky to one's recovery and avoiding them; and, self care practices such as diet, exercise, and meditation.

Example. Warren often isolates in his house and uses drugs as a result. After hearing Sylvia discuss how helpful her sponsor from Alcoholics Anonymous is during times of cravings, Warren decided to attend a self-help group and obtain a sponsor. As a result of doing so, Warren now has a sober support who he contacts when he begins moving towards a relapse.

The eighth therapeutic factor is *cohesiveness.* This is one of the more powerful factors. A cohesive group is one where members feel a sense of belonging, acceptance, and validation, which are important conditions for personal growth.

Cohesiveness and substance abuse treatment. Community, camaraderie, and support are essential components in successful, long-term recovery. A cohesive group provides the platform where clients can take risks, share struggles, and gain insight into sober living. Such cohesion allows for other therapeutic factors to occur.

Example. Maddie thinks about the group when she feels overwhelmed by thoughts of using. Her accountability to the group's goal of abstinence, her relationships with group members and her overall connection to the group process keep her from using. Upon her return to group, she shares her "close call" and her appreciation of the group.

The ninth therapeutic factor is *existential factors.* Members take responsibility for their own lives and the implications for their decisions.

Existential factors and substance abuse treatment. Some clients will blame others for their substance abuse and related behaviors. This is not beneficial to their recovery because it does not allow for an honest inventory of growth areas, particularly behaviors that might lead back to the use of alcohol or drugs. Through feedback and light confrontation from the counselor and group members, clients might begin to take responsibility for their behaviors and decisions, and feel empowered to do things differently.

> *Example.* Luisa lost custody of her children as a result of her crack use and irregular attendance at parenting workshops. Although Luisa initially denied that her absenteeism at the workshops was her fault or that she endangered her children by using crack, group feedback helped move her towards taking more responsibility for her choices.

The tenth therapeutic factor is *catharsis.* Members express uninhibited emotion, and might feel a relief from feelings of shame or guilt as a result of the support extended.

Catharsis and substance abuse treatment. Clients often use alcohol or drugs as a means of numbing their emotions, particularly painful emotions related to relationships. In early recovery, the expression of emotion is unfamiliar, uncomfortable, and scary without the use of alcohol or drugs. Group interactions and the power of a safe and supportive environment provide an opportunity for the uninhibited expression of emotion, which might be the first expression of feelings for many group members in years. Many clients will report feeling "relieved" and as if a "weight has been taken off their shoulders" after catharsis.

> *Example.* Joy felt a great amount of regret for not being sober or physically present during the final months of her father's life. She has carried around this regret, guilt, and shame for years, and it is in her counseling group where she finally disclosed these feelings after hearing another group member share similar regret. This was the first time in ten years that Joy cried without using alcohol or drugs.

The eleventh therapeutic factor is *interpersonal learning.* Members might achieve a greater level of self-awareness and personal insight as a result of interacting with others and receiving feedback from the counselor and peers.

Interpersonal learning and substance abuse treatment. Peer interactions in substance abuse treatment help clients learn about their strengths and areas for growth, particularly related to behaviors that could lead to a relapse in their alcohol and drug use. This gain in insight is a crucial starting point for change.

> *Example.* Carl attributes group counseling to his increased understanding of how he ineffectively manages his anger. Through group activities and personal reflection, Carl became aware that he learned his anger management from his father. As a result, he committed to unlearning ineffective ways to manage anger, and to learning more effective ways. Such insight and subsequent behavioral change positively affected his marital relationship.

THE LOGISTICS OF
GROUP THERAPY IN ADDICTIONS

TYPES OF GROUPS

Group counseling is delivered in a variety of formats in substance abuse settings. According to the Center for Substance Abuse Treatment,[3] five group models are common in substance abuse treatment. First, *psychoeducational groups* educate clients about substance abuse including the effects of alcohol or drug use on the body, the mind, and relationships. Lectures or DVDs are often used to introduce specific topics, and follow-up discussions are facilitated to help clients explore how the information relates to them personally and with each other in the group.[2] Second, *skills development groups* teach the skills necessary for sober living, as some clients began using alcohol or drugs during their adolescence, interfering with the development of their interpersonal skills necessary for adulthood. Skills development groups provide a useful tool for those who use alcohol and drugs as a way of coping with their perceived weak interpersonal styles.[7] Examples of skills development group topics are managing anger and identifying people, places, and things that could lead to relapse. Third, *cognitive-behavioral groups* help clients identify faulty thoughts and actions that lead to the use or abuse of substances, and teach them how to substitute maladaptive behaviors with healthier ones. Fourth, *self-help* or *support groups* bring together individuals who are moving towards or already in recovery to share information about maintaining abstinence and coping with every day issues of sober living. Support groups are valuable adjuncts to substance abuse treatment. For an in-depth discussion of a self-help group, see Chapter 19. Lastly, *interpersonal process groups* allow for personal work in a group format related to developmental issues, relationships, and other issues that impact or interfere with recovery. Group counseling, regardless of its format, contributes to the client's movement away from the use and abuse of alcohol and other drugs and towards sober living, and is an important component of substance abuse treatment.

GROUP ENROLLMENT

Counseling groups can also be closed or open enrollment groups.[12] *Closed enrollment groups* begin and end with the same members, excluding those who drop out from the group over time. They are conducted for a predetermined period of time, which usually corresponds to the prescribed treatment (e.g., treatment is ten weeks, group counseling is ten weeks). Once the group terminates at the end of its predetermined schedule, a new group is formed. On the other hand, *open enrollment groups* include members who join and leave throughout the course of the group. Since membership is constantly evolving, there is no definite amount of time that the group meets. It is worth mention that the open enrollment format can be disruptive for both the members of the existing group who have an established pattern for interacting and the new group member who has not yet acclimated to the norms and style of the group. It is suggested that no more than two members of a group be added at any one time to minimize the impact on group dynamics.[2]

Based on the author's (GW) experience in community agency settings, open enrollment groups are more common than closed groups, mainly for two reasons. First, open groups are more cost-effective because more clients can be treated and for longer periods of time. Second, following a clinical rationale, clients are more likely to engage because they can enter group counseling shortly after admission while not having to wait for a group to end and begin anew.

GROUP FORMATS

Group sessions can be lead in a number of ways by using an unstructured or structured format. An *unstructured format* includes a here-and-now focus where members share thoughts and feelings they have in the group at that moment. Through the use of skills, the group leader uses a "need-and-thread" approach where he or she identifies themes, and deepens the focus of those themes. Without using exercises or planned activities, the group leader allows for a natural group process where most relevant personal or group issues can surface.

A *structured format* might include exercises, which provide a topic, direction, and purpose for that group session. Through skilled leadership, the group facilitator works to draw out members, initiate and link member disclosure, and encourage feedback based on the information solicited through the use of exercises. Both the unstructured and structured format of group are effective ways to run a group counseling session; however, it is vital that the group leader who facilitates an unstructured group continuously keeps the group members on topic, while it is essential that the group leader who uses exercises is prepared to abandon his or her plan if a client is in crisis, or if the group calls for a specific clinical focus either related or unrelated to the exercise.

CRITERIA FOR CLIENT PLACEMENT IN GROUPS

General criteria for placing individuals into groups include the size and composition of the group related to its purpose, personal characteristics of those in the group, and the level of functioning of individuals.[6] However, the overarching rationale guiding placement is dependent on two primary criteria: the person's ability to benefit from the group and the impact of the individual's participation on the success of the group. A person must be placed in a group that meets his/her needs, while not compromising other members in the group. Although, it should be recognized that placement is a constantly changing process based on the client's progress, setbacks, and continued commitment to recovery.

Decisions regarding placement should begin with a thorough assessment of the person in terms of characteristics and needs; this assessment should continue throughout their participation in group therapy with adjustments made over time for their progress.[3] The assessment should include information such as demographics, needs and preferences, social networks (i.e., eco-map or sociogram), subjective, objective, and collateral assessment instruments, stage of recovery and group work history, and commitment to change. This information will round out a profile of a person's appropriateness and readiness for group interventions.

Group therapeutic techniques are conducive for those in addictions treatment because of the shared feeling of "sameness" in experience, which can be used as the basis for trust building.[10] Other aspects of "sameness" may be desired by a person seeking out a group. Placement may be made based on a person's stage of recovery, level of comfort/communication, or specific demographic variable—all of these factors relating to the unique needs of the client. One common practice is to form groups on the basis of gender, age, or culture. For example, women may prefer a women-only group because of the greater stigma related to substance abuse for their gender, differences in relational style attributed to gender, or because of a history of trauma (usually at the hands of a man). Placement of women in these groups is appropriate, but leaders should be cognizant that the safety of the group cannot be mirrored in society so the leaders will have to prepare the women for re-entry into society.[3] Groups specifically for adolescents are also common because of their variant psychosocial and developmental needs, scheduling concerns related to school, and laws relating to minors. This is not to say that groups need to be homogeneous to be "safe." Heterogeneity of groups can add richness to the process and perspectives, provided that those comprising the group are people with similar needs.

The type of group has implications for matching a person based on his or her comfort and needs. For example, those who are earlier in their recovery or are still ramping up their motivation to change, most often benefit more from psychoeducational and support groups. Those who are further along in their recovery and have demonstrated a solid commitment to change would benefit more from interpersonal process and relapse prevention groups to suit their stage in recovery.[3] As mentioned before, the addition of members to an existing, open enrollment group can be a disruptive process, especially for those who are new to the group experience. According to Couch,[3] four aspects should be incorporated into pre-group screening to smooth this transition:

◊   Identify client needs, expectations, and commitment;
◊   challenge myths and misconceptions about group, to reduce anxiety and increase safety;
◊   convey information about procedures and expectations; and
◊   screen the clients for their willingness to participate and desires for outcomes.

This on-the-spot assessment will ensure a solid fit and increase the preparation of the entering member.

CONFIDENTIALITY

Confidentiality is first addressed by the group facilitator during the informed consent process. In obtaining consent from participants, the facilitator outlines his/her responsibilities and theoretical orientation, procedures and policies of the agency, ethical/legal obligations and limitations, and the nature of the group. Counselors within a group setting are still legally bound by the same standards of confidentiality as they are in individual counseling. Counselors are still required to report intent to harm self and others. However, the bounds of confidentiality within the group process are different from those of an individual counseling session because the contract is not only between the counselor and the client, but among all members of the group. The expectations of confidentiality should be reviewed each time a new member is added to the group. Now with some of the general terminology and logistics of groups understood, let us turn to the skills, process, and dynamics of group counseling.

THE GROUP EXPERIENCE

GROUP LEADERSHIP

The role of the group facilitator is to do just that—facilitate. The leader is there to provide structure, organization, and direction.[10] The shape this role takes depends on a number of characteristics. The style of leadership a person employs over the course of a group changes with the needs and purpose of the group. While leaders may be more active and supportive in the earlier phases of therapy, they should be less so in the later stages of recovery when individuals should be assuming more responsibility for their recovery. In the case of facilitating groups of youth, the leader may act as an "information giver" to bring the group members to a point of discovery, whereas leaders for those who are exiting long-term substance abuse treatment may be serving the function of a "sounding board," providing questions that provoke personal inquiry and challenge.

The function of the leader is to be responsive and understanding and create an environment of consistency for consumers to explore their recovery. Leaders must have a firm understanding of their own identities, so that the focus of the group is on the members and not on them. Approaches to group leadership can fall along the lines of leader-directed or group-directed.[10] Groups that are *leader-directed* focus on the perceived needs of the group to select activities and dialogue that will facilitate members toward progress. Leaders seek to find the themes and links between individuals to aid in individual and group recovery. Groups that are *group-directed* allow the members to determine the direction and content of the group, although this approach might not be appropriate for those who are beginning in group treatment, are only meeting for a limited number of sessions, or do not have a clear understanding of their needs from group treatment.

Effective group leaders are going to possess the characteristics typical of effective counselors, such as warmth, flexibility, objectivity, and patience. Being in a group rather than one-on-one counseling calls for the person to also be comfortable with being in a position of authority; this includes the ability to take control and responsibility for the progress of the group. A leader must also be personally and psychologically healthy, as the various issues raised in a group situation might be emotionally impacting. Jacobs and colleagues[10] delineated the following other traits necessary for group leaders:

◊ Experience with diverse individuals;
◊ experience with groups;
◊ planning and organizational skills;
◊ knowledge of the topic and relevant content;
◊ good understanding of basic human conflicts and dilemmas; and
◊ a good understanding of counseling theory, as a basis to understand the behaviors of group members.

In essence, a group leader must understand how individuals think, feel, and behave, but also the impact that groups have on behavior and how individuals interact and coexist.

GROUP LEADERSHIP SKILLS

According to Milsom,[11] leaders must carry out the functions of:
◊ Administrating the group;
◊ helping members to gain insight and attribute meaning;
◊ stimulating emotions;
◊ focusing on the here-and-now; and
◊ promoting interaction.

These tasks are accomplished through the application of specific group counseling skills. The skills of a group leader are similar to basic counseling skills, although different because these skills are applied with multiple individuals at the same time. The responsibilities of a group leader are to set a tone and agenda for the group, facilitate active sharing, clarify perspectives, and manage conflicts.[11] Below are examples of principle techniques that are employed in counseling settings, with sample dialogue as appropriate.

Active listening involves tuning into the content of verbal messages, as well as the non-verbal messages of the individual speaking and group members listening. In a group situation, the leader must be attentive to what the person speaking is saying, but must also be aware of what other members are feeling and thinking in response to what they are hearing.

Jackson: I feel that this is just a huge struggle for me to be staying sober day in and day out because it was such a huge part of who I was.

Counselor: (nodding) Uh-huh.

Jackson: But the worst part of it all is the feelings of guilt that continue to overwhelm me every time I think about the effect that it has had on my kids.

Counselor: (noticing that others have now looked up and are nodding) It seems like you might have hit on something that strikes a chord with others. Let's spend a few minutes here.

Reflection/empathizing is used to convey that you understand the message or feelings of a person, as well as help a person become more aware of their own messages. In the group context, a leader may reflect on what an individual has said, what two or more individuals have said, or an overall theme that the whole group appears to be experiencing.

Lucy: Even though I've been sober for over four months and am getting my life back on track, I'm sick of the looks that I get from other parents in the school yard, the people in my building...it's like I'm the worst Mom in history.

Charlotte: I know that feeling. At the last family gathering, everyone is making small talk with you, but you know that as soon as you're out of earshot, the gossip is flying.

Counselor: You both seem to be sharing that despite the progress you know you are making, others are not as accepting of the change and progress you have made.

Clarification and *questioning* can also be used to draw out more information from a person to make their message more understandable to the rest of the group members. This is also a way to move from understanding what an individual has shared to probing about that same issue for the group as a whole.

Shawn: I don't think you realize what it takes for me to keep coming here. I'm not a 'people person'—I mean I used to drink just so I could *be* social. It's all I can do to just show up and I don't think I'm even getting anything out of this.

Counselor: I'm hearing that this group might be a bit of a stretch for you, but you've had the courage to keep coming back, even though you have some question about what you're getting out of the experience. You said that the group wouldn't understand how hard this is for you. Can you share with us a little more so that we might be able to understand better?

Shawn: I get that you're all here to help me—well, help me to help myself, but to be honest, drinking is what I know and it definitely isn't as hard. I feel like I don't have much of a reason to stay sober since I've already lost my wife, my kids won't talk to me, and I can't remember the last time I had steady work.

Counselor: Shawn, you've been through it all and you still keep coming back. I have a feeling, and based on some of the nods I'm seeing around the room, others have spent a little time in similar shoes. So I'd like to turn it back to the group to share a little bit about what has kept each of you motivated to keep coming back each week.

Summarizing is a way to tighten the focus of the group by highlighting key points in a discussion by one or more members. This can also be a technique used to shift the topic of the group from one to another.

Counselor: Although we started the group today talking about our plan for maintaining sobriety over the holidays, several of you have specifically mentioned some fears about your family and significant others trusting you. Bob and John, you shared that your partners are becoming increasingly anxious. Dave, Tom, and Phil talked about some of their concerns about seeing their children. Why don't we split up into pairs for a few minutes and help each other understand a little bit more about our feelings about family and loved ones before we go back to talking about our plans.

Linking is the way to connect members together and facilitate bonding. The leader may point out commonalities between members to develop alliances among members. The task here is to get the discussion moving and assist individuals to find ways to relate to one another. As the bonding and cohesiveness increases, the group leader can eventually move the responsibility of connecting to the members of the group.

Counselor: Dan, I know that you're feeling a little unguided right now with how to discuss your treatment with your son when you return, but I think that Nikki was sharing some of the same concerns last week when she was talking about returning to work and facing her coworkers. Does that seem on target, Nikki?
Nikki: You know, even though coworkers aren't the same as family, I've been working with them for almost a decade, so they are my family in a way. Where is your head at right now? What are you thinking of doing?
Dan: I'm not really sure where to start, honestly. This seems like such a huge step, that I really only get to do once.
Nikki: Maybe we can talk through "breaking the ice" a little more together later and I think we'll both feel a little more comfortable with it.

Setting the tone and *modeling* are ways of creating the mood of the group. As alluded to earlier, it is the responsibility of the leader to determine how formal, supportive, or task-oriented a group will be. This lays the groundwork for a positive and trusting environment, where mutual goals can be achieved. Providing rules and structure is one way to create a tone for the group, but a leader's adherence to the rules models appropriate behavior within the group. Leaders who are prepared, display professionalism toward those who co-lead, and contribute to the energy of the group demonstrate commitment to the progress and success of the group.

STAGES OF GROUP
Groups move through a series of stages as members interact and work together

as a system. Referred to as group development, this movement is determined by individual participation, group dynamics, leadership style, level of trust, and self-disclosure. The stages of development usually include a *beginning stage* where attention is given to establishing a safe environment where members can work on their personal issues; a *transition stage* where conflict occurs in the group, and members interact to successfully work through it; a *working stage* where members experience a number of therapeutic factors resulting from successful conflict resolution among the group and increased feelings of trust and safety; and, a *termination stage*, where members reflect on their overall experience and growth, and plan for long-term application of newly acquired skills.[5] The working stage is where the majority of personal work and growth are experienced and, therefore, use of group leadership skills are of particular importance during this stage. Follow-up in the form of a group session is ideal as it brings together the group to discuss progress towards goals and continued abstinence (or relapses). A post-group session also keeps members feeling accountable about their commitment to their treatment goals after discharge. Individual meetings or phone follow-ups are appropriate if a post-group session is not possible. For a more in-depth discussion of group development see Brooks and McHenry[2] or Corey.[5]

Closed enrollment groups are more likely to move through the stages of group development since membership is consistent. Open enrollment groups will need to address new member concerns as they join the group thus impacting group development. Regardless of the group structure, movement through the aforementioned stages is fluid and continuous, and it is not uncommon for a group one week to experience deep sharing of experiences and feelings with the next week involving disagreements and conflict. Such interactions are characteristic of the group process and set the platform for corrective emotional experiences, interpersonal learning, and overall change.

GROUP PROCESS AND CONTENT

The power cell of group counseling is its process.[14] Group process may be defined as "an activity in which individuals and groups regularly examine and reflect upon their behavior in order to extract meaning, integrate the resulting knowledge, and thereby improve functioning and outcome."[13,p. 104] It is important to differentiate process from content. Content in group counseling consists of the issues presented, the words used, and the arguments that might ensue. Content is important insofar as it provides the material for process to begin. But process is where the action and power are found. It feeds the group. It teaches members life lessons. Group process helps answer the following questions: Who am I in this group? or Who are we together? Without content, members have nothing to process. Without process, members will not experience a gain in sight and subsequent personal growth from the content they shared. Therefore, content and process make for a healthy partnership in group counseling.

With regard to leadership, an effective group counselor is not necessarily concerned with the content of group members' disclosure, but rather the "how" and "why" of their words and communication.[14,p.143] Particular attention is given to the metacommunicational aspect of the interaction such that interest is warranted on why a group member made a comment to a specific group member in a specific manner.[14] A major mistake that group counselors make when leading groups is not tending to the process component of group, particularly neglecting to address the "here-and-now" of the group experience.

According to Yalom and Leszcz,[14] the here-and-now focus of group consists of experiencing and illumination: group members are living in the here-and-now as they interact with each other. They develop strong feelings towards each other, the leader, and the group as a whole. The "there-and-then" focus, as it has been coined, is when group members discuss people, experiences, or issues which are outside the group. This often happens in the form of story-telling, preventing the group from interpersonal interactions that lead to interpersonal learning. Often, there-and-then discussions feel safer for group members and have to be confronted and blocked by the counselor in order for the group to transition back into the here-and-now. The here-and-now allows for the provision of feedback, confrontation, catharsis, self-disclosure, and, risk-taking. Illumination is a form of reflection on the here-and-now. It facilitates an in-depth analysis of the interactions that took place in the here-and-now. This provides invaluable lessons on interpersonal communication. Illumination is complex in that it must "transcend pure experience and apply itself to the integration of that experience."[14,p.142] Below is an example of a counselor whose response facilitates the here-and-now of the group, and an illumination of the group's experience.

> **Martha:** Whenever we give you feedback, Jim, you send it back to us with a "but" or "I don't think that would work." I am at a point of not wanting to help you anymore because you don't want to help yourself.
> **Jim:** This isn't the first time I am hearing that...my friend complains that I always use "but" in response to her advice, which she says is because I am not listening and not willing to really look at myself.

At this point, the group leader could move forward in two ways: respond to the situation Jim is describing with his friend, which could facilitate the there-and-then, or bring his experience with his friend to the here-and-now of the group interactions, which would be the more effective intervention.

> **Counselor:** Jim, what feelings come up for you as you share this with the group?
> **Jim:** I feel a little embarrassed. It's as if I have a spotlight over me and everyone sees my weaknesses.
> **Counselor:** It sounds like you feel vulnerable. Tell us more about this feeling.
> **Jim:** It's unsettling. Scary. Like I want to run out of this room and get a drink.

The group leader turns to the group and asks all members to sit for a moment in silence, and think of a time in group when they felt vulnerable, either in the group or out of the group. She continues to challenge group members to stay with thoughts of that experience of feeling vulnerable, and use it to feel empathy towards Jim's current position in the group.

> *Counselor:* Would anyone like to share how you are feeling in this moment as a result of Jim's disclosure of feeling vulnerable, and your own identification of a time in or out of this group when you felt similarly?

As a result of processing Jim's feelings about disclosing his experience with his friend in the here-and-now of group rather than the content of the experience, other members felt more comfortable to describe times in or out of the group when they felt vulnerable. This led to universality among members, particularly Jim; goal-setting such that Jim shared his desire to work on accepting constructive criticism; and, an overall movement towards a more cohesive group.

It is very important that the group leader sets the norm for the here-and-now early in the group experience. The group might need more guidance from the leader in its beginning stages, but as the group develops, the group will be less dependent on the leader's guidance and more likely to thrust itself into and maintain its stay in the here-and-now. Illumination, on the other hand, might provoke more resistance from group members since they may view the facilitation of reflection as the role of the leader. It is appropriate and beneficial for the leader to model such facilitation throughout the life of the group with hopes that group members will imitate such behavior, thereby relying less on the facilitation of the leader. For more in-depth reading on the here-and-now of group counseling, particularly techniques for the facilitation of the here-and-now, see Yalom and Leszcz.[14]

USE OF ACTIVITIES TO PROCESS IN GROUPS

Using exercises in group counseling can enhance the overall treatment experience by making group more "meaningful and interesting."[10,p.205] From the current authors' own clinical experience running group counseling, group members respond well to innovative, thought-provoking, and structured opportunities to interact with each other. According to Jacobs,[10] there are at least seven reasons to use exercises in group counseling:

To increase the comfort level. Often group members feel anxious when they begin a new group. Using dyads (pair of group members) or triads (three group members) to discuss a topic such as introductions, or hopes, fears, and expectations of group, can be more useful and calming for gathering information.

To provide the leader with useful information. Using creative activities that involve the completion of tasks might help group members feel more at ease when disclosing personal information, thus leading to an increase in self-disclosure and more useful information for the group counselor.

To generate discussion and focus the group. Groups often interact and function more effectively when a topic is proposed to them. A topic such as anger management integrated with an exercise allows for members to discuss their challenges and consequences associated with managing their anger. Having an identified topic keeps the group focused and decreases the likelihood that the members will talk about irrelevant or "there-and-then" topics.

To shift the focus. Using exercises in a group session also enables a group counselor to change the focus when the group begins talking about unhelpful topics, or appears to have stalled in its group development. Shifting the focus of a group might also work with resistance of the group or individual members to a particular topic.

To deepen the focus. Just as a group counselor can shift the focus when necessary, he or she can deepen the focus when the group appears to be benefitting or could benefit from a particular group topic. For example, when family roles emerge as a topic in a relapse prevention group, the group counselor can invite a group member to sculpt his or her family, with particular focus on relationships. Such an experiential portrayal and acting out of family dynamics can help the group member as well as other members become more aware of the family system and its role in substance abuse.

To provide an opportunity for experiential learning. Choosing, using, and processing an exercise that helps group members think outside the box of how they usually behave can be very powerful. Utilizing a role play to practice a desired behavior as part of sober living and using other group members as actors in that role play is priceless.

To provide fun and relaxation. It is hard to deny that using collages as a means to introduce ourselves is creative and fun, far more exciting than just using rounds where one member at a time speaks about his or her likes, dislikes, et cetera. There is something therapeutic about picking up crayons and cutting photos out of magazines that makes collages effective in variety of ways.

Group counselors who use activities in a group session must effectively introduce, facilitate, and process the exercise. Simply giving the group a task (e.g., talk about the role of Alcoholics Anonymous in treatment, in dyads) is not enough; the counselor must address the group's interactions during the task, themes that emerged, and ways in which members can apply the knowledge and awareness gained from the exercise to their lives outside of the group. The following are examples of activities that can be used effectively in groups. For a more in-depth list and description of the exercises, see Jacobs et al.:[10]

◊ Written exercises, such as sentence-completion, making lists, and writing your own obituary;

◊ movement exercises, such as values continuum, family sculpture and changing seats;

◊ dyad or triad exercises and rounds;

◊ creative props and arts and crafts;

◊   fantasy exercises, such as imagined house and hot-air balloon fantasy;

◊   reading exercises;

◊   feedback exercises, such as first impressions and written feedback; or

◊   moral dilemma exercises, such as shipwreck.

When introducing an exercise, simple and meaningful directions on how to complete the task are helpful for group members. It is not necessary to expose the hidden lesson of the exercise to the group; rather, give enough information about the plan of the exercise to allow members to give their informed consent, and follow the steps of the task. Be specific with details when relevant; provide a time-frame within which members will work; and, disclose how the exercise will be processed insofar as within dyads or triads, or within the larger group. For example, after writing the statement "every moment is another opportunity for change" on the whiteboard in a group session, a group counselor instructs the group to break into triads to discuss the meaning of that statement with relation to their recovery. Before beginning triad discussions, the group counselor encourages members to identify one similar viewpoint and one different viewpoint that will later be shared with the larger group. By using specific details to introduce the exercise, group members are prepared to participate, and aware of how the exercise will be processed.

When facilitating an activity, group counselors should use a diversity of group leadership skills to draw out members, deepen the focus of the topic, shift the focus if necessary, and link group members' experiences. As previously mentioned, it is essential that counselors effectively process an activity in order to bring the group to a close and to a point where clients feel comfortable leaving the treatment setting. If a group counselor does not effectively process an activity, the purpose and goal of the exercise might not be met, or group members might run the risk of leaving the treatment setting with unfinished business from that group session, which could increase members' risk for unhealthy behaviors (i.e., relapse, isolation). For example, after all group members shared their lists of recent unsuccessful efforts at managing their anger, the group counselor found no time to further explore these efforts and thus process the activity. Without the process component of the group session, group members who felt anger in the "here-and-now" of group, having not discussed their lists, left the room with that anger unaddressed and unresolved. Thus, group members were not able to receive encouragement, support, and feedback on their behaviors and how to manage anger in healthy ways. It is important to note that feeling anger in the group session was not an inappropriate dynamic; in fact, having group members feel anger while in the group session could have facilitated an excellent discussion and experiential learning opportunity (i.e., practice anger management through role-playing). Without balancing the time of the group session to allow for the sharing of lists *and* follow-up discussion (i.e., process), the anger in the "here-and-now" of the group session was not used effectively.

Multiple models have been proposed to help group counselors' process exercises. One model of note, The PARS model,[9] provides a "road map" for group processing.[p.15] Not only is this model popular among group counseling courses in graduate programs as a means of training group counselors, but the authors have had success in utilizing this model in their own group work. The PARS model is composed of three stages (reflecting, understanding, and applying) and three specific focus areas (activity, relationships, and self). The purpose of this model is to help members process a particular activity, the relationships, and various interactions that occurred as part of the activity, and how members can apply what they learned in group to their lives outside the group. First, *reflecting* takes place by retracing the steps of a particular activity (i.e., what did we do?), followed by a description of the actions taken by the group as well as individual members and how members interacted with one another. Second, *understanding* refers to the members gaining insight into the interactions that took place during the exercise, including their reactions and observations of group dynamics (i.e., who did what?). Group members also are beginning to work toward their individual goals and what the group means for them. Third, *applying* what is learned through the experiential component of group is encouraged as a means to help members realize the impact of the experience and what they will take back to their personal lives to make a difference. The PARS model offers group counselors a conceptual framework inclusive of direction and structure, which are both important characteristics of effective group processing. For a more in-depth discussion of the PARS model and an example of how the PARS model can be applied, see Glass and Benshoff.[10]

SPECIAL CONSIDERATIONS FOR GROUP THERAPY IN ADDICTIONS

ADDRESSING DIVERSITY ISSUES IN GROUP

"Diversity" can have multiple definitions within the counseling context as we try to understand the individuals with whom we work in the most holistic way. Competency with diversity issues within a group setting stretches a person beyond the traditional meaning of cultural competence, because the group leader must understand the interplay and impact of diversity on the group dynamic. Issues pertinent to group counseling skills include personal cultural awareness and competence, exploring diversity issues with individuals, understanding the perspectives of foreign-born clients, and the need for homogeneous vs. heterogeneous groups.

To be effective in today's group therapeutic milieu, it is incumbent on the facilitator to have developed the knowledge, awareness, and competence for understanding, and addressing diversity issues in the group process.[8] Group leaders should engage in a thorough self-assessment of their feelings, assumptions, and reactions to cultural/diversity characteristics. Leaders must be aware of how their own culture and personal characteristics influence their skills and attitudes, including how their cultural background will be perceived by those in the group. If the culture of the counselor is going to be perceived as a barrier to effective communication and trust building, the use of a co-facilitator from the members' culture might be beneficial in terms of allaying fears, providing insights, and serving as a role model.

Those providing group therapy should also be knowledgeable about the cultural and diversity backgrounds of others. Primary cultural characteristics may include age, gender, culture, sexual orientation, and physical/mental ability level. Secondary diversity characteristics to consider include religious background, social class, and involvement in the criminal justice system.[3] These are the characteristics that may be variable for a person over time. Using general cultural frameworks or "stereotypes" to apply to individuals of diverse background provides a useful starting point for understanding. This allows a group leader to understand some of the typical cultural values of a person. Leaders must then understand how the person relates to that stereotype and adjust their conceptualization accordingly.

In addition to understanding "domestic" issues of diversity, counselors need to consider the inclusion of individuals from other countries and their points of view. Those who are less acculturated or newer to the country may have language issues and may require specific program considerations. Those clients who are foreign-born may have a history of abuse or trauma prior to immigration, many times as a result of the government in their countries of origin. This results in a mistrust of authority and systems as being helpful, which may cause aversion to treatment. Another barrier to seeking and engaging in services is the stigma that those from other countries associate with mental health disorders. Individuals may feel that the diagnosis will bring shame to their family or make them appear to be less desirable.[6] Counselors need to be cognizant of these worldviews and take additional time for foreign-born clients to acclimate, and not mistake their behavior for resistance.

Cultural differences may need to be considered in making appropriate group placements. Determining whether to place individuals of diverse background into homogeneous or heterogeneous groups should be made on a case-by-case basis of needs. We do not want to group people together under the assumption that those who are similar will work better together, unless this is necessary. Working with a heterogeneous group may make some participants more guarded because they do not have experience with interacting with different individuals or may err on the side of political correctness. Conversely, working with homogenous groups may retain the strong aspects of that culture and influence the group process (e.g., reverence to older members may lead younger members to share less or always defer to the opinions of their elders). Group leaders must be able to accommodate for these scenarios.

WORKING WITH CHALLENGING CLIENTS

Certain individuals will pose a greater barrier to the group process based on personality characteristics, ulterior motives, or because they are not participating in the treatment by choice. Clients often present with behaviors that create a challenge to group process and dynamics including those who cannot stop talking, who interrupt, who refuse to share, or who flee from the session to avoid feelings. Resistance to treatment is a natural occurrence as individuals explore their road to recovery. Some individuals offer more of a barrier in this area. The following is a brief overview of some challenging clients and approaches to dealing with their resistance and behavior. For a more comprehensive overview for dealing with problem situations in group, consult Jacobs et al.:[10]

◊ *Mandated clients*: In addictions treatment, oftentimes clients are mandated as part of a court order to attend group therapy. These individuals may have little interest in being present due to lack of control regarding their participation or feel that they do not have a problem with addiction. These individuals may arrive habitually late or talk about their continued interest in using substances.[4] To address these problems, the counselor should speak with the client individually to discuss issues and benefits of treatment from a personal perspective, focusing on what they can gain "since they have to be here"; move the client to a group that is in an earlier stage of development, as not to derail clients who have progressed in their recovery; or engage the group in a discussion of the impact of the client's presence to expound on the positives and negatives that the person has on the group experience, to explore the issues of group cohesion.

◊ *Angry clients*: Individuals may challenge or offend others in the group with their words and behaviors. This might include yelling, interrupting, or insulting others. It is the responsibility of the leader to be able to manage the emotions that individuals bring to groups, especially when they disrupt the energy, calm, or safety of the group. The key in these situations is for the counselor to remain in control and not respond with similar behavior, address the behavior and not the content of the message, and concretely state the policy and consequences regarding such behaviors. The message to other members of the group is that they are protected, and to the disruptive client that the behavior will not be tolerated.

◊ *Withdrawn clients*: Fear, shame, and cultural values may be at the root of a person's reluctance to share in group. Others may be uncomfortable or not able to understand the pace of the group. The reason for lack of participation should be assessed and addressed appropriate to the root for the withdrawal. A counselor may provide mentoring/role modeling to improve participation, provide more concrete questions for the person to respond to, or assign a partner for dyad exercises who can help draw the person out. If the person is not participating because of difficulty with language and comprehension, then a referral for individual interventions might be warranted.

REFERENCES

[1]Association for Specialists in Group Work. (2009). *Professional standards for the training of group workers.* Retrieved from http://www.asgw.org/PDF/training_standards.pdf

[2]Brooks, F., & McHenry, B. (2009). *A contemporary approach to substance abuse and addiction counseling: A counselor's guide to application and understanding.* Alexandria, VA: American Counseling Association.

[3]Center for Substance Abuse Treatment. (2005). *Substance abuse treatment: Group therapy.* Treatment Improvement Protocol (TIP) Series 41. DHHS Publication No. (SMA) 05-3991. Rockville, MD: Substance Abuse and Mental Health Services Administration.

[4]Center for Substance Abuse Treatment. (2006). *Substance abuse treatment: Clinical issues in intensive outpatient treatment.* Treatment Improvement Protocol (TIP) Series 47. Rockville, MD: Substance Abuse and Mental Health Services Administration.

[5]Corey, M. S., Corey, G., & Corey, C. (2008). *Groups: Process and practice* (8th ed.). Belmont, CA: Brooks/Cole:

[6]Craig, R. J. (2004). *Counseling the alcohol and drug dependent client: A practical approach.* Boston, MA: Pearson Education.

[7]Doweiko, H. E. (2008). *Concepts of chemical dependency.* Belmont, CA: Wadsworth Publishing.

[8]Gladding, S. T. (2007). *Groups: A counseling specialty* (5th ed.). Upper Saddle River, NJ: Prentice Hall.

[9]Glass, J. S., & Benshoff, J. M. (1999). PARS: A processing model for beginning group leaders. *The Journal for Specialists in Group Work, 24,* 15-26.

[10]Jacobs, E. E., Masson, R. L., & Harvill, R. L. (2009). *Group counseling: Strategies and skills* (6th ed.). Belmont, CA: Brooks/Cole.

[11]Milsom, A. (2010). Leading groups in the schools. In B. T. Erford (Ed.) *Group work in the schools.* Boston, MA: Pearson.

[12]Morgan-Lopez, A. A., & Fals-Stewart, W. (2008). Analyzing data from open enrollment groups: Current considerations and future directions. *Journal of Substance Abuse Treatment, 35,* 36-40.

[13]Ward, D. E., & Litchy, M. (2004). The effective use of processing in groups. In J. L. DeLucia-Waack, D. A. Gerrity, C. R. Kalodner, & M.T. Riva (Eds.), *Handbook of group counseling and psychotherapy* (pp. 104-119). Thousand Oaks, CA: Sage.

[14]Yalom, I. D., & Leszcz, M. (2005). *Theory and practice of group psychotherapy* (5th ed.). New York, NY: Basic Books.